The Beauty of Thy House

by
Mark Alessio

"I have loved, O Lord, the beauty of Thy house;
and the place where Thy glory dwelleth."
(Psalm 25:8)

A perfect woman – Thine be laud!
Her body is a Temple of God.
At Doom-bar dare I make avows:
I have loved the beauty of Thy house.
(Francis Thompson, *Domus Tua*)

For my parents,
Bruno & Angela Alessio

Table of Contents

INTRODUCTION

This book was written out of gratitude. In fact, every word I have ever written about the Mother of God has been penned in gratitude, as will be every word I write about her in the future.

In that sense my approach to the Virgin Mary is a very practical one. To me, She is not a nice "facet" of the Catholic Faith, nor is She a theological abstraction. She is living, vibrant and loving. I found that out for myself one dark night in the year 1988. Having lived my entire adult life far away from the Faith into which I had been baptized and educated, I was confronted then with a rather potent understanding of the true import of being "far away" from Christ and His Church. For some reason which I still do not understand, I called out to the Blessed Virgin that night, even though I hadn't given her a second thought since my childhood. On the contrary, I shudder to remember the blasphemies I had heaped upon her as an adolescent in the name of "humor."

Suffice it to say that something occurred as a result that changed my life forever. I knew then that Jesus Christ was "real," and I discovered something else — namely, that the way to reach Him is through His Mother. But I didn't recognize this fact immediately as a "doctrine." At that point in my life, as a bonafide lapsed Catholic of many years standing, I knew nothing about the Church's teachings on Mary's Mediation, or her Universal Motherhood. Whatever I had learned, I had forgotten. In truth, I wasn't even aware that I still remembered the words to the Hail Mary until they came to my lips. What I *did* know — unmistakably — was that something unique had happened, and it seems to have been arranged in such a providential way that Jesus and Mary would figure in it *together*.

No, there was no "theory" or "theology" coloring the event. But, later on, as I thought about the debt I owed to this wonderful Woman who stooped to help me even after I had given her nothing but a lifetime of indifference and insults, I became hungry to learn about her, and I began devouring every book I could find about her. At the beginning, this was an indiscriminate process. But, after years of reading various volumes and scouring bibliographies for more titles, I began to get a "feel" for the subject and to know which authors were reliable and which were not. It was an enjoyable journey and, for over a dozen years, I devoured books on Our Lady *every* day, relishing especially the old, out-of-print tomes that were truly worthy works dedicated to the Virgin.

As I gradually learned the theology behind our Marian doctrines, I never found any of it strange or distant. Sure, the language and terminology in some of these books went over my head, but the doctrines all made sense, because I had *lived* them. I didn't need a theologian to tell me that Mary intercedes for us, because I had found that out from concrete experience. I didn't need a treatise to tell me that She looks upon us as her own children. I *lived* that! Yet, I came to understand that a study of the "technical" aspects of our Marian doctrines is not only important but crucial. In such a study, we learn how our Marian doctrines form part and parcel of our Christological and Ecclesiological beliefs, how doctrines relate to doctrines in such a seamless and perfect fashion.

I found my personal study of Our Lady to be so rewarding that I wanted to synthesize what I had learned and share it with those who may not have the time or inclination to delve into the nitty-gritty, but who still thirst for knowledge about God's Mother and ours.

I could never claim to be a "Mariologist." There are no academic titles or letters after my name. I don't pretend to be anything other than what I am — a garden-variety sinner blessed with an affection for the Mother of God. I'm truly grateful to Our Lord for the fact that my return to the Church was accompanied by circumstances which have given me an appreciation for Mary. I wish I could say that I've been a faithful son and servant to her in the years that have passed since that night in 1988. I wish I could say that I've served her and her Divine Son as they *deserve* to be served. I wish I could say I have become a paragon of Catholic manhood since then.

Sure!

I'm still a traveler in this "vale of tears," and my only hope for any strength or joy lies in the Sacred Heart of Jesus, the only Lord and Savior this world has ever known or will ever know. That's just a fact, not poetry. If I had a dollar for every time Our Lord and Our Lady showed mercy to me after I had turned away from them to walk less "narrow" paths, I would buy my own island. But, being Who they are, they continue lovingly to place me in a debt to them that I can never repay.

Jesus without Mary? The Gospels, the most sound Catholic theology, and my own experience tell me that it just doesn't work that way, and I feel sorry for the misguided souls who believe that Our Lady can ever "detract" from her Son. The Truth is quite different. A love of Mary can kindle a hope in Jesus even in the most desperate or forlorn heart. To profess love for Jesus without loving Mary is to play a fruitless "spiritual game," however well-intentioned, for it is Mary only who teaches us the true joy of hoping in her Son. Our Lord desires to see us at *her* side.

Jesus without Mary? That's just not the way the world works ... *DEO GRATIAS!*

In closing, I would like to thank those who have encouraged and supported my writing in many ways. They're fine Catholic folks all, and their acquaintance and friendship has made my own sojourn through this "valley of the shadow of death" a blessed one.

My thanks to my good friend, Willam L. Biersach, who suggested one day that I write a "booklet" on Our Lady. That "booklet" turned into *The Beauty of Thy House!*

Also, my fondest thanks go to Douglas Bersaw, Sharon Rose Bersaw, Charles Coulombe, Jeannette Coyne, Fr. Gommar A. DePauw, Jesse Griffiths, Anne Hale, Vincent P. Lewis, Michael Malone (R.I.P.), Bro. Andre Marie, M.I.C.M., Michael Matt, Fr. Kenneth Novak, Gary Potter, Jack Skiffington (R.I.P.) and John Vennari.

Ad Jesum Per Mariam!

Mark Alessio
Point Lookout, New York
July 26, 2004
(Feast of St. Anne, Mother of the Blessed Virgin Mary)

Chapter One

One True God

False gods, ancient and modern – The True God, the God of Revelation – The Incarnate Son of God, truly visible, truly tangible

After the fall of our first parents, mankind, dulled with original sin, fell easily into the worship of idols and false gods. The early history of the world is filled with such "gods": the Philistines' *Dagon*, half-human, half-fish; *Moloch*, to whom the Ammonites sacrificed their own children in flames; the Phoenician *Baal*, whose worship, indulged in even by some Israelites, was attended by human sacrifice, homosexuality and prostitution; the eerie animal-headed deities of the Egyptians; the salacious, sadistic members of the Greek pantheon; and the nature spirits of the ancient Romans.

In such company, the student of ancient or "comparative" religion will find much to ponder. There is a cultural dimension to this proliferation of deities. "Gods" of defeated enemies were either banished or incorporated into the victor's pantheon. The ancient Romans employed a practice called *Evocatio*, a solemn ceremony intended to summon gods away from an enemy city under siege and to bring them over to the Roman side. This was used against Rome's mortal enemy, Carthage, during the Third Punic War (146 BC). The historian Livy described the behavior of the Roman troops after their conquest of the wealthy Etrurian city of Veii (c. 392 BC):

> "When all property of value belonging to men had been taken from Veii, work began on the removal of what belonged to the gods – the temple treasures and the divine images themselves. It was done with the deepest reverence; young soldiers were especially chosen for the task of conveying Queen Juno to Rome; having washed their bodies and dressed themselves in white, they entered her temple in awe." (*The Early History of Rome*)

Certain "gods" of the ancient world, carried off to other lands, would change their names, functions and characteristics to suit their new environs, while some Roman emperors would be "deified" after their death, thereafter described by the title, "divine".

These considerations are interesting, and they display the influence that religious sentiment can have on secular affairs even if only for cultural or ceremonial ends, but they are meaningless if removed from a *spiritual* framework – from the realm of absolutes, of Truth and Error – for the "gods" of the ancient world were not neutral beings: "For all the gods of the Gentiles are devils." (Ps. 95:5) "But the things which the heathens sacrifice, they sacrifice to devils and not to God." (1 Cor. 10:20) Yet St. Paul also wrote, "We know that an idol is nothing in the world and that there is no God but one." (1 Cor. 8:4) Are these teachings contradictory?

No, because the worship of idols – of anything that is *not* God – is a means of drawing souls away from the Truth. The ancient gods of stone were dumb, but they were still potent weapons of hell:

> For the beginning of fornication is the devising of idols, and the invention of them is the corruption of life. . . . For either they sacrifice their own children, or use hidden sacrifices, or keep watches full of madness. So that now they neither keep life, nor marriage undefiled, but one killeth another through envy, or grieveth him by adultery. And all things are mingled together, blood, murder, theft, and dissimulation, corruption and unfaithfulness, tumults and perjury, disquieting of the good, forgetfulness of God, defiling of souls, changing of nature, disorder in marriage, and the irregularity of adultery and uncleanness. For the worship of abominable idols is the cause, and the beginning and end of all evil. (Wis. 14:12,23-27)

These words apply to the present as well as to the age in which they were first written; they read like a check-list of the ills and evils befalling nations which spurn God and His Truth. In the midst of it all, there is a voice that speaks in a different tone:

> As one whom the mother caresseth, so will I comfort you. (Is. 66:13) I will feed my sheep, and I will cause them to lie down. (Ez. 34:15) I will deliver them out of the hand of death. (Os. 13:14) He that toucheth you, toucheth the apple of my eye. (Zac. 2:8) I have loved thee with an everlasting love, therefore have I drawn thee, taking pity on thee. (Jer. 31:3)

This is the voice of the True God, the voice of absolute might, tempered by a mercy that can only be called "divine". It is the voice of the God of *Justice*, whose mercy is all the more wonderful because it is tendered in the most prosaic, even brutal, of circumstances – a God of Passion, of Majesty, of Love so profound it challenges every mortal conception of the term.

Each and every human being must come to terms with this God, for He is not a deity that can be controlled or manipulated, like the false gods of old, which were little more than mouthpieces for both demons and men. He is the Power behind all power, the Nature behind all nature ... and, the Love behind all love. To underestimate this God, or take Him lightly, is the height of folly, and of the deadliest kind: "It is a fearful thing to fall into the hands of the living God." (Heb. 10:31)

The neo-pagan revival of the late twentieth century (an amalgam of various anti-Catholic agendas disguised as alternative "spiritualities"), when not openly hostile to the very idea and name of God, appeared to tolerate a "spiritual" mind-set whose logo was a "god" of sorts – a tame, ingratiating, celestial puppet-on-a-string, a being with all the substance of an "imaginary friend", who always seems to agree with his keepers, who never voices an opinion or ever challenges mankind on *anything*, particularly on questions of morality. This "god", whenever he is trotted out to attest to the "spiritual" dimension of the pagan-revival agendas, is more "silent partner" than divine being.

There is another word for this type of "spirituality": atheism . . . to be more precise, "scientific and historic atheism". This is what Pope St. Pius X (†1914) called it in his encyclical against Modernism, *Pascendi dominici gregis* (1907), in which he taught that Modernism – the "synthesis of all heresies" – relegates "any divine intervention in human affairs" to some innocuous, abstract realm of *faith*, which is not the same as factual, and therefore unpredictable, *history*. This philosophy will have no part of a God who is vibrant, unfathomable, awesome. For a *real* "god", like a real husband, wife, or friend, may sometimes make demands upon his "followers", perhaps even inform them that some of their desires or goals are *wrong*. Imaginary "gods", like imaginary friends, are usually more pliant, and certainly more convenient.

It is true that, with the Incarnation of the Second Person of the Blessed Trinity, God would become visible, approachable, meek and humble. It is true that He would call us "friends," and even allow Himself to suffer at the hands of mortals. It is true that the divine humanity would be God's gift *of Himself* to a ravaged world. However, to lose sight of the immensity which characterizes the Living God, simply because that immensity has been hidden in "the form of a servant", is the greatest mistake a child of Adam and Eve can make.

Furthermore, a remembrance of the immensity and grandeur of God, even when this God can be observed eating at a wedding feast, sleeping in a boat – or being scourged mercilessly by soldiers – will, paradoxically, make His humanity even more endearing, by reminding us of the unfathomable love behind the gift of God-made-Man: "Therefore because the children are partakers of flesh and blood, He also Himself in like manner hath been partaker of the same: that, through death, He might destroy him who had the empire of death." (Heb. 2:14)

Through the Scriptures, through revealed Truth and the doctrines and dogmas taught by the Roman Catholic Church, and received with good will, we can achieve an appreciation of the immensity of God – "appreciation", not "understanding", for only a fool would claim to understand God. Yet as rational creatures capable of deductive reasoning, we are *obligated* to study the things which God has *revealed* to us, in the hopes of understanding as much as our limitations allow: "All Scripture, inspired of God, is profitable to teach, to reprove, to correct, to instruct in justice." (2 Tim. 3:16) "Search ye diligently in the book of the Lord, and read." (Is. 34:16)

An honest, diligent study of the things of God *will* yield fruitful results. This has been promised to us by Our Lord: "Seek, and you shall find." (Mt. 7:7) "They that trust in Him, shall understand the truth." (Wis. 3:9)

Chapter Two

The Blessed Trinity

THE TRINITY: FATHER, SON AND HOLY GHOST – THE MAJESTY OF GOD – ALL THREE PERSONS HAVE ONE MAJESTY, ONE ALMIGHTY POWER

St. John Eudes (†1680) wrote, "Whoever sees Jesus sees Mary, and he who sees Mary beholds Jesus!" If no treatise had ever been written about Mary, if no sermon had ever been preached about her, we would still be faced with the task of contemplating the Woman who was *and is* the "Mother of Jesus", as she is referred to with deep respect by the Evangelist St. John. Therefore, before turning our sights towards the Blessed Virgin, we will focus them on Jesus Christ, her Son:

> In the beginning was the Word, and the Word was with God, and the Word was God. The same was in the beginning with God. All things were made by Him: and without Him was made nothing that was made. In Him was life, and the life was the light of men. . . . And the Word was made flesh, and dwelt among us, and we saw His glory, the glory as it were of the only begotten of the Father, full of grace and truth. (Jn. 1:1-4,14)

In all the books ever written since these words were first penned, there has never been a stronger, more concise, more eloquent defense of the Divinity of Jesus Christ. "The Word was with God, and the Word was God." How can Our Lord be *with* God and also *be* God? As the Second Divine Person of the Blessed Trinity!

The True God, the Living God, is *One*: "The Lord our God is one Lord." (Dt. 6:4) This divine essence, or substance, is shared by *Three* Divine Persons. Therefore God is called the "triune" God; He is One "in three distinct Persons", *not* "distinct in three Persons" (Pope Pius VI, *Auctorem Fidei*, 1794). The divine essence has always been, and remains, undivided, as was taught in the Creed of Faith of the Council of Toledo XI (675):

> Therefore, the three are one, that is, in *nature, not* in *person*. We must not, however, consider these three Persons separable, since we believe that no one before the other, no one after the other, no one without the other ever existed or did anything. For, they are found inseparable both in that which they are, and in that which they do, because between the generating Father and the generated Son and the proceeding Holy Spirit we believe that there was no interval of time in which either the begetter at any time preceded the begotten, or the begotten was lacking to the begetter, or the proceeding Holy Ghost appeared after the Father or the Son.

This is taught clearly in the *Nicene Creed*, where the Church proclaims her belief in *One God*, "the Father almighty, maker of heaven and earth . . . Jesus Christ, the only-begotten Son of God . . . begotten, not made; consubstantial with the Father . . . the Holy Ghost, the Lord and giver of Life, Who proceedeth from the Father and the Son."

The nature of the Triune God is already evident in the very beginning of Sacred Scripture. In the first verses of *The Book of Genesis*, we read that ". . . the Spirit of God moved over the waters." (1:2) After the earth and the beasts had been created, God said, "Let *us* make man to *our* image and likeness." (1:26) When Adam was created, he was given a fully human form, the same form and nature that, one day, would be assumed by the Incarnate Word in the womb of the Virgin Mary.

Does mankind benefit by apprehending in God the distinct Persons of Father, Son and Holy Ghost? The Council of Toledo taught that, "These three, therefore, are called persons, as our ancestors define, *that they may be recognized*, not that they may be separated." Fallible, limited human beings are invited to contemplate the perfections and labors of the Godhead as manifested in the Three Divine Persons.

And what matters to consider! There is God the Father, the Creator of all things. There is the Son, the Uncreated Wisdom, "by Whom all things were made", the Redeemer and Restorer of the world. There is the Holy Ghost, the "Giver of Life", the Sanctifier, the Divine Spirit animating the Church and rejuvenating the hearts and souls of Catholics. Because of the triune nature of God, we can "recognize" God in a way unimaginable to the Israelites of the Old Testament – "And because you are sons, God hath sent the Spirit of His Son into your hearts, crying: *Abba*, Father." (Gal. 4:6)

The gift of considering and "apprehending" one God in three distinct Persons is not one intended for popes and theologians only. As a subject for contemplation, God's triune nature is a bottomless cornucopia. It can be viewed through the lens of theology, where extreme scrutiny yields a precise, though sometimes dense, language. It can also be viewed through the poet's lens, which yields a different "language":

> For God, you know, can be compared to a hand; listen and find out how this can be so. The Father was, from the first, like a *fist*, with one finger bent, until he saw fit to unbend his finger, and put it forth, as an extension of the palm, in whichever direction that it should be required. The palm itself is the whole hand, and also puts out the fingers, to carry out whatever task the hand purposes. This makes it, we can safely say, an accurate emblem of the Holy Spirit of heaven: he resembles the palm. The *fingers*, that are free to bend and perform actions, make an apt symbol for the Son, who was sent down to earth. He, as the palm instructed, made direct, intimate contact with our Lady, the Virgin Mary, and assumed from her his human nature. (William Langland, d. c.1386, *Piers Plowman*)

There is an important corollary to this gift of recognizing God in His triune nature. Each Divine Person *is* GOD. They are not aspects, or facets, or "parts" of God: "Our God is one Lord." (Deut. 6:4) While it is a fact that the voice of the True God shone like a beacon of love and mercy from among the false "religions" of the ancient world, it must not be forgotten that this merciful God is "awesome", "terrible", the very essence of might and majesty:

> Behold the heaven, and the heavens of heavens, the deep, and all the earth, and the things that are in them, shall be moved in His sight, the mountains also, and the hills, and the foundations of the earth: when God shall look upon them, they shall be shaken with trembling. (Ecclus. 16:18-19)

These words apply to the Father, and to the Son, and to the Holy Ghost, and it is the reason why, in the *Preface* of the Mass, the priest says that "in the confession of one true and eternal Godhead, we adore distinctness in persons, oneness in essence, *and equality in majesty.*" In the case of the Second Divine Person, it is even more important to remember this "equality in majesty", because He came to earth in humility – He "emptied Himself, taking the form of a servant, being made in the likeness of men, and in habit found as a man." (Phil. 2:7) He was born in the most humble of settings, and was raised in a quiet place, so that His own neighbors would one day exclaim: "How came this man by all these things? And what wisdom is this that is given to Him, and such mighty works as are wrought by His hands? Is not this the carpenter, the Son of Mary?" (Mk. 6:2-3)

Chapter Three

Christ the Redeemer

TWO NATURES IN CHRIST – HIS OBEDIENCE UNTO DEATH – THE FALL OF ADAM AND THE PLAN OF REDEMPTION – DISOBEDIENCE AND DEATH – THE DEATH OF CHRIST RESTORED LIFE – THE OBEDIENCE OF MARY REVERSES THE DISOBEDIENCE OF EVE

Jesus Christ referred to Himself as "meek and humble of heart" and, throughout His public ministry, when awesome wonders accompanied Him, He remained the perfect Teacher of humility, because He practiced the virtue pre-eminently: "And whereas indeed He was the Son of God, He learned obedience by the things which He suffered." (Heb. 5:8)

In an awesome paradox, even Our Lord's mighty works – the raising of the dead, the curing of the blind, the healing of the sick – were performed with a certain "divine humility". They were never attended by any fanfare, with the thunder and lightning associated with the pagan deities. The Truth they attested to was never forced upon anyone. On the contrary, there was a time when Our Lord would not even perform many miracles in His own country "because of their unbelief". (Mt. 13:58)

The Redeemer's supreme act of humility was His death on Calvary: "He humbled Himself, becoming obedient unto death, even to the death of the Cross." (Phil. 2:8) Even in the midst of His Passion, when the Lamb of God was preparing for the journey to Calvary, the divinity of Jesus, the might and majesty of the Godhead, were not permitted to go unrecognized. During His betrayal on Mount Olivet, Jesus said, "Thinkest thou that I cannot ask my Father, and he will give me presently more than twelve legions of Angels?" (Mt. 26:53) Lest any of His enemies dare presume that such words were mere empty boasting, Jesus allowed an infinitesimal portion of His power to be made manifest when the armed mob dispatched by the chief priests arrived, announcing that they were seeking Jesus of Nazareth. St. John relates that when Our Lord replied, "... I am He, ..." the mob "... went backward, and fell to the ground." (Jn. 18:6)

The two natures – divine and human – united in the one Person of Jesus Christ, are united in what is called the *Hypostatic Union*, whereby neither of these natures is in any way altered or diluted. Therefore, Our Lord is rightly called "True God *and* True Man." As True Man, the Redeemer could suffer and die in reparation for mankind's sins; Jesus "... by His own Blood, entered once into the Holies, having obtained eternal redemption." (Heb. 9:12) As True God, He could offer a sacrifice pleasing to the Father, because its merits were infinite: "For God indeed was in Christ, reconciling the world to Himself." (2 Cor. 5:19) To contemplate the Incarnation of the Second Person of the Blessed Trinity is to ponder the miracle of God *becoming* one of us, sharing in our human nature, in every way: "His Son, Who was made to Him of the seed of David, according to the flesh." (Rom. 1:3)

An omnipotent God could have redeemed the world in an infinite number of ways. That it needed to be redeemed is an indisputable fact. A complete definition of *justice* must include not only the idea of "fairness" but also "the administration of what is just, as by assigning merited rewards or punishments". The key word is *merited*. In societies divorced from Catholic Truth, there is prevalent a puerile mentality that perceives in the God of justice a type of ogre, an unfair and tyrannical "father-figure", who first imposes arbitrary restrictions on his children, then steps back, stick in hand, just waiting for them to transgress.

The facts, as recorded in the account of the fall of Adam and Eve, do not bear out this skewed vision. Possessed of free will, our first parents were trusted to use their intellects, their reason *and their experience of God's goodness*, in making their decisions. Was the prohibition against eating of the tree "in the midst of Paradise" an unreasonable burden? If we were to make up a check-list contrasting the gifts bestowed upon Adam and Eve with any "restrictions" on their "freedom", we would discover the following: (Gen. 1:12, 21, 24, 28; 2:8)

Gifts:

God created a new world. On this world was land, on which could be found "the green herb, and such as may seed, and the fruit-tree yielding fruit after its kind", not to mention "cattle, and creeping things, and beasts of the earth." Also on this world was the sea, containing such marvels as the "great whales, and every living and moving creature, which the waters brought forth."

There is more. Adam and Eve were given life, an existence, where before they had *none*. And they were given a special place in this fertile, teeming planet in which to live – "a paradise of pleasure". This existence was free from pain, disease and corruption.

There is still more. They were given the governance of this beautiful new world: "Fill the earth and subdue it, and rule over the fishes of the sea, and the fowls of the air, and all living creatures that move upon the earth."

Restrictions:

Adam and Eve were to stay away from one tree.

Comparing these two lists, it is difficult to conceive on what basis the enemies of God have constructed His supposed mean-spirited or whimsical persona. The lists tell us that God gave all the most exquisite gifts of His creation to Adam and Eve. He fulfilled all their needs, to the point where they would never lack either for food, or even for the purely aesthetic nourishment of flora, fauna and landscape. Adam was commanded to "dress" and "keep" the Garden, which did not indicate the hard toil and labor of the later farmer, but was a pleasurable activity, by which man could avoid idleness even as he lived in friendship with His Maker.

And what was the "catch?" Adam and Eve were to avoid eating the fruit of one solitary tree, "the tree of the knowledge of good and evil". Imagine someone giving his neighbor a million dollars, then removing a twenty-dollar bill from the huge stack of bills. Placing the twenty-dollar bill on the table, he informs the neighbor, "The rest of the ten million dollars belongs to you, just as long as you don't spend this twenty." Would anyone call the man "unfair" because of this arrangement? Does the twenty-dollar bill suddenly become *so* desirable merely because it has been labeled "forbidden", to the point where it is worth sacrificing the rest of the bounty?

The very idea is absurd. The million dollars *belongs* to the one who offers to bestow it on his neighbor; although it is freely offered, it is at the disposal of the giver, and the conditions accompanying it are *his* to make. Whoever chose the twenty-dollar bill over the million would relinquish wealth that was not his by right, but that had been *offered* to him; choosing freely, he would prove himself undeserving of the opportunity originally granted him. The "stakes" in Eden were beyond measure: life and friendship with God, or death, the death of the soul. Was this a harsh choice? On the contrary, it was completely fair. God is justified in saying, to those who complain that the enjoyment of Paradise carried with it a condition, the same words spoken by the man in the parable:

"Is it not lawful for me to do what I will? Is thy eye evil, because I am good?" (Mt. 20:15)

One who chooses to oppose God in any manner *decides* to separate himself from God. Even the serpent in the Garden could not force such a decision from Eve. Instead, he turned to subterfuge by asking her, "Why hath God commanded you, that you should not eat of every tree of paradise?" (Gen. 3:1) The serpent knew full well that God did not forbid Adam and Eve to eat of *every* tree; He denied them only *one* lone tree. The word "every" makes God seem unfair, and so do His opponents describe Him to this day.

The fall of Adam and Eve was not the result of a malicious trick, the springing of a "trap" set by the Creator as some sort of primordial "sting operation" meant to catch His children being unfaithful. It was the result of mankind (for Adam and Eve constituted the entirety of mankind at that time) freely and deliberately turning away from God. Our first parents believed the word of the serpent, who gave them nothing, over that of God, Who gave them everything. Of such import was this turning away from God that human nature itself would suffer. Like a body that is denied proper nourishment or sunlight, human nature became enfeebled, sickly, as a result of this original sin.

God was not the author of the fall, nor was He the "cause" of original sin. "Justice" implies the *administration* of what is just, which includes the meting out of either rewards or punishments. The need for "justice," for a balancing of the scales, is rooted in the human heart. During the Sermon on the Mount, Our Lord would acknowledge this need: "Blessed are they that hunger and thirst after justice: for they shall have their fill." (Mt. 5:6) A God Who did not administer rewards or punishments would not be a *just* God. A man who cared nothing for right or wrong, who did not even distinguish between the hero and the criminal, would be more monster than man. Who would dare posit such a *God* ?

"Unhappy man that I am, who shall deliver me from the body of this death?" cried St. Paul. (Rom. 7:24) This is the cry of *all* the children of Adam and Eve, burdened with the grim inheritance of Eden. Yet, because of this calamity, whereby human nature had become weakened, diseased, God took upon Himself this *same* nature: "Therefore because the children are partakers of flesh and blood, He also Himself in like manner hath been partaker of the same." Why? "That, through death, He might destroy him who had the empire of death, that is to say: the devil." (Heb. 2:14)

Through death, the Incarnate God would *destroy* the one who had the "empire of death." We are recalled back to Eden here, but the new events are occurring with a retrograde motion. In the Garden, the serpent triumphed *over human nature*, and *death* was visited upon the human race through the *disobedience* of a man and a woman. On Calvary, human nature, glorified at the Resurrection of Jesus, triumphed *over the serpent*, and *life* was visited again upon the human race because of the *obedience* of a Man ("My Father . . . Thy will be done") and a Woman ("Let it be done to me according to thy word").

This retrograde motion, in which the fall is "reversed" (at the Rising of the Savior from the tomb), made possible the completion of the cry of St. Paul: "Who shall deliver me from the body of this death? *The grace of God*, by *Jesus Christ, Our Lord*." (Rom. 7:24–25)

Chapter Four

Christ, the Divine Victim

THE OFFENCE: INFINITE MAJESTY DISOBEYED BY THE NOTHINGNESS OF THE FIRST MAN – THE REQUIREMENT OF JUSTICE – THE OFFENDED IS GOD, THE CREATOR; THE OFFENDER IS MAN, THE CREATURE – THE RECONCILIATION CAN ONLY BE ACHIEVED BY A GOD-MAN – GRACE RESTORED THROUGH THE MERITS OF JESUS CHRIST

There are many descriptions of Jesus Christ preserved in the Gospels, and the most powerful of them came from His own lips:

> I am the Good Shepherd. The Good Shepherd giveth His life for His sheep. (Jn. 10:11)
>
> I am the living Bread which came down from heaven. If any man eat of this Bread, he shall live forever: and the Bread that I will give is my flesh, for the life of the world. (Jn. 6:51-52)
>
> Jerusalem, Jerusalem, that killest the prophets, and stonest them that are sent to thee, how often would I have gathered thy children as the bird doth her brood under her wings, and thou wouldest not? (Lk. 13:34)
>
> They that are in health need not a physician, but they that are ill. Go then and learn what this meaneth: I will have mercy, and not sacrifice. (Mt. 9:12-13)

When reading the life of Jesus, we are struck by the combination of humility and authority, of meekness and might, which permeates His every action and word. Above all, though, we are drawn to His humanity. We think of Him – of *God* – with a certain familiarity, a familiarity which was not given to His servants before He took human nature to Himself. Pope St. Leo the Great (†461) wrote:

> The Son of God entered into these lowly conditions of the world, after descending from His celestial throne,

> and though He did not withdraw from the glory of the Father, He was generated in a new order and in a new nativity. In a new order, because invisible in His own, *He was made visible in ours*; incomprehensible, *He wished to be comprehended*; permanent before times, *He began to be in time*; the Lord of the universe assumed the form of a slave, concealing the immensity of His majesty; the impassible God did not disdain to be a passible man and the immortal to be subject to the laws of death. (*Lectis dilectionis tuae,* 449)

God had spoken to Abraham and to Moses; these loyal servants were granted the blessing to be God's friends. *The Book of Exodus* says that "the Lord spoke to Moses face to face, as a man is wont to speak to his friend." (Ex. 33:11) This phrase "face to face" is meant to indicate only that they conversed in a very personal manner. Later, when Moses asked to see the "glory" of God, he received *this* reply:

> Thou canst not see my face: for man shall not see me and live. . . . Behold there is a place with me, and thou shalt stand upon the rock. *And when my glory shall pass, I will set thee in a hole of the rock, and protect thee with my right hand, till I pass*: And I will take away my hand, and thou shalt see my back parts: but my face thou canst not see. (Ex. 33:20-23)

Compare these words with those recorded by St. John: "And the Word was made flesh and dwelt among us, *and we saw His glory*." Something radical has happened in the dealings between God and men.

Unfortunately, many people stop short at the familiarity accorded us by the Incarnation. The accessibility of Jesus and His humility are too often regarded apart from His divinity, from His very purpose in coming to earth to die the death He did. Because of this widespread forgetfulness, the opponents of Christ often find themselves on the reverse side of the same coin as those who claim to follow Him, but do so on the basis of sheer sentimentality. In the end, those who deny the Virgin Birth at Bethlehem are not much farther from the mark than those who will not link it to the sacrifice on Calvary, or the sacramental life of the Church. Both push aside the Divine Christ, replacing Him with a mere human paragon – the "good teacher", "moral activist", or "religious reformer."

The Second Divine Person came to earth as a man for a purpose, and His Incarnation was part of a plan that transcended time and space: "Blessed be the God and Father of our Lord Jesus Christ, Who hath blessed us with all spiritual blessings in heavenly places, in Christ: As He chose us in Him, *before the foundation of the world.*" (Eph. 1:3-4) This Man, Jesus of Nazareth, Who healed the sick and allowed Himself to be led away to Calvary without a word of protest, *is the Eternal God.* The One Who broke bread with the apostles, Who walked along dusty roads, Who cured the blind and the lame, was and is *God* – "And there are three Who give testimony in heaven: the Father, the Word, and the Holy Ghost. *And these three are one"* (1 Jn. 5:7) – and His advent was the very cornerstone for all of human history:

> Behold the Lord hath made it to be heard in the ends of the earth, tell the daughter of Sion: Behold, thy Savior cometh: behold, His reward is with Him, and His work before Him. (Is. 62:11) All things are delivered to Me by My Father. (Mt. 11:27)

Jesus Christ, the only-begotten Son of God *and* the only Son of Mary, *is* Hope and Truth. As TRUE GOD, His presence permeates creation and history. As TRUE MAN, He was the awaited Savior. "Search the Scriptures, for you think in them to have life everlasting," said Our Lord to the Jews, "and the same are they that give testimony of Me." (Jn. 5:39)

The demands of Justice required reparation to God for the events of Eden. It was incumbent upon *mankind*, or its representative, to make this reparation, since the original offense had been committed by mankind. There is no instance here of an arbitrary punishment being inflicted upon an arbitrary victim. In fact, the Scriptures teach us that God, like a good and loving parent, takes no delight in the chastisements called forth by His Justice: "For He hath not willingly afflicted, nor cast off the children of men." (Lam. 3:33) Yet, even in the everyday, natural sphere of earthly existence, Justice requires that "the equation be balanced."

This put mankind in a bind: How to balance the equation when its repercussions had an infinite dimension, when the offense had been committed against *God*? What did fallen humanity possess of enough value to make a suitable return to God? The only honest answer was *nothing*:

> All flesh is grass, and all the glory thereof as the flower of the field. The grass is withered, and the flower is fallen, because the Spirit of the Lord hath blown upon it. Indeed, the people is grass: The grass is withered, and the flower is fallen: but the word of our Lord endureth for ever. (Is. 40:6-8)

The primordial turning away from God, the original sin committed by our first parents, was of such import that it literally scarred human nature from that day forward. The results were plain to see: "Man born of a woman, living for a short time, is filled with many miseries." (Job 14:1) "All his days are full of sorrows and miseries, even in the night he doth not rest in mind." (Eccles. 2:23)

Unable to raise himself up from these spiritual, moral and physical depths, how was man ever to regain the friendship of God, which could only be won by the repayment of the "debt" incurred by Adam and Eve? How could the scales of justice ever be balanced? We are told how in *The Prophecy of Isaias:*

> Take courage, and fear not: behold your God will bring the revenge of recompense: *God Himself will come and will save you*. (Is. 35:4)

The recompense, the satisfaction, the demands of justice *will* be met by mankind. Reparation will be made, and friendship re-established between God and His children. God *Himself* would save mankind. And, since the offense had to be atoned for by humanity, then the unimaginable would happen. God would become man, would assume this human nature and make the perfect offering, the perfect sacrifice through which He would gather His children to Him again, renewed, refreshed and without blemish . . . a *redeemed* humanity. In this way, it could never be said that the Justice of God was lacking, that He would ever ignore right and wrong. At the same time, the mercy of God would shine forth in a splendor unheard of in the ages before or since.

Job spoke of "Man *born* of a woman . . ." (14:1) whose days were saddled with constant misery. St. Paul wrote: "When the fullness of the time was come, God sent His Son, *made of a woman.*" (Gal. 4:4) The retrograde motion in human affairs was ready to begin. Human nature, with its attendant sorrows and miseries, was ready to become glorified; the *cause* of human sorrow was about to become the *answer* to human sorrow. God was ready to give the world the greatest gift that He could ever give anywhere, anytime: *Himself.*

Mankind was not the "offended party" in the fall; the human race was in debt to the Blessed Trinity. Why, then, was God taking upon Himself the sins of the world? St. John told us why: "*For God so loved the world*, as to give His only begotten Son . . . that the world may be saved by Him." (Jn. 3:16-17)

God's love for mankind is the reason for the Incarnation. Divine Love is the reason that the Redemption, which could have been effected in any manner chosen by God, was accomplished on the Cross. When Abraham took his son, Isaac (a figure of Christ), to Mount Moria, he said, "God will provide Himself a victim for an holocaust." (Gen. 22:8) With the advent of Our Lord, born of the Virgin Mary at Bethlehem, these words were fulfilled in their deepest sense.

It is Divine Love which causes God ever to seek out His children. In Eden, we observe God calling out to Adam, "Where art thou?" Of course, God knew where Adam was, but what a beautiful image is preserved in this calling out, in this seeking of Adam. Throughout the history of Israel, God would continue seeking out His people, sending angels, prophets and judges to instruct and guide them in His ways. After the Resurrection, when the apostles were still smarting from their cowardice and inconstancy in the face of their Lord's Passion, the Risen Savior went to them. And what were His first words to those who had forsaken Him? – "Peace be to you." (Jn. 20:19)

Although God conversed with Moses as a man speaks "to his friend", the *complete* "friendship" between God and mankind – possible only when human nature is vivified by the life of grace – was broken in Eden, with the fall of Adam and Eve. It was to be restored in a manner which would not only raise human nature to glory, but would teach a weary world something precious about its God and His mercy: "God is Faithful." (Deut. 32:4) This God delights to be with His people: "I will be in glory in the midst thereof." (Zach. 2:5) To that end, the friendship severed in Eden would be renewed and proclaimed from God's own lips:

> I will not now call you servants: for the servant knoweth not what his lord doth. *But I have called you friends*: because all things, whatsoever I have heard of my Father, I have made known to you. (Jn. 15:15)

Chapter Five

The Spiritual Enmity Between the Woman and the Devil

ADAM AND EVE CAST OUT OF EDEN – A SAVIOR IS PROMISED BY GOD – THE "WOMAN" TO COME IS ANNOUNCED; SHE WILL CRUSH THE HEAD OF THE SERPENT – LUCIFER'S PRIDE – THE TWO KINGDOMS AND SPIRITUAL WARFARE

After the fall, God's Justice was made instantly manifest: "And the Lord God sent him out of the paradise of pleasure, to till the earth from which he was taken. And He cast out Adam." (Gen. 3:23-24) But the primal tragedy of Eden was not to be the end of hope. On the contrary, it would set the stage for the greatest Hope the world would ever know:

> But not as the offense, so also the gift. For if by the offense of one, many died; much more the grace of God and the gift, by the grace of one man, Jesus Christ, hath abounded unto many. . . . Where sin abounded, grace did more abound. (Rom. 5:15, 20)

The gifts of grace which would be given to *many*, to the countless descendants of Adam and Eve, on account of the Incarnation of the Second Divine Person, would dwarf the dire sin committed by *one* in Eden. "O Happy fault," sings the Church on Holy Saturday, "that was worthy to have such and so great a Redeemer!"

God's mercy was made manifest immediately after the fall of Adam and Eve. The Creator did not let His children wallow in their guilt and self-pity. In their presence, He cursed their enemy, the serpent: ". . . thou art cursed among all cattle, and beasts of the earth." (Gen. 3:14) But a curse was not the only thing to be pronounced in the hearing of Adam and Eve. In the midst of their misery, the God of mercy also prophesied hope, the very substance and epitome of hope. He did this in words, still addressed to the serpent, whose import was so profound for the entire human race, that they are referred to as the *Proto-evangelium*, the "First Gospel":

> I will put enmities between thee and the woman, and thy seed and her seed: she shall crush thy head, and thou shalt lie in wait for her heel. (Gen. 3:15)

This *Proto-evangelium* was the announcement of the Incarnation of Christ. It is the first prophecy recorded in Scripture, and it proclaims God's unending love for His own. Of the "seed" prophesied here, St. John would write, "For God so loved the world, as to give His only begotten Son." In the midst of the inexorable unfolding of Divine Justice, and the righteous anger of God against both the serpent and our first parents, there is the promise of forgiveness and life. The Father would *not* leave His children in despair.

We are struck immediately in the *Proto-evangelium* by the prominent place of the "Woman". She is not a mere afterthought, or a grudging necessity required in order for her "seed" to be generated. God Himself said this: "I will put enmities between thee *and* the woman."

The "thee" addressed by God in the Proto-Gospel is the serpent. In his *Apocalypse*, St. John leaves no doubt as to this creature's true identity: "And that great dragon was cast out, that old serpent, who is called the devil and Satan, who seduceth the whole world." (Apoc. 12:9) The serpent is the angel who was once called *Lucifer*, the "Lightbearer". At the dawn of time, he was created by God, along with St. Michael and the rest of the heavenly host, in unimaginable splendor:

> The first visibility of the invisible God was but an instantaneous flash, and there lay outspread the broad world of angels, throbbing with light, and teeming with innumerous and yet colossal life. The brightness that silvered them was the reflection of Infinite Beauty. From It and because of It they came. Out of It they drew their marvelous diversity of graces. (Fr. Frederick William Faber, d. 1863, quoted in *St. Michael and the Angels*)

Of Jesus Christ, St. John taught that, "All things were made by Him: and without Him was made nothing that was made." (Jn. 1:3) This, of course, applies to the hosts of angels as well: "Let us first understand this, that the demons were not made as demons, for God made nothing bad. And they also were created beautiful, but fell from heavenly wisdom." (St. Athanasius, †373)

One-third of this host, luminous with the reflected light of the Godhead, succumbed to pride. "A third of that creation of purest light," wrote Fr. Faber, "has, it is maintained, refused to adore the Incarnate Word, and is flung speedily into the dread abyss." In the *Apocalypse*, we read that the Dragon's tail "drew the third part of the stars of heaven, and cast them to the earth." (Apoc. 12:4)

The results of Lucifer's willful rejection of God are chronicled in the sacred texts. The Prophet Isaias wrote: "How art thou fallen from heaven, O Lucifer, who didst rise in the morning." (14:12) These words, addressed to the proud king of Babylon, also have a *spiritual* sense to them, and are applied by the Church to Satan. The celestial being who was once the "bearer of light", cast into hell by St. Michael and the good angels, lost his brightness and became corrupt in every sense of the word. In the *Inferno*, Dante Alighieri (d. 1321) observed of Satan, "If he was once as beautiful as now he is hideous, and still turned on his maker, well may he be the source of every woe!"

The corrupted nature of the fallen angel was described by Our Lord: "He was a murderer from the beginning, and he stood not in the truth; because truth is not in him . . . for he is a liar, and the father thereof." (Jn. 8:44) St. Peter described Satan as "a roaring lion . . . seeking whom he may devour." (1 Pt. 5:8) Fallen angels – i.e., demons – are referred to as "unclean spirits" in the Gospels.

It is Catholic teaching that Lucifer's pride caused him to reject the Incarnation, to refuse homage to God *united to human nature*. Testimony to the truth of this can be found throughout the Scriptures, in the obsessive and unrelenting assaults of Satan upon mankind, upon human beings whose model, or "template", is the Sacred Humanity of the Incarnate Word, through which Jesus associated Himself with His creatures. "Lucifer became a rebel against his Creator," taught St. Francis de Sales (†1622), "and therefore against *the image of his Creator*, who is man."

"As long as you did it to one of these my least brethren, you did it to me." (Mt. 25:40) Our Lord could very well be addressing Satan with these same words. In his twisted way, the fallen angel goes up against God, against the Sacred Humanity he had rejected, each time he attacks a human being: "Let us make man to our image and likeness." (Gen. 1:26) This explains why an angel, possessed of intellectual and supernatural powers superior to those of men, can be obsessed with attacking beings he would consider his "inferiors".

It is not the will of the Father "that one of these little ones should perish." (Mt. 18:14) However, He will not deny the exercise of free will to His rational creatures:

> Before man is life and death, good and evil, that which he shall choose shall be given him. (Ecclus. 15:18) If it seem evil to you to serve the Lord, you have your choice: choose this day that which pleaseth you, whom you would rather serve. (Jos. 24:15)

Men and women *can* choose to separate themselves from God . . . and for eternity. The devil, the enemy of humanity, of human *nature* itself, works towards that one end, the separation of God's *human* children from their birthright: "If you be Christ's, then you are the seed of Abraham, heirs according to the promise." (Gal. 3:29)

St. Paul wrote to the Romans:

> For I am sure that neither death, nor life, *nor angels, nor principalities, nor powers,* nor things present, nor things to come, nor might, nor height, nor depth, nor any other creature, shall be able to separate us from the love of God, which is in Christ Jesus, our Lord. (Rom. 8:38-39)

The love of God is of such power and endurance that no outside force can compromise or budge it, whether creatures or circumstances. But our birthright as *children* of God, co-heirs to His kingdom with Christ, can be freely *given* away. In *The Book of Genesis*, the story is told of Esau, the son of Isaac, who sold his birthright to his brother Jacob for a bowl of lentils. As the first-born was entitled to double portions of his father's wealth, as well as the father's special blessing, this attitude of Esau betrayed little appreciation for such gifts.

The denial of mankind's *spiritual* birthright is of infinitely more import, and Our Lord gave us a very specific warning regarding it:

"Fear ye not them that kill the body, and are not able to kill the soul: but rather fear him that can destroy both soul and body in hell." (Mt. 10:28) The ruination of the soul, the rejection of Truth and the choosing of Satan over Christ, is the only way in which a "separation" from God can be effected, the separation which, otherwise, would be impossible to imagine, as St. Paul reassured the Catholics of Rome.

Ousted from Paradise for eternity, it is intolerable for the serpent to imagine eternal beatitude visited upon creatures whose very "persons" are dependent upon their souls being *united* to the despised human nature. The ruin of human souls, then, the souls of men and women created in the image of God, is the means by which he wreaks his revenge:

> For the devil was exulting in the deceit he had practiced on man, causing him to lose the divinely given gifts. Man had stripped himself of the gift of immortality and could look forward only to the sentence of death. Perhaps the devil found some comfort in having a partner in crime! (Pope St. Leo the Great, †461, *Second Sermon on the Nativity of Our Lord*)

The devil sets his feet upon this ruinous road with a firm resolve. In *The Book of Job*, Satan says to God, "I have gone round about the earth, and walked through it." (Job 1:7) Well might St. Peter have added, "seeking whom he may devour."

The ruin of souls is carried out much like a well-planned military campaign. In *The Letter to the Hebrews*, Satan is referred to as " . . . him who had the empire of death . . ." (Heb. 2:14) The word *empire* is significant; it tells us something about the nature of what is quite literally "the devil's work". It reveals that there is a "kingdom" of darkness, opposed to God's kingdom, that both men and angels can be found in the opposing camps: "For God created man incorruptible, and to the image of His own likeness He made him. But by the envy of the devil, death came into the world: And they follow him that are of his side." (Wis. 2:23-25)

A constant state of *war* exists between these kingdoms, and Satan will employ for his ends only the most effective tactical methods:

Deception – "For Satan himself transformeth himself into an angel of light." (2 Cor. 11:14)

The Dissemination of Unreliable (though sometimes partially accurate) Information – "For God doth know that in what day soever you shall eat thereof, your eyes shall be opened." (Gen. 3:5)

The Use of Agents: "And when He had dipped the bread, He gave it to Judas Iscariot, the son of Simon. And after the morsel, Satan entered into him." (Jn. 13:26-27)

The struggle between humanity and hell is not a mere allegory for temptation or man's inclination to vice. Because its principal arena is the invisible human soul, this *supernatural* struggle is easily dismissed as fiction by those who tend to exalt their own rationalism. On the contrary, the battle for souls bears all the hallmarks of a true war, in which each side can only advance through vigilance and perseverance.; and the onset of this struggle took place in Eden.

Chapter Six

The Wages of Sin

THE DEVIL WAS CREATED GOOD AND FELL FROM GRACE – THE WAGES OF SIN – CHRIST IS THE ANTIDOTE TO DEATH – EVE FREELY DISPOSED HERSELF TO SIN

Common usage mistakenly portrays God and Satan as "exact opposites." On the one hand is good and "light"; on the other is evil and "darkness". There is God, the ultimate power for good; there is Satan, the ultimate power for evil. This sense that there is something like an "equality" between God and the devil is an ancient error; it contradicts not only the teachings of Scripture and the Catholic Church concerning the primeval battle between St. Michael and Lucifer, but also regarding the very beginning of Creation, where the One God created *all* things and "saw that it was good." The third-century *Manichean* heresy held that there existed an eternal "Principle of Evil", not a fallen being, but *essential* evil. This error was addressed by the Council of Braga (561):

> If anyone says that the devil was not first a good angel made by God, and that his nature was not a work of God, but says that he came forth from darkness, and does not have any author of himself, but is himself the origin and substance of evil, as Manichaeus and Priscillian have said, let him be anathema. (*Anathemas against Heretics*)

Pope Innocent III (1198-1216) taught that "the devil was made evil not through creation *but through will.*" He is not the "substance of evil", as though "Evil" were a disembodied reality on a par with "Good". He is a creature who, at one point in time, freely and deliberately rejected God forever, by rejecting God-made-Man. This *rejection of Christ* is the beginning and foundation of all evil: "I am the light of the world: he that followeth Me, walketh not in darkness. . . . Why do you not know My speech? Because you cannot hear My word. You are of your father, the devil, and the desires of your father you will do." (Jn. 8:12,43-44)

The Gospels teach plainly that there is a kingdom, an "empire", whose head is Satan. While tempting Jesus in the desert, showing Him ". . . all the kingdoms of the world in a moment of time," (Lk. 4:5) the devil said, "For to me they are delivered, and to whom I will, I give them." (Lk. 4:6) This was no idle boast, for our Lord Himself referred to Satan as ". . . the prince of this world . . ." (Jn. 12:31) Yet, the Scriptures proclaim, "O Lord God of hosts, who is like to Thee?. . . Thine are the heavens, and *Thine* is the earth." (Ps. 88:9,12) How can the earth "belong" both to God and Satan?

When Christ stood before Pontius Pilate, the governor of Judea, He said: "Thou shouldst not have any power against me, unless it were given thee from above." (Jn. 19:11) This is a remarkable statement, for the Son of God did not state merely that the governor held no power that was not granted from above; He said, "Thou wouldst have no power *against* me." Our Lord taught that opposition to Him is allowed to exist.

If the respective kingdoms of God and the devil can never be equal, then what is the nature of the "opposition" between them? Job lamented that, "The earth is given into the hand of the wicked. . . ." (Job 9:24) Satan *is* the "prince of the world"; that is, the "prince" of the *fallen* world. When he tempted Jesus in the desert, he said: "To Thee will I give all this power, and the glory of them; for to me they are delivered." (Lk. 4:6) What is the "power and the glory" of mankind after the fall? The picture is not pretty:

> Their thoughts, and fears of the heart, their imagination of things to come, and the day of their end: From him that sitteth on a glorious throne, unto him that is humbled in earth and ashes: From him that weareth purple, and beareth the crown, even to him that is covered with rough linen: wrath, envy, trouble, unquietness, and the fear of death, continual anger, and strife. (Ecclus. 40:2-4)

As a warlord who levels an entire city, then moves in to occupy the remains, so did the devil with the fallen earth. Having become "the prince of this world" through treachery, through human pride and neglect, he mounted his throne: "There is no power upon earth that can be compared with him who was made to fear no one. He beholdeth every high thing, he is king over all the children of pride." (Job 41:24-25) Behind him goes an angelic host, for God ". . . spared not the angels that sinned, but delivered them, drawn down by infernal ropes to the lower hell, unto torments. . . ." (2 Pt. 2:4) St. Athanasius wrote that these fallen angels "envy us Christians and move everything to hinder us from the way to heaven, lest we mount to where they fell from."

If, then, the respective kingdoms of God and the devil can never be equal, on what "battlefield" do they contend? What arena can provide opportunities for *both* to make conquests? There is only one such theatre: the immortal rational soul united to a body of flesh and blood – i.e., the human *person*. These two "kingdoms," then, each have deeply *interior* aspects:

> My kingdom is not of this world. . . . For this was I born, and for this came I into the world; that I should give testimony to the truth. Every one that is of the truth, heareth My voice. (Jn. 18:36-37)

> I will go forth, and be a lying spirit. (3 Kg. 22:22) And when an unclean spirit is gone out of a man he walketh through dry places seeking rest, and findeth none. Then he saith: I will return into my house from whence I came out. (Mt. 12:43-44)

In his encyclical on the Kingship of Christ, Pope Pius XI contrasted the two kingdoms: "Indeed, this kingdom is presented in the Gospels as such, into which men prepare to enter by doing penance; moreover, they cannot enter it except through faith and baptism, which, although an external rite, yet signifies and effects an interior regeneration; it is opposed only to the kingdom of Satan and to the powers of darkness." (*Quas Primas,* 1925)

Of course, a kingdom with solely an interior vitality, without any external manifestation as a *visible* society, would not be a complete kingdom, and Pope Pius followed this observation on the interior nature of the Kingship of Christ by stating that anyone would be committing a gross error "who should deprive Christ, the man, of power over all civil affairs, since He has received the most absolute right over created things from the Father, so that all have been placed under His authority."

However, the kingdom of God is established firstly in the heart and soul of the human person, through "the grace of God, life everlasting in Christ Jesus, our Lord." (Rom. 6:23) This is the principal foundation. From there, its vitality flows into the temporal sphere, into the kingdom of God seen as the "perfect society" on earth, the Catholic Church: "You are the light of the world. A city seated on a mountain cannot be hid." (Mt. 5:14) The Church *Militant* (its members still living on earth) is no less integral a part of God's kingdom than is either the Church *Suffering* (the souls in purgatory) or the Church *Triumphant* (the blessed in heaven). Therefore, it is absolutely necessary to remain a part of this kingdom or society while still living on earth, if one desires to enter the *eternal* kingdom forever: "Be thou faithful until death, and I will give thee the crown of life." (Apoc. 2:10)

The grace of God, life everlasting, in Christ Jesus, Our Lord. This is the antidote prescribed by St. Paul for "the wages of sin" – death. Pope St. Pius V (†1572) taught that through sanctifying grace a sinner is "vivified" and is thereby "made a living branch on the vine for Christ." Supernatural *life* is restored to the sinner via this grace; therefore, the man or woman thus "vivified" is considered a participant in "the life" of the Blessed Trinity:

> In this we know that we abide in Him, and He in us: because He hath given us of His Spirit. And we have seen, and do testify, that the Father hath sent His Son to be the Savior of the world. (1 Jn. 4:13-14)

"If anyone love Me, he will keep My word, and My Father will love him," said our Lord during the Last Supper, "and We will come to him *and will make Our abode with him.*" (Jn. 14:23) To keep the word of our Lord is to seek out and cultivate a life of grace. The prerequisite for such a life is the sacrament of Baptism: "Amen, amen I say to thee, unless a man be born again *of water* and the Holy Ghost, he *cannot* enter into the kingdom of God." (Jn. 3:5) Fallen human nature, tainted with original sin, can never cleanse itself of the contagion. In Baptism, such a purification can occur, through the merits of the sacrifice on Calvary: "Know you not that all we, who are baptized in Christ Jesus, are baptized in His death?" (Rom. 6:3)

Even infants, as descendants of Adam and Eve, are "truly baptized unto the remission of sins, so that which they have contracted from generation may be cleansed in them by regeneration." (*Canons against the Pelagians*, approved by Pope St. Zosimus, †418)

What, then, is the "work" of the baptized Catholic? "If you keep My commandments," our Lord said, "you shall abide in My love; as I also have kept My Father's commandments and do abide in His love." (Jn. 15:10) After Baptism, fidelity to the teachings of Christ, to the Truth, is the way in which individuals keep His commandments. This entails a life-long struggle to "remain in" the love of God, to participate in the supernatural "life" of the Blessed Trinity – i.e., to cultivate and maintain the "state of grace". It is indeed a struggle, and the stakes literally dwarf those of the most momentous and bloodiest military campaigns of history.

This is why the "arena" in which the kingdoms of Christ and Satan meet is the human person, composed of body *and* soul. The operatives of one kingdom work to separate the person from the life of grace (and from his birthright as "heir" to the kingdom). It started in Eden when the serpent suggested that Eve could do better for herself than simply following the commandments of God, a perfect example of the interior nature of the struggle. There was no physical coercion exerted by the serpent. In fact, his first lie, that God had spitefully forbidden our first parents the use of *every* tree in Paradise, was challenged and corrected by Eve: "Of the fruit of the trees that are in paradise we do eat." (Gen. 3:2) She displayed here an understanding of God's commandment: "But of the fruit of the tree which is in the midst of paradise, God hath commanded us that we should not eat lest perhaps we die." (Gen. 3:3)

Eve's disposition to disregard God's commandment occasioned the fall, "And the woman saw that the tree was good to eat." (Gen. 3:6) Yet, we refer to this as the "sin of Adam," for it was he who *ratified* the rebellion from God's commandment when the fruit was offered to him "who did eat." In the fall of Adam and Eve can be seen, in microcosm, the struggles of each and every one of their descendants against sin, against the serpent. There are the first stirrings of temptation, which obscure the beauty and importance of grace, when God's words seem unfair or restrictive: "Why hath God commanded you, that you should not eat of *every* tree of Paradise?" (Gen. 3:1) Gaining ground during this growing apathy to grace is a feeling of "unfairness," the sense that God has tricked us, by backing us into a corner through cruel and unnecessary laws and commandments, leaving sin the only release: "The woman, whom *Thou* gavest me to be my companion, gave me of the tree, and I did eat." (Gen. 3:12) There is the often intoxicating allure of a life "independent" from God, when sin appears like a tree whose fruit is ". . . good to eat, and fair to the eyes, and delightful to behold. . . ." (Gen. 3:6)

Finally, there is the "payoff", the grim jackpot guaranteed to come when the mind, heart and soul confer and discover that they have been duped: "And the eyes of both of them were opened: and when they perceived themselves to be naked, they sewed together fig-leaves, and made themselves aprons." (Gen. 3:7) So was established the "empire of death", best symbolized by withered sterility, as opposed to the *fertile*, life-restoring kingdom of the Creator of all things:

> I am the vine; you the branches: he that abideth in Me, and I in him, the same beareth much fruit: for without Me you can do nothing. If any one abide not in Me, he shall be cast forth as a branch and shall wither, and they shall gather him up and cast him into the fire, and he burneth. (Jn. 15:5-6)

The devil is not a divine being, and can *never* attack God directly. But he can attack the "life of God" in *creatures* – the supernatural life, the life of grace. In order to enter this battlefield – i.e., humanity – God sent His only-begotten Son, ". . . made of a woman . . ." (Gal. 4:4) ". . . made in the likeness of men, and in habit found as a man." (Phil. 2:7)

The struggle between the two "kingdoms," established in Eden, affects all souls of all times and, though its effects are easily observable in daily life, it has an *eternal* dimension that renders its importance inestimable. As far as our place within this battle goes, there is, quite literally, nothing in creation nearly as important: "Thus saith the Lord: Behold, I set before you the way of life, and the way of death." (Jer. 21:8)

Chapter Seven

The "First Gospel"

THE PROTOEVANGELIUM – MORE ON THE ENMITY BETWEEN THE WOMAN AND THE DEVIL – THE "SEED" OF THE WOMAN IS JESUS CHRIST

In light of the foregoing observations, the words of the first prophecy ever uttered on earth, the *Proto-evangelium* spoken by God Himself to the serpent, deserve close scrutiny:

> I *will put* enmities between thee and the woman, and thy seed and her seed: she shall crush thy head, and thou shalt lie in wait for her heel. (Gen. 3:15)

God is not announcing solely that an enmity already exists between the Woman and the serpent, that human and fallen angelic natures are at odds as a result of what happened between Adam, Eve and the serpent, between those who had been deceived and the one who deceived them. God did not say, "There *are* enmities between thee and the woman." He said, "I *will put* enmities between thee and the woman."

God is establishing, sanctioning, ordaining a particular enmity between the Woman and her seed, and the devil and his seed. "God has established only one enmity," wrote St. Louis de Montfort (†1716), "but it is an irreconcilable one which will last and even go on increasing to the end of time." This "enmity" will be mirrored in the millions of men and women who will struggle on either side of it throughout the ages, but the prototype is to be found here, in the enmities prophesied by God and *involving distinct individuals.*

It is interesting to note that the phrase "thee and the woman" should be spoken independently of the phrase "and thy seed and her seed". The Woman is an important element in this divinely-established enmity: the Woman *and* her seed.

Who is this Woman? She is not Eve. The Woman of the *Protoevangelium* will be at war against the serpent; an enmity so profound, so all-encompassing, will exist between them, that she will *crush* his head. Eve, instead, saw her sorrows multiplied and Paradise lost because of her collusion with the devil. She and Adam will be vindicated one day, but they could not possibly vindicate themselves.

Is the Woman the Church? The early *Acta Martyrorum*, records of the deaths of the martyrs, refer to the Church as "Mother". A letter composed about the year 177, which told of the persecutions of Catholics in Gaul, refers to the Church as "Virgin Mother". A reprieve had been given to the Christians suffering in the amphitheater at Lyons when it was learned that one of them was a Roman citizen. The letter describes how this time was spent:

> For them this was not a time of gainless idleness, but through their patient endurance the boundless compassion of Christ was made manifest; for through the living, the dead were brought back to life, and those who had accepted martyrdom begged graces upon those who had refused it. And great joy came to their Virgin Mother: those whom she had brought forth dead through miscarriage, these were restored to her alive. Through the martyrs, the majority of those who had disowned her became hers once more; they were conceived again and rekindled with the glow of life. *(Epistola Ecclesiarum Viennensis et Lugdunensis)*

St. Irenaeus (†202) observed that "where the Spirit of God is, there is the Church and all grace . . . wherefore, those who do not partake of the Spirit, are neither nourished by the Mother's breasts."

However, a very specific prophecy is contained in the *Protoevangelium*, and reference was made, not to a "people" who will possess or exhibit certain traits of constancy or righteousness, but to *individuals* – to one, unique Mother, who will bear one, unique Son. "I will put enmities between thee *and the woman*, and thy seed *and her seed*." The seed is, of course, Jesus Christ, ". . . His Son, who was made to Him of the seed of David, according to the flesh." (Rom. 1:3)

Since the "seed" is an *individual*, a unique Man with a name, so will the Mother be an *individual*, a unique Woman with a name. She will not be a mere representation of "maternity," a symbol for spiritual regeneration. Moreover, she will join her "seed," her Child, in the enmity against the serpent. If Our Lord is the *seed*, who is the *Woman*? The genealogy of Jesus, as recorded by St. Matthew, concludes with the words, "And Jacob begot Joseph the husband of Mary, *of whom was born Jesus*, Who is called Christ." The "Woman" of the *Proto-evangelium* is the Blessed Virgin Mary.

It stands to reason that a prophecy spoken by God will reveal truth in "three-dimensions", so to speak – in a manner vivid, rich and multi-layered, where past and future events will illuminate each other's meaning and depths. God does not begin by saying to the serpent, "I will put enmities between you and My Son." He says, "I will put enmities between you and the Woman . . ." – between you and Mary.

When God speaks, there is no question of a "mental lapse", or any verbal confusion. Of course, the war will rage between the kingdom of *Christ* and the "empire of death" (i.e., the kingdom of the devil). God does not intend here to "usurp" the rightful place of Jesus. And yet, we are faced with the fascinating Divine proclamation, "I will put enmities between thee *and the Woman*," between the devil and Mary. Furthermore, this is a fact that *must* be confronted even by those who, despising the authority and inspiration of the most learned Church Fathers, Doctors, popes, saints and theologians, insist on translating the following verse as, "*He* shall crush thy head, and thou shalt lie in wait for *His* heel."

Our Lady is mentioned first in the *Proto-evangelium*. Curiously, Our Lord is mentioned specifically in opposition to the "seed" of the serpent. Since Jesus is True God, and Mary a creature who derives *all* her grace and privileges from Him, this appears like a "reverse" order. It is not. On the contrary, it is based on the soundest of theological principles, for it draws our attention inescapably to the *Incarnate* God – not solely to the Word, eternally begotten of the Father, but to the "seed", the *Person* of Jesus Christ, the Word *united to human nature*. Our Lord's death and Resurrection were rendered possible only because of the union of humanity and divinity. Through the one, He died; through the other, He rose again. Through one, He atoned for the sin of Adam, a man making reparation for the sin committed by a man; through the other, this sacrifice assumed the dimension necessary to satisfy the justice of the infinite God:

> And despoiling the principalities and powers, He hath exposed them confidently in open shew, triumphing openly over them *in Himself.* (Col. 2:15) But Christ, being come an high priest of the good things to come, by a greater and more perfect tabernacle not made with hand . . . by *His own Blood,* entered once into the Holies, having obtained eternal redemption. (Heb. 9:11-12)

The human person, struggling against a fallen nature, is the battleground for the two kingdoms. Although Christ triumphs "openly" over the powers of darkness, such a triumph does not mean that these powers will desist from hostilities. A nation subordinated to another, more powerful one, can still rebel; in our Lord's day, the occupying Roman army had its hands full with the zealots of Palestine. This is the case even in the supernatural realm: "Woe to the earth and to the sea, because the devil is come down unto you, having great wrath, knowing that he hath but a short time." (Apoc. 12:12) Therefore, St. Louis de Montfort described the enmity established in Eden as "an irreconcilable one which will last and even go on increasing to the end of time." This reveals quite clearly that the importance of the *Woman* – of the Blessed Virgin, Mother of God – will not suddenly cease or diminish after the birth of her Son.

Freedom from eternal ruin, redemption from the curse which is the legacy of Adam and Eve – all was dependent upon the Incarnation of the Second Divine Person: "For He is our peace, Who hath made both one, and breaking down the middle wall of partition, the enmities in His flesh." (Eph. 2:14) This phrase, describing the uniting of Jew and Gentile as one people *in Christ,* also gives us pause to consider how the "partition" separating God and man after the fall was broken down in the "flesh" of the Incarnate Word, which, having been pierced on Calvary, ransomed human nature from the "empire of death".

Chapter Eight

The Church

THE CHURCH – THE BODY OF CHRIST – SONS OF GOD

Throughout history, God has called upon men and women to *co-operate* with Him in the accomplishment of His designs. Moses led the Israelites out of Egypt; judges, prophets and kings made the Divine Will known to the people. "For we are God's coadjutors," (1 Cor. 3:9) wrote St. Paul to the Catholics of Corinth. A coadjutor is more than an assistant; the word implies a right of succession. The very existence of an ecclesiastical hierarchy, of an ordained priesthood, is a testimony to the central place of human "cooperation" in God's designs.

Through the papacy, Our Lord would provide His Church with a visible head, a *visible* head for a *visible* society. St. Peter and his successors would rule and govern by the very authority of Christ. Through the priesthood, the sacraments are made available to the faithful. Through the efforts of Catholic parents, children are reared in the True Faith. Through the efforts of the laity, the doctrines of the Church can be taught and defended according to the opportunities occasioned by their station in life. In each case, the ultimate aim is the sanctification of souls, which is nothing else than a participation in the Divine Life of the Blessed Trinity. The proper end of man's cooperation with God, then, is to "involve" souls *directly* in the sacrifice on Calvary, that they may benefit *directly* from the Redemption won for us by Christ.

Born in original sin and living debased lives on that account, we are "children of wrath" by *nature*: "Wherein in times past you walked according to the course of this world, according to the prince of the power of the air . . . by nature children of wrath." (Eph. 2:2-3) The enmities established in Eden have left their mark on the world, and men of all times and places fall into one of the two opposing "camps":

> What if God, willing to shew His wrath, and to make His power known, endured with much patience vessels of wrath, fitted for destruction. That He might shew the riches of His glory on the vessels of mercy which He hath prepared unto glory? (Rom. 9:22-23)

Some people remain vessels of wrath, others become vessels of glory, yet they live side-by-side: "Suffer both to grow until the harvest, and in the time of the harvest I will say to the reapers: Gather up first the cockle, and bind it into bundles to burn, but the wheat gather ye into my barn." (Mt. 13:30) There is only one thing that can transform vessels of *wrath* into those of *glory*: "The grace of God, by *Jesus Christ Our Lord*. . . . For the law of the Spirit of Life, *in Christ Jesus*, hath delivered me from the law of sin and of death." (Rom.7:25; 8:2)

"*Who shall deliver me from the body of this death*?" cried St. Paul. Unless some suitable reparation is made first, the offending party in a dispute cannot rightfully seek favors from the one who has been offended. In the interests of justice, humanity had to atone for the sin of Adam. The answer to St. Paul's question is the beginning and foundation of all hope:

> The grace of God, by Jesus Christ our Lord. . . . If God be for us, who is against us? . . .Who is he that shall condemn? Christ Jesus that died, yea that is risen also again; Who is at the right hand of God, Who also maketh intercession for us. (Rom. 7:25; 8:31, 34)

"O death, where is thy victory? O death, where is thy sting? Now the sting of death is sin . . . But thanks be to God, Who hath given us the victory through our Lord Jesus Christ." (1 Cor. 15:55-57) Our Lord made a perfect atonement for the sin of Adam. In the *Person* of Jesus Christ, crucified and risen, death is stripped of its "sting," like a defeated general surrendering his sword. On Calvary, our judge became our advocate as well. *If God be for us, who is against us?*

The word "redemption" implies the paying of a price or debt in order to free a captive. The price for mankind was paid superabundantly by Jesus on the Cross, when He ". . . gave Himself a redemption *for all* . . ." (1 Tim. 2:6) Men remain free to approach Jesus or not. God desires that His creatures do so: "O taste, and see that the Lord is sweet." (Ps. 33:9) But He will never trample upon the free will of His children, even while exhorting them: "I have set before you life and death, blessing and cursing. Choose therefore life." (Deut. 30:19)

How important, then, are those who "cooperate" in the unfolding of God's designs, who teach children their first prayers, who defend sound doctrine, who invite prodigals to return to the True Church, who baptize, hear confessions and celebrate the Holy Sacrifice of the Mass? There is no question here of "impersonal" forces at work, or of abstract lessons offered as intellectual exercises: "*God Himself will come* and will save you." To these words recorded in *The Prophecy of Isaias* must be added others, just as powerful, which, completing the thought, strike us with a heightened sense of wonder because of what they reveal: "For *the Son of Man* is *come* to seek and to save that which was lost."(Lk. 19:10) Note well our Lord's words. The Son of MAN is come to save that which was lost. God *Incarnate* . . . God, the Son of Mary . . . comes to save.

"I and the Father are one." (Jn. 10:30) "In Him dwelleth all the fullness of the Godhead *corporeally*". (Col. 2:9) The gift of God-made-Man was the ultimate gift given to the world by the Blessed Trinity: "For God so loved the world, as to give His only begotten Son; that whosoever believeth in Him may not perish, but may have life everlasting." (Jn. 3:16) What is too often overlooked is God's *condescension* towards His creatures.

The Son of God ". . . emptied Himself, taking the form of a servant, being made in the likeness of men, and in habit found as a man." (Phil. 2:7) One of the most sublime aspects of the Incarnation is the fact that it was effected *for eternity.* The Second Person of the Trinity remains True God *and* True Man *forever.* He did not shed His humanity after "the job was done," and He ascended to the Father: ". . . this *Man* offering one sacrifice for sins, *forever* sitteth on the right hand of God." (Heb. 10:12)

Jesus Christ, Who "being in the form of God," did not consider it "robbery to be equal with God," (Phil. 2:6) and yet descend to earth to become Man . . . forever. At the Incarnation, Divinity humbled Itself, so that human nature could be exalted. Man could not raise himself to heaven by his own devices, so God came down to earth to lift him. At one time, God placed man in a terrestrial paradise. Through Christ, the way was opened to another paradise, of which Eden was a mere shadow: "I will draw them with the cords of Adam, with the bands of love: and I will be to them as one that taketh off the yolk on their jaws: and I put his meat to him, that he might eat." (Osee 11:4) This awesome gift, the Word *Incarnate*, was presented to the world by one person and one person only – the Blessed Virgin Mary. She was a "cooperator" with God, but, applied to her, the term barely scratches the surface. Sacred Scripture teaches that men and women are called to different levels of cooperation. St. Paul even wrote that, through his own sufferings, he would "fill up those things that are wanting of the sufferings of Christ, in my flesh, for His body, which is the Church." (Col. 1:24)

For the Church . . . the sufferings of the Redeemer were in no way deficient for the restoration of the entire human race, past, present and to come, so St. Paul is careful to qualify his statement, by saying that the sufferings that are "wanting" are the sufferings of the *members* of the Church. These members, living mortal lives in a veil of tears, can unite their sufferings to the supreme sacrifice made on Calvary: "Know you not that all we, who are baptized in Christ Jesus, are baptized in His death?" The sacrament of Baptism *incorporates* souls into the Church – i.e. it makes them members of *one* Body, whose head is Christ: "Christ is the head of the Church. He is the Savior of His Body." (Eph. 5:23)

The Church as the "body of Christ" is not merely a metaphor for the relationship between the Redeemer and the redeemed. It is a visualization of a concrete reality, for the relationship between Christ and Catholic individuals exhibits the hallmarks of a single corporeal entity: "Let the peace of Christ reign in your hearts, wherein also you are called in one body." (Col. 3:15) As the head and members of a natural body share in the vicissitudes of mortal existence, in both peace and suffering, so the "supernatural body" composed of Christ and His Church is bonded in peace and suffering. Because of this, that peace ". . . which surpasseth all understanding . . ." (Phil. 4:7) which can come only from Jesus, is communicated to His body, the Church . . . and the "things that are wanting of the sufferings of Christ," the sufferings of the Church, are joined to those which redeemed creation: "For unto you it is given for Christ, not only to believe in Him, but also to suffer for Him . . . " (Phil. 1:29)

Because the members of the Church form a single Body, with Christ as Head, there is a marvelous interplay within this mystical organism: "For as the body is one, and hath many members; and all the members of the body, whereas they are many, yet are one body, so also is Christ . . ." (1 Cor. 12:12) ". . . Head over all the Church, which is His body, and the fullness of Him Who is filled all in all." (Eph. 1:22-23)

So, grace from the head is communicated to the "limbs," the individual members – by which they are "vivified" and "made a living branch on the vine for Christ" (Pope St. Pius V) – while the sufferings of these members (such as the trials of the holy martyrs), united in Christ, can benefit *all*: "And if one member suffer any thing, all the members suffer with it; or if one member glory, all the members rejoice with it." (1 Cor. 12:26) Because the Head of the Mystical Body ". . . is not the God of the dead, but of the living," (Mt. 22:32) the living members can pray for the dead in purgatory – "It is therefore a holy and wholesome thought to pray for the dead, that they may be loosed from sins" (2 Mac. 12:46) – while those in heaven can intercede for those still on earth through "the prayers of all saints upon the golden altar, which is before the throne of God." (Apoc. 8:3)

This intimate and unprecedented relationship between God and mankind, Creator and creature, the "Head" of the Church and His "Body", was made possible only by means of the human nature given freely and lovingly to her Lord by the Blessed Virgin: "The Son of *MAN* is come to seek and to save that which was lost." (Lk. 19:10) Because of the Incarnation, mankind can say, "And of His fullness we all have received, and grace for grace." (Jn. 1:16) Also because of the Incarnation, the Eternal Word can say, "sacrifice and oblation Thou wouldst not: but a body Thou hast fitted to me." (Heb. 10:5) The result was the possibility of a new life for men and women caught in the grip of concupiscence and mortality: "For you have not received the spirit of bondage again in fear; but you have received the spirit of adoption of sons, whereby we cry: Abba (Father)." (Rom. 8:15)

It was in the blessed womb of Mary, then, that the psalm was fulfilled pre-eminently: "Mercy and truth have met each other: justice and peace have kissed." (Ps. 84:11) Through the flesh He took from His Mother, our Lord satisfied Divine Justice, while giving the world the perfect example of Divine Mercy. At the moment of the Incarnation, the womb of the Virgin became the center of all creation, the pivot of history and the focal point of all hope for humanity. Pope St. Pius X wrote:

> In the same holy bosom of His most chaste Mother, Christ took to Himself flesh, *and united to Himself the spiritual body formed by those who were to believe in Him.* Hence Mary, carrying the Savior within her, may be said to have also carried all those whose life was contained in the life of the Savior. Therefore all we who are united to Christ, and as the Apostle says, "are members of His body, of His flesh and of His bones," have issued from the womb of Mary like a body united to its head. Hence, in a spiritual and mystical fashion, we are all children of Mary, and she is Mother of us all. (*Ad diem illum laetissimum*, 1904)

These observations recall the striking words set down so many centuries earlier by one of the great Fathers and Doctors of the Church. "God has become man," wrote St. Augustine (†430), "that man might become God."

Chapter Nine

The Immaculate Conception

Enmity, more than mere hostility – Genesis 3:15, the first of all prophecies – God will prepare the Woman for the warfare – The Immaculate Conception – The definition of Bl. Pius IX – Her first triumph – The effects of original sin on men – An ongoing conflict to last until the end of the world – Christ, the Redeemer of all men

Of course, God in no way "minimized" His Son by mentioning the Blessed Virgin first in the *Proto-evangelium*, or by giving her a unique place in that primeval prophecy. Therefore, since God is the best of all models to imitate, we will follow His example and consider this singular woman, the Virgin Mary. By doing so, her *place* in the prophecy spoken in Eden will become apparent. At the same time, her *person* will shine forth in splendor, and we will glimpse why, from out of the millions of women to have walked the earth throughout the centuries, the Lady of Nazareth, "espoused to a man whose name was Joseph, of the house of David," (Lk. 1:27) was chosen to hear the greeting of the Angel Gabriel.

I will put enmities between thee and the Woman. "Enmity" implies more than simple "hostility". The word designates opposition, a *mutual* antagonism between two parties. A person may be hostile towards a particular political platform or party, but he can only feel *enmity* for another individual, say a representative of that platform or party, someone with conflicting values or goals. In the *Proto-evangelium*, the first of all prophecies, God revealed that *enmities* – mutual antagonisms – were to be established between the serpent and the Mother of the Redeemer, the Son sent "to seek and to save that which was lost."

The kingdom of Christ is characterized by the restoration of life: "And where the Spirit of the Lord is, there is liberty." (2 Cor. 3:17) "Death is swallowed up in victory." (1 Cor. 15:54) The reign of the serpent, *who is called the devil and Satan,* is described in the inspired texts as the "empire of death". What characterizes this kingdom? – "Now the sting of death is sin." (1 Cor. 15:56) This empire was inaugurated in Eden with the original sin which was the matrix for all others to follow: the rejection of God in pursuit of false idols, self-idolization, and willing collaboration with the serpent.

Therefore, to be at enmity with the "empire of death" is to be at enmity with *sin. I will put enmities between thee and the Woman.* God Himself established this enmity; it will be a *work of God*, not a mere abiding state of mutual ill-will resulting from the fall. The Omnipotent God will *cause to be* this enmity, because of who this prophesied woman will be: "I will put enmities between thee and the woman, and thy seed *and her* seed." She will bear the Redeemer, the Son of God, "made of a Woman." St. Paul did not write that Our Lord is "a god, made of a woman." He says that "when the fullness of time was come, God sent *His Son*, made of a woman."

The Godhead will not merely "reside" in Jesus, or "possess" Jesus, or "manifest" itself somehow through Jesus. God Himself will deign to be "*made* of a woman." He will even refer to Himself as "the Son of Man." At the Incarnation, and only in the womb of the Holy Virgin, Divine and human natures will be *united* in such a manner that neither one is diluted in the process:

> Humanity has been united to divinity through the unity of Person, not through the ascension or resurrection or baptism, *but within the Mother, in her womb*, and – even more – in the Virginal Conception itself. Because of this unity of Person, it happens that what is proper to God is ascribed to the man, and what is proper to the flesh is ascribed to God – *indifferently and without distinction*. Therefore, as it is written in Holy Scripture, "He that descended from heaven, the Son of Man who is in heaven," (Jn. 3:13) and "crucified the Lord of glory" (1 Cor. 2:8) on earth. Furthermore, since the body of the Lord was made and created, it is said that the "Word" of God Himself was "made" (Jn. 1:14), His wisdom filled up (Eccl. 24:35), His knowledge created (Eccl. 1:4, 24:36); therefore do the prophetic writings refer to His hands and feet as "pierced". (Ps. 21:17) (St. Vincent of Lerins, †445, *The Commonitories*)

I will put enmities between thee and the woman, and thy seed and her seed. The seed born of Mary was sinless: "There is none holy as the Lord is."(1 Kg. 2:2)

The holiness of Christ is the supreme sanctity of the Godhead, the fullness from which all other holiness is derived: "Holy, holy, holy, the Lord God of hosts, all the earth is full of His glory." (Is. 6:3)

The Mother of Christ, by God's command, would be at enmity with "him who had the empire of death," Satan. Because of the intrinsic natures of the "kingdoms" of Christ and Satan, this enmity can be expressed as the opposition between sin/spiritual death and grace/spiritual life. Scripture teaches that ". . . to every one of us is given grace, according to the measure of the giving of Christ." (Eph. 4:7) Grace is bestowed as God sees fit, freely and in accord with the end for which it is granted: "Of His fullness we all have received." (Jn. 1:16) "My grace is sufficient for thee." (2 Cor. 12:9)

The *Proto-evangelium* prepares us for the coming of a unique "Woman." God, from whom all grace flows, will *Himself* prepare her to be at war with the serpent and his "empire". When the fullness of time has arrived, God will descend into her womb and unite Himself there with a human body *formed from her own flesh and blood.* She will give birth, not to a man blessed with divine characteristics, but to a man who *is* God. Although God is eternal, existing without any "beginning", and the Blessed Virgin was and is, like us, possessed of a human nature only, she is *and will always be* the Mother of God.

If God Himself bestows "sufficient" grace on His children to facilitate a particular good work or result, how much would He render to the Woman who, by His own admission, will be at war with the beast whose pleasure is to rip souls from the grace that is their birthright as "co-heirs" of the kingdom of God? If the grace of God is "sufficient" for all souls, and their labors, proceeding from that "fullness" which could only exist in the Godhead, what amount of grace would be *sufficient* to prepare a human being to give birth to GOD?

If Moses was commanded to remove his shoes before the burning bush, because he was standing on "holy ground", then how holy was the "ground" in which rested the Incarnate Word? If the earth on which Moses stood was sanctified by the presence of the Godhead manifested in the bush, what level of sanctity would we hope to encounter in the womb in which resided the Divine Person of Jesus Christ, in Whom could be found "... all the fullness of the Godhead corporeally?" (Col. 2:9)

The Dogma of the Immaculate Conception, defined by Blessed Pope Pius IX in the Apostolic Constitution, *Ineffabilis Deus* (1854), proclaims that the Virgin Mary was conceived *immaculately* in the womb of her mother, St. Anne. It teaches that the infant Mary bore no trace of original sin at her conception, that her soul was unstained by any taint of the sin of Adam. Furthermore, in order for this conception to be truly an "immaculate" one, Our Lady's soul would have to have been stainless from the very *first* instant of her conception. If she had been burdened with original sin even for a moment of her existence, we would not be able to speak of an immaculate *conception*; we would, then, be able to celebrate only the time of her *sanctification* in the womb of her mother.

Pope Pius IX defined the dogma in these words:

> We declare, pronounce, and define that the doctrine which holds that the most Blessed Virgin Mary, in the first instant of her Conception, by a singular grace and privilege granted by Almighty God, in *view of the merits of Jesus Christ, the Savior of the human race*, was preserved free from all stain of original sin, is a doctrine revealed by God and therefore to be believed firmly and constantly by all the faithful.

At the beginning of this document, the Holy Father placed the dogma in its historical framework:

> God ineffable ... having foreseen from all eternity the lamentable wretchedness of the entire human race which would result from the sin of Adam, decreed, by a plan hidden from the centuries, to complete the first work of His goodness by a mystery yet more wondrously sublime through the Incarnation of the Word ... in order that what had been lost in the first Adam would be gloriously restored in the Second Adam.

The plan of Divine Mercy, the Incarnation, had been formulated "from all eternity", and consisted of the Eternal Word assuming human nature, thus both atoning for the sin of the "first" Adam, and drawing His creatures to Himself through the bond of human nature, in a *Mystical* Body:

> For by a man came death, and by a man the resurrection of the dead. And as in Adam all die, so also in Christ all shall be made alive. (1 Cor. 15:21-22) As He chose us in Him *before the foundation* of *the* world. . . . Who hath predestinated us unto the adoption of children, through Jesus Christ. (Eph. 1:4-5)

Pope Pius IX continued, directing our thoughts back to the "enmities" prophesied in Eden:

> From the very beginning, and before time began, the Eternal Father chose and prepared for His only-begotten Son a Mother in whom the Son of God would become incarnate and from whom, in the blessed fullness of time, He would be born into this world. And indeed it was wholly fitting that so wonderful a mother should be ever resplendent with the glory of most sublime holiness and so completely free from all taint of original sin *that she would triumph utterly over the ancient serpent.* To her did the Father will to give His only-begotten Son – the Son whom, equal to the Father and begotten by Him, the Father loves from His heart – and to give this Son *in such a way that He would be the one and the same common Son of God the Father and of the Blessed Virgin Mary.* It was she whom the Son Himself chose to make His Mother.

Had Our Lady not been conceived immaculately in the womb of St. Anne, how could she "triumph utterly over the ancient serpent"? In the *Proto-evangelium,* we learn that the "Woman" will crush the *head* of the serpent, the ruler of the "empire of death". What does this "head" signify? "The sting of death is sin," wrote St. Paul. Sanctification, the triumph of grace over sin, of life over death, is the means by which Satan, "the old serpent", is defeated. Each human soul that seeks out and struggles to preserve sanctifying grace is a threat to the dominion of the devil, who ". . . was a murderer from the beginning, and he stood not in the truth; because truth is not in him." (Jn. 8:44) The "murder" committed by the devil is spiritual death, the loss of sanctifying grace – ultimately, the eternal ruin of the soul: "Fear ye not them that kill the body, and are not able to kill the soul: but rather fear him that can destroy both soul and body in hell." (Mt. 10:28)

A penitent soul, receiving grace, heeds the admonition of *Deuteronomy* to "choose therefore life." Of such import is this freely made decision that ". . . there shall be joy before the angels of God upon one sinner doing penance." (Lk. 15:10) The baptized infant, the adult convert, the penitent prodigal – each of these robs hell of the spoils of the fall. Each sanctified soul is a victory for the Church, a thing to rejoice the angels, a sharing in the victory of the Redeemer: "For we are buried together with Him by baptism into death; that as Christ is risen from the dead by the glory of the Father, so we also may walk in newness of life." (Rom. 6:4)

Souls are cleansed and renewed through sanctifying grace: "For if by one man's offense, death reigned through one; much more they who receive abundance of grace, and of the gift, and of justice, shall reign in life through one, Jesus Christ." (Rom. 5:17) However, there is here no "crushing" of the serpent's head, no complete, life-long eradication of all vestiges of sin, for these souls were first stained with sin, then cleansed through the merits of Christ (the treasury of graces won by His Passion and death). Although sanctified souls have been made ". . . whiter than snow", (Ps. 50:9) it was not always so, for we are born "children of wrath".

Human beings, composite creatures formed from the union of soul and body, do not emerge from their bout with original sin unscathed. A man who has survived a life-threatening illness often carries some physical effect of the illness with him throughout the remainder of his life, and the debilitating effects of original sin, a "life-threatening condition" in the fullest sense of the term, likewise persist:

> I find then a law, that when I have a will to do good, evil is present with me. For I am delighted with the law of God, according to the inward man. But I see another law in my members, fighting against the law of my mind, and captivating me in the law of sin that is in my members. (Rom. 7:21-23) There was given me a sting of my flesh, an angel of Satan, to buffet me. (2 Cor. 12:7)

Such is the lot of the sons and daughters of Adam and Eve. The baptized Catholic does not cease to be human. Sanctification occurs within the *framework* of mortality. Through the sacrament of Baptism, the soul is truly cleansed ". . . by the laver of water in the word of life." (Eph. 5:26) But the *person* thus spiritually vivified remains mortal. He is still a participant in human nature and weakness, and their attendant ills and troubles. The Council of Ephesus (431) taught that:

> In the transgression of Adam all men lost their "natural power" and innocence, and no one can rise from the depth of that ruin through free will *unless the grace of a merciful God raise him up.* . . . No one even after having been restored by the grace of baptism is capable of overcoming the snares of the devil and subduing the concupiscenses of the flesh. (*Concerning the Grace of God*)

The lot of mortal men can be characterized, then, as an *ongoing* struggle against the "empire" of the serpent – against sin. Individuals can lose sanctifying grace, can chase after idols – can even consciously reject God. But mankind is not left high and dry. We are treated each and every day to the divine bounty referred to by the Council of Ephesus as "the grace of a merciful God". This is *actual* grace, by which God inspires souls to turn to Him, to seek out sanctifying grace and the sacraments, to ride out the storms of mortal existence: "Now our Lord Jesus Christ Himself, and God and our Father, Who hath loved us and hath given us everlasting consolation, and good hope in grace, exhort your hearts, and confirm you in every good work and word". (2 Thes. 2:15-16)

Cooperation with grace brings with it a taste of the sweet fruit of perseverance: "If you keep my commandments, you shall abide in my love, as I also have kept my Father's commandments, and do abide in His love." (Jn. 15:10) More often than not, inconstancy is the rule of the day: *When I have a will to do good, evil is present with me*. This endless skirmishing, during which individuals progress, fall back, regroup, charge with renewed vigor, fall back again – this is the dynamic of a *redeemed* world, a world that had once been held captive, but was later restored.

The "Woman" of the *Proto-evangelium* is given a far different role in the battle than that of the rest of mankind. She *will* be redeemed by her Son, but she has also been designated by God as a *direct* cooperator in the Redemption. The Blessed Virgin alone was given the task of participating in bringing about the Redemption *itself*. A Catholic who teaches or defends the Faith cooperates with the Blessed Trinity, but God descended *into Mary's virginal womb*, and united His divine nature with *her* very own substance, taking His humanity from her:

> Being united from the womb itself, He is said to have endured a generation in the flesh in order to appropriate the producing of His own body. Thus [the Holy Fathers] did not hesitate to speak of the holy Virgin as the Mother of God. (The Council of Ephesus, *The Incarnation*, 431)

"Do not accept the testimony of a man," wrote St. Cyril of Jerusalem (†386), "unless you are taught by Sacred Scripture about the Virgin, about the where, the when, and the how." If Our Lady is not the *Mother* of God, if she is not the real Mother of the one *Person* in whom are united (and which does not merely "contain") two natures, divine and human, then the sacrifice on Calvary was not a propitiation for the sins of mankind, for St. Peter taught in no uncertain terms: "Christ also died once for our sins . . . being put to death indeed *in the flesh,* but enlivened in the Spirit." (1 Pt. 3:18) St. John wrote, "The Word was *made* flesh." *The Epistle to the Hebrews* states that Christ "by *His own Blood*, entered once into the Holies, having obtained eternal redemption."

"Christ *died* for all." (2 Cor. 5:15) There is no redemption without the supreme sacrifice of Jesus Christ, without God *made Man*, for it was only in His human nature that God could suffer and die:

> For the sake of paying the debt of our creation, an inviolable nature was joined to a passible nature; so that [He] . . . both could die by reason of the one, and could not die on account of the other. Accordingly, in the whole and perfect nature of true man, true God was born, complete in His own, complete in ours. (Pope St. Leo the Great, *Lectis dilectionis tuae*, 449)

At the Incarnation, when Mary was overshadowed by the Holy Ghost and received God into her womb, she was brought to the very frontier of divinity. No being, human or angelic, *could* possibly get closer to God than the one who became His Mother. "Above Mary, God only," wrote St. Anselm (†1109), "beneath Mary, all that is not God." Such is the wonder which took place because of the consent of the young Virgin to the Angel Gabriel, at which time her holy womb became literally the *center of all creation*.

This is "cooperation" of a completely new order. This is a unique, never-to-be duplicated cooperation *in the Redemption*, in the establishing of the redemptive order, the "fullness of time", the mission of the Incarnate Word.

Chapter Ten

The Vocation of Mary

"I [Christ] have chosen you" – Mary chosen from all eternity – Her Divine Maternity – Jesus is Mary's Savior and Redeemer – Preservative and restorative redemption – The New Eve: Testimony of fathers and doctors on Mary's Immaculate Conception – The Essence of the Hypostatic Union – "God sent His Son made of a woman"

The words of Jesus to His apostles at the Last Supper apply firstly and preminently to the "Woman" of *Genesis*, His own Mother: "I have chosen you; and have appointed you, that you should go and should bring forth fruit; and your fruit should remain." (Jn. 15:16) The dogma of the Immaculate Conception is the first manifestation of the "tandem" of Woman and seed, of the relationship and "partnership" between Mother and Son foretold by God after the fall.

The Immaculate Conception of the Blessed Virgin was possible only because of the Redemption won for mankind by Jesus. When he defined the dogma, Pope Pius IX wrote that God, "having foreseen from all eternity" the misery of fallen humanity, decreed the restoration of mankind "through the Incarnation of the Word". St. Paul taught that we are chosen in Christ "before the foundation of the world". All redemption, all life comes through Jesus Christ, through God-made-Man.

If the Redemption was ordained "from all eternity . . . before the foundation of the world," then the humanity of the Incarnate Word was likewise ordained from all eternity: "O eternal God, Who knowest hidden things, Who knowest all things before they come to pass." (Dan. 13:42) "He declareth the things that are past, and the things that are to come, and revealeth the traces of hidden things." (Ecclus. 42:19)

Because the humanity of the Savior was given to Him by (and *only* by) His Mother, the Virgin Mary was therefore also present to the Divine Intellect from before the foundation of the world as the mother of Christ. As such, she appears prophetically as the "Woman" of the *Proto-evangelium*, as the "Spouse" of *The Canticle of Canticles*, as the "Virgin", foretold by the Prophet Isaias, who ". . . shall conceive and bear a son." (Isaias 7:14)

Because Mary was part (indeed, a focal point) of the Divine Plan set in place from the very beginning, we also find her represented prophetically in the *Sapiential* ("Wisdom") books of the Old Testament, speaking through the inspired words bequeathed to us by the Holy Ghost. While the figure of Wisdom personified inhabiting these texts can refer to Christ or the Holy Ghost, it also has a very definite "Marian" application, recognized by the Church since the days of the Fathers:

> This occurs so far as Wisdom is represented as the beginning of all the ways of God and the first-born of God's whole creation. In virtue of her first and highest origin from God, she is His most perfect image and likeness, partner and helper, thus in an eminent manner "daughter of God", i.e., child and bride at the same time, the one in the form of the other, and as such she is to the world queen of all things and mother of life and light.
>
> Wisdom thus occupies a central place between God and creation in which it appears as existing and working outside God, not haphazardly . . . but in a most particular way, similar to the essential characteristics and workings of a mother. It is like a mother, who in the fulfillment of her task, the arrangement of her household, the care and government of the inmates, and above all the care of the children, acts as the main figure of the family and becomes a child with, and among, her children. (Rev. Matthias J. Scheeben, *Mariology*, Vol. I, 1946)

In one of these books, Our Lady rejoices that, from eternity, she was cherished by God and regarded as the Mother of His only-begotten Son: "From the beginning, and before the world, was I created, and unto the world to come I shall not cease to be, and in the holy dwelling place I have ministered before Him. . . . I am the Mother of fair love, and of fear, and of knowledge, and of holy hope." (Ecclus. 24:14,24)

"Before I formed thee in the bowels of thy mother, I knew thee." (Jer. 1:5) said the Lord to the Prophet Jeremias. This truth provides the historical context for the Immaculate Conception. Before Mary was formed in the womb of St. Anne, Our Lord "knew" her. He knew and loved her as one of His creatures. He knew and loved her as one for whose soul He would one day suffer and die. But here, any similarities between Mary and all other sons and daughters of Adam and Eve end.

"From the very beginning, and before time began," wrote Pope Pius IX, "the Eternal Father chose and prepared for His only-begotten Son a Mother in whom the Son of God would become incarnate and from whom, in the blessed fullness of time, He would be born into this world." Our Lord "knew" Mary from the very Beginning as His creature, as one of the redeemed . . . and He also knew and loved her from the beginning *as His Mother*. The One Who commanded men to ". . . honor thy father and mother" (Deut. 5:16) would be born of a human Mother, would be raised by a human Mother, and would spend all but three years of His earthly life in the company of a human Mother. With the Incarnation, the Eternal God would enter into a new relationship with mankind: "Greater love than this no man hath, that a man lay down his life for his friends. . . . I have called you friends." (Jn. 15:13,15) This new relationship began with that singular relationship existing between Jesus and His Mother, Mary.

Throughout the history of salvation, throughout the history of the Catholic Church, we encounter many examples of the servants of God being prepared for their roles. Before the birth of St. John the Baptist, the Angel Gabriel told Zachary that his son ". . . shall drink no wine nor strong drink: and he shall be filled with the Holy Ghost, even from his mother's womb." (Lk. 1:15) After St. Francis of Assisi (†1226) renounced the world and left his father's house, he spent four years tending to lepers, rebuilding ruined chapels and preaching, before finally writing his Rule and seeking papal approval. Such were the preparations for the Precursor of the Lord, and for one of his most faithful servants, to whom was granted the stigmata.

The Virgin Mary was chosen to be the *Mother* of this Lord. What "preparation" would suffice for the future Mother of God? How does the Creator of the Fourth Commandment "honor" His own Mother? The answer to these questions hinges on the observation made by St. Augustine, in his response to the *Pelagian* heresy, which denied the universality of original sin (and, therefore, posited any number of sinless individuals by professing that men can live without committing sin). St. Augustine wrote that even the greatest saints, "all those holy men and women", if asked, would have been compelled by their love of Truth to admit their sin:

> With the exception of the holy Virgin Mary, in regard to whom, *out of respect for the Lord*, I do not propose to have a single question raised on the subject of sin – after all, how do we know what greater degree of grace for a complete victory over sin was conferred on her who merited to conceive and bring forth Him Who all admit was without sin. (*De natura et gratia*)

Mary's Divine Maternity, the unique relationship existing between her and the Second Person of the Blessed Trinity, is the foundation for the Dogma of the Immaculate Conception. According to the papal definition of the dogma, Our Lady was redeemed, preserved free from any stain of original sin, "in view of the merits of Jesus Christ, the Savior of the human race". This is entirely in accord with the teachings of Sacred Scripture: "Christ died for *all.*" (2 Cor. 5:15) "Who gave Himself *a redemption for all.*" (1 Tim. 2:6)

In this way, the curse of Eden, subjection to the "empire of death", the dominion of the serpent, was not visited upon the Woman of the *Proto-evangelium*. In this way, *and only together with her "seed", her Son*, the Woman crushed the head of the serpent, the sting of death . . . sin. The ancient prophecy is fulfilled, and the role of Jesus Christ as Savior of the *entire* human race is safeguarded.

"And as *in Adam*, all die, so also in Christ all shall be made alive." (1 Cor. 15:22) Death was the legacy of our first parents. As a daughter of Adam and Eve, the Blessed Virgin inherited the *debitum incurrendi maculam*, the "debt of incurring the stain" of original sin. In *Adam, all die*. However, Jesus, her Son and her Savior, paid that debt: *In Christ, all shall be made alive*. And, while He paid that debt for all mankind, He did so in a unique way for His Mother. Our Lady was redeemed from that *same* treasury of grace and merit won by Jesus on Calvary, but in a completely singular way, at the very instant of her own conception. This privilege was decreed because the young girl who gave her "*fiat*" to the archangel became, as a result, the *Mother of God.*

We are indebted to two great defenders of the Immaculate Conception – William of Ware (d. c.1305) and Bl. John Duns Scotus († 1308) – for a clearer understanding of the manner in which Our Lord applied the merits of His redemptive sacrifice to His Mother. William of Ware examined the doctrine in light of its fittingness to both the majesty and power of God. Since God *could* create a sinless being, had He left His future Mother stained with original sin, He would have deliberately created for Himself a Mother inferior to one He *could* create, therefore "what He could do, it was fitting that He should do and from this it follows that He did do it; for the Son should honor the Mother."

William pointed out that, even in this unique form of preservative redemption, Mary "needed the Passion of Christ, not on account of any sin that was in her, but on account of that which would have been in her, had her Son not preserved her through faith." Duns Scotus explained how God was able to ensure that the Blessed Virgin should never find herself in the state of original sin:

> Original sin does not reside in a soul that has grace. God could have conferred as much grace on her in the first moment of her soul's existence as He does on another soul at circumcision or baptism; in that moment, then, the soul would not have had original sin, as it would not have it afterwards when the person was baptized. (*Ordinatio III*)

This important distinction between *preservative* and *restorative* redemption places the Immaculate Conception in its proper framework as the first-fruits of the sacrifice on Calvary. From the first moment of her conception, Our Lady was sinless, and like other men and women, she was redeemed by her Son, Jesus Christ. However, because of the immense dignity of her future role of *Theotokos* (Mother of God), Our Lord applied His merits to His Mother in the form of a "preservative" redemption, while the remainder of mankind enjoys "restorative" redemption. In *restorative* redemption, the person is "restored" to the life of grace – i.e., redeemed *after* contracting original sin. In the *preservative* redemption which was a unique privilege of Our Lady, Mary was "preserved" *from* contracting original sin. In both cases, the person is redeemed by the sacrifice and merits of Christ.

The best analogy is a simple mud puddle. One person falls into the mud, and is then pulled out by a friend; this person is *restored* to cleanliness after being stained with filth. Another person, who is just about to fall into the mud, is snatched away from the edge of the puddle at the last moment, and never actually falls in. This second individual is *preserved* from being stained; if his rescuer does not act, he plunges into the mud without fail. *In both cases, a "savior" is required* – both to pull someone out of the mud, and to keep someone from falling in.

St. Francis de Sales, championing the *preservative redemption* of Mary, wrote that "at the instant of her Conception, He [Jesus] placed Himself between her and sin – or rather, one might say, *under* her, to prevent her from falling into Original Sin." Bishop Jacques Bossuet (d. 1704) wrote:

> Jesus Christ is her Savior . . . but Jesus Christ is also her Son, and therefore she must be separated *from* others: if others are delivered from evil, she must be preserved from it, so that its very course may be hindered. How can this be, except by some more special communication of her Son's privileges? (*On the Conception of the Blessed Virgin*)

And so, when Pope Pius IX defined the Immaculate Conception, he observed that the privilege was granted to Mary by God "in view of the merits of Jesus Christ, *the Savior of the human race*."

Scripture teaches that "the glory of children are their fathers." (Prov. 17:6) With the Woman prophesied in Eden, we are presented with a prodigy. God will assume her flesh, and reside in her womb, the One True God of Whom Scripture proclaims: "Who shall not fear Thee, O Lord, and magnify Thy name? For Thou only art holy." (Apoc. 15:4) Of the holy Presence of God, we read that "there shall not enter into it any thing defiled." (Apoc. 21:27) God Himself proclaims, "Behold, I make all things new." (Apoc. 21:5)

The early Church Fathers referred to Mary as the "New Eve", contrasting her obedience and cooperation in the Redemption with the disobedience and cooperation in the fall of the first Eve. In God's dealings with men, His people are instructed clearly *and at the appropriate time* on the means of pleasing Him and, therefore, benefiting themselves. During the early centuries of her history, the Church was occupied with specific tasks. She followed Christ's mandate to baptize all the nations, and defended herself from doctrinal innovators and the heresies spawned by their teachings. There was little cause for detailed studies of the Blessed Virgin's sanctity to be produced then.

Beginning in the fourth century, more elaborate testimonies to the Virgin's sanctity appear, and one senses an impetus on the part of the Fathers to extol it. There are the famous words of St. Ephrem of Syria († c.373): "Only you and your Mother are more beautiful than everything. For on you, O Lord, there is no mark; neither is there any stain in your Mother." Similar unfettered praises are found in the writings of St. Epiphanius († 403): "God alone excepted, she is superior to all beings. By nature she is more beautiful than Cherubim and Seraphim and all the angelic hosts. . . . O Holy Mother, immaculate lamb, you have brought forth the Incarnate Lamb of God; Christ."

This desire to highlight and extol the holiness of Mary continued unabated throughout the history of the Church, and only a fool would deny the inspiration of the Holy Ghost behind these praises. "Mary, since she was blessed," wrote St. Paschasius Radbertus († c. 850), "had not the corrupting stain, and hence gave birth to Christ without sorrow or corruption." St. Peter Damian (†1072) taught that the flesh of Mary "did not admit of the stain of Adam." St. Anselm (†1109) said that Mary possessed a purity "than which none can be imagined greater" below that of God, and his good friend, Eadmer (d. 1130), asked who would dare to assert that the Mother of God "was in the beginning of her conception deprived of the grace and illumination of the Holy Ghost"?

It was not only saints and theologians who felt their hearts turned to Mary's sanctity like flowers to the sun. The crafters of verse also proclaimed it in glowing terms. The Byzantine *Akathist Hymn* (c. 6-7th century) calls Mary "the beginning of Christ's wonders". The Old

English poet, Cynewulf (d. c. 825), referred to her as "a stainless maiden, whom He chose for Mother." Adam of St. Victor (d. 1180) described her as "Sprung from thorns, but thornless thoroughly."

Any denial of Our Lady's Immaculate Conception reflects even more on Jesus Christ than it does on Mary herself. The Flesh and Blood of the spotless Lamb of God, the vehicle which redeemed mankind and restored a fallen world, was imparted to Him by His Mother:

> And she brought forth her first-born Son, and wrapped Him up in swaddling clothes. (Lk. 2:7) You were not redeemed with corruptible things, as gold or silver. . . . But with the precious Blood of Christ, as of a lamb unspotted and undefiled, foreknown indeed before the foundation of the world, but manifested in the last times for you. (1 Pt. 1:18-20)

God born of a sinner? God residing for nine months in the womb of a woman whose body and soul had been tainted and weakened by original sin? The *Mother* of the Infant Lord lamenting, "When I have a will to do good, *evil* is present with me?" To admit such things is to make a liar out of God: "There is none holy as the Lord is: for there is no other beside Thee, and there is none strong like our God." (1 Kg. 2:2)

In the Gospels, we read of the abysmal treatment inflicted upon Jesus Christ by those He came to earth to die for. "They spit in His face, and buffeted Him: and others struck His face with the palms of their hands." (Mt. 26:67) The humility displayed here by the Omnipotent God almost defies description, and it required nothing less than a prophet to give us some small understanding of it: "He was offered because it was His own will, and He opened not His mouth: He shall be led as a sheep to the slaughter, and shall be dumb as a lamb before his shearer, and He shall not open His mouth." (Is. 53:7)

This *offering* of Himself, where the Almighty and Eternal One becomes a sacrificial Lamb, was effected only through the Incarnation. Regarding solely His Divinity, such abuse directed towards God is *unimaginable. The Book of Exodus* needed few words to describe the awesome might of the God of Israel: "And the Egyptians pursuing went in after them, and all Pharaoh's horses, his chariots and horsemen through the midst of the sea. And now the morning watch was come, and, behold, the Lord, looking upon the Egyptian army through the pillar of fire and of the cloud, slew their host." (Ex. 14:23-24)

The One Who "overthrew the wheels of the chariots" of the Egyptian soldiers, is the same Who allowed Himself to be spit upon and scourged. The Incarnation was not a means by which God merely "disguised" Himself as a human being, as some of the early heretics alleged. The Second Person of the Blessed Trinity "*emptied* Himself"; He "humbled Himself, *becoming obedient* unto death, even to the death of the Cross"; He "*learned obedience* by the things which He suffered." The Incarnation was no masquerade. As *Man,* God suffered, died, and rose again. As Man, God *could* be touched by unclean hands, subject to all the cruelty human minds can conceive.

But it was not God *already* incarnate Who entered Mary's womb. Jesus Christ was "conceived" in her womb by the power of the Holy Ghost. God, in His full Divinity, *met* Our Lady's humanity at the instant of conception, and the Scriptures teach that no "defiled" thing shall enter God's presence. There is no basis for comparison between the uniquely intimate relationship inaugurated between God and Mary, after she gave her "*fiat*" to the Angel Gabriel, and the deeply personal relationship existing between God and certain of his servants (Moses, Abraham, etc.) before He became incarnate in the Virgin's womb. *Behold, I make all things new*. Because of *who* she was, and *what* she would become, the Blessed Virgin Mary was the very first to be made "new", by the privilege of the Immaculate Conception.

The *Hypostatic Union* by which two natures, divine and human, were united in the one Person of Jesus Christ was not a union in name only. The natures were not somehow "attached" to each other, merely "co-existing" in one corporal shell. The humanity of Christ did not exist independently for any amount of time, to be "joined" later on to the eternal divine nature (such as at His Baptism in the Jordan River). The Son of God was "born of the Father before all ages . . . begotten not made; of one being with the Father," as is recited in the *Nicene Creed*. The Divine Person of Jesus Christ, the Redeemer and Savior, was born in *time*, on a certain day, at a certain hour, in Bethlehem. He was (and is) the Son of God, and the Son of Man. He is *God* ". . . made in the likeness of men, and in habit found as a man". (Phil. 2:7) He is *Man* "Who is over all things, God blessed forever." (Rom. 9:5)

We do not distinguish or segregate the two natures united in the Person of the Redeemer: "In *the name of Jesus* every knee should bow, of those that are in heaven, on earth, and under the earth." (Phil. 2:10) "Because of this Unity of Person," wrote St. Vincent of Lerins, "it happens that what is proper to God is ascribed to the man, and what is proper to the flesh is ascribed to God – *indifferently and without distinction.*" The Divine nature of Christ could *never* become "defiled" by contact with original sin. Yet, He chose to be "made in the likeness of men". He chose to take flesh of a human woman, a daughter of Eve . . . and still come into the world sinless, "a lamb unspotted and undefiled".

If, as St. Vincent of Lerins taught, "what is proper to the flesh is ascribed to God" by means of this marvelous Unity of Person, then the Immaculate Conception is the means by which the honor of the *Person* of Jesus Christ is preserved. In addition, there is maintained a fitting symmetry, consistent with the unfolding of the economy of salvation. As the only Son of God, Our Lord was "born of the Father before all ages . . . begotten not made," the very essence of perfect purity. As the only Son of Mary, He was born in time, His flesh formed from the immaculate flesh of His Mother, in whom no taint of sin (original or actual) was *ever* to be found. Therefore, purity and holiness are the hallmarks of both the eternal *and* the temporal generations of Jesus.

"What concord hath Christ with Belial?" (2 Cor. 6:15) asked St. Paul. The denial of Mary's Immaculate Conception implies quite a concord between Christ and Satan. It implies that the Mother of the Redeemer was *selected* from among the subjects of the devil, a representative of the "empire of death": "He chose the Mother He had created; He created the Mother He had chosen." (St. Augustine)

Even a denial which would attribute to the Virgin a *complete* sanctification mere moments *after* she was conceived in the womb of St. Anne, or at a later time, such as during the Annunciation, implies a collaboration; the Blessed Trinity searching among the "children of wrath" for the future Mother of the Incarnate Word. Such a compromise on the part of God, Who orders all things in creation, is inconsistent with His dignity. The Unity of Person, God-made-Man, the salvation effected by the shedding of *God's own Precious Blood*, do not allow for any denial of the Dogma of the Immaculate Conception. On the contrary, they lead us inescapably to the sentiments expressed by St. Louis de Montfort: "Mary is the earthly Paradise of Jesus Christ, the new Adam, where He became man by the power of the Holy Ghost, in order to accomplish in her wonders beyond our understanding."

Furthermore, if the Woman of the *Proto-evangelium* is to stand at the side of her Son against the "empire" of the serpent, and if her opposition to him has been established by God Himself – "I will put enmities between thee and the Woman" – can she ever have belonged to the devil's "empire", even for a moment?

"It was wholly fitting that so wonderful a mother should be ever resplendent with the glory of most sublime holiness and so completely free from all taint of original sin that she would triumph utterly over the ancient serpent," wrote Pope Pius IX. Truly, the Mother of God was a prodigy, even at her birth, which was an occasion of intense joy:

> What festive jubilation for all the angels when they saw her born whom God had made known to them from the beginning, as the one through whom the ruin sin had made among them should be repaired! What ravishing consolation for the souls of the holy Patriarchs and prophets, and the other holy Fathers detained in Limbo, for Adam and Eve, Abel and Noe, for Abraham, Isaac and Jacob, Joseph, Moses and David, when their good Angels revealed to them the birth of her by whose mediation they should soon be delivered from those obscure prisons wherein they languished. (St. John Eudes, *The Wondrous Childhood of the Most Holy Mother of God*)

The appearance on earth of the "Woman" of the *Proto-evangelium*, the one mentioned in the first part of the ancient prophecy, heralded the redemption at hand: "There shall come forth a rod out of the root of Jesse, *and a flower shall rise up out of his root*. And the Spirit of the Lord shall rest upon Him." (Is. 11:1-2)

The despoiling of the "empire of death" would not commence until the *fullness of time was come*, when *God sent His Son, made of a woman*. Since the fall, the world had been waiting for one thing with an ardent desire: "For we know that every creature groaneth, and travaileth in pain, even till now." (Rom. 8:22) The wait was over, at last, the moment a pure, wise, amiable and charitable young girl voiced the words that would alter reality forever: "Behold the handmaid of the Lord; be it done to me according to thy word." (Lk. 1:38)

Chapter Eleven

"That the Scriptures Might Be Fulfilled"

Our Lord's twofold affection for His mother – Christ fulfilled the Law – He is "the end of the Law"

God knows each one of his creatures even before they are conceived: *Before I formed thee in the bowels of thy mother, I knew thee.* Omniscient and unfettered by the limitations of time and space, the Blessed Trinity knows each of us *in detail* from all eternity, who we are and what we will be. When Rebecca, the wife of Isaac, concerned over the sons growing in her womb, went to consult the Lord, she received this reply: "Two nations are in thy womb, and two peoples shall be divided out of thy womb, and one people shall overcome the other, and the elder shall serve the younger." (Gen. 25:23) These words prophesied not only the coming struggles between Esau and Jacob, but of their descendants (physical and spiritual) as well. Esau, the first-born, was as much a son of Isaac as was Jacob, yet his descendants would not become God's favored people. It was Jacob, the younger, who represented the elect, and whose posterity would be favored by God.

Our Lord knew His Blessed Mother before she was conceived in the womb of St. Anne. He loved her *as only the Perfect Son could love His Immaculate Mother* from "before the foundation of the world". In Mary's heart, the love of a creature for her Creator merged with that of a mother for her child. Throughout her life, "adoration fused with human love, and was not separate," as the poet Fr. John W. Lynch (d. 1970) put it so aptly. The love of Jesus for Mary reciprocated this twofold affection, combining the love of God for one of His creatures with the love of a human Son for His Mother.

Our Lord never placed Himself in opposition to the Law: "Do not think that I am come to destroy the law, or the prophets. I am come not to destroy, but to fulfil." (Mt. 5:17) The religion of the Pharisees would come to naught, and its rituals mere empty rites, but the moral precepts of the Law would endure forever: "*But the word of the Lord endureth forever*. And this is the word which by the Gospel hath been preached unto you." (1 Pt. 1:25) "For amen I say unto you, till heaven and earth pass, one jot or one tittle shall not pass from the law, till all be fulfilled." (Mt. 5:18)

Jesus Christ fulfilled the Law through His own obedience: ". . . Suffer it to be so now," He said to St. John the Baptist before His Baptism on the banks of the Jordan, "For so it becometh us to fulfil all justice . . ." (Mt. 3:15) He fulfilled the Law also by justifying weak human beings, who were otherwise powerless to do so: "But also for us, to whom it shall be reputed, if we believe in Him that raised up Jesus Christ, our Lord, from the dead, Who was delivered up for our sins and rose again for our justification." (Rom. 4:24-25)

St. Paul wrote that ". . . the law is spiritual; but I am carnal, sold under sin." (Rom. 7:14) The law is a *holy* thing, yet, through its neglect, human *iniquity* is made manifest: "Is the law sin? God forbid! But I do not know sin, but by the law; for I had not known concupiscence, if the law had not said: Thou shalt not covet." (Rom. 7:7)

This is the plight of fallen man, bewailed by St. Paul. It is the omnipresent human drama of facing up to the Law, knowing that we are rightfully condemned by it: "If Thou, O Lord, wilt mark iniquities: Lord, who shall stand it?" (Ps. 129:3) How can man, prone to vice even when he would choose virtue, approach the Law? A practical solution to this "existential" dilemma exists for one reason only, because "God so loved the world, as to give His only begotten Son; that whosoever believeth in Him may not perish." In the Body of God-made-Man, Creator and creature were reconciled forever, "For by Him we have access both in one Spirit to the Father." (Eph. 2:18)

Christ *rose again for our justification*. The breach between God and men was repaired in the Body of the Savior, given up as a propitiation for all the sins of the world. Individual men and women are called to form *one* Body with this Savior: "Christ is the head of the Church. He is the Savior of *His* body." (Eph. 5:23) Therefore, *in and with Jesus*, fallen mankind faces the Law, not as slaves bound by sin, but as *released* captives:

> For the law of the spirit of life, in Christ Jesus, *hath delivered me from the law of sin and of death.* For what the law could not do, in that it was weak through the flesh, God, sending His own Son in the likeness of sinful flesh and of sin, hath condemned sin in the flesh; *That the justification of the law might be fulfilled in us* who walk not according to the flesh, but according to the Spirit. (Rom. 8:2-4)

"The end of the law," wrote St. Paul, "is Christ." (Rom. 10:4) Because of this, the merciful Redeemer could say to sinful individuals: "For my yoke is sweet and my burden light." (Mt. 11:30) "If thou wilt enter into life, keep the commandments." (Mt. 19:17) Left to our own devices, the following of God's precepts and laws is not a "light" burden. In Jesus, through the grace, strength and perseverance that can come only from *Him*, this yoke ceases to be a dead weight.

Speaking prophetically in the Psalms, Our Lord says: "In the head of the book it is written of Me that I should do Thy will: O My God, I have desired it, and Thy law in the midst of My heart." (Ps. 39:8-9) One of the most striking aspects of the Incarnation is the one that presents to our eyes a "humble" God – "Learn of Me, because I am meek, and humble of heart" – a God Who will so completely merge His Divinity with human nature, that He will practice the virtue of *obedience*: "He humbled Himself, becoming obedient unto death, even to the death of the Cross."

Love of the virtue of obedience. Love of the Father's will. Love for the Law and Commandments. Love for the human beings redeemed by His Precious Blood. This characterizes the Son of God and Son of Mary – God incarnate – God *seen* and *touched* by His creatures. Therefore, if we wish to obtain even the merest glimpse of the love of Jesus Christ for the Blessed Virgin, we can read what the Scriptures teach regarding the relationship between parent and child. What we find there was (and always will be) observed by the Savior, the One Who came not to destroy, but to fulfil the Law and the prophets.

As we note with what honor and respect Jesus regarded His own Mother, we can truly learn of Him, keeping in mind His admonition to "Go, and do thou in like manner." (Lk. 10:37)

Chapter Twelve

Honor Thy Mother

THE FOURTH COMMANDMENT – THE COMMAND TO HONOR ONE'S MOTHER ECHOED THROUGHOUT SCRIPTURE – THE MEANING OF "HONOR" – IN THE IMMACULATE CONCEPTION GOD HIMSELF HONORS HIS MOTHER

> Honor thy father and thy mother, that thou mayest be long-lived upon the land which the Lord thy God will give thee. (Ex. 20:12)

This is the wording of the Fourth Commandment. In the generation and rearing of children, parents are, in a sense, the "ministers" of God, and worthy of honor on this account, in addition to that arising from ordinary sentiment. This commandment is echoed throughout the inspired texts:

> My son, hear the instruction of thy father, and forsake not the law of thy mother: That grace may be added to thy head, and a chain of gold to thy neck. (Prov. 1:8-9)

> He that curseth his father, and mother, his lamp shall be put out in the midst of darkness. (Prov. 20:20)

> Honor thy father, and forget not the groanings of thy mother: Remember that thou hadst not been born but through them: and make a return to them as they have done for thee. (Ecclus. 7:29-30)

> He that honoreth his mother is as one that layeth up a treasure. (Ecclus. 3:5)

To "honor" can mean both *treating* a person honorably, and also *conferring* honor upon someone. God attributes great spiritual value to actions performed with a sincere good will. When the poor widow dropped her two mites into the temple treasury, Jesus told His disciples,

"This poor widow hath cast in more than all they who have cast into the treasury." (Mk. 12:43) On the other hand, we read in *The Acts of the Apostles* of a Roman Centurion named Cornelius, a convert, a religious man, ". . . giving much alms to the people." (Act. 10:2)

The poor widow showed no less good will than the prosperous Centurion: "And whosoever shall give to drink to one of these little ones a cup of cold water only . . . he shall not lose his reward." (Mt. 10:42) However, the means and station in life of Cornelius enabled him to express his charity in a different manner than the widow: "If thou have much, give abundantly; if thou have little, take care even so to bestow willingly a little." (Tob. 4:9)

The sincere love of a pauper for his mother is no less profound than that of a king for *his* mother. Station in life, means, and ability will determine just *how* this filial affection will be displayed. When the elder Tobias, believing his death to be imminent, called his son to him, he gave him these instructions:

> Thou shalt honor thy mother all the days of her life: For thou must be mindful what and how great perils she suffered for thee in her womb. And when she also shall have ended the time of her life, bury her by me. (Tob. 4:3-5)

These are simple instructions, capable of being observed by people of different means. They entail respect for the mother and solicitation for her needs until the end of her life. No one can be expected to do more . . . unless one is provided with the *means* to do so. Compare the words of Tobias with a description of King Solomon's behavior towards his mother, Bethsabee:

> The king arose to meet her, and bowed to her, and sat down upon his throne: and a throne was set for the king's mother, and she sat on his right hand. And she said to him: I desire one small petition of thee, do not put me to confusion. And the king said to her: "My mother ask: for I must not turn away thy face." (3 Kg. 2:19-20)

Tobias was instructed to render honor to his mother through filial love, care and attention. Such actions would be demanded also from Solomon. But as king, Solomon could also place his mother on a throne beside his, and see to it that her petitions are heeded and carried out. In both instances, it is a matter of filial love being expressed according to ability and opportunity.

The only Son of Mary, Jesus Christ, is also the only-begotten Son of God. Through the Unity of Person, the Child conceived in her womb, the Son she carried, bore, nursed and raised, was *God*. She regarded Jesus with a twofold affection – the love of a creature for her Creator, and the love of a Mother for her Child. Jesus regarded her also with a twofold affection – the love of God for one of his creatures, and the love of a Son for his own unique Mother.

If "honoring" someone means both treating that person honorably, as well as conferring honor upon her in *accord with one's abilities and station in life*, how does the Son of God – the glorious King of Kings and Savior – "honor" His Mother? How does God, to Whom all things are possible, honor the one who carried Him, gave birth to Him, and reared Him with the most tender affection and regard, the chosen Woman prophesied in *Genesis* and in the writings of the Prophet Isaias? This question must be answered very carefully, for to do so incorrectly is to malign the Sacred Humanity of Jesus, to question the very integrity and goodness of the Blessed Trinity.

As the Mother of God, Mary was endowed with gifts and graces impossible to enumerate. Her Divine Maternity is the foundation, the basis, for *all* her prerogatives. Yet, at the very beginning was that "primeval" honor granted by God, by which a human creature, a daughter of Eve, was chosen from among the millions of women ever to be born, to be the Mother of the Savior. "It is such that God could make a greater world, a greater heaven," wrote St. Bonaventure (†1274), "but He cannot exalt a creature more than by making her His Mother."

"What greater prodigy could the world behold than a woman become the Mother of God, and a God clothed in human flesh," asked St. Alphonsus Ligouri (†1787). A "prodigy" denotes the extraordinary, something to excite a sense of wonder. In the Blessed Virgin Mary, we discover a woman whose relationship to the Eternal God is one of *intimacy*, an intimacy undreamed of by the holiest, most gifted mystics ever to walk the earth. She will be the daughter of God the Father, but the first among daughters, destined to the highest honor from the beginning. She will be overshadowed by the Holy Ghost, will conceive by Him, thus cooperating personally *and directly* as His spouse in the presentation of God's greatest gift to the world. As Mother of the Son, she will hold her *God* in her arms, and the first words He speaks in His humanity will be words of affection meant for her ears only.

This promised Woman, being the future Mother of God, was truly a prodigy from the very beginning of her life, for God does all things well: "For by the greatness of the beauty, and of the creature, the Creator of them may be seen, so as to be known thereby." (Wis. 13:5) Because of the Divine Maternity which would be hers *when the fullness of time was come*, Our Lady's Immaculate Conception insured that "this Mother, ever absolutely free of all stain of sin, all fair and perfect, would possess that fullness of holy innocence and sanctity, than which one cannot even imagine anything greater, and which outside of God, no mind can succeed in comprehending fully." (Pope Pius IX)

Mary's Immaculate Conception was one way in which her Son "honored" her. It was in His power to prevent original sin, and the misery and concupiscence engendered by it, from harming His Mother. A leper once approached Jesus, saying: "Lord, if Thou wilt, Thou canst make me clean." (Mt. 8:2) Our Lord's reply was, "I will. Be thou made clean." *Men* do not limit God's power, or the manner in which it is manifested. When Queen Esther's people were in danger of being destroyed by their enemies, her uncle, Mardochai, asked her to petition King Assuerus on their behalf. At the time, any person entering the king's presence unbidden could be put to death by law. Yet, Esther received the consoling words of Assuerus: "Thou shalt not die: for this law is not made for thee, but for all others." (Est. 15:13) It was the right of this king to apply the law as he saw fit, or to extenuate its consequences, in the interests of justice.

It was the right and privilege of the King of Kings, Who answers to no one, to apply the graces and merits He would win on Calvary to His Mother at any time He chose, even *before* the Crucifixion, or His birth at Bethlehem, for, *as God*, He is not bound by the temporal progression of events: "Amen, amen I say to you, before Abraham was made, I am." (Jn. 8:58) The curse of original sin, the debt incurred at the fall, is the lot of *all* men and women. As a daughter of Eve, this debt belonged to Our Lady as well. However, at her Immaculate Conception, the Savior seems to say to His Mother: "Thou shalt not die, for this law is not made for thee, but for all others. . . . Be thou made clean."

The Book of Ecclesiasticus plainly bids us to honor our parents *and* to "make a return to them as they have done for thee." We are not, then, to honor our mothers with words only, but actively, by making a *return* to them. Our station in life, means and ability to make this return will determine its form. A man of modest means will give his mother a home and the things she needs to be happy and well. A king can give her a throne, and fulfill her wishes. Both will strive to keep their mothers healthy, safe and contented.

The ravages of original sin are concupiscence, disordered passions, unhappiness, spiritual and temporal death. If an earthly king saw his mother in the grip of sickness, or in danger of dying, would he spare any expense to procure only the best physicians and medicines? Do we dare to expect anything less from Jesus Christ, King of Kings and the supreme Physician, by His own declaration: "They that are in health need not a physician, but they that are ill." (Mt. 9:12) Does the perfect Son allow His Mother to waste away with the degenerative sickness of original sin, when He can spare her such misery? Is that the "return" the Son of God makes to His Mother?

> God did more for the Blessed Virgin than merely correct in her an unhealthy tendency inherited from her first parents. He did not merely give her a remedy for disease, He *gave her health*. By His preventing action He removed the very principal of inward weakness. That, indeed, is saying too little. From the first instant of her life He so regulated the passions and appetites of that privileged being that they were always entirely under her control. Holy and pure, she was able to face all difficulties without danger, prepared to conquer in all. (Fr. A. Vermeersch, *Meditations and Instructions on the Blessed Virgin*, Vol. II, 1911)

Our Lord fulfilled the Fourth Commandment completely and perfectly. He honored His Father by His words and actions:

> Father, the hour is come, glorify Thy Son, that Thy Son may glorify Thee . . . I have glorified Thee on the earth; I have finished the work which Thou gavest Me to do. (Jn. 17:1, 4)

Could the Incarnate Word, Who fulfilled the Law perfectly, consider only *half* of the Fourth Commandment worthy of observance? Impossible, for "God is faithful and without any iniquity, He is just and right" (Deut. 32:4); He is the One Who declared, "My counsel shall stand, and all My will shall be done." (Is. 46:10) Our Lady's own Son – her Lord and the Physician of souls – made the only return to His Mother that we would expect from Uncreated Wisdom, from the God of Love. He endowed her with a *plenitude* of grace and, never miserly in His goodness, He did so at the very moment of her conception, making His Mother all beautiful, within and without.

In the safeguarding of His Mother, in the honor shown to Mary by Jesus in accordance with the Law, the honor of the Son is also safeguarded. "The glory of children are their fathers," says *The Book of Proverbs*. The reason St. Augustine would not include Our Lady in any discussion of sin was "out of respect of Our Lord." Had Our Lady belonged to Satan even for a moment of her life, the Accuser – the serpent – would have held this one victory over the Woman and her seed.

When Our Lord fasted in the desert after His Baptism, the devil prefaced his temptations with an assault on the humility of Jesus. "If *Thou be the Son of God*, command that these stones be made bread. . . . *If Thou be the Son of God*, cast Thyself down." (Mt. 4:3, 6) Had Jesus done either of these things, He would *not* have glorified the Father through His obedience: "Not as I will, but as Thou wilt. . . . Thy will be done." (Mt. 26:39, 42) It is the Luciferian philosophy, the hatred of human nature and any expressions of it, that was being vented in these temptations. The Son of God and Mary was called upon to deny and despise His own humanity, and no wonder – that very nature would became the vehicle for the liberation of souls from the devil's kingdom.

A denial of filial affection on the part of Jesus for His Mother, a denial of His *desire* to honor her in accord with both the Law *and His own ability and means to do so*, a denial of His love for her, which combines supernatural and natural fullness – such a denial is of a piece with that proposed in the desert by the Accuser of men. To deny the feelings of Jesus for Mary is to deny the Sacred Humanity. This is exactly what Satan hoped to gain in the desert.

Chapter Thirteen

The Unique and Exquisite Holiness of Mary

Mary prepared directly by God for her vocation – The Almighty has done "great things" for her – To minimize Mary is to insult her Son – She had the use of reason from her conception – Mary's most blessed childhood – Her formative years at the temple – Mary was full of the grace she received as a creature – compared to God Mary is nothing – No original or actual sin in Mary – The integrity of her soul – Mary could only be tempted by exterior sources – Mother and Child; an enternal covenant in an order all its own

The life of the Virgin Mary prior to the Annunciation was a life spent in *preparation* to receive the Son of God as her own cherished Son. Throughout history, God prepared His servants for their labors. Samuel "ministered before the face of the Lord" from a very young age, and he ". . . advanced, and grew on, and pleased both the Lord and men." (1 Kg. 2:18,26) The courageous Judith, who slew Holofernes, the general of the Assyrian army and sworn enemy of Israel, was the widow of Manasses. She ". . . made herself a private chamber in the upper part of her house, in which she abode shut up with her maids. And she wore haircloth upon her loins, and fasted all the days of her life, except the Sabbaths, and new moons, and the feasts of the house of Israel." (Jth. 8:5-6) The history of salvation is replete with men and women who were *prepared* to do the work of God.

The Blessed Virgin was prepared to "mother" God Himself, to bear Him and raise Him. Although she was "Full of Grace" from the first instant of her conception, she is not a divine being. Mary could increase in virtue and holiness with every sigh of her Immaculate Heart, which was in constant adoration of God, especially so after the Incarnation. Not only with every act of charity did Mary advance immeasurably in grace, but with every act of faith and hope. In His human nature, Jesus could not grow in, nor could He have, the theological virtues of faith or hope, for He had the beatific vision of God in His created mind from the moment of His conception. He could not believe without seeing, for He always saw God. He could not hope that God would reward Him or be true to His promises because He already knew God in that eternal life which He, as the God-Man, was one with on account of the union of His divine and human nature in the eternal Person of the Son. Nor could He increase, as man, in grace (or the virtue of charity, i.e., love of God) because His Sacred Heart was filled with every possible grace and all possible charity on account of the same divine and hypostatic union. When one reads in the *Gospel of Luke* that Jesus "advanced in wisdom and age and grace with God and men" (2:52) it simply means that, as man, He manifested His fullness of wisdom and grace in complimental proportion to His age. Pope St. Gregory the Great was voicing the traditional teaching of the Church when he explained this verse thusly:

> Not that He was wiser at any future period of His life, than He was at the moment of His conception, but this is said, because He chose to manifest increasing signs of wisdom as He increased in years. In the same manner also He increased in grace, by displaying, as He advanced in age, the gifts of grace with which He was endowed; and by this excited men to the praise of God, from the consideration of favors God had bestowed upon Him; and thus He conduced to the honor of God, and the salvation of men.

Though perfect at her conception, the future Mother of Jesus could still prepare herself diligently. Even before she knew that the prophesies were to be realized in her own womb, she was preparing herself day by day for her role, by living a life consecrated to God, even in its most prosaic situations and actions. Her Immaculate Conception allowed her to do this to an extremely fine degree: "All she did throughout the course of her life tended to cooperate with her Divine Son in the work of our salvation, *or to dispose her soul for this marvelous cooperation.*" (St. John Eudes)

Our Lady's consent to the Incarnation, and the maternal love she lavished on her Child, were not foregone conclusions, somehow "programmed" into her at her Immaculate Conception. The absence of sin does not make one less human or "free" but more so. Mary's obedience to God, and her love of Jesus, were heartfelt, passionate, beyond comprehension.

A pious nature in an individual, or a person's desire to consecrate himself to God, does not render that individual "aloof", like the infamous "plaster saints" cited as examples of unattainable holiness or unreasonable expectations. The simple truth is that it is not *holiness* that makes one less human; it is *sin* that does so. There were no "plaster saints". They were all, each man and woman, genuine, complex human beings. They knew anxiety and fear. They also knew hope. When we read their homilies or treatises on theology or devotion, we are not reading the "ideas" of people who never sinned, or abstract utopian agendas that are impossible to realize in "real life".

On the contrary. In the lives of the saints, we see proof that ". . . no word shall be impossible with God." (Lk. 1:37) As St. Paul taught so well, it is a struggle for sinful human beings to turn away from sin. He likened the struggle to a "race" for an imperishable crown, unlike the ephemeral crowns of laurel leaves given to victorious athletes. Yet there is glory in the fight. The struggle for holiness is engaged, not to become something cold, less human or passionate, but to become *fully* human, fully alive *in Christ*, Who raised and glorified our nature: "And you, when you were dead in your sins. . . . *He hath quickened together with Him*, forgiving you all offenses." (Col. 2:13)

There are those unfortunate souls whose hostility towards the Mother of God manifests itself in a denial of her Immaculate Conception, on a spurious supposition that the dogma grants her "divine" status, or turns her into a type of "paragon", chiseled in stone and far removed from earthly cares. This is, at bottom, an expression of the perverse belief that *sin* is the real quality of mercy, of endearment . . . the real goal of the human heart. This belief produces, in turn, a very definite effect: the automatic branding *as hypocrites* of all those who struggle for holiness and obedience to Christ, but so often fall short. It is the mentality which prompted the arch-heretic Martin Luther to say, regarding "pious souls", that "it is more important to guard them against good works than against sin." This is in direct contrast to St. Paul's teaching that "Love therefore is the fulfilling of the law." (Rom. 13:10)

When we speak of the Blessed Virgin, then, and we marvel at her purity, at her wisdom, at her freedom from both original and actual sin, at the love of her maternal heart, we are awed not by a type of literary "construct", an amalgam of desirable traits molded into a composite "character" deemed worthy of her place in history. We are attracted not by myth, but by this *person*, this vibrant human being. We are awed by her intimacy with the Blessed Trinity, and all the prerogatives that flow from it, but it is not awe in the face of the *unreal*. It is a marveling at the works of God made manifest in and with this exquisite creature, an empathy with the words spoken to Mary by St. Elizabeth, under the inspiration of the Holy Ghost, "Blessed art thou that hast believed," (Lk. 1:45) which were echoed by the Virgin herself: "He that is mighty hath done great things to me." (Lk. 1:49)

Miserliness and hesitancy in the proclamation of God's works are not fruits of the Holy Ghost. The opposite is true: "Great is the Lord, and greatly to be praised." (Ps. 144:3) The denial of Our Lady's privileges, or a desire to minimize or ignore them, is therefore not a work pleasing to the Blessed Trinity.

The depths of each individual soul are known to God alone: "The searcher of hearts and reins is God." (Ps. 7:10) "The Lord is the weigher of spirits." (Prov. 16:2) However, with the Mother of God, we are given the *surety* of her freedom from original sin and its ravages. Therefore, while the depths of the Virgin's soul, and its workings, can be fathomed only by her Creator, we have set before us still the prodigy of the Immaculate Conception. Our reason, then, informed by the lessons of inspired Scripture, allows us to paint a portrait of Mary as she would have appeared to her relatives, friends and neighbors. Like any portrait, ours can never capture the myriad facets of our subject, but it *can* (again, like many portraits) present us with an accurate representation.

The removal of the debilitating effects of original sin is essentially the removal of the obstacles to a complete surrender to God. "To will is present with me," confessed St. Paul, "but to accomplish that which is good, I find not." (Rom. 7:18) He refers to his mortal body, weakened by original sin, as a "body of death", remembering that ". . . the wages of *sin* is death." (Rom. 6:23) Our Lady, freed from the unwholesome, destructive influence of concupiscence, disordered passions and clouded judgment, spent an entire life in preparation for her Divine Maternity.

As a child, Mary, her heart-strings "tuned" to God like those of a fine violin, would have followed all the Scriptural admonitions enjoining respect for parents and obedience towards them, which would one day be summed up by St. Paul: "Children, obey your parents in the Lord, for this is just." (Eph. 6:1) Many theologians, including Doctors of the Church, taught that she enjoyed the use of reason from her conception. Their reasons were summarized by Fr. Reginald Garrigou-Lagrange:

> It is not becoming to hold that Mary, Queen of patriarchs, prophets, apostles, and all the saints, lacked a privilege granted to St. John the Baptist. We read of him in Luke 1, 41 and 44, while he was still in the womb: 'When Elizabeth heard the salutation of Mary, the infant leaped in her womb. . . ." If, therefore, St. John the Baptist had the use of reason and will before his birth, because of his vocation as precursor of Christ, the same privilege can hardly be denied to Christ's mother.
>
> Mary's initial fullness of grace, virtues, and gifts which surpassed already the final fullness of the saints, could not have remained inactive at the beginning of her life. Such inactivity would appear opposed to the sweet and generous dispositions of Divine Providence in favor of the Mother of the Savior. But unless she had the use of her free will through infused knowledge, the virtues and gifts which she possessed in so high a degree would have remained inactive for a considerable part of her life (that is, the beginning). (*The Mother of the Savior and Our Interior Life*, 1948)

Because of who she was, and what wonders the Blessed Trinity would accomplish through her, it is fitting that our Lady recognize and render praise and obedience to God in a singular manner:

> Now there can be no doubt that, being chosen for a higher dignity than St. John, she had the use of reason in a more excellent manner. We other poor people are

> born in the greatest misery imaginable . . . but the sacred Virgin was born as our Queen, with the use of reason. (St. Francis de Sales, *Sermon on the Nativity of the BVM*)

> Hence from that first moment Mary, grateful to God, began to do all that she could do, by immediately and faithfully trafficking with that great capital of grace which had been bestowed upon her; and applying herself entirely to please and love the divine goodness, from that moment she loved Him with all her strength, and continued thus to love Him always. (St. Alphonsus Ligouri, *The Glories of Mary*)

Our Lady's early years, spent in the blessed company of Sts. Joachim and Anne, would have impressed upon her the outlines of a home in which God was loved and adored. According to the most ancient and reliable traditions, when Mary was three years old, her parents brought her to the Temple in order to dedicate her to the service of God: "Not wishing to separate ourselves even a little from the common teaching of the Church, we say that the Blessed Virgin was presented in the Temple in order to be perfectly educated there." (Pope Benedict XIV, 1740-1758, *De Festis BV*) This Presentation would have inaugurated a life of prayer and service, echoing the labors of the Israelite women in preparation for the making of the tabernacle to house the Ark of the Covenant: "The skillful women also gave such things as they had spun, violet, purple and scarlet, and fine linen." (Ex. 35:25)

Those years of service would have provided our Lady with numerous opportunities to practice obedience, humility and charity, and it is, perhaps, the image of the beautiful young Mary, working at her spinning and weaving, which underlies the vivid image of her as the "workshop" of the Incarnation:

> Being outside of the flesh, the Word of God took upon Himself the holy flesh from the holy Virgin; like a bridegroom, He prepared for Himself that garment

> which He would weave together with His sufferings on the Cross. (St. Hippolytus of Rome, †235, *Christ and Antichrist*)

> She is the awe-inspiring loom of the Incarnation, whereon in a way unspeakable was woven the garment of the Hypostatic union, with the Holy Ghost as weaver; the overshadowing power from above, the connecting thread; the ancient fleece of Adam, the wool; the undefiled flesh from the Virgin, the threaded woof; the shuttle, the immeasurable grace of her who bore, with the Logos as artist. (St. Proclus of Constantinople, †446, *Encomium on the All-Holy Mary, Mother of God*)

> But what is the workshop of this economy? The body of a holy Virgin. And what are the active principles of this birth? The Holy Ghost and the overshadowing power of the most high. (St. Basil the Great, †379, *On the Holy Generation of Christ*)

To souls directed towards God, each day is an occasion to approach Him more ardently, to progress in virtue and grace. This was so for Mary, as well. She was conceived "Full of Grace". Now, a cup that is full of water, and a barrel that is full of water, are both completely "full"; one is not "more full" than the other, but the *capacity* to hold water increases as one goes from cup, to bucket, to barrel, to pond, etc. Mary could merit such an increase of grace. Of course, as a finite creature, she was ever open to the *reception* of grace:

> The Blessed Virgin *was endowed* with a *threefold* perfection of grace. The first was by way of preparation that she might be worthy to be the Mother of Christ. The second perfection of grace was because of the presence of the Son of God Incarnate in her womb. The third is her final perfection, that of glory. That the second perfection is greater than the first, and the third greater than the second, is evident. (St. Thomas Aquinas, †1274, *Summa Theologica*)

> With her cooperation the Blessed Virgin increased many times over the grace bestowed upon her. . . . Her industry in this labor of meriting was also the greatest possible, for there was found in her no indifferent or indeliberate act. This was because of the perfect dominion she had over her faculties and their operations. Still less was there to be found in her any blameworthy act, or even any imperfection. She ever acted with all the strength of the actual graces given her at the time, and with all the virtue of the habits of grace which had been infused into her or which she had acquired. Moreover, the stimulus of sin and every other hindrance to well-doing were quite wanting in her. So she must have gone forward in her meriting like the light of day that, in a moment, reaches to the limits of the horizon. (Fr. John Peter Pinamonti, d. 1703, *The Immaculate Heart of Mary*)

"With the whole Church I acknowledge that Mary, being a mere creature fashioned by the hands of God, is, compared to His infinite majesty, less than an atom," wrote St. Louis de Montfort, "or rather is simply nothing, since He alone can say, 'I am He Who is.'" Being fully human, the Blessed Virgin stands in relation to God as creature to Creator. A new dimension was added to this creature-Creator relationship at the Incarnation: "You have received the spirit of adoption of sons." (Rom. 8:15) "I live, now not I; but Christ liveth in me." (Gal. 2:20)

If the relation between God and man has been changed through the Incarnation, then the Virgin must hold a unique place, as she stands in an intimate relation to the Incarnation *itself*. God "has decided to begin and accomplish His greatest works through the Blessed Virgin," wrote St. Louis de Montfort. The saving work of the Blessed Trinity, the Redemption of fallen mankind by the death and Resurrection of Jesus Christ, was dependent upon the Incarnation. In preparation for such a work, nothing was left to chance. A people was gathered to God and instructed throughout the centuries, a race from which would spring the Mother of God, the "Rod of Jesse". Mary herself was conceived immaculately, making her a fit dwelling for the sinless Redeemer.

As Our Lady matured, she approached nearer and nearer to the day she would be greeted with great reverence by the Archangel, and invited to cooperate with the Blessed Trinity in the Redemption of the world. Her sinlessness did not make her *less* free to accept the Divine Maternity. That God chose a Mother for His Son is fact; that the chosen woman would be asked to *consent* to the Divine Maternity is also fact: "God made man from the beginning, and left him in the hand of his own counsel." (Ecclus. 15:14)

The future Mother of Jesus was free from both original and actual sin. This is taught in Sacred Scripture, where we learn that the "Woman" of the *Proto-evangelium* would be at enmity with the serpent, whose head was crushed at the Savior's Resurrection (for the Immaculate Conception was the first fruit of the *Resurrection*), allowing Our Lady to be conceived without any trace of original sin in her pure soul – i.e., to be redeemed "in *view of* the merits of Jesus Christ". (Pope Pius IX) As the one destined to crush the serpent's head (i.e., sin, whose wages are spiritual death) in tandem with her Divine Son, "to her more grace was given than was necessary to conquer sin completely." (Pope Pius IX)

The idea of *actual* sin being attributed to the Blessed Virgin, then, is out of the question; it is both un-Scriptural and unreasonable. What rational mind can imagine these words issuing from the mouth of the Woman chosen to raise the Savior: "For I do not that good which I will; but the evil which I hate, that I do." (Rom. 7:15) On the contrary, Scripture and sound doctrine teach incontrovertibly that Mary was "the only daughter of life, the tabernacle most holy, not made by hands of man, preserved incorrupt, and blessed from the head to the feet." (St. Dionysius of Alexandria, †265)

Our Lady was always lovable, in the truest sense of the word, always beloved of God. Even as a child, she "performed her smallest actions *according to her measure of grace*" and thus "rendered very great glory to God even in the smallest things." (St. John Eudes) Had our Lady lived her life as a sinner, even avoiding all mortal sin, what would we make then of her *preparation* to bear, nurture and raise the Son of God? Even the least serious of sins take on a habitual character in time. As such, they work to turn the will away from God. Had our Lady been wont to turn away from God, even in fleeting moments, turning her eyes instead towards the borders of the "empire of death", we would find the future Mother of God *denying* Him on occasion. This is NOT the belief bequeathed to the Church either by Scripture or Tradition:

> The nearer a thing approaches to its principle, the more does it partake of the effect of that principle. But Christ is the principle of grace, and Mary is nearest to Him, since He received from her His human nature. Hence she ought to receive from Christ a greater fullness of grace than anyone else. (St. Thomas Aquinas, *Summa Theologica*, Book III)

Our Lady's plenitude of grace was not a stagnant "supply" of grace bestowed upon her at her conception, and from which she would draw as from a receptacle whose contents diminish as they are used. Her cooperation with grace, her continued practice of virtue, her allegiance to God and His laws, would last throughout her earthly life – a life in which there was no room for sin of *any* kind. "Being far exalted above others," wrote St. Cyprian (†258) concerning the Holy Virgin, "she partook of their nature *but not of their sin*."

Because temptations can arise either internally, externally (through the senses), or from the suggestions of unclean spirits, we may well believe that Mary – like her Divine Son in the desert – experienced temptations arising from *external* sources only:

> In the case of Jesus Christ and of His Mother Mary, any such onslaught *from within* was impossible, as it was also to our first parents before the fall. In Our Lord, His human nature was hypostatically united to the Godhead. In the soul of His Immaculate Mother, from the first moment of her being, there reigned the perfect harmony which could suffer no disturbance. But both to Jesus and Mary temptation might come, and did come, from the visible world and also from the direct onslaughts of Satan. . . . Merits are heaped up through correspondence with the grace of God, even though the

> correspondent may, at the moment, present no difficulty. Still, there is no doubt that when a struggle is necessary, *it enormously enhances merit.* We have a High Priest Who is able to compassionate us because He too was tempted – so were all His saints – so was His spotless Mother. . . . But as the temptations of Jesus in no way tarnished His ineffable Sanctity, so was it with the temptations – however severe and terrible they may have been – of His Mother Mary. They all belonged to the economy of God's dealings with her sinless soul. (Fr. O.R. Vassall-Phillips, *The Mother of Christ*, 1936)

The Immaculate Conception prepared Mary to carry God in her own body. Preliminary to this, it prepared her to consecrate herself to God freely and unselfishly; it prepared her to receive and consent to the Annunciation; it prepared her to make a home in which *God*, in His Sacred Humanity, would dwell for thirty years. The only reasonable *and possible* description for such a woman is that given by Pope Pius IX: "The Blessed Virgin was, through grace, entirely free from every stain of sin, and from all corruption of body, soul and mind . . . she was always united with God *and joined* to Him – an *eternal covenant* . . . she was never in darkness but always in light." (*Ineffabilis Deus*)

Joined to Him – an *eternal covenant.* The bond between Jesus and Mary, still one between God and creature, is of a different order than that between Jesus and the remainder of the souls redeemed by His Precious Blood. The Woman and her seed were prophesied in Eden, and again by the Prophet Isaias: "Behold a Virgin shall conceive, and bear a Son." (Is. 7:14) Finally, mankind knew that salvation was truly at hand when, *and only when*, the Shepherds and Magi ". . . found the Child with Mary His Mother." (Mt. 2:11)

Chapter Fourteen

Saint Joseph

THE HOLY FAMILY AT NAZARETH – THE HOLY MARRIAGE OF JOSEPH AND MARY AND THEIR VOW OF VIRGINITY – THE GLORIES OF ST. JOSEPH THE "JUST MAN" – HIS VIRGINAL INTEGRITY – HIS TRIAL – TESTIMONY OF FATHERS AND DOCTORS CONCERNING JOSEPH'S HUMILITY IN THE FACE OF SO GREAT A MYSTERY – JOSEPH'S ADVANCE IN VIRTUE MERITS THE VISIT OF AN ANGEL

The home in which the King of Kings was raised was never given over to the disorders, frustration and regret occasioned by sinful lapses and episodes. To attribute such a lack of foresight and preparation to the Omniscient Godhead is ludicrous. King David prayed to God: "If I ascend into heaven, Thou art there: if I descend into hell, Thou art present. If I take my wings early in the morning, and dwell in the uttermost parts of the sea: Even there also shall Thy hand lead me." (Ps. 138:8-10) God was present, *in the flesh*, inside that modest home in Nazareth.

St. Luke records that, after Mary and Joseph discovered the Child Jesus in the Temple, "He went down with them and came to Nazareth and was subject to them." (Lk. 2:51) The Living God made Himself *subject* to His parents, to a human man and a human woman. It would be worthwhile, then, to turn our attention briefly to this man, St. Joseph, the one chosen from among all others to protect and provide for "the Child and His Mother" and thereby arrive at a clearer appreciation of his relationship with the Blessed Virgin.

Though chaste, the marriage of Joseph and Mary was not a merely symbolic one, a legal expedient to provide the Holy Family with proper social credentials. *The Catechism of the Council of Trent* states that "the nature and force of marriage consist in the tie and obligation; and that, without consummation, the consent of the parties . . . is sufficient to constitute a true marriage." The virginal conception of Jesus did no violence to Mary's role as the wife of Joseph, for the Catechism also observes that "the word *matrimony* [Latin, "mater" – mother] is derived from the fact that the principal object which a female should propose to herself in marriage is to become a mother; or from that fact that to a mother it belongs to conceive, bring forth and train her offspring."

Our Lady accepted the Divine Maternity. St. Joseph accepted the awesome roles of husband of the Immaculate Conception and "foster-father" of the Incarnate Word. However, this title of Joseph's, *foster-father,* should not be confused with or likened to the title, "adoptive father", which does *not* apply to St. Joseph. Although, like an adoptive father, Joseph accepted and reared as his own a Child Whom he did not physically generate, yet the similarity ends there. The virginal union of Mary and Joseph was a prerequisite for the coming of the Redeemer – i.e., God the Father had ordained that His Son would be born to a *legally married couple.* Although Joseph did not participate in the natural generation of the Incarnate Word born of the Virgin, it remains a fact that Jesus was born to the Woman *who was the wife of St. Joseph.* Although a husband may adopt a child which had been born to his wife outside of their marriage, our Lord was born *while Mary and Joseph were legally married*:

> Jesus was born *in Joseph's own marriage* while Joseph was still living. . . . The outstanding difference between a human adoptive father and St. Joseph is this: An adopted son is a stranger or alien to the marriage of his adoptive parents, or to one of them. . . . *Yet Jesus was by no means alien to the marriage of Joseph and Our Lady.* The very purpose of the virginal union as determined by God was that it should prepare for Our Lord's coming, should receive Him in its midst, and should rear Him to adult manhood. (Fr. Francis L. Filas, *Joseph: The Man Closest to Jesus*, 1962)

> Every good of marriage was fulfilled in the parents of Christ: offspring, loyalty, and the sacrament. We recognize the offspring in Our Lord Jesus Christ Himself; the loyalty, in that no adultery occurred; and the sacrament [i.e., the indissolubility], because of no divorce. Only conjugal intercourse did not take place. (St. Augustine, *De. nup. et concup.*)

Now, we know that the Blessed Virgin was descended from the royal house of David, because the Archangel Gabriel had told her that her Son would inherit "the throne of David His father", and St. Paul wrote that Jesus was made "of the seed of David, according to the flesh." When our Lord was born, however, it was the custom to trace a child's genealogy through the *father*. Therefore, in the *legal* sense, Joseph would have been considered the direct ancestor of Jesus – i.e., our Lord would have held hereditary rights over Joseph's goods. St. Luke tells us that Joseph also was "of the house and family of David". Here is yet another example of the manner in which the Blessed Trinity ordered all things to perfection for the Incarnation. Our Lord was the "Son of David" both *legally* and *humanly* speaking, through Mary *and* Joseph . . . through His Mother and through His "earthly" father. Therefore, no foundation whatsoever was lacking in Our Lord's fulfillment of *all* the Messianic prophecies which heralded His human birth.

Here, again, we find the Divine Symmetry at work, ordering all things to the glory of God. In His divinity, Our Lord was "born of the Father before all ages . . . true God of true God . . . begotten, not made." This perfectly pure generation of the Second Divine Person is represented, or "mirrored", on earth by the virginal integrity of St. Joseph. "We may say," wrote St. Francis de Sales (†1622), "that the Holy Family was a Trinity on earth, which in a certain way represented the heavenly Trinity Itself." If we consider St. Joseph's relationship to the Blessed Trinity and his place in the created order, then we must, in good faith, admit that his relationship to Jesus Christ, Whom he loved with a father's heart, is a truly intimate and unprecedented one, second only to that between Jesus and His Mother, Mary:

> Herein we see manifested the great love of the Three Persons of the Blessed Trinity for our saint and the confidence They reposed in him; for the Eternal Father committed wholly into his charge His well-beloved Son; the Divine Son delivered Himself entirely to his care and to his will; the Holy Ghost consigned and committed to him His most immaculate Spouse; so that this Holy Family,

> of which Joseph became the head, was another Triad on earth, a resplendent image of the Most Holy Triad in heaven, the Ever-Blessed Trinity: Joseph representing the Eternal Father, Jesus representing and being in very truth the Eternal Word, and Mary representing the Eternal Love, the Holy Ghost. (Edward Healy Thompson, M.A., *The Life and Glories of St. Joseph*, 1888)

When he sat down to his supper after a long day of work, his gaze rested upon the beautiful Queen of heaven and earth, and upon his Lord and God, Who, with a Heart filled with filial affection, gladly called him "father":

> As Joseph has been united to the Blessed Virgin by the ties of marriage, it may not be doubted that he approached nearer than anyone else to the eminent dignity by which the Mother of God so nobly surpasses all created natures. For marriage is the most intimate of all unions, which essentially imparts a community of gifts between those joined together by it. Thus, in giving Joseph the Blessed Virgin as spouse, God appointed him to be not only her life's companion, the witness of her virginity, the protector of her honor, but also, by virtue of the conjugal tie, a participator in her sublime dignity. (Pope Leo XIII, *Quamquam pluries*, 1889)

The fact that *God* would be raised in an earthly home supports the Church's ancient belief that St. Joseph was sanctified while in his mother's womb, in preparation for his becoming the foster-father and guardian of the Redeemer. The Mass for the feast of "St. Joseph, Spouse of the Blessed Virgin Mary" accommodates this Old Testament text (in praise of Moses) to Joseph: "He glorified him in the sight of kings, and gave him commandments in the sight of his people, and shewed him His glory. He sanctified him in his faith, and meekness, and chose him out of all flesh." (Ecclus. 45:3-4)

One day Joseph would hold parental authority over Jesus. If "all paternity in heaven and earth is named" (Eph. 3:15) for God the

Father, what are we to make of the one man chosen to represent Him, physically, in the raising and care of His Son, the Word Incarnate? Is it reasonable to picture a home for our Lord wherein either His Mother *or* His foster-father would say, "The good which I will, I do not; but the evil which I will not, that I do . . . I find then a law, that when I have a will to do good, evil is present with me." (Rom. 7:19,21)

God provides "sufficient" graces to His servants and, therefore, a *pre-natal* sanctification of St. Joseph (which has Scriptural precedents in the persons of the Prophet Jeremias and St. John the Baptist) is in keeping with God's consistent method of preparing His special servants. John Gerson (d. 1429), priest and chancellor of the University of Paris, spoke of St. Joseph's pre-natal *sanctification* in a discourse delivered at the Council of Constance (1414), while carefully pointing out that it was not of the same order as the singular *conception* of the Mother of God: "As Mary before her birth was sanctified in her mother's womb, so may we believe was also her virginal spouse, Joseph, although not in an altogether similar manner." St. Peter Julian Eymard (†1868) observed that "St. Joseph was the holiest of men, for it was fitting that God should choose a man most perfect and the most worthy to confide to him so high a mission over Jesus and Mary."

St. Joseph's sanctification would have prepared him also to consecrate his virginity to God. That he did so is not to be doubted, for he was chosen to be the husband of the *Ever-Virgin* Mary, Mother of God. To suggest that Joseph would have been chosen to be the husband of Mary, had he desired anything other than a chaste life, is to fly in the face of reason. This was stressed by St. Jerome (†420), in his reply to Helvidius, who had denied Mary's perpetual virginity:

> You say that Mary did not remain a virgin. I, instead, claim to affirm something even more: namely, that Joseph also remained a virgin for Mary's sake, so that a virgin Son might be born from a virginal marriage. For if there was no place for fornication in a holy man like Joseph, and if it is not written that he had another wife, and if for Mary, who was considered his wife, he was a guardian rather than a husband, we conclude that, along

> with Mary, he who merited to be called father of the Lord remained a virgin. (*De virginitate perpetua*)

St. Thomas Aquinas also taught that St. Joseph had made a vow of virginity. He reasoned that our Lady's initial vow would have been a "conditional" one, dependent upon God's desire and His acceptance of her offering. Thus, both Mary's *and* Joseph's vows would have become "absolute" vows *after* the Annunciation:

> The Mother of God would not have made a simple vow without the condition "insofar as it is pleasing to God". When she knew that it was acceptable to God because of the message of the Annunciation, she made the vow absolutely. . . . After the espousal, by mutual consent, they both vowed absolute virginity. (*Summa Theologica*)

The virginal integrity of St. Joseph is a recurring theme in sound Catholic thought down through the ages. St. Augustine wrote, "Rejoice, Joseph, in the virginity of Mary, you who alone merited to possess the virginal affection of your spouse, because by the merit of virginity you have been separated from the embrace of a wife, that you might be called the father of the Savior." St. Francis de Sales summarized well the Church's understanding of the chaste marital union between our Lady and her husband: "Both had made a vow to preserve virginity for their entire lives, and it was the will of God to join them in the bond of holy marriage, not in any way to revoke their vow, but rather to confirm it."

The Gospels sum up the virtues and character of St. Joseph in one brief phrase which speaks volumes. St. Matthew tells us that he was "a just man". The usual definitions for the word *just* – "upright", "conscientious", "honest" – do not capture fully the concept as embodied in the Scriptures. In the inspired texts, the "just" man is oriented towards the precepts and commandments of God; he loves God and delights in obeying Him. *The Book of Proverbs*, in describing the *just man*, presents a vivid portrait of the head of the Holy Family: "The blessing of the Lord is upon the head of the just. . . . The work of the just is unto life. . . . The lips of the just teach many. . . . The expectation of the just is joy.

. . . The strength of the upright is the way of the Lord. . . . The Lord is far from the wicked: and he will hear the prayers of the just."

When the *Infancy Narratives* of the Gospels are read with an eye fixed upon Joseph, the following passage stands out as the most significant:

> Now the generation of Christ was in this wise. When as His Mother Mary was espoused to Joseph, before they came together, she was found with child, of the Holy Ghost. Whereupon Joseph her husband, being a just man, and not willing publicly to expose her, was minded to put her away privately. But while he thought on these things, behold the angel of the Lord appeared to him in his sleep, saying: Joseph, son of David, fear not to take unto thee Mary thy wife, for that which is conceived in her, is of the Holy Ghost. (Mt. 1:18-20)

The common opinion regarding the actions of St. Joseph is that they are the result of his being troubled at the pregnancy of his espoused wife, a pregnancy he had nothing to do with. In this scenario, Joseph refuses to make the Virgin's supposed "shame" public in order to shield her from both malicious slander and any legal punishment for adultery.

The Book of Numbers describes the "trial of jealousy," a rite in which a woman accused of adultery was given "the most bitter waters" to drink, which consisted of holy water into which was mixed "a little earth of the pavement of the tabernacle." If the woman was innocent, the drink would not harm her; if she were guilty, the effects of the drink would be deadly.

The ancient apocryphal texts, in their less sublime moments, allude to the testing of the Virgin for a supposed "infidelity". *The Gospel of Pseudo-Matthew* (c. 3rd century) goes so far as to depict Mary and Joseph, the subjects of scandalous rumors, being taken before the chief priests by the ministers of the Temple, where the Virgin, after protesting her innocence, "approached the altar of the Lord with confidence, and drank the water for drinking, and went round the altar seven times, and there was found no spot in her."

In *The Book of James* (c. 3rd century), we encounter a distraught Joseph lamenting: "Who hath done this evil in mine house and hath defiled the virgin? Is not the story of Adam repeated in me? For as at the hour of his giving thanks the serpent came and found Eve alone and deceived her, so hath it befallen me also." Needless to say, such displays of self-pity on the part of the future Patron of the Universal Church do not resonate with the general portrait of St. Joseph as handed down through tradition.

However, considering that Joseph was unwilling "to expose" Mary, instead deciding to "put her away privately," are such sentiments and scenarios the only logical interpretation of St. Matthew's account? No. In fact, there is another opinion, cherished as well from antiquity, in which St. Joseph is not so quick to judge Mary as having been unfaithful.

At the time of the Incarnation, Mary and Joseph were "espoused" or betrothed. This espousal constituted a formal contract between the future bride and groom, and required a bill of divorce in order to be terminated. A year after this arrangement was entered into, the nuptials would be solemnized in a wedding ceremony, at which time the bride would be conducted to the home of her husband, dressed in her finest clothes, an earthly symbol of the heavenly marriage between Christ and His Church: "And I, John, saw the holy city, the new Jerusalem, coming down out of heaven from God, prepared as a bride adorned for her husband." (Apoc. 21:2) On this festive day, the friends and relatives of the betrothed couple would have some respite from the normal cares of life, and enjoy a time of laughter, good food and dancing.

During the period of espousal, the betrothed couple lived apart and the sexes did not intermingle with the intimacy and frequency of modern times. The crime of adultery was considered a heinous one, carrying different penalties depending upon whether it was committed during the time of betrothal or after the marriage had been solemnized. The punishment for infidelity during the period of espousal (recorded in *The Book of Deuteronomy*) was described by the historian Josephus (d. 93): "If she be one of the people, for not having kept chaste guard over her virginity up to her lawful marriage, let her be stoned." (*The Jewish Antiquities*) When a woman taken in adultery was brought before Jesus, He said to her accusers, "He that is without sin among you, let him first cast a stone at her," (Jn. 8:7) indicating that she could have been an *espoused* wife.

Much ado is made over St. Matthew's statement that Joseph, learning that his betrothed was with child, and ". . . not willing publicly to expose her, was minded to put her away privately." (Mt. 1:19) Since the espousal was recognized as a legal union, and its termination, therefore, required a bill of divorce, it is readily assumed that Joseph had planned to issue a *private* bill of divorce to Mary, which would have required the presence of only two witnesses.

However, before considering the matter closed, it would be useful to recall here an elementary fact of the Catholic faith, namely, that it rests on a twin foundation of Sacred Scripture *and* Sacred Tradition. Tradition tells of St. Joseph's holiness, of his sanctification before his birth, in order that he might worthily exercise parental authority over the Incarnate God and become a chaste husband for the Immaculate Conception. It tells of his free acceptance of a life of chastity, a life of service to Jesus and Mary . . . a life *consecrated* to God. To underscore his character and virtues, the Church, the sole authoritative interpreter of Scripture, accommodates certain Old Testament texts to St. Joseph.

In *The Book of Genesis*, Joseph, the son of Jacob, is considered a "type," or foreshadowing, of St. Joseph. The first Joseph was exiled into Egypt through the treachery of his brothers, who sold him into slavery; St. Joseph went into exile in Egypt because of the treachery of Herod. God revealed His designs to the first Joseph through dreams; the Angel of the Lord spoke to St. Joseph, and directed him, through dreams. The first Joseph was made ruler over all Egypt by Pharaoh, and he saved his land from famine; St. Joseph was constituted head of the Holy Family, Patron of the Universal Church (by Pope Pius IX), and he, too, in saving the Infant Redeemer from the murderous wrath of Herod, helped save his people from spiritual famine. The words addressed to the first Joseph by Pharaoh resound to the honor of the Guardian of Jesus and Mary:

> Can we find such another man, that is full of the Spirit of God. . . . Seeing God hath shewn thee all that thou

> hast said, can I find one wiser and one like unto thee? Thou shalt be over my house. (Gen. 41:38-40)

That St. Joseph experienced some sort of deep internal conflict when he discovered the condition of Mary is obvious from the simple fact that he felt it imperative to take some action on that account, an action involving specifically a "separation" from Mary. There is a strong, clear voice echoing down the ages, which speaks of this remarkable time in the life of St. Joseph with great insight and reverence.

According to this voice, whose cadence can be heard in the writings of the Church Fathers, Joseph is still caught in a real dilemma, but it is not that of the betrayed husband; it is the dilemma of one who must reconcile the testimony of his eyes with that of his reason, a not uncommon trial for those who strive to live lives of faith. It calls us to consider St. Joseph, not as an isolated character who takes center-stage in one dramatic Gospel episode, but rather our minds and hearts attuned to the devotional and doctrinal legacy of the Church, it invites us to follow the lead of St. John Chrysostom (†407), who wrote in one of his *Sermons*:

> Joseph is a man of sublime philosophy, far above the tyranny of passion or suspicion. But what Joseph faced was a fact, not a suspicion. Even so he was a man of such purity of intention and so elevated above worldly judgments that no shadow of suspicion ever crossed his mind. Although he lived under the Law, his thoughts rose far above the Law. With the coming of grace into the world, we might expect to see more sublime examples of life also coming forth.

There is a paradox caused by the commonly accepted understanding that Joseph had decided to *formally* repudiate Mary. Such an action would readily become known in the small village of Nazareth. Yet St. Matthew informs us that the point of the proposed "separation" of Joseph and Mary was to *protect* her reputation! How would the reputation of a young betrothed woman, beginning to show signs that she carries a child, be safeguarded by her receiving a bill of divorce from her intended husband? A formal repudiation would have achieved the opposite of what Joseph intended.

Yet, without a doubt, the phrase "put her away privately" implies a *separation* – i.e., a parting of the ways:

> It is the word, for instance, used in the Gospel of St. Matthew xix.5: "For this cause shall a man leave (*dimittet*) father and mother," where, assuredly, the term *dimittet* could not signify to put away or divorce. Neither can it be the meaning in the case of which we are speaking. Joseph could not have repudiated Mary by a private bill of divorce, or any other form, without its becoming known, and therefore without defaming or publicly exposing her, the very thing which, it is said, he was not willing to do. (Edward Healy Thompson, *The Life and Glories of St. Joseph*, 1888)

However, there is a scenario in which Joseph could "separate" himself from his betrothed without causing any undue attention to Mary, and it is grounded on the ancient belief that Joseph did NOT imagine Mary to have been unfaithful in any way whatsoever:

> But, if she were innocent, why does he not remain with her? The reason, as we have said, is clear. Having become persuaded from so many signs that she is the mother of the Messias, he, reckoning himself unworthy to abide under the same roof with her, and with the Desired of all nations, comes to the determination to leave her privily, so that her reputation may remain undamaged. . . . Departing thus quietly, people might actually suppose that his work had called him away for a time, and that he was executing some order which he had received in the neighborhood, or possibly, that for some cause or another he was making a fresh journey into Judea. (Thompson, *The Life and Glories of St. Joseph*)

Whereas a bill of divorce could not help but place a spotlight on Our Lady, there would be nothing amiss about the absence of a tradesman for any length of time. But, a huge question remains. *Why*? Why would Joseph wish to depart from Mary?

St. Joseph was not omniscient, but he was a holy, clear-thinking individual, and Mary was no *stranger* to him. "For every tree is known by its fruit." (Lk. 6:44) A young man would be naturally curious concerning his intended bride, and Joseph would have observed first-hand, albeit discretely, Mary's exceptional character, her sanctity and charitable demeanor. The very idea of the young Virgin being unfaithful, and dishonest in the bargain, was simply beyond the range of Joseph's experience, and opposed to the dictates of his reason.

From the apocryphal texts comes a "solution," echoed by later writers, which does not imply any thought on the part of Joseph that Mary was unfaithful to him. It paints Joseph as a man filled with self-recrimination, because he had failed to protect Mary's chastity, had failed as the guardian of his young espoused bride. In *The Book of James*, Joseph cries out, "With what countenance shall I look upon the Lord my God, and what prayer shall I make concerning this maiden, for I received her out of the temple of the Lord my God a virgin, and have not kept her safe."

This "solution" is not a very good one. First of all, an espoused wife who had been the victim of coercion was in no danger of incurring a penalty under the Law: "If a man find a damsel that is betrothed, in the field, and taking hold of her, lie with her, he alone shall die: The damsel shall suffer nothing . . . for as a robber riseth against his brother, and taketh away his life, so also did the damsel suffer." (Deut. 22:25-26)

But there is a more cogent argument against this interpretation. If the face of Moses beamed with light after his conversation with the Lord, what expressions of serenity, of deep and complete joy, must have animated the features of Mary, as God rested *in* her holy womb? The *Sibylline Oracles*, Greek verses dating from the second century, depict a beautiful change in our Lady's countenance after she gave her *fiat* to the Angel Gabriel:

In stillness she stood trembling
bewildered, as one lost,
the while her heart did throb
to hear the wondrous news.
Then jumped her heart with joy
to find comfort in those words.
She smiled, with blushing cheek,
delighting in her joy,
heart filled with gentle modesty.

Would a man like St. Joseph readily mistake the countenance of the Immaculate Mother of God for that of a woman who had been deprived of all serenity by any act of coercion? The only logical alternative is that he had somehow intuited the presence of a supernatural work in his espoused wife, Mary.

Does this supposition seem far-fetched or overly pious? When Mary and Joseph brought the Divine Infant to the Temple to present Him to the Lord, they encountered there the venerable Simeon. The old man, inspired by the Holy Ghost, had gone to the Temple. There, he was confronted with nothing other than a dignified young couple and their infant son, yet, he took the Child in his arms and said, "Now thou dost dismiss thy servant, O Lord. . . . *Because my eyes have seen thy salvation.*"

The prayerful Simeon *knew* that he was in the presence of the Divine. Therefore, is it reasonable to deny to St. Joseph the discernment attributed to him by St. John Chrysostom? – "For a man who had meditated at length on the words of the prophet, the miracle of a Virgin Mother ceased to seem novel and became something familiar."

In this approach to the Gospel narrative, then, the primary cause of St. Joseph's distress is not Mary's condition, but her *silence*, a silence born from a complete trust in the providence of her God. This silence placed Joseph in the position in which we encounter him in St. Matthew's Gospel. Whereas Mary had spoken to the Archangel before she had given her *fiat*, St. Joseph was placed before the greatest Mystery of all creation all *alone*, so to speak. He would also hear the words of the angel, but not until he had pondered and prayed upon the events unfolding before his eyes.

This treatment of Joseph by God may seem odd at first, akin to someone being taught to swim by getting pushed into a lake. The Great mystery of Creation unfolds . . . and Joseph, a central player in this drama, is left to "figure things out" for himself. Yet this was a divinely-ordered state of affairs, and it is precisely in his actions, as recorded by St. Matthew, that we can observe how truly St. Joseph fulfills the requisites of the "just man" of the Scriptures, who waits upon the Lord with patience. This was a time of *trial*: "For gold and silver are tried in the fire, but acceptable men in the furnace of humiliation." (Ecclus. 2:5) The mettle of Jesus' earthly father, the humility of his heart before God and His works, were tested here and the outcome is plain to see: "For that which is at present momentary and light of our tribulation, worketh for us above measure exceedingly an eternal weight of glory." (2 Cor. 4:17)

One day, after the birth of Jesus, St. Joseph would require nothing more than a few words from an angel in order to pack up the Holy Family and set out into an alien land, with no idea as to how long their exile would last. A few more words from the Lord's messenger would find him leading the Family back to their homeland, happy at their return, but still wary over the safety of the Child and His Mother: "But hearing that Archelaus reigned in Judea in the room of Herod his father, he was afraid to go thither: and being warned in sleep retired into the quarters of Galilee. And coming he dwelt in a city called Nazareth." (Mt. 2:22-23)

The guardian of the Savior and His Mother needed no detailed instructions or guarantees before he would obey God for the security of his family. Prudence and the disposition to place everything in God's hands were the motivating factors in the life of St. Joseph throughout the *Infancy Narratives*. Why deny these virtues to him in the face of his first trial? The conclusion that Joseph suspected "foul play" when he first learned that Mary was expecting a child need not – in fact, should not – be the first one that comes to mind. If Joseph was awaiting some enlightenment regarding the situation *and his place in it*, it is no great wonder that he was "not willing publicly to expose her."

The writings of the early Fathers testified to St. Joseph's powers of discernment. A homily attributed to Origen (d. c. 254) states that Joseph "wished to dismiss her since he knew that the power of mystery and some marvelous sacrament was in her, which he thought himself unworthy to approach." St. Basil the Great wrote:

> Before they came to live together, she was found with child by the working of the Holy Ghost. Joseph found both things: both the conception and its cause, namely, the intervention of the Holy Ghost. Therefore, fearing to be called the husband of such a woman, he "wanted to send her away quietly," not daring to make public what had happened to her.
>
> But being just, it was his lot to have mysteries revealed to him. For "while he was thinking of these things, the angel of the Lord appeared to him in a dream, saying: 'Do not fear to take Mary as your wife.'" You should not have thought it necessary to conceal a fault from wicked and suspicious people. For you have been called just: it would not be the action of a just man to pass over sins in silence. "Do not fear to take Mary as your wife." Joseph showed that he had not disdained her, nor had he showed disgust at her, *but that he feared because she was full of the Holy Ghost*. "That which is born of her is of the Holy Ghost." (*On the Holy Generation of Christ*)

"Joseph understood that this was an admirable work of God," wrote St. Ephrem of Syria. One of history's greatest Scripture scholars, St. Jerome, seconds these thoughts, while calling attention specifically to Joseph's prudence:

> How could Joseph be called a just man if he were going to conceal his wife's crime? Here it is not the case at all. *This is a testimony to Mary*, because Joseph knew her chastity and marveled at the wonderful event that had occurred. He preferred to be silent about a mystery that he did not understand. (*Commentary on Matthew*)

Joseph, a holy man, intuiting the presence of a prodigy, the physical proximity of the divine, *did* experience a real, deep-seated distress, but not because of jealousy or nervous ire. He was already betrothed to this marvelous young woman, Mary, but his humility caused him to ponder his place in an event that certainly transcended any plans of mortal men. A proposed separation, then, as opposed to a formal "divorce", would have been the means by which St. Joseph reposed all his trust in the goodness and wisdom of God, according to the Scriptures: "Judge me, O Lord, for I have walked in my innocence, and I have put my trust in the Lord, and shall not be weakened." (Ps. 25:1) It was not decided upon lightly.

St. Bernard (†1153) summarized the true nature of Joseph's trials:

> Why did he want to put her away? Take the answers of the Fathers, rather than my opinion. Joseph wanted her out of his life for the same reason that St. Peter begged our Lord, "Depart from me, O Lord, for I am a sinful man." It was the same reason the Centurion used in discouraging our Lord from coming to his home, "O Lord, I am not worthy that you should come down under my roof."
>
> Just so, St. Joseph considered himself an unworthy sinner, and he felt deep inside that he should not force his friendship on so great a woman in such a marvelous and mysterious matter. He understood and drew back in awe at these definite traces of the Divine presence. (*Second Homily on the Missus Est*)

One day, after the Child raised by Joseph and Mary had ascended to His heavenly Throne, one of His apostles would write a hymn to charity, praising this virtue that "is patient, is kind . . . beareth all things, believeth all things, hopeth all things." (1 Cor. 13:4,7) There is no exegetical mandate to attribute to St. Joseph any rash judgment of the Blessed Virgin. His trial was real, of that there can be no doubt, according to the inspired Gospel account. But the *just* man need never fear that God will allow him to dwell in uncertainty: "The Lord God is my helper, therefore am I not confounded . . . He is near that justifieth me." (Is. 50:7-8) Throughout the *Infancy Narratives*, St. Joseph relied on God and, fittingly, he left it to God, and not to his own devices, to determine his fitness as a husband for Mary, whom he knew to be a woman truly blessed.

"But being just," wrote St. Basil concerning Joseph, "it was his lot to have mysteries revealed to him." The *just* man does not presume or judge rashly, but rather waits upon the Lord, holding fast to the precepts of the sacred texts: "Cast thy care upon the Lord, and He shall sustain thee: He shall not suffer the just to waver for ever." (Ps. 54:23)

During those early days of the Savior's earthly sojourn, the future guardian of the Holy Family (and Patron of the Universal Church) was able to practice and advance in the virtues of prudence, patience and humility, and his trial came to an end when "the angel of the Lord appeared to him in his sleep, saying, Joseph, son of David, fear not to take unto thee Mary thy wife, for that which is conceived in her, is of the Holy Ghost." With this reassurance, the Scriptures were fulfilled quite literally, and the Guardian was confirmed in his role: "Thou hast proved my heart, and visited it by night, thou hast tried me by fire, and iniquity hath not been found in me." (Ps. 16:3) The reassurance that, indeed, the proper place for Joseph was at the side of Mary, is a beautiful and fitting climax to this episode.

Divine condescension will never demean itself in the practice of humility. Filial obedience to someone caught in the web of sin and confusion is out of the question for God. It is true that the adult Savior was "betrayed into the hands of sinners", but the subjection of the Lamb of God to His persecutors was not obedience to *sinners*. It was obedience to the *Father*: "Nevertheless not as I will, but as Thou wilt." (Mt. 26:39) The voluntary "subjection" of Jesus to His Mother and earthly father was an act of love . . . love for Mary and Joseph, and love for the Commandments.

Chapter Fifteen

The New Ark of the Covenant

NOT DEPOSITED, JESUS CHRIST WAS TRULY CONCEIVED IN MARY'S WOMB – SHE WAS THE NURSE OF HIM "WHO NURTURES THE WORLD" – THE ANNUNCIATION – MARY IN PROPHECY – "A WOMAN SHALL COMPASS A MAN" – MARY IS THE NEW "ARK OF THE COVENANT" – ST. GABRIEL, THE MESSENGER, SENT BY GOD FORMALLY TO THE VIRGIN MARY – HER VOW OF VIRGINITY – HER PERPETUAL VIRGINITY – THE "BRETHREN" OF THE LORD – HER "FIRST-BORN SON" – OUR LADY'S *FIAT* – THY WILL BE DONE

At the moment of the Incarnation, the womb of Mary truly became the first tabernacle, fashioned by God, upon which all later tabernacles built by the hands of men to house the Blessed Sacrament would be modeled.

At the dedication of the great Temple in Jerusalem, King Solomon exclaimed aloud to God, "If heaven, and the heavens of heavens cannot contain Thee, how much less this house which I have built?" (3 Kg. 8:27) At that time, the "glory of the Lord", in the form of a cloud, had filled the Temple. In the pure womb of the Virgin Mary, God, Whom the heavens could not contain, rested for nine months, present *physically*, the divine and human natures of Jesus united forever. "O virgin Mother of God", proclaims the Gradual for the *Common of the Blessed Virgin Mary*, "He Whom the whole world containeth not, becoming man, shut Himself in thy womb." St. Epiphanius asked, "How shall we not proclaim her great, who held within her the uncontainable One?"

So precious was this dwelling for the Infant Christ, this holy place beneath the heart of His Mother, that the great Fathers and saints have consistently referred to Mary's womb as a new "Paradise" (made for Christ, the *second* "Adam"), far surpassing in splendor the terrestrial Paradise in which had resided the "first" Adam: "*You* yourself are more glorious than paradise! For paradise was the cultivation of God; but you cultivated God Himself, according to the flesh." (St. Proclus of Constantinople) In the *Akathist Hymn* (c. 6-7th century), the Byzantine Church addresses our Lady, "Hail, Meadow Land yielding a rich harvest of mercies!" St. John Chrysostom wrote: "As the first soil produced for us the garden of paradise without any seed, so the Virgin gave birth to Christ for us without receiving any manly seed."

In the unfathomable mystery of the Incarnation, Mary received the Son of God in her womb, not as a mere "receptacle", an outside agent or functionary employed to effect the human birth of the Redeemer. Such a debased, utilitarian mentality is refuted in the *Nicene Creed*, when we profess belief in Jesus Christ, "Who for us men, and for our salvation, came down from heaven, *and was incarnate by the Holy Ghost of the Virgin Mary*, and was made man." The Savior was not "deposited" in the womb of Mary; He was *conceived* in her womb by the power of the Holy Ghost. The bond uniting the Incarnate Word and His Mother – the Woman and her seed – which was held in the Divine Intellect from "before the foundation of the world", became flesh in Mary's womb. This bond is an eternal one, stretching back to the Beginning, and forward throughout time.

In the face of Mary's Divine Maternity, then, there are only two acceptable reactions – awed silence or some attempt, however feeble, to render it fitting praise: "It is enough, O Virgin, to be called the Mother. It suffices to be the nurse of Him Who nurtures the world. It is a great thing to have held within your flesh the One who upholds all things." (St. Amphilocius of Iconium, †c. 394)

Our Lady was loved by God from the beginning as the future Mother of His Son, "from all eternity joined in a hidden way with Jesus Christ in one and the same degree of predestination." (Pope Pius XII) The writings of Catholic theologians and mystics relate that the angelic host was made privy to the counsels of God regarding the future Incarnation of His Son. Those angels who sang "Glory to God in the highest" at the birth of Christ were the same who had stood before the throne of God since the dawn of creation, the hosts observed by Daniel in his vision: "Thousands of thousands ministered to Him, and ten thousand times a hundred thousand stood before Him." (Dan. 7:10) The angels also knew that a prodigy, a singularly beautiful Mother, would one day be born into the world, whose chaste womb would bear *their* Lord:

> Since there is no mystery after the Incarnation which is second in dignity, worth, wisdom or power to the glory

> of the most Blessed Virgin, this grace of perfection was not denied the angels. Since the angels were shown the great mystery of Christ as man, they were also shown the mystery of Mary's excellence. . . . Just as they always contemplate the Word, they always venerate and love her. It was revealed to them that God would become man; it was equally revealed that He would be the Son of the Virgin. (Francis Suarez, d. 1617, *Treatise on the Angels*)

The world, weary with sin and groaning in its trials, was awaiting its redemption, the time when, ". . . as sin hath reigned unto death; so also grace might reign by justice unto life everlasting, through Jesus Christ our Lord." (Rom. 5:21) It waited, with no recourse other than prayer and perseverance, for that day, unknown to all, when a Virgin would "bear a Son". One day it happened, the event of which the prophets had dreamed. The Virgin ". . . brought forth her first-born Son, and wrapped Him up in swaddling clothes," (Lk. 2:7) and she and St. Joseph "called His name Jesus." (Mt. 1:25)

Mary had lived a life set apart for God. Because she was sinless, she was "human" in the most profound sense of the word, for her humanity was characterized not by self-interest, anger or regret, but by warmth, compassion and an intellect whose appreciation of creation would be the envy of any scientist or naturalist. If a poet can see the world "in a grain of sand", what understanding must have illuminated the mind of our Lady, who saw the hand of God *everywhere*, in all things?

The Scriptures offer a glimpse of the youthful Mary, living a life in preparation for that moment in which the Archangel would come to her, when she would be asked to consent to the Incarnation for the salvation of the world. Even though these words were written down long before our Lady was born, we can apply them to her with no hesitation whatsoever. They are some of the most famous words to be found in the Old Testament; in fact, they encapsulate the spiritual duties enjoined upon Israel by God. They reveal concisely what is pleasing to Him, not in theological terms, but in the language of daily life, of common everyday activities. The Virgin, her mind always clear and focused, her heart ever turned towards her Creator, would have observed these admonitions wholeheartedly, as would St. Joachim and St. Anne, who were chosen to be her parents:

> Hear, O Israel, the Lord our God is one Lord. Thou shalt love the Lord thy God with thy whole heart, and with thy whole soul, and with thy whole strength. And these words which I command thee this day, shall be in thy heart: And thou shalt tell them to thy children, and thou shalt meditate upon them sitting in thy house, and walking on thy journey, sleeping and rising. (Deut. 6:4-7)

When our Lord quoted this text, He added something: "Thou shalt love the Lord thy God with thy whole heart, and with thy whole soul, and with thy whole *mind.*" (Mt. 22:37) Mary would have fulfilled this injunction, too. If the greatest saints deemed it beneficial to meditate before the Blessed Sacrament, what profound meditations would have occupied the mind of Mary during those nine months she contemplated daily the mercy of God as He rested in her womb, or watched the Savior of the world sleeping in His crib?

"I meditated also on Thy commandments, which I loved." (Ps. 118:47) These words describe the attitude of Mary, her love for God plumbing new depths with each passing day. St. Luke would write of her that, regarding the events surrounding the life of her Son, "Mary kept all these words, pondering them in her heart." (Lk. 2:19) Her love of the precepts of God, her deep understanding of His mercy and goodness, served Our Lady well on the day of the Annunciation. Her reaction to the Angel Gabriel, the few words spoken by her, even the very manner in which she consented to the Divine Maternity – all these display not only discernment and fortitude in the face of something awe-inspiring, but also prudence and a faith that runs deeper than can be imagined.

The first reaction of the Virgin at the Archangel's greeting is one of holy fear: "Who having heard, was troubled at his saying, and thought with herself what manner of salutation this should be." (Lk. 1:29) What was the greeting that troubled her? – "Hail, Full of Grace, the Lord is with thee: blessed art thou among women." This greeting is reverent. It also expresses joy, for the word translated in the Vulgate Bible as *Ave* ("Hail") was originally the Greek word, *Chaire*, which, when used as a greeting, has the same sense as the word, "hail." But, it can also be translated as "rejoice," a sense which harmonizes Gabriel's greeting with the words recorded by the Prophet Zacharias, describing the entry of Christ into Jerusalem: "Rejoice greatly, O daughter of Sion, shout for joy, O daughter of Jerusalem: BEHOLD THY KING will come to thee, the Just and Savior: He is poor, and riding upon an ass, and upon a colt, the foal of an ass." (Zach. 9:9)

In a sense, both the prophet and the Angel are concerned with an entry of Christ into "Jerusalem". Zacharias prophesied the triumphal entry of Christ into Jerusalem, His holy city, before the hour was at hand which would see Him victorious over death. In the *Apocalypse*, the Church Triumphant, comprising the citizens of heaven (both human and angelic), is called the *New Jerusalem*: "And I, John, saw the holy city, the new Jerusalem, coming down out of heaven from God, prepared as a bride adorned for her husband." (Apoc. 21:2) This description recalls the Spouse of the *Canticles*, the beloved of God, representing both the Church *and* the Blessed Virgin: "Thou art beautiful, O my love, sweet and comely as Jerusalem." (Cant. 6:3)

"Rejoice greatly, O daughter of Sion . . . Hail (rejoice), Full of Grace." The words of the prophet were addressed to the children of Israel, the "daughter of Sion"; those of Gabriel were addressed to Mary, the *first* among the children of Israel, the first Daughter of God the Father. Zacharias had prophesied the entry of the Savior into the holy city on the first Palm Sunday. In order for that to have occurred, in order for salvation to be visited upon the children of Israel (and the world) – in order for mankind to be able to enter the new, heavenly Jerusalem – Christ had first to enter another "Jerusalem", the immaculate body of His Mother. The Incarnation of the Second Person of the Blessed Trinity is the pivot upon which *all* prophecies revolve.

Immediately after delivering his greeting, Gabriel said to Mary, "The Lord is with thee." It was not the first time these words were addressed to a human being. Not long before the death of Moses, God had allowed the patriarch, along with a small force of Israelites, to destroy the Madianites, an enemy which had led God's people into debauchery and idol-worship. At the time of Gedeon, the Madianites had again come to power, and the children of Israel became subject to them, as a chastisement from God. One day, an angel appeared to Gedeon and said: "*The Lord is with thee*, O most valiant of men. . . . Thou shalt deliver Israel out of the hand of Madian." (Jg. 6:12,14) Gideon subsequently destroyed the altar of Baal and defeated the Madianites with a force of only three hundred men.

When the Prophet Jeremias, hearing the call of the Lord, protested that he was unable to speak as a prophet should, God told him not to be afraid: "I *am with thee* to deliver thee, saith the Lord." (Jer. 1:8) The "company" of God is ever the great consolation of His people. It is a pledge of strength: "The Lord Thy God in the midst of thee is mighty, He will save." (Soph. 3:17) It is a pledge of God's favor: "In Thy mercy Thou hast been a leader to the people which Thou hast redeemed." (Ex. 15:13)

Josue, who would lead the force that captured the city of Jericho, and whose command caused the sun and moon to stand still in the heavens during the battle against the Amorrhites, heard these words from the Lord: "Take courage, and be strong: for thou shalt divide by lot to this people the land, for which I swore to their fathers, that I would deliver it to them. . . . Fear not and be not dismayed: *because the Lord thy God is with thee* in all things whatsoever thou shalt go to." (Jos. 1:6,9)

In the Scriptures, individuals who are called to God's work are encouraged at the reminder that the Lord is "with" them; the loftiness of their mission is implicit in such a greeting. Gedeon, a Judge of Israel, delivered his people from an enemy who, at one time, had drawn them *away* from God. Jeremias prophesied the birth of the Redeemer: "For the Lord hath created a new thing upon the earth: A WOMAN SHALL COMPASS A MAN." (Jer. 31:22) After enduring his own persecutions and trials, he would preserve the Ark of the Covenant from capture by hiding it in a cave. Josue was chosen by Moses himself to lead the Israelites as his successor, and his praises were sung in the holy books: "Valiant in war was Jesus (Josue) the son of Nave, who was successor of Moses among the prophets, who was great according to his name, very great for the saving the elect of

God, to overthrow the enemies that rose up against them, that he might get the inheritance for Israel." (Ecclus. 46:1-2)

A judge, a prophet, a warrior – each one selected to serve the Lord, and doing so valiantly, laboring for His people in the midst of great trials. The Blessed Virgin heard the greeting, "*the Lord* is *with thee*," too, because she had reached that point in her life when the call of God, the invitation to bear the Redeemer and, later, to stand by Him as He died, would be made explicit. But all comparisons end there, for "there is an infinite difference between the Mother of God and the servants of God." (St. John Damascene, † c.750) Gedeon destroyed the Madianites, who had led the people into idolatry; Mary would crush the head of the serpent himself. Jeremias preserved the original Ark by hiding it in a cave; Mary, the "new" Ark, would be preserved from the corruption of the grave and assumed into heaven after her earthly race was run. Josue's command caused the heavens to stand still; Mary's "fiat" brought the Son of God to earth, into her womb.

There is a "formal" quality to the Annunciation. Gabriel is a messenger, "sent from God". and his words to Mary are deliberate, not conversational. He is *relating* the greeting and message entrusted to Him and meant solely for the ears of the Virgin. *Hail, Full of Grace* is the proclamation of a title. *The Lord is with thee* is the proclamation of the exalted state of the person addressed. *Blessed art thou among women* recognizes the unique place and role in the history of salvation to which Mary is being called. The Archangel appears in the Annunciation narrative as the "courtier" of God, the one who attends to the wishes of His Lord. Therefore, his reverential and respectful demeanor *is in keeping with the wishes of His Master*. Gabriel approaches Mary in this manner precisely because God *decrees* that she be approached in this manner. It stands to reason, then, that *any* manner of regarding the Blessed Virgin which is not characterized by profound reverence and respect can in no way be pleasing to God.

The holy fear of Mary at the greeting of the Angel was not that of timidity or anxiety. The Scriptures teach that ". . . the fear of the Lord is the lesson of wisdom: and humility goeth before glory." (Prov. 15:33) This fear is a stimulus to the practice of the virtue of prudence. Our Lady, troubled at the angel's greeting, displays this prudence, and a maturity beyond her years, by questioning him: "The prudent shall look for knowledge." (Prov. 14:18)

This manner of searching after knowledge does not indicate doubt or incredulity. Mary deftly expresses both her willingness to serve God ("How shall this be done . . ."), and her vow of perpetual virginity, by which she already intended to serve God all the days of her life (". . . because I know not man?"). She did not inform Gabriel that she had not *known* any man, the logical objection for a virgin to make. She declares that she does not *know* man. Had Mary *not* consecrated her virginity to the Lord, she would not have said this, for, ordinarily, a young woman betrothed to a young man and ready to enter into matrimony would have no need to inquire as to *how* she would come eventually to bear a child:

> She does not refuse to believe the angel; neither does she move away from her convictions. She says: I have given up any contact with man. . . . If Joseph had taken her to be his wife, for the purpose of having children, why would she have wondered at the announcement of maternity, since she herself would have accepted becoming a mother according to the law of nature? (St. Gregory of Nyssa, †c.394, *On the Holy Generation of Christ*)

Although St. Thomas Aquinas held that our Lady's vow of virginity was a "conditional" one until her espousal to St. Joseph, Rev. Matthias J. Scheeben offered a different opinion, based on the fact that a conditional vow expresses a certain degree of uncertainty on the part of the person making it as to whether or not it will be pleasing and acceptable to God:

> We are not compelled to accept this uncertainty. Even before the betrothal she could have known this through divine revelation, just as she could have been certain, through such an inspiration, or even through a previous agreement with her bridegroom, that she did not expose her virginity to danger in this marriage, but rather would find a protection. . . . It may well be presumed

> that Mary took the vow not only out of love for virginity in general, but also because of a clear knowledge that God had called her to take it. For otherwise this vow is usually taken with the knowledge that God will not merely accept it with complacency, but will also expect it of the person who takes it. This view must be expected still more with regard to Mary, who was predestined by God from the beginning to be His bride and mother. (*Mariology*, Vol. I)

Opponents of the belief that Mary had consecrated her virginity to God claim that such a vow was not in keeping with the times. Children were the greatest blessing a husband and wife could receive from the Lord, while barrenness was considered a curse. Israel had been awaiting its salvation, and each child born brought the day of deliverance closer.

This argument is faulty in its basic premise, for it assumes that God could not, or would not, inspire His future Mother with a desire to practice the virtue of virginity merely because the majority of women living at the time would not have opted for such a sacrifice. It ignores that clarity of thought and empathy with God's will which characterized the Blessed Virgin because of her Immaculate Conception. It assumes, oddly enough, that the growth and practice of virtue in the Mother of God must somehow remain "fixed" in predetermined boundaries – not boundaries set by God, but by men!

That Mary's reply to the Archangel – "How shall this be done, because I know not man?" – is proof that she had made a vow of virginity at some time in her life prior to the Annunciation merely follows the dictates of reason:

> Since then Mary, when the angel tells her from God that she, a woman betrothed according to Jewish customs, is to conceive a Son, appeals to her virginity as a difficulty, there is only one possible explanation: Mary finds herself in the presence of a complication. God foretells that she will conceive a Son, and yet *she is bound in conscience* so that she cannot cooperate naturally in this conception.

> This is possible only if her resolution to remain a virgin had the character of *a vow*, in which case she would have to be released from her promise by God Himself, or else God would have to make some other provision. (Fr. C. Friethoff, *A Complete Mariology*, 1958)

> These words . . . clearly show that not only had the Virgin formed a resolve not to know man, but also that she was so bound or impeded that she could not licitly do so. For even though up to that time she had not known man – even supposing she had formed the resolution – yet if it were completely within her discretion to know man licitly by her own free choice, there would have been no reason why she should so anxiously ask: "How shall this be done?" For the angel could easily have replied to her that she was free to know man in order to conceive a son. Therefore, the meaning of these words is "I do not know man"; that is, it is not permissible for me to know him, nor is this any longer up to my will. (Francis Suarez, *The Mysteries of the Life of Christ*)

And what of the relation of such a vow to Mary's marriage to Joseph? Saurez continued:

> Consequently, as a vow of itself and by its very nature seems to be in opposition to the fidelity and justice of marriage, so is the resolve not to render the marriage debt in conflict with the same virtues. For what is more unjust than to be in debt without the disposition and intention of paying it? Therefore, if from the beginning the Virgin had the unchangeable resolve of virginity, she could not without changing her resolution have contracted marriage unless she had received a divine illumination and revelation by which it was clear to her that Joseph would never request the debt but rather would consent to this resolve of virginity. Granted this

> revelation, matrimony is neither incompatible with the resolution nor with the vow.

In *The Acts of the Apostles*, St. Paul traveled to Caesarea. There he visited Phillip, who "... had four daughters, virgins, who did prophesy." (21:9) A footnote in *The Haydock Bible* states: "It is supposed that these daughters of S. Philip had made a vow of virginity, or at least remained in that state out of a motive of religion." With the advent and arrival of God Incarnate in the world, it must be expected that certain individuals would be inspired to consecrate themselves to Him, body and soul, regardless of the prevailing attitude of the times concerning virginity.

"Before He was conceived," wrote St. Augustine, "He chose to be born of a woman already consecrated to God." Christ Himself taught that "... there are eunuchs, who have made themselves eunuchs for the kingdom of heaven." (Mt. 19:12) Of His Mother's virginity, can He not rightly say, "Mary hath chosen the best part, which shall not be taken away from her?" (Lk. 10:42)

> Is it, however, so extraordinary that, under the influence of grace, Mary should feel herself attracted by an ideal which at that time was very vital in certain Jewish circles, at least among men, as we now know better since the discovery of a monastery of Essenes at Qumran, on the shores of the Dead Sea, some kilometers from the traditional location where St. John the Baptist preached? (Fr. S. Lyonnet, quoted in "The Perpetual Virginity of the Mother of God" from *Mariology*, Vol. 2 – Fr. J. Carol, ed., 1957)

Would the future Mother of the Redeemer be any *less* worthy of such divine inspirations to chastity, to a complete consecration of herself to her Lord? On the contrary, the Church sees Mary's vow of virginity as the template for all later vows professed by men and women entering the religious life: "We exhort all priests, religious men and women, to entrust themselves to the special protection of the holy Mother of God, who is the Virgin of virgins, the 'teacher of virginity', as Ambrose says, and the most powerful Mother of those in particular who have vowed and consecrated themselves to the service of God." (Pope Pius XII, *Sacra Virginitas*, 1954)

Our Lady's *Perpetual* Virginity is one of the Church's most ancient and cherished doctrines, and we defend it because we know, from the question she asked the Angel Gabriel at the Annunciation, that it is very close to Mary's heart. When she appeared to St. Juan Diego (†1548), Our Lady of Guadalupe announced herself as "the perfect *and perpetual* Virgin Mary, Mother of the true God." The history of the Church teems with references – in liturgical texts, Council documents, the writings of popes and saints, etc. – to the "Ever-Virgin Mary, Mother of God".

Throughout the ages, the Church has guarded with zeal the doctrine of the Perpetual Virginity of the Blessed Virgin by carefully defending the three aspects of Mary's virginity: virginity *ante partum* (before birth, or parturition), virginity *in partu* (during birth) and virginity *post partum* (after birth). These three aspects are clearly set forth in the dogmatic definition of the Perpetual Virginity proclaimed at the First Lateran Council (649):

> If anyone does not properly and truly confess in accord with the holy Fathers, that the holy Mother of God and ever Virgin and immaculate Mary in the earliest of the ages conceived of the Holy Ghost without seed [virginity *ante partum*], namely, God the Word Himself specifically and truly, who was born of God the Father before all ages, and that she incorruptibly bore Him [virginity *in partu*], her virginity remaining indestructible even after His birth [virginity *post partum*], let him be condemned.

"Those who love Christ," wrote St. Basil the Great, "will not brook the assertion that the Mother of God ever ceased to be a virgin." This sums up the Catholic attitude towards the doctrine of Mary's Perpetual Virginity, one that will not tolerate specious or malicious attempts to compromise it to any degree. The Council of Trent described as "depravity" and "iniquity" any denial that the Virgin Mary "did not always persist in the integrity of virginity, namely, before bringing forth, at bringing forth, and *always* after bringing forth." (Pope Paul IV, *Cum quorundam*, 1555) St. Hilary of Poitiers (†368) referred to those who denied Mary's Perpetual Virginity as "irreligious individuals, utterly divorced from spiritual teaching," while St. Epiphanius asked, "Was there ever anyone who dared pronounce the name of holy Mary without immediately adding the title 'Virgin'?"

St. Peter warned us of those "unlearned and unstable" ones who fixate on certain scriptural passages with malicious intent, and who ultimately "wrest" the holy books "to their own destruction". (2 Pt. 3:16) There are enemies of Christ who direct their attacks at His Mother, at her dignity, purity and virginity, often claiming that such attacks have a "scriptural" basis. As "proof" that Mary bore other children after giving birth to the Son of God, these malcontents refer to certain Gospel verses which speak of the "brethren" of Jesus:

> Behold Thy mother and Thy brethren without seek for thee. (Mk. 3:32)

> Is not His mother called Mary, and His brethren James, and Joseph, and Simon, and Jude: And His sisters, are they not all with us? (Mt. 13:55-56)

"According to the Hebrew language," wrote Rev. M.J. Scheeben, "this expression [brethren] does not require that these 'brothers' should be considered children of the same parents. It is also used in a wider sense for relatives in general." Because the Hebrew language has no word for "cousin", the term "brethren" can be interpreted like the Latin word, *consanguis* ("kindred" or "relations"). To demonstrate this widespread application of the term "brethren", we need only turn to *The Book of Genesis*: "Abram therefore said to Lot: Let there be no quarrel, I beseech thee . . . for we are brethren." (Gen. 13:8) Lot was Abraham's *nephew*, not his brother. Later on, we find Laban saying to his *nephew*, Jacob, "Because thou art my brother, shalt thou serve me without wages?"(Gen. 29:15)

The "brethren" of Jesus mentioned in the Gospels are His relatives; they are *not* his actual brothers and sisters. James and Joseph, for instance, are the sons of Mary, the wife of Cleophas (cf. Mt. 27:56), who is referred to as the *sister* of Our Lady by St. John the Evangelist (19:25). St. Hegesippus, a Jewish convert of the second century (quoted by Eusebius in his *History of the Church*, 325 A.D.), recorded that Cleophas was a brother of St. Joseph. If this were the case, Mary of Cleophas would have been the sister-in-law of St. Joseph; she and Our Lady, her "sister", would not have been siblings, though they would have been related by marriage. James and Joseph, then, would have been the cousins of Jesus. The "James" mentioned by St. Paul as "the brother of the Lord" in his *Epistle to the Galatians* (1:19) is the son of Alphaeus (cf. Mt. 10:3); he is called "James the Less", to distinguish him from James, the brother of St. John the Evangelist.

A similar "wresting" of Scripture often occurs regarding St. Luke's description of the Nativity – "She brought forth her first-born Son" – as though a first-born must be the first of many. However, "first-born" was a *legal* term, not a numerical qualification; it did not indicate how many sons were in the family, or imply the existence of any sons born *after* the "first-born". A first-born son held certain special privileges and bore certain duties. The term merely designated the first son's *standing* in the family, *as the first male to issue from the womb of the mother*: "Thou shalt set apart all that openeth the womb for the Lord." (Ex. 13:12) An only child can be a first-born son.

Another supposed "proof" against the Perpetual Virginity of Mary is this quote from St. Matthew's Gospel: "And he knew her not till she brought forth her first-born Son." (1:25) By this reasoning, if St. Joseph did not engage in conjugal relations with Mary *until* Jesus was born, then they must have done so afterwards. Yet, the mere fact that a particular condition or situation prevails up to a certain point in time does not demand that the situation change after that point. If a person claims that his neighbor never touched a drop of alcohol "until the day he died," he is merely describing the neighbor's *abiding* condition as an abstainer from spirits.

We also find in the inspired Scriptures this description of Michol, the daughter of King Saul: "Therefore Michol the daughter of Saul had no child to the day of her death." (2 Kg. 6:23) This certainly does not imply that Michol bore children *after* she died. The intent of

St. Matthew was to *highlight* the virginal conception of Christ, not to compromise the virginal integrity of the Mother of God. The Evangelist had simply stated that the conception of Jesus was miraculous – i.e., the Virgin had not "known" any man before the conception and birth of her Divine Son. To suggest that there was any intent on his part to deny Our Lady's Perpetual Virginity is to misread the holy book with slanderous intent.

In his epistle, *Accepti litteras vestras* (392), to Anysius, Bishop of Thessalonica, Pope St. Siricius wrote:

> Surely, we cannot deny that regarding the sons of Mary the statement is justly censured, and your holiness has rightly abhorred it, that from the same virginal womb, from which according to the flesh Christ was born, another offspring was brought forth. . . . For he who imputes this, imputes nothing other than the falsehood of the Jews, who say that He could not have been born of a virgin.

The sheer perversity which insists – in the face of Scripture and Tradition – upon placing the Ever-Virgin Mary in carnal scenarios was dealt with magnificently by St. Jerome in his reply to Helvidius, a heretic who insisted that Our Lady did not remain a virgin throughout her life:

> There are things which, in your extreme ignorance, you Helvidius had never read, and therefore you neglected the whole range of Scripture and employed your madness in outraging the Virgin, like the man in the story who, being unknown to everybody and finding that he could devise no good deed by which to gain renown, burned the temple of Diana: and when no one revealed the sacrilegious act, it is said that he himself went up and down proclaiming that he was the man who had applied the fire. The rulers of Ephesus were curious to know what made him do this thing, whereupon he replied that if he could not have fame

> for good deeds, all men should give him credit for bad ones. Grecian history relates the incident. *But you do worse*. You have set on fire the temple of the Lord's body, you have defiled the sanctuary of the Holy Ghost from which you are determined to make a team of four brethren and a heap of sisters come forth. In a word, joining in the chorus of the Jews you say, "Is not this the carpenter's son? Is not his mother called Mary? And his brethren James and Joseph and Simon and Judas? And his sisters, are they not all with us?" The word *all* would not be used if there were not a crowd of them. Pray tell me, who, before you appeared, was acquainted with this blasphemy? Who thought the theory worth two-pence? You have gained your desire and have become notorious by crime. (*The Perpetual Virginity of Blessed Mary, Against Helvidius*)

A rather blunt statement by St. Ambrose (†397) makes for an appropriate footnote to this impassioned defense of Mary's honor: "And Joseph, the just man, assuredly did not so completely lose his mind as to seek carnal intercourse with the Mother of God."

The Scriptures attest to the Perpetual Virginity in verses which foreshadow the Mother of God. In *The Prophecy of Ezechiel* is found this passage, describing the eastern gate of the Temple: "And the Lord said to me: This gate shall be shut, it shall not be opened, and no man shall pass through it: because the Lord the God of Israel hath entered in by it." (44:2) In *The Canticle of Canticles*, these descriptions are applied by the Beloved (Christ) to His Spouse: "My sister, my spouse, is a garden enclosed, a garden enclosed, a fountain sealed up." (4:12) The Church applies these figures to Mary, and to her virginity before, during and after childbirth. Medieval and Renaissance depictions of Our Lady often employed such Old Testament imagery as background objects. In 1498, a German edition of the *Speculum humanae salvationis* (an illustrated history of salvation, originally composed in 1324) was published, containing a woodcut in which the actual figure of the Virgin is not even portrayed; the illustration depicts only an enclosed garden and a sealed fountain, which indicate Mary's "presence" nonetheless.

During the Annunciation, the high regard in which the Archangel held the Blessed Virgin can be noted in the fact that it is only *after* she questions him that his own manner of speaking becomes less formal. He even addresses her by her name: "Fear not, Mary, for thou hast found grace with God." That Gabriel actually *awaits* her consent is evident in his final statement to her. After speaking of the virginal conception of the Redeemer, and of St. Elizabeth's pregnancy, he says, "Because no word shall be impossible with God." (Lk. 1:37) After that, silence. Mary's prudence has been rewarded, her concern for her virginity has been addressed, and the Angel has concluded his message, appropriately, with praises of his Lord's might. He has carried out his mission and spoken to Mary as God's intermediary, as a "courtier".

Holy fear, *born of humility*, resolves itself, not into anxiety, but into a blessed peace: "The fear of the Lord is honor, and glory, and gladness, and a crown of joy." (Ecclus. 1:11) This peace, born of a complete trust in God, characterizes Our Lady's *fiat*, "Behold the handmaid of the Lord; be it done to me according to thy word." Honor, glory, gladness, a crown of joy? These would all belong to Mary; they were her birthright. But, in her consent to the Incarnation, one thing shines above all others: humility. *Behold the handmaid.* Gabriel had informed her that she would be the Mother of God. An Archangel approaching a young girl, he had spoken to her with reverence becoming a queen. Yet, in the face of such professions of her dignity, Mary proclaimed herself a servant of the Lord. One day, her Son will make a similar pronouncement: "The Son of Man is not come to be ministered unto, but to minister." (Mt. 20:28)

Our Lady's words, by which the Incarnation was effected in her womb, *Be it done to me according to thy word*, are the faithful echo of the words of Jesus at the beginning of His Passion, "Not as I will, but as Thou wilt." These pledges of obedience to the Father cannot be separated. One clothed the Redeemer in human flesh; the other saw that Flesh offered for the restoration of the world.

Chapter Sixteen

The Holy Family

The Child and His mother – With Mary and Joseph Jesus gave glory to His Father for thirty years of hidden life – The Son of God "emptied Himself" – Life in Nazareth was part of the work Jesus was sent to do – Mary is the perfect "valiant woman" of Proverbs – The domestic imagery of the parables – Other valiant women, St. Anne – Mary's character clearly seen at the Annunciation: *the handmaid of the Lord* – More on the Holy Family – Obedience to the Law

In Bethlehem, Jesus and Mary – united in the mind of God *always*, united throughout Mary's own childhood by bonds of measureless grace, united as Infant and Mother at the Incarnation – were presented to a weary world as a living icon of salvation: "The Child and His Mother". The "Woman" of the *Proto-evangelium* now had a name: Mary, the daughter of Joachim and Anne. The "seed" of the *Proto-evangelium* also had a name, and "there is no other name under heaven given to men, whereby we must be saved:" (Act. 4:12) Jesus, the Son of God and the Son of Mary.

The venerable image of the Madonna and Child, cherished as much by those who walked the torch-lit passageways of the ancient catacombs as by Catholics today, is only secondarily a devotional image. It is principally theological, for it represents the *surety* that God was made man, that the Redeemer had at last come among His people. Up until the birth of Christ, people of good will had remembered the prophecy of the Woman and her seed, of the Virgin who would bear a Son. This Son was to be their Life, the only life that mattered – a Savior, not a political functionary.

The days of the devout Simeon were spent "waiting for the consolation of Israel." Like the Shepherds and Magi, he knew this consolation was at hand when, inside the Temple, he witnessed the living icon of Madonna and Child, when "His parents brought in the Child Jesus, to do for Him according to the custom of the law," (Lk. 2:27) when Our Lady and St. Joseph brought the Infant to the Temple for the prescribed rite of circumcision.

For the first thirty years of Jesus' life, the Mother and Son were inseparable. This fact is worthy of serious consideration. Our Lord came to earth as a man to do His Father's will, to restore humanity to life and friendship with God through His Supreme sacrifice of Love: "And what shall I say? Father, save me from this hour. But for this cause I came unto this hour. Father, glorify Thy name." (Jn. 12:27-28)

Each and every action performed by Jesus Christ was done in union with the Father: "I and the Father are one." (Jn. 10:30) "The Son cannot do anything of Himself, but what He seeth the Father doing: for what things soever He doth, these the Son also doth in like manner." (Jn. 5:19) Moreover, each and every action performed by Jesus was done to the greater glory of the Father: "I have glorified Thee on the earth; I have finished the work which Thou gavest me to do." (Jn. 17:4)

Each day our Lord spent in the company of Mary, then, was a day in which He gave glory to the Father, in which He practiced perfect obedience to the Father. The "hour" for which our Lord came to earth – His death on the Cross – was the consummation of the work He had "finished", the work His Father had given Him to do. Thirty-three years would elapse between the Nativity and the Crucifixion. Each minute of those thirty-three years spent by Jesus, each minute spent by *God on earth*, was of infinite worth. The work of the Redeemer was consummated on Calvary, but it began at His birth.

When the young Jesus was found in the Temple by our Lady and St. Joseph, He said to His Mother, "I must be about my Father's business." (Lk. 2:49) What did He do then, immediately after announcing that He must do His *Father's* work? – "He went down with them and came to Nazareth and was subject to them." (Lk. 2:51) The years spent by Jesus in filial obedience to Mary and Joseph were not "throw-away" years during which God "waited" for His chance to act. His infancy, His boyhood, His manhood – each stage of the life of the Savior is, in itself, an encyclopedia of lessons, His Father's work.

Principal among the lessons of Our Lord's youth is that of *humility*: "Who being in the form of God, thought it not robbery to be Himself equal to God: But emptied Himself, taking the form of a servant, being made in the likeness of men." (Phil. 2:5-7) He was subject to Mary and Joseph, and He lived a very "human" life of honest toil and simplicity, to the point where His neighbors would say, "Is not this the carpenter, the Son of Mary," in the face of His wisdom and works.

When His "hour" had come, this humility would not diminish, but would shine incandescently: "He humbled Himself, becoming obedient unto death, even to the death of the Cross." (Phil. 2:8)

The "subjection" of Jesus to His Mother began well before His youth at Nazareth. The discerning mind marvels that *God* should obey a human man and woman, humbling Himself before their authority. How much more to be wondered at, then, was the initial "subjection" of Jesus to Mary, the *dependence* of the Eternal and Almighty One on one of His creatures for sustenance and safety? God became Man. God became Man in the womb of Mary and, in doing so, paid her the unequaled tribute of trusting her in *the weakness He assumed out of love for mankind*:

> A wonder is Your mother: the Lord entered her and became a servant; He entered able to speak and He became silent in her; He entered her thundering and His voice grew silent; He entered Shepherd of all; a lamb He became in her; He emerged bleating. The womb of Your mother overthrew the orders: The Establisher of all entered a Rich One; He emerged poor. He entered her a Lofty One; He emerged humble. He entered her a Radiant One, and He put on a despised hue and emerged. He entered, a mighty warrior, and put on fear inside her womb. He entered, Nourisher of all, and He acquired hunger. He entered, the One who gives drink to all, and He acquired thirst. Stripped and laid bare, He emerged from her womb, the One who clothes all. (St. Ephrem of Syria, *Hymns on the Nativity*, 11)

Let no one imagine that the thirty years spent by Jesus in the sweet company of His Mother was "down time", unrelated to His salvific work. When the disciples, fearful for their lives, awakened Jesus as He slept in the storm-tossed boat, His first words to them were: "Why are you fearful, O ye of little faith?" (Mt. 8:26) He spoke these words even before He calmed the winds and waves. In His Sacred Humanity, Jesus, "made in the likeness of men," slept, ate, felt weariness and pain. Pope Innocent III wrote:

> He Who was in the Divinity the Son of God the Father, true God from the Father, was in the humanity the son of man, true man from a mother, having true flesh from the womb of His Mother and a human rational soul; at the same time of each nature, that is God and man, one Person, one Son, one Christ, one God with the Father and the Holy Ghost, the author and ruler of all, born from the Virgin Mary in a true birth of the flesh; He ate and drank, He slept and, tired out from a journey, He rested, He suffered in the true passion of His flesh. (*Eius exemplo*, 1208)

In His Divinity, the disciples in the boat were never out of the thoughts of Jesus, "true God from the Father", even for a moment: "Neither let Him slumber that keepeth thee." (Ps. 120:3)

Because He is True God, as well as True Man, every action performed by Jesus is the work *of God*. We are admonished to learn from Him. Therefore, we are bound in conscience to observe the Blessed Virgin closely, to imitate Jesus in honoring her and remaining by her side, to view her, not as an "incidental" footnote to the Redeemer's work, but as a particularly worthy part of salvation history, created and put in place by the Blessed Trinity, and done so with the regard that only *God* could show to a Mother, Daughter and Spouse.

The Scriptures are not as silent as some would like to think concerning the character of the Blessed Virgin. In order to understand something of the home chosen by God as the only refuge and sanctuary His Son would ever know on earth, we need only look at the Mother whose Immaculate Heart imparted to this home so much of its character. The Scriptures describe her for us:

> Who shall find a valiant woman? Far, and from the uttermost coasts is the price of her. . . . She hath sought wool and flax, and hath wrought by the counsel of her hands. . . . She hath tasted, and seen that her traffic is good: her lamp shall not be put out in the night. She hath put out her hand to strong things, and her fingers have taken hold of the spindle. She hath opened her hand

> to the needy, and stretched out her hands to the poor. . . . She hath opened her mouth to wisdom, and the law of clemency is on her tongue. She hath looked well to the paths of her house, and hath not eaten her bread idle. (Prov. 31:10-27) As the sun when it riseth to the world in the high places of God, so is the beauty of a good wife for the ornament of her house. (Ecclus. 26:21)

Our Lord, Who had spent so many years living in daily concourse with Mary, often spoke in parables after He went forth to gather His disciples to Him and seek out His Bride, the Church. Many of these parables are clothed in domestic imagery, and it would be strange, indeed, if the image of the Blessed Virgin, going about her daily labors in the holy house at Nazareth, did not lie behind these scenes:

> The kingdom of heaven is like to leaven, which a woman took and hid in three measures of meal, until the whole was leavened. (Mt. 13:33)

> Or what woman having ten groats, if she lose one groat, doth not light a candle and sweep the house and seek diligently till she find it? (Lk. 15:8)

> Neither do men light a candle and put it under a bushel, but upon a candlestick, that it may shine to all that are in the house. (Mt. 5:15)

> And nobody putteth a piece of raw cloth unto an old garment. For it taketh away the fullness thereof from the garment, and there is made a greater rent . . . neither do they put new wine into old bottles. (Mt. 9:16-17)

The Scriptural descriptions of the "valiant woman", the good wife, paint a portrait of integrity. The "valiant woman" is industrious, wise, charitable. She is skilled both in the ordering of the household, with its myriad responsibilities and decisions, as well as in the trades she pursues by the industry of her own hands. Her charity extends beyond her own door, to her neighbors and the needy. There is only one characteristic left to include in this admirable portrait, but it forms the basis and motivation for *all* the others: "As everlasting foundations upon a solid rock, so the commandments of God in the heart of a holy woman." (Ecclus. 26:24)

These traits – industry, charity, determination, piety – are not "idealized" ones, incapable of being realized in ordinary, flesh-and-blood human beings. On the contrary, history discloses some striking examples. Here is how St. Augustine described his mother, St. Monica, in his *Confessions*:

> Whenever she could, she showed herself to be a great peacemaker between persons who were at odds and in disagreement. . . . Whoever among them knew her greatly praised You, and honored You, and loved You in her, because they recognized your presence in her heart, for the fruit of her holy life bore witness to this. She had been the wife of one husband; she repaid the duty she owed to her parents; she had governed her house piously; she had testimony for her good works; she had brought up children, being as often in labor in birth of them, as she saw them straying from you.

Memorable examples of "valiant" women are found in the noble mother of the Machabees, in the widow Judith, and in the heroic Martyr of the English "reformation", St. Margaret Clitherow. The Machabees were seven brothers, faithful to God, who incurred the wrath of King Antiochus by refusing to eat swine's flesh; their mother encouraged her sons to meet the trials of martyrdom for the love of God, and, finally, suffered martyrdom herself. (2 Mac. 7) When the city of Bethulia was besieged by General Holofernes, the people agreed to surrender if they were not rescued in five days. Judith confronted them for this, saying, "And who are you to tempt the Lord?" She went to Holofernes, waited until he slept in a drunken stupor, and delivered her people:

> Saying: Strengthen me, O Lord God of Israel, and in this hour look on the works of my hands, that as Thou hast promised, Thou mayest raise up Jerusalem Thy city:

> and that I may bring to pass that which I have purposed, having a belief that it might be done by Thee. . . . And she struck twice upon his neck, and cut off his head, and took off his canopy from the pillars, and rolled away his headless body. (Jth. 13:7,10)

St. Margaret Clitherow (†1586) was the wife of a butcher, and helped him run his shop. She was imprisoned repeatedly for holding fast to the True Faith, and taught herself to read while in prison so that she might be better able to give her children a sound Catholic education. She sent her son to study with the Catholic exiles in Douay and harbored fugitive priests who celebrated Mass in her home. Charged with treason, she was told that she would be spared if only she would embrace the false new religion promulgated by the "reformers". St. Margaret refused and was executed when the following sentence was read to her, then carried out:

> You shall return to the place from whence you came, and in the lower part of the prison be stripped naked, laid down on your back to the ground, and so much weight laid upon you as you are able to bear, and thus you shall continue three days; the third day you shall have a sharp stone put under your back, and your hands and feet shall be tied to posts that, more weight being laid upon you, you may be pressed to death.

The ancient traditions of the Church portray St. Anne, the mother of the Blessed Virgin, as a woman worthy of honor and admiration. St. John Damascene described Anne as "the chosen one, a woman worthy of all manner of praise", and he certainly followed his own admonition:

> O glorious womb of Anna, in which the most holy fetus grew and was formed, silently increasing! O womb in which was conceived the living heaven, wider than the wideness of the heavens. (*Homily on the Nativity*)

If these holy women, and others down through the ages, embody with such steadfastness the virtues and characteristics of the "valiant woman" of the Scriptures, to what degree would this figure be embodied in the Mother of God, conceived immaculately, free from all distractions of a sinful nature, her thoughts and affections directed to God like a compass needle to the north? If we admire the mother of the Machabees, who stood courageously while her sons were killed before her eyes, and Judith, who cut off the head of her people's oppressor, with what greater admiration should we contemplate our Lady, who watched her only Son die on the Cross, *knowing that He was God*, and who crushed the head of Satan, the worst oppressor of all, both at her Immaculate Conception and when she gave birth to the One Who would topple the "empire of death".

A cynical age portrays someone desiring to belong to God as little more than a "follower" or an automaton, an unoriginal thinker depending upon rules written centuries ago for values and guidance. The truth is, as usual, something much grander in its essence and manifestation. The valiant women of *all* ages sought after and followed the commandments of God, not thoughtlessly, but *passionately*, acting not from some type of emotional "programming", but out of *love* for God, with generosity and courage. There was fire in the hearts of these women, not a trance-like attachment to abstract principles, and we can almost hear them crying out to God, "How sweet are Thy words to my palate! More than honey to my mouth." (Ps. 118:103)

The home of Jesus, Mary and Joseph in Nazareth was a piece of heaven on earth. Its centerpiece was the center of all creation, God Himself. The Mother whose spirit and maternal warmth filled it is *the* Valiant Woman, the blueprint for all others, for her image was cherished by God *from before the foundation of the world*, right beside that of the Son. "Behold the handmaid of the Lord," was the declaration *she* made, which initiated the restoration of the world. The words of the psalmist seem to have been written to give voice to her own desire for this Lord Who came to rest in her womb:

> O how have I loved Thy law, O Lord! It is my meditation all the day. . . . I have understood more than all my teachers: because Thy testimonies are my meditation. I

> have had understanding above ancients: because I have sought Thy commandments. (Ps. 118:97,99-100)

Of course, her understanding far surpassed that of others. "This Woman is invested with the all-burning, but non-consuming flame of Divine Love," wrote St. Bernard. Proof that Our Lady "had understanding above ancients" is seen in the simple fact that the Angel Gabriel *waited* upon her consent to the Incarnation. He had laid at the feet of a young girl the most profound Mystery of all: "Thou shalt conceive in thy womb, and shalt bring forth a Son. . . . He shall be great, and shall be called the Son of God. . . . And of His kingdom there shall be no end." As Mary, a descendant of King David, pondered the words, her thoughts would have raced back through the history of her people, through ages of yearning, to alight on the cadences of a psalm: "The Lord hath sworn truth to David, and He will not make it void: *of the fruit of thy womb* I will set upon thy throne." (Ps. 131:11) This prophecy, fulfilled in part by King Solomon, had another, deeper dimension, a spiritual one which pointed to the advent of the Redeemer.

The words of Church Fathers, Doctors, theologians, popes and Councils have placed the Incarnation into a necessary verbal framework which can be discussed, explained and, most importantly, taught. Yet, perhaps, with twenty centuries' worth of treatises, homilies and studies behind us, we are sometimes too casual in offering clinical descriptions of the Incarnation. Who can imagine the thoughts in the mind of a young girl confronted with a heavenly messenger, as the Incarnation is spoken of, not as a theological subject or a prophetic possibility, but as an imminent reality *waiting to happen*?

The Annunciation occurred in "real time". Mary would ponder it all the days of her life, but as she stood before the Angel Gabriel, the Incarnation, ordained from all eternity, was on the verge of becoming reality. History was about to be changed forever. *And she was being asked to initiate the most momentous event in all of Creation*! Since the fall of Adam, the world had been waiting for one thing only: for Mary to say "yes" . . .

> *This is conclusion, and the fires that scorched*
> *The Prophet's lips, the old consuming fires*

That burned in Israel's blood might now be cooled;
For prophecies are ending, and the dreams
That throbbed above the great unfinished music
Of the Psalms are quieted, and psalms
At last resolve, like chords that come to rest.
This is fulfillment, and upreaching hands
May now be folded, and the long desires
That beat, half heard in need, through all the veins,
May now be eased. New testament is made,
New visitation, and a full new world
That holds much more of mystery, and more
Of consequence than that which answered first
From nothingness.

(Fr. John W. Lynch, *A Woman Wrapped in Silence*)

Some young women would have turned away in confusion or begged for time in which to think it over; others would have been overwhelmed at the sheer responsibility. The demeanor of Mary during the Annunciation tells us much of her character. Both humble and prudent, she is "troubled" at the exalted greeting of the Angel. Yet she listens to all he says calmly. She asks one question only, briefly and to the point; this question concerns her vow of Perpetual Virginity, a matter of such import to her that it *had* to be asked. Mary listens; she understands; she gives her consent as a servant of God.

A hymn from the *Little Office of the Blessed Virgin* describes God as "the great Artificer Divine", and *The Book of Proverbs* says, "Wisdom hath built herself a house, she hath hewn her out seven pillars." (Prov. 9:1) In the womb of Mary, the Incarnate Wisdom took to Himself a fully *human* body and, while walking among His people, instituted the seven sacraments. The Incarnation was not a theological "topic" for Our Lady. It was a flesh-and-blood reality that would find her one day holding the warm, gently breathing body of *God* in her arms, His gaze returning her own, His voice sounding in her ears.

Mary's penetrating intellect, far from making her complacent or proud in the face of divine mysteries, only whetted her desire to ponder them. As one becomes more knowledgeable about a subject, he becomes, not *less* interested or passionate about it, but more so. When the object of right desire is God, for Whom our souls were created, the same principle applies, but with a special sweetness: "Thy testimonies are wonderful: therefore my soul hath sought them." (Ps. 118:129)

The earthly home of the Redeemer, after which He had no place "to lay His head", was characterized by this intense love of God. Jesus loved God as His Father. Mary loved God as her Son. St. Joseph, *a just man*, the most distinguished of all saints, was given the gift of contemplating daily God-made-Man . . . and the Mother of God, as well. In the most chaste and selfless manner, he loved Mary as a wife and Jesus as a Son, lavishing the affection of a Guardian upon both.

The Holy Family rendered praise and thanksgiving to the Father as their brethren did and always had done. We are told that they "went every year to Jerusalem, at the solemn day of the Pasch." (Lk. 2:41) After the birth of Jesus, Mary, sinless but obedient to the Law, freely submitted to the ancient rite of "purification", even though, from birth, she – the *Immaculate Conception* – was free from all defilement of body and soul. This "purification" was a *ritual* purification incumbent upon women after childbirth, the details varying according to the sex of the child:

> If a woman having received seed shall bear a man child, she shall be unclean seven days . . . and on the eighth day the infant shall be circumcised: But she shall remain three and thirty days in the blood of her purification. She shall touch no holy thing, neither shall she enter into the sanctuary, until the days of her purification be fulfilled. (Lev. 12:2-4)

"If a woman *having received seed* shall bear a man child, she shall be unclean seven days." It is wrong to attribute even a "legal" or ritual defilement to the Virgin Mother, whose Son was conceived by the Holy Ghost, not with the seed of man: "The Virgin was not subject to the law of purification . . . since without human generation she became Emmanuel's Mother." (St. Basil) However, in accord with the dictates of the Law, Mary, the holiest creature after her Son, would have refrained from touching any "holy thing" or from entering the Temple during her purification, so we read that, ". . .*after* the days of her purification, *according to the law of Moses*, were accomplished, they carried Him to Jerusalem, to present Him to the Lord." (Lk. 2:22)

According to *Leviticus*:

> And when the days of her purification are expired, for a son, or for a daughter, she shall bring to the door of the tabernacle of the testimony, a lamb of a year old for a holocaust, and a young pigeon or a turtle for sin, and shall deliver them to the priest . . . And if her hand find not sufficiency, and she is not able to offer a lamb, she shall take two turtles, or two young pigeons, one for a holocaust, and another for sin: and the priest shall pray for her, and so she shall be cleansed. (Lev. 12:6,8)

The "holocaust" was an offering of thanks to God; the offering for sin dealt with ritual or *legal* impurity, an imputed status associated with the process of childbirth. Any spurious reasoning which accepts Mary's "sin offering" as an admission of sinfulness must also accept our Lord's baptism by St. John the Baptist as an admission on *His* part of sin, for those who went to St. John "were baptized by him in the Jordan, confessing their sins." (Mt. 3:6) The servant, the *handmaid*, is not greater than her Lord, nor has she ever presumed to be.

When our Lord was born, "there was no room for them in the inn." (Lk. 2:7)

> Look at the grotto of Bethlehem. Is it perhaps a suitable dwelling place even for modest artisans? Why these animals, why these bundles used for travel, why this absolute poverty? Is this what Mary and Joseph had dreamed of in the intimate sweetness of their home in Nazareth for the birth of the Child Jesus? It is more than likely that Joseph had, for many months, been collecting some pieces of wood which he had sawn, planed, cleaned and then made into a cradle. And we may well believe that Mary, who from childhood was trained in the temple in womanly handiwork, had like every other woman

> about to become a mother cut, hemmed and lovingly embroidered the layette for the Desired of Nations! (Pope Pius XII, *The Lesson of Bethlehem*, 1940)

"Look at the grotto of Bethlehem." Such humility, worthy of the Son of God, was shared by His Mother and foster-father. Mary and Joseph *knew* Who was about to be born, yet they took the "last place" without complaint, knowing that, wherever the Divine Infant was, there was *everything* that mattered. One day, the Son born in that place would say: "But when thou art invited, go, sit down in the lowest place; that when he who inviteth thee cometh he may say to thee: Friend, go up higher." (Lk. 14:10)

Chapter Seventeen

Mary Is Our Treasure

To imitate Christ be close to Mary – to honor one's mother is to "store up a treasure" – To imitate Christ be "subject" to Mary – *Behold thy mother* – Members of the Body of Christ, His mother is our mother, God is our Father

Venerable Thomas à Kempis (†1471) began his great spiritual classic, *The Imitation of Christ*, with this reflection:

> "He that followeth Me, walketh not in darkness," saith Our Lord (John 8:12). These are the words of Christ, by which we are admonished, that we must imitate His life and manners, if we would be truly enlightened, and delivered from all blindness of heart.

No period in the life of Christ is excluded here. His entire life, in all its particulars, is worthy of veneration and imitation. His very first minutes on earth proclaimed the mercy of God, Whose love of humility, and for mankind, saw Him lying in a manger. The obedience and respect He rendered to His parents as a youth, by submitting to their parental authority, is another quality to be emulated. The long years He spent in obscurity, plying the carpenter's trade, is itself an encouragement for all people to give God a place in daily life, regardless of the particular labors occasioned by different stations in life.

Jesus lived in filial intimacy with the Blessed Virgin for most of His earthly life. This is a fact which *cannot* be overlooked or ignored if one desires to practice any sort of an "imitation" of Christ:

> God the Son came down into her virginal womb as a new Adam into His earthly paradise, to take His delight there and produce hidden wonders of grace. God-made-Man found freedom in imprisoning Himself in

> her womb. He displayed power in allowing Himself to be borne by this young maiden. He found His glory and that of His Father in hiding His splendors from all creatures here below and revealing them only to Mary. *He glorified His independence and His majesty in depending upon this lovable virgin* in His conception, His birth, His presentation in the temple, and in the thirty years of His hidden life. (St. Louis de Montfort, *True Devotion to the Blessed Virgin*)

The lesson is straightforward and valuable. It is *good* to be with the Blessed Virgin Mary, to have a "personal relationship" with the Mother of God. To be more precise, it is *essential* to have this relationship. Our Lord, "by whom all things were made," the One Who needs no creature to supplement His might, knowledge or majesty, nevertheless made the Virgin the "center" of His human existence until He was ". . . about the age of thirty years", (Lk. 3:23) when He was baptized by St. John the Baptist, after which He fasted in the desert and began His *public* ministry:

> And He came to Nazareth, where He was brought up: and He went into the synagogue, according to His custom, on the sabbath day; and He rose up to read. . . . And He began to say to them: This day is fulfilled this Scripture in your ears. (Lk. 4:16,21)

The "Hidden Life" of the Savior, the Son of God – even the phrase is tantalizing. *God* living on earth as a Man, day after day, week after week, month after month . . . *year after year,* stretching into decades. Who would not wish to be able to observe just one of those days in the life of Jesus, one day out of thousands of such days, complete from dawn to dusk?

"O eternal God, Who knowest hidden things, Who knowest all things before they come to pass," (Dan. 13:42) cried out Susanna, when her chastity had been maliciously impugned by the corrupt elders of her people. God plans all things perfectly, comprehending all aspects, details and consequences of His designs before they come to pass. The years spent by the Savior in the company of Mary and Joseph were years decreed by the Blessed Trinity. Decreed to what end? St. John the Evangelist wrote of Our Lord in His agony on Calvary: "Afterwards, Jesus knowing that all things were now accomplished, . . . said: I thirst." (Jn. 19:28)

The accomplishing of *all* things, the "consummation" announced by Jesus from the Cross, was the fulfillment of the Scriptures. The Life and Passion of the Redeemer was one continuous unfolding of prophecy, one unbroken series of Scriptural truths made flesh. He was born in Bethlehem of a virgin; He was called out of Egypt, where His parents had taken Him for safety; He fulfilled the Law, in all its particulars, perfectly; He went to His death like a silent Lamb, the "Suffering Servant" of Isaias; He brought the serpent down low, despoiling the principalities, the "empire of death".

The "Hidden Life" of Jesus was valuable in all its particulars, directed to the glory of the Father "that the Scripture might be fulfilled":

> Why do you think Our Lord spent only a few years here on earth and nearly all of them in submission and obedience to His Mother? The reason is that "attaining perfection in a short time, he lived a long time," [Wis. 4:13] even longer than Adam, whose losses He had come to make good. Yet Adam lived more than nine hundred years! Jesus lived a long time because He lived in complete submission to His Mother and in union with her, *which obedience to God His Father required.* The Holy Spirit tells us that the man who honors his mother is like a man who stores up a treasure. [Ecclus. 3:5] (St. Louis de Montfort, *True Devotion to the Blessed Virgin*)

Because of the Incarnation, God Himself can be *made of a woman, made under the law*, and Jesus Christ, the Source of all graces and treasures, can yet *increase* in *wisdom, and age, and grace with God and men*. Because of the Incarnation, we can read that *God* became hungry and thirsty, and that He wept at the death of His friend, Lazarus. Also, because of the Incarnation, God can honor His Mother "like a man who stores up a treasure":

> Which shall we admire first? The tremendous submission of the Son of God, or the tremendous God-given dignity of the Mother of God? Both are marvels: both amazing. When God obeys a woman, it is humility without precedent. When a woman commands her God, it is sublime beyond measure. In praising virgins, we read that they follow the Lamb wherever He goes. How can we possibly praise sufficiently the Virgin who leads Him? (St. Bernard, *First Homily on the Missus Est*)

The first lesson to be learned here is an obvious one, and it was stated by St. Bernard, after he wonders at the humility of Christ in His submission to the Virgin: "Learn, O man, to obey; learn, O earth, to be subject; learn, O dust, to bow down. . . . Blush, proud ashes, for God humiliates Himself and you exact yourself. God submits to men, but you, ignoring His example, seek to dominate your fellow men." Another lesson was stated by St. Louis de Montfort: "The man who honors Mary, his Mother, to the extent of subjecting himself to her and obeying her in all things will soon become very rich, because he is amassing riches every day through Mary who has become his secret philosopher's stone."

Because of the *Hypostatic Union* (by which divine and human nature were *united* in the Person of Jesus), and His saving work, we are obliged to accept all the pronouncements spoken by Jesus "in a universal" context, as directed towards mankind, though sometimes spoken to individuals. "Unless a man be born again of water and the Holy Ghost," said our Lord to Nicodemus, "he cannot enter into the kingdom of God." (Jn. 3:5) These words were not intended solely for Nicodemus. When asked by St. Peter how many times a brother must be forgiven, Jesus replied, "I say not to thee, till seven times; but till seventy times seven times." (Mt. 18:22) This instruction was not meant for St. Peter only.

"Behold thy Mother," was the pronouncement made to St. John by Jesus, as He hung on the Cross. It was not meant for St. John alone, but was directed through him to mankind at large, to each and every man and woman with a soul to save. "When you shall have lifted up the Son of Man," said Jesus, "then shall you know that I am

He and that I do nothing of Myself, but as the Father hath taught Me, these things I speak." (Jn. 8:28) *Behold thy Mother* – words "taught" by the Father, words spoken on Calvary when the Son of Man had been lifted up. They are as important as the other words He spoke throughout His life, words whose truth would be attested to by His death and Resurrection.

From the Cross, our Lord said to His Mother, indicating St. John, "Woman, behold thy son." He said to the Beloved Disciple, indicating the Holy Virgin, "Behold thy Mother." Mary already *had* a Son: Jesus. St. John already *had* a mother: Mary Salome. These were *natural* relationships. The Redeemer was establishing, from the Cross, a new "filiation" – a *spiritual* one – and not merely entrusting Mary to the "care" of John (although this was a happy result). Mary and John are constituted by God Himself as "Mother" and "Son", for Mary is not the *natural* mother of John, yet she is proclaimed as such. This is a new filiation, one made possible "in the order of grace", one made possible *because the Catholic Church is the Mystical Body of Christ.*

The Church does not merely "resemble" a human body; she *is* the Body of Christ: "He is the Savior of His Body." (Eph. 5:23) This "corporal" image is not an analogy, or a metaphor, for the Church. It is a *diagram* of a concrete reality: "But now God hath set the members, every one of them, in the Body as it hath pleased Him. And if they all were one member, where would be the Body? But now there are many members indeed, yet one body." (1 Cor. 12:18-20)

Thus, grace flows from the head of the Church to His Body, not as though emanating from an impersonal, outside source, but through this very union:

> So we, being many, are one Body in Christ, and every one members one of another. And having different gifts, according to the grace that is given us. (Rom. 12:5-6) But all these things one and the same Spirit worketh, dividing to every one according as He will. For as the Body is one and hath many members; and all the members of the Body, whereas they are many, yet are one Body, so also is Christ. (1 Cor. 12:11-12)

This mystery of divine charity, whereby God deigns to form one body with His creatures in Christ, results in an all-encompassing intimacy between Divinity and humanity, infusing even purely human relationships:

> Know you not that your members are the temple of the Holy Ghost, Who is in you, Whom you have from God, and you are not your own? (1 Cor. 6:19) For as many of you as have been baptized in Christ, have put on Christ. There is neither Jew nor Greek: there is neither bond nor free: there is neither male nor female. For you are all one in Christ Jesus. (Gal. 3:27-28)

The Catholic Church, being the Body of Christ, can rejoice, then, in the supernatural *life* animating this Body:

> But you are not in the flesh, but in the Spirit, if so be that the Spirit of God dwell in you. . . . And if Christ be in you, the body indeed is dead, because of sin; but the spirit liveth, because of justification. And if the spirit of Him, Who raised up Jesus from the dead, dwell in you; He that raised up Jesus Christ from the dead shall quicken also your mortal bodies, because of His spirit that dwelleth in you. . . . For none of us liveth to himself; and no man dieth to himself. For whether we live, we live unto the Lord; or whether we die, we die unto the Lord. Therefore, whether we live or whether we die, we are the Lord's. For to this end Christ died and rose again; that He might be Lord both of the dead and of the living. (Rom. 8:9-11;14:7-9)

Individuals are able to form a Mystical Body with Jesus Christ only because He assumed our human nature at the Incarnation: "Therefore because the children are partakers of flesh and blood, He also Himself in like manner hath been partaker of the same." (Heb. 2:14) The relationship between God and man can assume, for the first time, a "fraternal" aspect. The members of the Church are "sons" of God and, therefore, "brothers" of Jesus:

> For whosoever are led by the Spirit of God, they are the sons of God. For you have not received the spirit of bondage again in fear; but you have received the spirit of adoption of sons, whereby we cry: Abba (Father). (Rom. 8:14-15)

As brethren of Jesus, the members of the Church can rightfully call God "Father" and are invited to share the glorious inheritance won by the Savior, to become co-heirs with the Only-Begotten Son, "heirs indeed of God, and joint-heirs with Christ." (Rom. 8:17) "If you be Christ's," wrote St. Paul, "then you are the seed of Abraham, *heirs according to the promise.*" (Gal. 3:29) How can we be considered sons of *Abraham*? Because, in Christ, "there is neither Jew nor Greek . . . bond nor free . . . male nor female." The members of the Mystical Body receive "the spirit of adoption of sons".

Abraham had two sons, Ismael and Isaac. Ismael was born to the servant, Agar. Only *one* son was the natural child of the *promise* made by God to Abraham – Isaac, born to Sara. But, Abraham was promised descendants as *numerous* as the stars, a promise gloriously fulfilled in the Catholic Church, of which St. Paul wrote: "Now we, brethren, as Isaac was, are the children of promise. . . . We are not the children of the bondwoman, but of the free: by the freedom wherewith Christ has made us free." (Gal. 4:28,31)

Through the Incarnation of the Eternal Word, St. Paul could write, "Now therefore you are no more strangers and foreigners; but you are fellow-citizens with the saints, and the domestics of God." (Eph. 2:19)

Chapter Eighteen

Children of Mary

MOTHER OF THE CHURCH: ORDAINED FROM ALL ETERNITY – ST. PIUS X: "WE ARE CHILDREN OF MARY – TO SEE THIS TRUTH WE MUST RETURN TO CALVARY AND HEAR THE WORDS OF JESUS IN AGONY

During His final agony on Calvary, Jesus said, *Behold thy Mother*. He spoke to St. John. He spoke to the Church, for these words would form forever part of the Gospel's inspired canon. St. Paul placed this Mother in context:

> Now I say, as long as the heir is a child, he differeth nothing from a servant, though he be lord of all; but is under tutors and governors, until the time appointed by the father. So we also, when we were children, were in bondage, under the elements of the world. But when the fullness of the time was come, God sent His Son, *made of a woman*, made under the law: that He might redeem them who were under the law: *that we might receive the adoption of sons*. And because you are sons, God hath sent the Spirit of His Son into your hearts, crying: Abba, Father. Therefore now he is not a servant, but a son. And if a son, an heir also through God. (Gal. 4:1-7)

Pope Pius XI wrote of our Lady, "Since she brought forth the Redeemer of the human race and of all of us, *whom the Lord Christ has willed to regard as brothers*, she is our most beloved Mother." (*Lux veritatis*, 1931) Therefore, the Incarnation of the Word, and the incorporation into one Mystical Body of the individual members of the Church, will bring mankind into a deeply "personal" relationship with Mary, the Mother of God.

The Crucified Savior said to Mary, "Woman, behold thy son," and we cannot believe for a moment that our Lord, who said to

St. Paul, "My grace is sufficient for thee," (2 Cor. 12:9) would leave our Lady unprepared for such a role, the Spiritual Motherhood of the Church. On the contrary, just as she was prepared by her Immaculate Conception and a plenitude of grace for her *Divine* Motherhood, so was she prepared also for her *Spiritual* Motherhood:

> She is the mighty Mother of God. But – what is still sweeter – she is gentle, exquisite in tenderness, and of a limitless love and kindness. *As such God gave her to us.* Having chosen her for the Mother of his only-begotten Son, He taught her all a mother's feelings that breathe nothing but pardon and love. Such Christ desired that she should be, for He consented to be subject to Mary and to obey her as a son does a mother. As such He proclaimed her from the Cross when He entrusted to her care and love the whole of the race of man in the person of His disciple John. And as such does she prove herself by her courage in gathering the heritage of the enormous labors of her dying Son, in accepting freely the office of Mother towards all. (Pope Leo XIII, *Octobri mense*, 1891)

The "heritage" of Jesus was gained through His Passion and death. He deigned to be "made under the law", to pay the debt owed by mankind to its Creator, "that we might receive the adoption of sons." By this "adoption", we are constituted not only sons of God – but sons of Mary as well.

Pope Pius XII taught that God "from all eternity regards Mary with a most favorable and unique affection." "Before time began," wrote Pope Pius IX, "the Eternal Father chose and prepared for His only-begotten Son a Mother in whom the Son of God would become incarnate. . . . Above all creatures did God so love her that truly in her was the Father well pleased with singular delight." This Woman, beloved by God and destined to be the "Cause of Our Joy" (as the *Litany of Loreto* addresses her) by bringing the Savior to us, was included in that same primeval decree which had ordained the Incarnation of the Word, "from all eternity joined in a hidden way with Jesus Christ in one and the same decree of predestination." (Pope Pius XII)

As Our Lord was destined from all time to come to earth as man, to suffer, die and rise again, *and to found His True Church*, then Mary, whose Spiritual Motherhood of this Church was proclaimed by *the Son of God Himself* from the Cross, was always "Mother of the Church" in the eyes of God:

> For is not Mary the Mother of Christ? Then she is our Mother also. And we must in truth hold that Christ, the Word made flesh, is also the Savior of mankind. Now, as the God-Man, He had a material body like that of any other man; and as Savior of the human family, He had a spiritual and mystical body, the society, namely, of those who believe in Christ. "So we, being many, are one body in Christ." [Rom. 12:5] Now the Blessed Virgin did not conceive the Eternal Son of God merely in order that He might be made man, taking His human nature from her, but also in order that by *means of the nature assumed from her, He might* be *the Redeemer* of men. . . . Therefore, in the same holy bosom of His most chaste Mother, Christ took to Himself flesh, *and united to Himself the spiritual body formed by those who were to believe in Him.* Hence Mary, carrying the Savior within her may be said to have also carried all those whose life was contained in the life of the Savior. Therefore all we who are united to Christ, and as the Apostle says, ". . . are members of His body, of His flesh and of His bones," [Eph. 5:30] *have issued from the womb of Mary like a body united to His head.* Hence, in a spiritual and mystical fashion, *we are all children of Mary*, and she is Mother of us all. (Pope St. Pius X, *Ad diem illum laetissimum*, 1904)

To appreciate this fully, let us return to Calvary on the first Good Friday, when a fallen world was being restored by the shedding of the Precious Blood. Our Lord hung on the Cross to ". . . deliver them, who through the fear of death were all their lifetime subject to servitude," (Heb. 2:15) during three hours of torment whose intensity cannot even be hinted at in words.

Jesus spoke from the Cross. *Father, forgive them, for they know not what they do*, He said, as the soldiers cast lots for His garments, testifying to a Mercy so profound that the mind, incredulous, halts before it. *Amen I say to thee, this day thou shalt be with me in Paradise*, was addressed to the penitent thief, an encouragement for sinners of all times to persevere, even when all seems lost. *I thirst*, spoken in torment, were words which fulfilled the Scriptures.

My God, My God, why hast Thou forsaken Me? This cry testified to the *humanity* of Jesus Christ, a warning to all later heretics who denied that the Savior was, indeed, True God *and* True Man, who denied that we were "not redeemed with corruptible things, gold or silver . . . But with the precious Blood of Christ." This cry is commonly, and unfortunately, referred to as one of "despair", yet the complete abandonment of hope suggested by the term can not be attributed to the Son of God. The words are a quotation from the *Psalms*: "O God, my God, look upon me: why hast Thou forsaken me? Far from my salvation are the words of my sins." (Ps. 21:1-2) This psalm is a prophetic depiction of Christ's Passion, yet in what sense could the Divine Redeemer say, *Far from my salvation are the words of my sins*? St. Peter provides the answer:

> Because Christ also suffered for us, leaving you an example that you should follow His steps. Who did no sin, neither was guile found in His mouth. . . . *Who His own self bore our sins in His Body upon the tree*: that we, being dead to sins, should live in justice: by Whose stripes you were healed. (1 Pet. 2:21-22,24)

Our Lord's cry *was*, indeed, a cry from the heart, but it testified to the truth that, as God *and* Man, He took upon Himself all the sins of the world, for which he atoned on the Cross. The sinless One "became" sin for our sake, insofar as He took it upon Himself to pay the debt for sin, and we can hear faint premonitions of the cry of Jesus from the Cross in words spoken before His Passion: "I have a baptism wherewith I am to be baptized: and how am I straitened until it be accomplished?" (Lk. 12:50) Throughout His agony on Calvary, Our Lord, Whose "mercy is from generation to generations," thought only of the sinners for whom He suffered, hence His cry.

The final words of the psalm quoted by Jesus turn from His redemptive suffering to its glorious fruits: "There shall be declared to the Lord a generation to come: and the heavens shall shew forth His justice to a people *that shall be born*, which the Lord hath made." (Ps. 21:32) This refers to the Church, the souls redeemed by Christ, who have Mary for their Mother. There is no "birth" – natural or spiritual – without a mother.

The words of Jesus to the Blessed Virgin and the Beloved Disciple – *Woman, behold thy son. . . . Behold thy Mother* – were important enough to be proclaimed during the Passion, from the height of the Cross. St. John recorded his reaction to these words: "And from that hour the disciple took her to his own." Clearly, then, the Catholic doctrine of the Spiritual (or "Universal") Motherhood of Mary can be traced back to Apostolic times, certainly to St. John the Evangelist.

Chapter Nineteen

Mother of the Church

The Church is one body – Pius XII's *Mystici Corporis* – the visible Church – Christ, the Head is entire in each and every living member and entire in the whole body of the Church – Mary labors to form Christ in us – She brings forth the members of His body spriritually and nourishes them as a mother – The Mother of the Church is also a member – Testimony of saints and Scripture – She is the Great Sign of the Apocalypse

Why did Christ leave His Church with a Spiritual Mother? The Holy Ghost would guide the Church throughout the ages. The Vicar of Christ, the Successor of St. Peter, would reign in Christ's stead, protecting the deposit of Faith. The sacraments would nourish souls and restore sanctifying grace, allowing them to continue sharing in the very life of the Blessed Trinity. Why a Spiritual Mother?

The Latin adjective, *"mysticus"*, denotes an intimate communion with God. The Body of Christ, the Church, is a supernatural entity, *grounded in the natural* – i.e., in human beings. It is "mystical" in the sense that its core – the Divine life of God – remains "hidden", as the soul of a human body animates and sustains it invisibly. Just as the complete human person must have his spiritual and visible components in a union of one integral substance, so the Mystical Body of Christ cannot be called a "Body" without its corporeity.

> It is the Spirit of Christ that has made us God's adopted sons, [cf. Rom. 8:14-17; Gal. 4:6-7] that someday "we all beholding the glory of God with open face may be transformed into the same image from glory to glory" [II Cor. 3:18]. Moreover, to this Spirit of Christ *as to no visible principle* is this also to be attributed, that *all parts of the Body are joined to one another as they are with their exalted head;* for He is entire in the head, entire in the Body, entire in the individual members, and with these He is present, and these He assists in various ways, according to their various duties and offices, according to

> the greater or less degree of spiritual health which they enjoy. He is the one who by His heavenly grace is to be held as the principle of every vital and in fact every salutary act in all the parts of any body. (Pope Pius XII, *Mystici Corporis*, 1943)

Unlike the Protestants' fanciful "invisible church of all believers", which is alleged to include various denominations, even conflicting doctrinal interpretations and authority figures, the Catholic Church founded by Jesus Christ, while animated and invigorated by the Spirit of Christ, is meant to exist as a structured, *visible* society, as a Body whose works can be seen and evaluated, a singular entity which can be recognized and approached:

> You are the light of the world. A city that is set on a mountain cannot be hid. Neither do men light a candle and put it under a bushel, but upon a candlestick, that it may shine to all that are in the house. So, let your light shine before men, that they may see your good works, and glorify your Father Who is in heaven. (Mt. 5:14-16)

A person does not spring into existence fully grown, like some pagan deity. There are stages in the formation of a human being: conception, gestation, birth, infancy, growth, maturity. Scripture is quite clear that the growth of the Body of Christ, which is dependent upon the growth of its members, follows the same series of stages. "He that received the seed upon good ground, is he that heareth the word, and understandeth, and beareth fruit, and yieldeth the one a hundred-fold and another sixty, and another thirty." (Mt. 13:23)

The one who hears the Truth is described as one receiving "seed"; this is an image of conception. From then on, each soul will bear fruit according to its kind, some a hundred-fold, some thirty. This is the sense of the words of Pope Pius XII: "He is entire in the Head, entire in the Body, entire in the individual members, and with these He is present, and these He assists in various ways, according to their various duties and offices, *according to the greater or less degree of spiritual health which they enjoy.*"

Christ is "entire in the Head, entire in the Body, entire in the individual members, and with these He is present." Each "member" of the Body, then, must grow in Christ *individually*, as each limb of a natural body must grow in proportion to the others. It does not happen automatically, any more than an infant turns into an adult overnight. "My little children," wrote St. Paul to the Galatians, ". . . of whom I am in labor again, *until Christ be formed in you.*" (4:19)

The relation of a natural mother to her offspring is one *which the mother gives of herself to the child, for the purpose of nurturing the child as it matures.* The mother nurtures, protects, teaches and raises the child – i.e., the mother *loves* the child, and *actively* promotes his welfare. In the womb, this bond exhibits its most radical and mysterious manifestation. The mother "feeds" the child with her very own substance. Her womb is the perfect home for the infant, in every detail; the mother and child live as one. This intimate bond was no less intense between the Infant Jesus and Mary than with any other mother and child. In fact, it was more so, for Jesus, having no earthly father, took *all* his human characteristics from His Mother. "He was known, doubtless, by His likeness to her, to be her Son," observed Cardinal John Henry Newman († 1890).

After the birth of the child, a mother protects him. She is the bridge by which the child enters human society. The Infant Jesus was God in the fullness of His Divinity, omniscient and omnipotent; He was also Man in the fullness of His humanity, suckled by a mother. God had given many valiant women to His people – Rachel, Esther, Judith, Deborah, the mother of the Machabees, etc. Yet, it was not until the Incarnation, until God had taken human nature upon Himself, that the words "Behold thy Mother" were spoken. They were not spoken by God from a pillar of flame, or through the mediation of judges or prophets. They were spoken by God *the Son*, the "Head" of His Body, the Church. This is no coincidence. They were spoken by God, "made of a woman" – by God *born of a Mother*. We are told that we must form one Body with this God "made of a woman". We are told, clearly and succinctly, during the most important event the world will ever know, that this "woman" is to be *our* Mother as well.

God "will have all men to be saved," wrote St. Paul to St. Timothy. The words and works of Jesus, the Son of God and Mary, were all directed to the glory of the Father, and their end was the good of souls: "Now this is the will of the Father Who sent Me: that of all that He hath given Me, I should lose nothing; but should raise it up again in the last day." (Jn. 6:39) Therefore God does not engage in meaningless gestures. If God the Son gave a mother to us, it is so that we may enjoy a *filial* relationship with her. We were not presented on Calvary with a woman who just *happened* to be the Mother of Jesus, given to mankind merely because it is "pleasant" to turn our attention on occasion to some sort of a consoling "maternal principle". We were presented with a woman who IS *our* mother. "Behold *thy* Mother!" The Church, the *Body*, was presented with the *same* Mother who had given birth to the *Head* of the Body.

This means that, by God's own desire and will, our Lady will perform for us the duties of a Mother. This also means that a genuine regard for Mary will consist of affections directed towards a *mother* (and not to a mere symbol). They will satisfy the individual heart, while observing the precepts given to us by God for the honoring of mothers.

How does Mary "mother" the Church? St. Louis de Montfort observed:

> If Jesus Christ, the head of mankind, is born of her, the predestinate, who are members of this head, must also as a necessary consequence be born of her. One and the same mother does not give birth to the head without the members nor to the members without the head, for these would be monsters in the order of nature. In the order of grace likewise the head and the members are born of the same mother. (*True Devotion to the Blessed Virgin*)

Where there is one Body, there is one Mother. Yet, our natural mothers have *already* given birth to us, to our persons. What does it mean to be "born" of the Blessed Virgin? We have the answer from the lips of Jesus. After being told that a man must be "born again" in order to see the kingdom of God, Nicodemus asked, "How can a man be born when he is old? Can he enter a second time into his mother's womb, and be born again?" Jesus replied:

> Amen, amen I say to thee, unless a man be born again of water and the Holy Ghost, he cannot enter into the kingdom of God. That which is born of the flesh, is flesh; *and that which is born of the Spirit, is spirit.* (Jn. 3:5-6)

The birth, *of the Spirit*, of the members of the Church is a supernatural birth. "It is the Spirit of Christ that has made us God's adopted sons," wrote Pope Pius XII, "His heavenly grace is to be held as the principle of every vital and in fact every salutary act in all the parts of any body." The seed planted in Baptism must be watered and tended "until Christ be formed" in individuals, after which they will bear fruit, "one a hundred-fold and another sixty, and another thirty."

It is the work of the Catholic Church – *Mother* Church, as she was called in saner times – to carry, nurture and bear her members, as any mother will do. "Conceived" in Baptism, the soul travels its earthly path, sometimes avoiding, often stumbling into the numerous pitfalls of sin dotting our mortal landscape. The Church raises up her soiled, bruised children in the sacrament of Penance. Throughout the child's life, she instructs and strengthens her offspring. The Holy Sacrifice of the Mass is the most exquisite example of this. At the altar, thanksgiving and worthy praise is rendered to God by sinful men and women, pardon is sought and obtained, and the members of the Church can commune with their Head in that singular union effected through the reception of Holy Communion. The brief prayers of the ancient Mass teach lessons on doctrine worthy of tomes many pages in length. The Church, as Mother, leaves nothing to chance in the education and protection of her own.

The Blessed Virgin is the Mother of the Church, but, as one of the redeemed, she is also a *member* of the Church. How can this be? "Before Abraham was made, I am," (Jn. 8:58) proclaimed Jesus to the Jews. The plan of salvation was set in place, not at the Annunciation or the Crucifixion, but from *before the foundation of the world.*

Therefore, we can recognize a foreshadowing of the sacrament of Baptism in the crossing of the Red Sea by the Israelites, or of the Crucifixion in the story of Abraham's willingness to sacrifice Isaac. We can make these connections because the entire history of the world resonated with the fall of Adam. All of history was, in effect, one vast preparation for the advent of the Savior, and it would have been strange, indeed, if the Old Testament did *not* contain people, objects and events whose significance went beyond the literal, in accord with the words of God recorded in *The Prophecy of Isaias*:

> I am, I am the Lord: and there is no Savior besides me. I have declared, and have saved. I have made it heard, and there was no strange one among you. You are my witnesses, saith the Lord, and I am God. *And from the beginning I am the same*, and there is none that can deliver out of my hand. (Is. 43:11-13)

The Church, present to the Divine Intellect from the Beginning, was to be the Body of the Savior, the Mystical Body of the Crucified One. Her existence presupposes the Incarnation. God, of course, apprehends all events of all times simultaneously: "For thus saith the High and the eminent that inhabiteth eternity." (Is. 57:15) "The measure of Him is longer than the earth, and broader than the sea." (Job 11:9) However, in order to discuss the things of God, the human intellect must apprehend them in a sequential framework. St. Paul wrote:

> Blessed be the God and Father of Our Lord Jesus Christ, Who hath blessed us with spiritual blessings in heavenly places, in Christ: As He chose us in Him before the foundation of the world, that we should be holy and unspotted in His sight in charity. Who hath predestinated us unto the adoption of children through Jesus Christ unto Himself . . . in Whom we have redemption through His Blood, the remission of sins, according to the riches of His grace . . . that He might make known unto us the mystery of His will, according to His good pleasure, which He hath purposed in Him, in the dispensation of the

> fullness of times, *to re-establish all things in Christ, that are in heaven and on earth, in Him.* In Whom we are also called by lot, being predestinated according to the purpose of Him Who worketh all things according to the counsel of His will. (Eph. 1:3-11)

God's mercy would be revealed at "the fullness of times", but souls are "predestinated" unto the adoption of children, chosen in *Christ* "before the foundation of the world". It is through the Catholic Church, a visible "society", that *all* things can be "re-established" in Christ, for such a labor requires unity of purpose, belief, doctrine and law: "The Church of the living God, the pillar and ground of the Truth." (1 Tim. 3:15) "*One body and one Spirit* . . . One Lord, one faith, one baptism." (Eph. 4:4-5)

From the Beginning, the sacrifice on Calvary was the means ordained for the Redemption, and the existence of the Church presupposes the *Crucified* Savior: "In Him, we have redemption *through His Blood*, the remission of sins." (Col. 1:14) The condition whereby GOD can *be* crucified, in the supreme sacrifice of which the earlier animal holocausts of Israel were but pale foreshadowings, presupposes the Incarnation: "sacrifice and oblation Thou wouldst not: but a body Thou hast fitted to Me." (Heb. 10:5) The Incarnation presupposes a *Mother*: "When the fullness of the time was come, God sent His Son, *made of a* woman . . . and she brought forth her first-born Son, and wrapped Him up in swaddling clothes."

The Catholic Church, then, presupposes the Blessed Virgin Mary, the Divine Maternity which clothed the Redeemer in the flesh that was to serve as the vehicle for the restoration of mankind to friendship with God and the life of the Blessed Trinity (the life of grace). Therefore, it is not strange that Our Lady should be both Mother *and* member of the Church. In a sense, when she gave us Jesus, she gave us the Church, for "He is entire in the Head, entire in the Body, entire in the individual members, and with these He is present." Of course, she was also *redeemed* by Jesus.

In the *Apocalypse*, St. John, the Beloved Disciple who took Mary "to his own", wrote of the *Great Sign*:

> And the temple of God was opened in heaven: and the ark of His testament was seen in His temple, and there were lightnings, and voices, and an earthquake, and great hail. And a great sign appeared in heaven: a Woman clothed with the sun, and the moon under her feet, and on her head a crown of twelve stars: And being with Child, she cried travailing in birth, and was in pain to be delivered. (Apoc. 11:19;12:1-2)

This woman represents the Catholic Church:

> The Church is clothed with the sun, that is, with Christ: she hath the moon, that is, the changeable things of the world, under her feet; and the twelve stars with which she is crowned, are the twelve apostles: she is in labor and pain, whilst she brings forth her children, *and Christ in them*, in the midst of afflictions and persecutions. (*The Haydock Bible*, footnote to *The Apocalypse of St. John*)

However, it is impossible to gain a comprehensive understanding of this "Woman" if we stop at the ecclesial dimension. The *Great Sign* of the Apocalyptic vision is also the Blessed Virgin Mary. St. John wrote that the Woman "brought forth a man child, who was to rule all nations *with an iron rod*". (Apoc. 12:5) In the Psalms, we read the following, which is fulfilled in Christ:

> The Lord hath said to me: Thou art my Son, this day have I begotten Thee. Ask of me, and I will give Thee the Gentiles for Thy inheritance, and the utmost parts of the earth for Thy possession. Thou shalt rule them *with a rod of iron*. (Ps. 2:7-9)

While the "child" brought forth by the "Woman clothed with the Sun" represents the Church, which will rule the world as a shepherd over its flock, Christ is also indicated here, for the One "begotten" by the Lord to rule over the entire earth is a *Messianic* image:

> "Behold the days come," saith the Lord, "and I will raise up to David a just branch: *and a king shall reign*, and

> shall be wise: *and shall execute judgment and justice in the earth."* (Jer. 23:5) He shall be great, and shall be called the Son of the most High; and the Lord God shall give unto Him the throne of David His father; and He shall reign in the house of Jacob forever. (Lk. 1:32)

Because Mary's Divine Maternity *precedes* the Church, we may conclude that the "Woman crowned with twelve stars" is *principally* the Virgin. St. John has recorded a potent "dual" image, in which are superimposed the Birth of Christ *and* the "birth" of the Spirit of Christ in *individual members of the Church*. Since the members are called to form one Body with Jesus, the Head, these two images are resolved in one "Woman". Our Lord had *one* Mother; Mary. Our Lady had only one *natural* Son: Jesus. Yet, this one Son, the very principle of the Church, will be "formed" over and over again in the souls of individuals. This formation takes on the characteristics of "birth", albeit of a *spiritual* nature: "Amen, amen I say to thee, unless a man be *born* again, He cannot see the kingdom of God." (Jn. 3:3)

Common usage often refers to metaphorical births – the "birth" of an idea, or the "birth" of a nation, etc. Our Lord did not speak symbolically, for He specifically mentioned "water and the Holy Ghost", when He spoke to Nicodemus. Whatever is truly *born*, is born from a *Mother*: "Honor thy father, and forget not the groanings of thy mother: Remember that thou hadst not been born but through them." The children of the Roman Catholic Church, the Bride of Christ, are "born" of her – they literally enter into new *life* (the life of grace) through her.

The Blessed Virgin formed the members of Christ's *human* Body; the Church forms members of His Mystical Body. The Catholic Church, then, in effect, recapitulates spiritually what Mary did physically:

> Holy Mother Church received you in her womb by the most sacred sign of the Cross, even as she received the brethren before you. She gives birth to you, the children-to-be, through the sacred waters of regeneration . . . Mother Church loosens the bond of death brought upon the children of disobedience. By her obedience, this Mother is a channel of love and Life. All the sacramental rites now

> preparing you for Baptism, the prayers and the canticles, the exorcisms and the penances, the humble garments and the prostrations, all of these prepare you for presentation to Christ, happily reborn of Holy Mother Church. In the Apocalypse of St. John the Apostle, we read that the dragon stood by the woman as she gave birth, ready to pounce upon her child. The dragon, of course, is the devil. The woman is the Virgin Mary, who, preserving her own virginal integrity, gave birth to the Virgin Head of the Church. In this, Mary symbolizes the Church. She, a virgin, brought forth a Son. Holy Mother Church, herself a virgin, constantly brings forth children, also remaining a virgin. (St. Augustine, *Treatise on the Creed for the Catechumens*)

In the Psalms, the Church is prefigured under the image of *Sion*, and the words used to describe her apply in full measure to Our Blessed Mother as well: "Shall not Sion say: This man and that man is born in her? And the Highest Himself hath founded her." (Ps. 86:5) The words of St. Augustine read like a commentary on this inspired text.

The Woman of the Apocalyptic vision "cried travailing in birth, and was in pain to be delivered." This detail is an arrow pointing to the Virgin Mary. Catholics hold that the Mother of God experienced no birth pangs at the Nativity of Jesus. Such pangs, inflicted upon Eve after the fall, were "reminders" of original sin to all generations, and it would be perverse to suggest that the joyful Birth of the Savior – "Him Who taketh away the sins of the world" – was nothing more than yet another instance in which mankind was to be reminded of original sin.

In addition, the *virginitas in partu* – the virginity *during* childbirth – of the Blessed Virgin has been taught throughout history in tandem with the Perpetual Virginity. The Lateran Council (649), for example, taught that Mary bore Jesus "incorruptibly". The Council of Trent taught that she persisted "in the integrity of virginity, namely, before bringing forth, *at bringing forth*, and always after bringing forth." (Pope Paul IV, *Cum quorundam*, 1555) St. Ephrem of Syria addressed Our Lady with these words: "Who loves you is amazed . . . the Virgin became a Mother while preserving her virginity."

How, then, can Mary be the Woman "travailing in birth" and "in pain to be delivered"? On Calvary, "there stood by the Cross of Jesus, His Mother." (Jn. 19:25) The Woman chosen *from before the foundation of the world* to be the Mother of Jesus, and endowed with a fitting plenitude of grace, stood by her Son. The Woman who initiated the glorious Redemption of mankind with her freely-given *fiat* to the Angel Gabriel, stood beneath the Cross. The Woman whose intercession occasioned our Lord's first public miracle at Cana was present when the Redeemer's work was "consummated".

Our Lady of Sorrows was present on Calvary because she was the natural Mother of Jesus, because she loved Him with every ounce of her being; she wanted to be with Him, and she knew that her face would be a beacon for Him in a sea of madness and obscenity. She was also present on Calvary as the Mother of the Church, and the "pangs" spared her during the birth of the Divine Infant would manifest themselves at the death of the Savior, *at the generation of His spiritual brethren*, when the radiant, serene Mother who knelt by the manger would stand in sorrow as the Queen of Martyrs.

Our Lord left His Church on earth, a Church He won for Himself by His Passion and death on the Cross: "Christ also loved the Church, *and delivered Himself up for it*: that He might sanctify it, cleansing it by the laver of water in the word of life: That He might present it to Himself a glorious Church, not having spot or wrinkle." (Eph. 5:25-27) He left this Church with a Mother: *Behold thy Mother.*

Of what character is the love of Mary for the Church, that she would undergo such horrible pangs, "travailing" in the birth of her spiritual sons and daughters? *Forget not the groanings of thy mother*, admonishes the Scriptures, and remember always that you would not be born but for her. Our Lady can rightfully speak of her "labor pains", but these are pains that wounded her beyond the physical level, and which were prophesied by Simeon in the Temple: "And thy own soul a sword shall pierce." (Lk. 2:35)

It was not until after the fall that Adam gave his wife the name, Eve, "because she was the mother of all the living." (Gen. 3:20) He had listened to the *Proto-evangelium*, spoken by God to the serpent. In the midst of his shame, and the expectation of death, Adam heard the prophecy of redemption promised to his descendants, the crushing of the head of the enemy who had plotted his ruin. St. Epiphanius called Mary the one "who raised up Eve and returned the exiled Adam to Paradise."

If Eve, the ancestor of our Lady, was called "the mother of all the living", how much more does that title belong to the Mother of God?

> Therefore, O Eve, hasten to Mary. O mother, hasten to your daughter. The daughter will answer for the mother, will take away the cloud. She satisfies for both the father and the mother. Man fell once, through a woman; now he is raised up through a woman. (St. Bernard, *Second Homily on the Missus Est*)

Chapter Twenty

Our Mother Mary

ROSA MYSTICA – OLD TESTAMENT MARIAN TEXTS – MEDIATRIX OF ALL GRACES – PRIESTHOOD OF CHRIST – SUBORDINIATE MEDIATORS – MARY IS OUR MOTHER IN THE ORDER OF GRACE – THE MEMBERS OF THE CHURCH ARE "THE REST OF HER SEED" – POEM BY FR. G. MANLEY HOPKINS

The Spiritual Motherhood of Mary is an *actual* Motherhood. In her Litany, she is called the *Rosa Mystica*, the "Mystical Rose". This intriguing title encompasses many facets of the "Mystery" of Mary. Chosen to bear God-made-Man, she was *hidden* in the bosom of the Blessed Trinity from *before the foundation of the world*: "The Lord possessed me in the beginning of His ways, before He made anything from the beginning. I was set up from eternity, and of old before the earth was made." (Prov. 8:22-23) For nine months, Jesus rested in her immaculate womb, and the two shared a *hidden* concourse undreamed of by their neighbors, and suspected only by St. Joseph and St. Elizabeth: "He that made me, rested in my tabernacle." (Ecclus. 24:12) After her glorious Assumption, she entered into an inheritance and glory whose full splendor remains *hidden* to earthbound creatures: "I dwelt in the highest places, and my throne is in a pillar of a cloud." (Ecclus. 24:7)

Our Lady has been granted the authority and means necessary to enable her to stand in a maternal relationship to the entire Church. The role of this Church is to call souls to her, and then restore, fortify and preserve the life of grace in them. It is a theological certainty (as taught by St. John through his Apocalyptic vision of the *Great Sign*) that the maternities of Mary and the Church are mirror images of one another. Therefore, the most powerful expression of Mary's maternal solicitude for sinful men is her role of *Mediatrix of All Graces*. There is a general confusion, particularly among non-Catholics, regarding the nature of mediation and its relation to the unique, salvific role of Jesus Christ. There are two facets to "mediation". On the one hand, the *intermediary*, the "mediator", works with opposing sides in order to resolve a dispute or effect a settlement; *mediation* can also involve the bringing about, influencing, or transmitting (as a physical process or effect) by acting as an intermediate or controlling agent or mechanism. The first aspect focuses on the PERSON of the mediator, one who must be able to represent properly *both sides* in a conflict. In a fable involving a dispute between wolves and sheep, we would not expect a wolf to be a proper "mediator" for both sides of the conflict. The second aspect focuses on the WORK of the mediator, as an intermediary who labors to bring about a desirable end, or transmit, as a physical process or effect, by *acting as a controlling agent*.

Our Lord is, as St. Paul wrote, the ". . . one mediator of God and men", (1 Tim. 2:5) and this applies to both definitions of the term. Being both True God *and* True Man, He was the only *Person* Who could properly intercede between God and humanity. He was the One Mediator, because God in His Divinity could not die for mankind, and a man in his mortality could never offer up a sacrifice of infinite merit; and so, "God indeed was in Christ, reconciling the world to Himself." (2 Cor. 5:19) However the present tense must also be used in this connection, for Jesus is, still and always, the One Mediator between God and men:

> And therefore He is the mediator of the new testament: that by means of His death, for the redemption of those transgressions which were under the former testament, they that are called may receive the promise of eternal inheritance. (Heb. 9:15) We have such an high priest, Who is set on the right hand of the throne of majesty in the heavens, a minister of the holies . . . For every high priest is appointed to offer gifts and sacrifices: wherefore it is necessary that He also should have something to offer. (Heb. 8:1-3)

Our Lord in His glory is called our "High Priest". It is the duty of a priest to offer sacrifice: *For every high priest is appointed to offer gifts and sacrifices.* Jesus offered Himself on the Cross and, as a result, He had "something to offer" the Father on behalf of mankind – the infinite merits and satisfaction of His Passion and death. The Scriptures also teach that we *have* a High Priest in heaven, that the priesthood of Jesus did not cease when He entered the true "Holy of Holies". Therefore, He still intercedes *as High Priest*:

> He, therefore, Our God and Lord, though He was about to offer Himself once to God the Father upon the altar of the Cross by the mediation of death, so that He might accomplish an eternal redemption for them, nevertheless, *that His sacerdotal office might not come to an end with His death*, at the Last Supper on the night he was betrayed, so that He might leave to His beloved spouse the Church a visible sacrifice (as the nature of man demands), whereby that bloody sacrifice once to be completed on the Cross might be re-presented and the memory of it remain even to the end of the world *and its saving grace be applied to the remission of those sins which we daily commit*, declaring Himself constituted "a priest forever according to the order of Melchisedech", offered to God the Father His own body and blood under the species of bread and wine, and under the symbols of those same things gave to the apostles (whom He then constituted priests of the New Testament), so that they might partake, and He commanded them and their successors in the priesthood in these words to make offering: "Do this in commemoration of me, etc.," as the Catholic Church has always understood and taught. (*The Council of Trent*, Sess. XXII, 1562)

The ordained priesthood is a participation in the priesthood of Jesus: *We have such an high priest, Who is set on the right hand of the throne of majesty in the heavens, a minister of the holies*. Each time the Holy Sacrifice of the Mass is celebrated, our Lord intercedes for the world as High Priest, acting through His human instruments: "Christ as Redeemer has acquired the Church by His Blood, and as Priest has offered and *continues* to offer Himself as a victim for our sins." (Pope Pius XI, *Quas primas*, 1925)

As True God *and* True Man, Jesus Christ alone could be the One Mediator between God and men. His humanity made Him one of us by *nature*; it allowed Him to be the Saving Victim: "He hath reconciled *in the body of His flesh* through death, to present you holy and unspotted, and blameless before Him." (Col. 1:22) His Divinity raised that nature from death to life: "The first man Adam was made into a living soul: the last Adam into a *quickening* spirit." (1 Cor. 15:45)

No saint or angel – not our Blessed Mother herself – could "create" or be the source of grace, of divine life. Jesus Christ, consubstantial with the Father and the Holy Ghost, is the *quickening spirit*, the meritorious Cause of grace: "Who hath predestinated us unto the adoption of children through Jesus Christ unto Himself . . . In Whom we have redemption through His Blood, the remission of sins, according to the riches of His grace." (Eph. 1:5,7)

The singular and principal mediatorship of the Incarnate Word is an obvious fact. The sacrifice of Jesus on Calvary was sufficient for all souls; past, present and to come. Each and every grace administered to individuals comes from that Treasury of Graces won by Christ: "And of His fullness we all have received, and grace for grace." (Jn. 1:16) "For if by one man's offense, death reigned through one; much more they who receive abundance of grace, and of the gift, and of justice, shall reign in life through one, Jesus Christ." (Rom. 5:17) The "superabundant" sacrifice on Calvary effected a never-to-be-duplicated act of mediation which requires nothing to complete or augment its efficacy or scope: "Christ was offered once to exhaust the sins of many." (Heb. 9:28) In the *Sequence* from the Mass for Easter Sunday, Jesus is described as the "Lamb unstained, unmeasured price hath paid."

St. Thomas Aquinas wrote: "There is no reason why certain others should not be called in a certain way mediators between God and Man, that is to say, in so far as they cooperate by predisposing and ministering in the union of man with God." In *The Epistle to the Hebrews*, the holy angels are described as "ministering spirits, sent to minister for them who shall receive the inheritance of salvation." (Heb. 1:14) We read in *The Gospel According to St. Matthew*: "And having called His twelve disciples together, He gave them power over unclean spirits, to cast them out, and to heal all manner of diseases, and all manner of infirmities, . . ." (Mt. 10:1) These words describe an active ministry, founded on the authority of Christ: "He *gave* them power."

The existence of "subordinate mediators", who are placed between Christ and mankind, is a simple fact of life: "He that receiveth you, receiveth me, and he that receiveth Me, receiveth Him that sent Me." (Mt. 10:40) A sick man or woman healed by St. Peter or St. John was healed by *Christ* through the mediation of His disciples. In *The Acts of the Apostles*, St. Peter healed a lame man with the words: "What I have, I give thee: *In the name of Jesus Christ* of Nazareth, arise, and walk." (Acts 3:6) To this day, Catholics hear similar words in Confession: "I absolve you in the name of the Father, and of the Son, and of the Holy Ghost." These life-restoring words are uttered for the simple reason that Christ said to His first priests: "Receive ye the Holy Ghost. Whose sins you shall forgive, they are forgiven them; and whose sins you shall retain, they are retained." (Jn. 20:22-23)

Jesus told His priests that whose sins *you* shall forgive are forgiven, that they are to dispense grace, to mediate, upon their own cognizance. Because the subordinate mediation of the apostles was founded upon the One Mediation of Christ, they were entitled and expected to act with authority. "What I have, *I* give thee," said St. Peter. "Whose sins *you* shall forgive, they are forgiven them," said our Lord. "I absolve you," says priest to penitent.

The ministry of apostles and priests is the ministry of the Church: "I baptize thee in the name of the Father, and of the Son, and of the Holy Ghost." The first Vicar of Christ heard the words, "Thou art Peter; and upon this rock I will build my Church . . . And I will give to *thee* the keys of the kingdom of heaven." (Mt. 16:18-19) This Church is to have ". . . one body and one spirit." (Eph. 4:4) "You are all one in Christ Jesus." (Gal. 3:28)

In *The Book of Exodus*, the Lord said to Moses: "Israel is My *son*, My first-born. . . . Go in to Pharaoh, and thou shalt say to him: . . . Let My *people* go to sacrifice to Me." (Ex. 4:22; 8:1) However, before his conversion, St. Paul (then known as Saul), a persecutor of the Church, heard Jesus say to him, "Why persecutest thou *Me*?" (Act. 9:4) Our Lord did not ask why Saul persecuted His "people", or His "sons", but why *He*, Jesus Christ, was being persecuted. This radical change in the relationship between God and His children was initiated in the womb of the Blessed Virgin, where the Eternal One took to Himself the very nature of His creatures.

If the members of the Church are truly *one* body and spirit . . . one Body with Jesus as Head . . . one Body quickened by the Spirit of Christ . . . then, of course, all acts of mediation performed for the good of the Church and its individual members will be a *sharing* in the One Mediation of Jesus, "For we, being many, are one bread, one body." (1 Cor. 10:17) As the supreme "controlling agent" who brings about, influences or transmits, our Lord has chosen to employ subordinate mediators, "agents" who act by His authority: "All power is given to *Me* in heaven and in earth. Going, therefore, teach ye all nations; baptizing them in the name of the Father, and of the Son, and of the Holy Ghost." (Mt. 28:18-19) Before His Ascension into heaven, Jesus said to His apostles, "You shall receive the power of the Holy Ghost coming upon you, and you shall be witnesses unto Me in Jerusalem, and in all Judea, and Samaria, and even to the uttermost parts of the earth." (Acts. 1:8) This promise was fulfilled on Pentecost. After the Descent of the Holy Ghost, St. Peter delivered his moving sermon to the crowds in Jerusalem, after which many souls were converted and baptized.

It is recorded that these early converts "were persevering in the doctrine of the apostles, and in the communication of the breaking of bread, and in prayers." (Acts 2:42) The term "breaking of bread" is used in the Scriptures to indicate the celebration of Holy Mass: "The chalice of benediction which we bless, is it not the communion of the Blood of Christ? And the bread which we break, is it not the partaking of the Body of the Lord?" (1 Cor. 10:16) "I am the living bread which came down from heaven. If any man eat of this bread, he shall live for ever; and the bread that I will give is my Flesh, for the life of the world." (Jn. 6:51-52)

Those first converts, then, began living as *Catholics*, learning the doctrines of the True Faith and assisting at the Holy Sacrifice of the Mass. "Do this for a commemoration of me," said our Lord to His first priests. Participating in the sacerdotal ministry of the supreme High Priest, Jesus Christ, the apostles, in the offering of the Mass and administration of the sacraments, were sharing in the *mediatorship* of the One Mediator: "Let a man so account of us as the ministers of Christ, *and the dispensers of the mysteries of God".* (1 Cor. 4:1) "We are God's coadjutors: you are God's husbandry; you are God's building." (1 Cor. 3:9)

The apostles and their spiritual descendants are the dispensers of the mysteries of God – by their preaching, guidance and administration of the sacraments. The Blessed Virgin was not ordained a *minister* (i.e. priest) of her Son's Church. She was made the *Mother* of His Church. To appreciate the singular manner in which the mediation of Mary participates in that of Jesus, and how it differs in quality and kind from that of all others, we need only ponder the words of St. John Damascene: "There is an infinite difference between the Mother of God and the servants of God."

A mother provides for *all* the needs of her child. She does not say, "I will feed my son, but not clothe him," or "I will clothe my daughter, but not educate her." On the contrary, the mother is all things to her children, a dispenser of whatever mercies, kindness, assistance, nourishment and chastisements are needed to raise and protect the child.

Jesus decreed that the Blessed Virgin Mary would be the *Mother of His Church*. This motherhood is *not* intended to be a merely symbolic one, for the works of God on behalf of mankind are directed towards a definite, concrete end, *salvation*: "For the Son of Man is come to seek, and to save that which was lost." (Lk. 19:10) If Christ made Mary the Mother of His Church, He did so for the *good* of the Church. She is, therefore, an *active* mother, taking an active role in the salvation of each and every Catholic soul. She is the "Mediatrix of *All* Graces" because God has ordained that she "mother" the entire Church, and a mother supplies *all* beneficial things to her offspring. "To every one of us is given grace, according to the measure of the gift of Christ," (Eph. 4:7) taught St. Paul. Mary was indeed *Full of Grace*, having already received at her Immaculate Conception "the abundance of all heavenly gifts poured from the treasury of His divinity." (Pope Pius IX)

When Jesus rested in His Mother's womb, He derived all His bodily sustenance from her. She generated His human body, sustained it and nourished it. As man, an Infant in the womb, Christ deigned to be completely dependent upon His Mother, and He did *not* consider this dependence in any way demeaning: "Who being in the form of God, *thought it not robbery* to be Himself equal to God: But emptied Himself, taking the form of a servant, being made to the likeness of men, and in habit found as a man." (Phil. 2:6)

Can a man "enter a second time into his mother's womb, and be born again," asked Nicodemus. Such a reversal of nature need not accompany a *spiritual* rebirth, through which the members of the Church come into their "inheritance" as joint-heirs with Christ: "But as many as received Him, He gave to them power to be made the *sons* of God. . . . Who are born, *not of blood, nor of the will of the flesh*, nor of the will of man, but of God." (Jn. 1:12-13) Our Lady was not chosen by God to be the *natural* mother of all the members of the Church, but to be their *supernatural* Mother, a Mother *in the order of grace*:

> This earthly existence is not, however, all of life. . . . The life which does not die is the supernatural life, the life *of grace*. Mary has been given to us for a model and for a mother in this new life *added to* the earthly life. (*The Imitation of Mary*)

A natural maternity results in a physical birth. A maternity in *the order of grace* results in a spiritual birth: "I am in labor again, until Christ be formed in you." Our natural mothers gave birth to our bodies, who are united to immortal souls created by God – i.e., to our complete *persons*, unified beings. Our Blessed Mother, who gave birth to the Head of the Mystical Body, gives birth also to the "members" of this Body, united to the Head, and to each other, by the "Spirit of Christ" – again, a unified "being". Mary labors with all her heart to "form" Christ in "the rest of her seed". This is the sense of the insightful verses of Fr. Gerard Manley Hopkins (d. 1889):

If I have understood,
She holds high motherhood
Toward all our ghostly good
And plays in grace her part

About man's beating heart,
Laying, like air's fine flood,
The death dance in his blood;
Yet no part but what will
Be Christ our saviour still.
Of her flesh he took flesh:
He does take fresh and fresh,
Though much the mystery how,
Not flesh but spirit now
And makes, O marvellous!
New Nazareths in us,
Where she shall yet conceive
Him, morning, noon, and eve;
New Bethlehems, and he born
There, evening, noon and morn –
Bethlehem or Nazareth,
Men here may draw like breath
More Christ and baffle death;
Who, born so, comes to be
New self and nobler me
In each one and each one
More makes, when all is done,
Both God's and Mary's Son.

(The Blessed Virgin Compared to the Air We Breathe)

Chapter Twenty-One

Grace and Baptism

More on Mediatrix of all Graces – Actual and sanctifying grace – Baptism – The indelible character – Our Lady's baptism

It would have been a peculiar thing, had Jesus directed us to Mary as to a mother, and then left her deficient in her ability to fulfill this maternal role. *To every one of us is given grace, according to the measure of the gift of Christ*; therefore, we *can* go to the Blessed Virgin as to a mother precisely because her Son has made her the Mediatrix of *All* Graces. The Mother of the Church possesses the heart, the charity, the wisdom and the power to rear her children and protect them.

The words of the Savior from the Cross – "Behold thy Mother" – keep these doctrinal teachings fully grounded in Mary's Spiritual Maternity. Jesus fulfilled the requirements for both definitions of the word *Mediator*. As *intermediary*, he effected a "settlement" between two parties, God and man. As the *controlling agent*, He brings about an effect – i.e., sanctification, distribution of the graces He merited on Calvary – through His Church and the subordinate mediation of individuals.

Because of *who* she is, and *what* she is, the mediation of the Blessed Virgin is in a class of its own:

> When we have recourse to Mary in prayer, we are having recourse to the Mother of mercy, who is so well disposed toward us that, whatever the necessity that presses upon us, especially in attaining eternal life, she is instantly at our side of her own accord, even though she has not been invoked. She dispenses grace with a generous hand from that treasure with which from the beginning she was divinely endowed in fullest abundance that she might be worthy to be the Mother of God. By the fullness of grace

> which confers on her the most illustrious of her many titles, the Blessed Virgin is infinitely superior to all the hierarchies of men and angels, the creature who is closest to Christ. "It is a great thing in any saint to have grace sufficient for the salvation of many souls; but to have enough to suffice for the salvation of everybody in the world is the greatest of all; and this is found in Christ and in the Blessed Virgin."[(St. Thomas Aquinas) (Pope Leo XIII, *Magnam Dei Matris*, 1892)

Sufficient grace for the salvation of all mankind is found "in Christ and in the Blessed Virgin", wrote St. Thomas in the words quoted by Pope Leo. The distinction is made carefully – in *Christ* "and" in Mary. Christ is the Source of grace, the meritorious Cause of grace. On Calvary, He won an abyss of graces for His Church, "in Whom we have redemption through His Blood, the remission of sins, according to the riches of His grace, Which hath superabounded in us." (Eph. 1:7-8)

Although the Redeemer's sacrifice was *superabundant*, and even one drop of the Precious Blood could have redeemed countless worlds, yet "not all receive the benefit of His death, but those only to whom the merit of His passion is communicated." (Council of Trent, *Decree on Justification*, 1547) The storehouse of grace merited by Christ is there always, bursting with its treasure, but it is one which, like all treasures, *must be distributed* to be of any practical benefit. It remains, then, for this treasury of Grace to be distributed to individuals: "For by grace you are saved through faith, and that not of yourselves, for it is the gift of God." (Eph. 2:8) The *Prayer* from the Mass for Easter Sunday highlights this distinction between the "objective redemption" (the sacrifice of Christ which atoned for *all* sin) and the "subjective redemption" (by which the merits of this sacrifice are dispensed to *individuals*): "O God, Who, this day by Thine only-begotten Son, vanquishing death, hast *unlocked for us* the gates of eternity, help us *to attain* the desires to which Thou hast led us by Thine inspiration."

The distribution of graces to the Mystical Body is analogous to the life-sustaining nourishment provided by a natural mother:

> If then the Most Blessed Virgin is the Mother at once of God and men, who can doubt that she will endeavor with all diligence to bring it about that Christ, "the head of the body, the Church," will transfuse His gifts into us, His members, and above all help us know Him and "live by Him". . . . When the supreme hour of the Son came, beside the Cross of Jesus there stood Mary, His Mother, not merely occupied in contemplating the cruel spectacle, but rejoicing that her only Son was offered for the salvation of mankind; and so entirely participating in His Passion that, if it had been possible "she would have gladly borne all the torments that her Son underwent." (St. Bonaventure) From this community of will and suffering between Christ and Mary "she merited to become most worthily the reparatrix of the lost world" (Eadmer) and dispensatrix of all the gifts that Our Savior purchased for us by His death and by His Blood. (Pope St. Pius X, *Ad diem illum laetissimum*, 1904)

For the Motherhood proclaimed by Christ on Calvary to be a true "motherhood", it must exhibit the hallmarks of motherhood – i.e., there must be a bond uniting Mother and children in which the mother sustains the offspring. In the natural order, this sustenance is of a bodily nature (complemented, of course, by a unique emotional and spiritual bond). In the supernatural order, the *order of grace*, this sustenance is the "life of grace", a sharing in the Divine life of the Blessed Trinity. Since superabundant graces were obtained for mankind by the Passion and death of Jesus, then what remains is the *distribution* of these graces. As the *intermediary* or "controlling agent" who brings about or transmits an effect, our Lord, the One Mediator, desires that the Blessed Virgin, proclaimed "Universal Mother" from the Cross, have a unique role in this distribution – a *maternal* role. This Spiritual Maternity comes to the fore in her role of *Mediatrix of All Graces*.

Men and women are dependent upon grace, not only for sanctification, but even for the very *desire* to seek God, to approach Him and, hopefully, submit to Him. Human beings are free beings. While our souls, created by God, are "oriented" towards Him, we are endowed with will and reason, which allow us to respond to or reject this innate "attraction" to our Creator.

Actual Grace is the "predisposing grace", a supernatural assistance given to individuals when, "aroused and assisted by divine grace, receiving faith 'by hearing', they are freely moved towards God, believing that to be true which has been divinely revealed and promised." (Council of Trent, Sess. VI, 1547) *Sanctifying Grace* is distinct from *Actual Grace*. Through it, "the guilt of original sin is remitted." (Council of Trent, Sess. V, 1546) It is conferred in Baptism, increased through the reception of the sacraments, and can be regained through the sacrament of Penance.

Pope St. Pius V outlined the distinction between these two manifestations of grace, "that distinction of a *twofold* vivification, the one, by which a sinner is vivified, when the resolution to penance and the beginning of a new life through the grace of God inspire him; the other, by which he is vivified who is truly justified and is made a living branch on the vine for Christ." (*Ex omnibus afflictionibus*, 1567) This distinction is taught in Scripture: "For it is God who worketh in you, both to will and to accomplish." (Phil. 2:13) "No man can come to Me, except the Father, Who hath sent Me, draw him." (Jn. 6:44) "According to His mercy, He saved us, by the laver of regeneration, and renovation of the Holy Ghost." (Titus 3:5)

Our Lord ". . . will have all men to be saved, and to come to the knowledge of the truth." (1 Tim. 2:4) God desires the instruction and salvation of souls. In order to bring this instruction and salvation to the billions of souls who would inhabit the earth throughout the ages after His Ascension into heaven, Jesus established His Church, leaving behind His own Mystical "Body" for all the world to see and approach. His love for this Church is described as that between a Groom and His Bride, a Bride which He "won" to Himself by His conquest over the "empire of death":

> Husbands, love your wives, as Christ also loved the Church, and delivered Himself up for it: That He might sanctify it, cleansing it by the laver of water in the word of life: That He

> might present it to Himself a glorious Church, not having spot or wrinkle, nor any such thing; but that it should be holy, and without blemish. (Eph. 5:25-27) Can the children of the bridegroom mourn, as long as the bridegroom is with them? But the days will come, when the bridegroom shall be taken away from them, and then they shall fast. (Mt. 9:15) Let us be glad and rejoice and give glory to Him; for the marriage of the Lamb is come, and His wife hath prepared herself. (Apoc. 19:7) And I, John, saw the holy city, the new Jerusalem, coming down from God out of heaven, prepared as a bride adorned for her husband. (Apoc. 21:2)

The Lamb and His Bride will celebrate their final nuptials one day, when all the redeemed will have joined their Savior in heaven, to spend eternity in His loving Presence. But, like a true marriage, this one began with a "betrothal", contracted at the Annunciation, when human and divine natures were joined in the holiest of bonds in the blessed womb of Mary. "Gabriel has been sent," wrote St. Gregory Thaumaturgus (†c. 275), "to contract the espousals between heaven and earth."

The sanctification of souls, the sacramental life of the True Church, friendship with God and a sharing in the divine life of the Trinity – all these things flow from Calvary, where the Groom "delivered Himself up" for His Bride. The Treasury of Grace, that superabundance of grace won by Christ and put into the keeping of the Catholic Church, is not merely a symbol for God's "favor". Someone "in a state of grace" is someone of good will who has been an actual *recipient* of grace, and is strengthened, enlightened, sanctified as a result.

Martin Luther taught that "the nature of man is so corrupted that it can *never* be regenerated. . . . God's all-powerful grace does *not* cleanse from sin," that God merely covers over, as with a blanket, men's sins, which still and always remain. This directly contradicts St. Paul's inspired teaching that Christ died for His Church "that He might sanctify it, cleansing it by the laver of water . . . that He might present it to Himself a glorious Church . . . holy, and without blemish." It also questions the integrity of God by denying the words of the *Apocalypse*, where Our Lord announces, "Behold, I make all things new," and His faithful are described as "a holy city . . . a bride adorned for her husband . . . there shall not enter into it any thing defiled."

In its reply to the perverse errors of Luther, the Council of Trent decreed, among others, the following canon:

> If anyone shall say that he who has fallen after baptism cannot by the grace of God rise again; or that he can indeed recover lost justice, but by faith alone without the sacrament of penance, contrary to what the Holy Roman and universal Church, taught by Christ the Lord and His apostles, has hitherto professed, observed, and taught: let him be anathema. (*Canons on Justification*, Sess. VI, 1547)

The sacrament of Baptism *does* remit original sin and actual guilt, though concupiscence, which does not of itself constitute sin, remains. St. Augustine, referring to the Baptism of Jesus in the Jordan River, wrote: "The Lord is baptized, not because He had need to be cleansed, but in order that, by the contact of His pure flesh, He might purify the waters and impart to them the power of cleansing." Moreover, sins can be remitted, and grace restored, through the sacrament of Penance:

> For each one has good reason to distrust the accuracy of his own judgment on his actions, and hence we could not but be very much in doubt regarding the truth of our internal penance. It was to destroy this, our uneasiness, that Our Lord instituted the sacrament of Penance, by means of which we are assured that our sins are pardoned by the absolution of the priest; and also to tranquilize our conscience by means of the trust we rightly repose in the virtue of the sacraments. (*The Catechism of the Council of Trent*)

Through the administration of sacramental absolution, the graces merited by Christ on Calvary flow generously to the members of the Church, the "members" of His own Mystical Body: "A contrite and humbled heart, O God, Thou wilt not despise." (Ps. 50:19) The grace bestowed in Baptism, and restored in the sacrament of Penance, presupposes other graces – the ones which lead the convert to the True Church and the waters of life, which invite parents to bring their infants to the Baptismal font, which lead the penitent to the confessional or the indifferent heart to desire once again the Blessed Sacrament.

Baptism is the "corridor through the Red Sea", through which each and every soul must pass in order to escape death and enter into Life. By making the soul a member of the Church – by *incorporating* it into the Body of Christ – Baptism marks the individual as belonging to Christ. This mark is an *indelible* one; it imprints the soul. St. Cyril of Jerusalem (†386) called it "the wondrous and salvific seal, at which demons tremble and which angels recognize," while St. Methodius of Philippi (†c. 311) wrote of those who have been baptized, "the likeness of the form of the Word is stamped upon them."

This indelible mark, conferred only by the reception of the regenerating waters of Baptism, stamps the baptized individual as a member of the Catholic Church:

> As the human body consists of many members, animated by one soul, which gives sight to the eyes, hearing to the ears, and to the other senses the power of discharging their respective functions; so the mystical body of Christ, which is the Church, is composed of many faithful . . . and Baptism, which is the seal of our Christian faith, is also one. (*The Catechism of the Council of Trent*)

The intimate connection between Baptism and actual, physical *membership* in the visible, hierarchical Church is made clear in *The Acts of the Apostles*. After the descent of the Holy Ghost on Pentecost, St. Peter preached to the crowd in Jerusalem, with the result that about three thousand souls were baptized. After their baptism, the new converts began living as members of the Church . . . as *Catholics*: "And they were persevering in the doctrine of the apostles, and in the communication of the breaking of bread, and in prayers." (2:42)

St. Paul reminds us that to be baptized is not only to become free from the stain of original sin, but to do so *in the context of belonging to the Church*: "Christ loved the Church, and delivered Himself up for it, that He might sanctify it, cleansing it by the laver of water in the word of life." (Eph. 5:25–26)

Tradition relates that our Lady was indeed baptized, not to sanctify her (as she had been conceived without the stain of original sin), but so that, like her spiritual children, she would be formally incorporated into the Church, her pure soul also marked forever with this distinctive seal. St. Euthymus, a fourth-century abbot from Palestine, reported that "some have written that Jesus Christ Himself baptized the Virgin and Peter." Christ *loved* the Church and, since His Mother was the first and most prominent member of this Church, it was only fitting that she receive the sacrament of Baptism:

> Our Lady must have borne the Character of her Divine Son, or she would have been "distinguished" – 17 set apart – from all her children in heaven. How could she who is full of grace lack that which is carried as a Divine Seal by all her children? Our heavenly Queen must have possessed the identifying mark of her Son, and have possessed it pre-eminently. For, it is the sacrament of water Baptism alone that marks us as members of Jesus Christ, and thus as members of His Mystical Body, the Roman Catholic Church, outside which there is no salvation whatsoever possible. (Michael Malone, *The Christening of Mary*)

Like us, Mary is a child of Adam and Eve, and was redeemed by her Son. She is both member of the Roman Catholic Church, and Mother of this Church. On the day of her Baptism, God the Father must have looked down with inexpressible love on His Beloved Daughter, in whom He was well-pleased.

Baptism opens the door to the Catholic life, to the reception of the sacraments, to eternity. Because God became man, the individual members of the Church are joined to Him in one Body and it is, then, *His* Spirit and strength which accomplish all good things, even in the face of human frailty: "For it is God Who worketh in you, both to will and to accomplish, according to His good will." The Church hails our Lady as the *Mediatrix of All Graces* because she dispenses grace, but we are right in thanking her also for bringing to us the very Source and Fountain of these countless graces. "Whoever could know God," asked St. Germanus of Constantinople (†c. 733), "were it not for you, O most holy Mary?"

Chapter Twenty-Two

Children of Mary

JESUS CHRIST: THE ONLY MEDIATOR OF JUSTICE – MORE ON OUR LADY'S MEDIATORSHIP – JESUS WOULD NOT LEAVE US ORPHANS – CHILDREN OF MARY – THE DRAGON'S WAR AGAINST THE WOMAN AND "THE REST OF HER SEED," HER SPIRIRTUAL CHILDREN – MARY, THE AQUEDUCT OF GRACE, THE "NECK" OF THE MYSTICAL BODY – TESTIMONY OF THE FATHERS AND DOCTORS OF THE CHURCH – SCRIPTURAL REFERENCES – THE "BRETHREN" OF THE LORD – JESUS, "THE FIRST-BORN SON"

The lot of mortal men and women is characterized by *struggle*, internal as well as external: "The life of man upon earth is a warfare." (Job 7:1) There are the easily perceived calamities of natural disaster, illness and uncertainty: "For the corruptible body is a load upon the soul, and the earthly habitation presseth down the mind that museth upon many things." (Wis. 9:15) There are the less easily discernible battles raging within each individual, struggles against sin, inclination, habit: "But I see another law in my members, fighting against the law of my mind and captivating me in the law of sin that is in my members." (Rom. 7:23)

"Greater love than this no man hath," said our Lord at the Last Supper, "that a man lay down his life for his friends." (Jn. 15:13) We are given a glimpse into the chasm of Divine Love by the Prophet Isaias:

> Surely He hath borne our infirmities and carried our sorrows: and we have thought Him as it were a leper, and as one struck by God and afflicted. But He was wounded for our iniquities, He was bruised for our sins: the chastisement of our peace was upon Him, and by His bruises we are healed. (53:4-5)

There is NO power on earth like that of God. There is NO goodness or beauty like that of God, and the Church is promised a share in this divine bounty: "Eye hath not seen, nor ear heard, neither hath it entered into the heart of man, what things God hath prepared for them that love Him." (1 Cor. 2:9) This is the promised inheritance spoken of in the Scriptures:

> And therefore He is the mediator of the new testament: that by means of His death, for the redemption of those transgressions which were under the former testament, they that are called may receive the promise of eternal inheritance. (Heb. 9:15)

Mankind struggles, groaning, to come into its spiritual inheritance. Men and women, powers and principalities, all engage in this daily contest, the outcome of which will determine eternity for each and every person ever born or to be born. The implications are staggering. Yet when Jesus spoke to the apostles after the Last Supper, knowing the turmoil they would endure after the Crucifixion, He did not give them intensive lessons in the virtue of fortitude, couched in theological terms. He said: "I will not leave you orphans, *I will come to you*". (Jn. 14:18) Can any discourse on perseverance or the love of God ever match the simple beauty and power of the Redeemer Himself saying, "I will come to you?"

I *will not leave you orphans* was the promise made by Jesus, Wisdom Incarnate, to His Church. As is only to be expected, He fulfilled this promise *completely*. We have a *Father* in heaven: "You have received the spirit of adoption of sons, whereby we cry: Abba (Father). . . . Thus therefore shall you pray: Our Father Who art in heaven." By the mercy of God, we also have a *Mother* in heaven: "And a great sign appeared in heaven: A Woman clothed with the sun, and the moon under her feet, and on her head a crown of twelve stars: And being with child, she cried travailing in birth . . . Behold thy Mother."

"Jesus Christ is the only Mediator of Justice. . . . Mary is the mediatrix of grace," wrote St. Alphonsus Liguori. This is a crucial distinction. The Treasury of Grace was *merited* by the Redeemer and "the dispensing of these treasures is the particular and supreme right of Jesus Christ, *for they are the exclusive fruit of His death*." (Pope St. Pius X) However, they are *administered*, or dispensed, by the Blessed Virgin, in her divinely-appointed role as *Mediatrix of All Graces*, so that "if we have any hope, any grace, any salvation, we should know that all comes to us by Mary." (St. Bernard) This is the labor undertaken with love by Our Blessed Mother, *formally* proclaimed "Mother of the Church" by the Crucified Savior:

> In me is all grace of the way and of the truth, in me is all hope of life and of virtue. Come over to me, all ye that desire me, and be filled with my fruits. For my spirit is sweet above honey, and my inheritance above honey and the honeycomb. (Ecclus. 24:25-27)

"Behold I am with you all days, even to the consummation of the world," (Mt. 28:20) promised our Lord. I *will not leave you orphans*, I *will come to you*. He is ever faithful to His word. He comes to us uniquely in the Blessed Sacrament. He comes to us each and every time His own beloved Mother distributes graces to "the rest of her seed", the men and women redeemed by His Precious Blood:

> *Thou art the Star, blazing with beames bright*
> *Above this world's dark waves so violent,*
> *Clearing the dark of sin with thy bright light,*
> *Man's Mediatrix with God omnipotent.*
>
> (Alexander Barclay, d. 1552, *Ballade to Our Lady)*

Woman, behold thy son. Our Lady beholds her own children each time she gazes upon the earth. As the Mother of both Jesus (the Head) *and* the Catholic Church (the Body), she follows the precept of her Son to a degree possible *only* to her: "As long as you did it to one of these my least brethren, *you did it to me*". (Mt. 25:40) Mary tends to her spiritual children as Mother and Mediatrix, and St. Paul's meditations on charity ably capture her disposition, as she watches over a weary, sinful world: "Charity is patient, is kind . . . Charity never faileth." (1 Cor. 13:4,8)

To be an adopted son of God, to be a "joint-heir" with Christ in the eternal inheritance of the kingdom of God, means to be *a child of Mary*, one of "the rest of her seed": (Apoc. 12:17)

> Just as in natural and bodily generation there is a father and a mother, so in the supernatural and spiritual generation there is a Father Who is God and a mother who is

> Mary. *All true children of God have God for their Father and Mary for their Mother*; anyone who does not have Mary for his mother, does not have God for his father. (St. Louis de Montfort, *True Devotion to the Blessed Virgin*)

These "children" of Mary – *the rest of her seed* – are the ones who overcome the "accuser of our brethren" (Satan), and they do so ". . . by the Blood of the Lamb, and by the word of their testimony." (Apoc. 12:11) *By the Blood of the Lamb*. There is no strength, truth, peace, hope or victory apart from Christ: "As the branch cannot bear fruit of itself, unless it abide in the vine, so neither can you, unless you abide in Me." (Jn. 15:4) The ransom purchased for fallen mankind with the Precious Blood was purchased once, but the *effects* of that Redemption reverberate down through the centuries:

> And He is the propitiation for our sins: and not for ours only, but also for those of the whole world. (1 Jn. 2:2) Because with the Lord there is mercy: and with Him plentiful redemption. (Ps. 129:7)

With the Lord there is *plentiful* redemption, the grace to predispose souls to the Catholic Faith, and the grace to renew and sanctify them after they have embraced this Faith. By making Mary the Mother of His Church, the *Mediatrix of All Graces*, Jesus placed in her keeping this "plentiful" Treasury of Grace. As a consequence, the saints have given her such titles as "Almoner" of God, and "Treasure" of God.

Because all graces pass through the hands of Mary, she has been called the "neck" through which graces flow from the Head of the Mystical Body to the members, after a verse from the *Canticles*, "Thy neck is as the tower of David". (4:4)

> The Blessed Virgin is the neck of our Head, through which all spiritual gifts are communicated to the mystical Body of her Son. (St. Bernardine of Sienna †1444)

> Christ is the Head of the Church and Mary is the Church's neck. All divine favors, all graces, all heavenly influences come to us from Christ, as from the Head.

> They all descend to the body by Mary, just as in the human organism it is by the neck that the head vivifies its members. In the body of man there are arms, shoulders and feet. There is only one head and only one neck. Similarly, in the Church I behold several apostles, many martyrs, many Confessors, many Virgins. There is, however, but one only Son of God, one only Mother of God. (St. Robert Bellarmine †1621, *De Nativitate BMV*)

Our Lady has also been called the "Aqueduct" which conveys streams of graces from their origin to thirsty souls on earth:

> Now what is this fountain of life if it be not Christ the Lord? This stream from the heavenly source descends to us through an Aqueduct; it does not indeed exhibit all the fullness of the Fountain; but it serves to moisten our dry and withered hearts with some few drops of the waters of grace, giving more to one, less to another. The Aqueduct itself is always full, so that all may receive of its fullness, (Jn. 1:16) yet not the fullness itself. . . . Let us, therefore, look more deeply into this matter, and let us see with what sentiments of tender devotion the Lord would have us honor Mary, in whom He has placed the plenitude of all good; so that if there is anything of hope in us, if anything of grace, if anything of salvation, we may feel assured it has overflowed unto us from her "who went up from the deserts flowing with delights." (St. Bernard, †1153, *Sermon for the Feast of the Nativity of the Blessed Virgin Mary*)

> There are various types of "fullness" of grace. Among them is the fullness which receives solely for the purpose of giving, and that is the fullness of the canal. Now the Blessed Virgin has this fullness: for all graces without exception pass by her hands. (St. Albertus Magnus, †1280)

> In her the secret mysteries of our reconciliation have been accomplished and the sight of her reminds God of

> His covenant and causes Him to be mindful of His mercy. Mary is that heavenly stream which brings to the hearts of wretched mortals all God's gifts and graces. (Pope Benedict XIV, *Gloriosae Dominae*, 1748)

This image also derives from the Scriptures, from verses inspired by the Holy Ghost, in which the Church discerns the "prophetic voice" of the Virgin:

> I, like a brook out of a river of a mighty water; I, like a channel of a river and like an aqueduct came out of Paradise. I said: I will water my garden of plants, and I will water abundantly the fruits of my meadow. (Ecclus. 24:41-42)

The "Aqueduct" is not the Source, but there is nothing to stop the refreshing waters from pouring through it constantly, inundating those below with an abundance of all necessary graces: "For if by one man's offense, death reigned through one; much more they who receive abundance of grace, and of the gift, and of justice, shall reign in life through one, Jesus Christ." (Rom. 5:17)

St. Alphonsus Liguori observed that "it is one thing to say that God cannot, and another that He will not, grant graces without the intercession of Mary." It is not for men to dictate or question the ways of God: "Shall the thing formed say to Him that formed it: Why hast Thou made me thus? Or hath not the potter power over the clay?" (Rom. 9:20-21) God *can* dispense grace in any manner He chooses, and He has chosen to do so solely through the mediation of the Woman designated by Him as "Mother of the Church". St. Alphonsus continues:

> We most readily admit that Jesus Christ is the only Mediator of Justice . . . and that by His merits He obtains us all graces and salvation; but we say that Mary is the Mediatrix of grace; and that receiving all she obtains through Jesus Christ, and because she prays and asks for it in the name of Jesus Christ, yet all the same whatever graces we receive, *they come to us through her intercession.* . . . It must now be evident to all that when these

> saints and authors tell us in such terms that all graces come to us through Mary, they do not simply mean to say that we "received Jesus Christ, the source of every good, through Mary" . . . but that they assure us that God, Who gave us Jesus Christ, wills that all graces that have been, that are, and will be dispensed to men to the end of the world through the merits of Christ, should be dispensed by the hands and through the intercession of Mary. (*The Glories of Mary*)

"In Christ all shall be made alive." (1 Cor. 15:22) "He is not the God of the dead, but of the living." (Mt. 22:32) The "Body" of which Christ is the Head is composed of the Church *Triumphant* (the blessed in heaven), the Church *Suffering* (the holy souls in purgatory) and the Church *Militant* (those members still struggling on earth). God sees and knows each member: "For the wisdom of God is great, and He is strong in power, seeing all men without ceasing." (Ecclus. 15:19)

There are no "dead limbs" attached to the Body of Christ. Those who have already gone to their reward do not cease thinking about or praying for those still bound by mortality. Those on earth do not imagine that the souls of the faithful departed have been "put on hold", but remember and pray either for or to them. When souls intercede for one another, it is the individual *members* of the Body of Christ who are interceding. This Body has one Father . . . and *one* Mother. Our Lady is as much the Mother of the blessed souls in heaven, as she is of the souls in purgatory, or those still walking the earth. Because the Second Person of the Trinity, the Head of the Church, is eternal, and His Incarnation was the one Hope for humanity from the very foundation of the earth, Mary is Mother also of those faithful souls who lived *before* the Incarnation, for their hope, too, resided in the advent of God-made-Man, God the Redeemer . . . God the *Son*.

St. Francis de Sales employed the Gospel narrative of the Visitation – when, at the sound of Mary's greeting, St. John the Baptist was sanctified in the womb of his mother – to underscore the unity of Christ's Body:

> But notice that St. Elizabeth received the Holy Ghost by means of the Virgin. Certainly we must avail ourselves of her as a mediatrix with her Son in order to obtain this Divine Spirit; and although we can go directly to God and ask for His graces without employing the mediation of the saints for this purpose, nevertheless Divine Providence has not willed that it happen so; but It has formed still another union, for God is One. . . . Therefore He has so united the Church Militant with the Church Triumphant *that the two make only one*, having only one Lord who rules, guides, governs and nourishes them, though in different ways. (*Sermon for the Feast of the Visitation*)

As loyal sons and daughters of the Catholic Church, the saints in heaven can be described in the succinct words of St. Louis de Montfort: "All true children of God have God for their Father and Mary for their Mother." Because of this relationship between the Head of the Church, the Members of the Church, and the Mother of the Church, we discern the labors of the *Mediatrix of All Graces* also in the charitable intercession of the saints. This was made evident in a discourse delivered by the Bishop of Orleans to the pilgrims present at the approval of the miracles for the canonization of St. Joan of Arc: (April 6, 1919)

> We think God has so disposed matters to remind the faithful that we must never forget Mary even when the miracle seems to be attributed to the intercession or the mediation of one who has been beatified or canonized . . . On one hand Our Lord shows us that even on this earth, which is confided to the care of His Blessed Mother, He can work miracles through the intercession of one of His servants; on the other hand, He reminds us that even in such cases it is necessary to postulate the intercession of her whom the Holy Father greeted as "*Mediatrix Mediatorum omnium.*"

"What all saints can do *with* you," wrote St. Anselm, addressing Mary, "you can do yourself and *without* them. . . . If you are silent, none can pray for me or help me; but if you do speak, all can pray for me, all can hasten to my aid." This is the consistent teaching of the Church; it is a natural corollary to the doctrines of Mary's Spiritual Maternity and the Church as Christ's Mystical Body.

When Jesus was told that His mother and relatives were waiting to see Him, He replied: "My mother and my brethren are they who hear the word of God and do it." (Lk. 8:21) The Virgin's detractors imagine that Jesus renounced His Mother with these words, or, at least, used them to place her on the same level as all His other followers. However, we read in *The Book of Proverbs*: "He that afflicteth his father, *and chaseth away his mother*, is infamous and unhappy." (Prov. 19:26) The word "infamous" here denotes, in the Hebrew, "a son of confusion and reproach". The one who presumes that Jesus, at *any* time, demeaned the place of His natural Mother, is effectively calling the Son of God "a son of confusion and reproach".

Jesus' statement that His mother and brethren are they who keep the word of God was *not* an occasion snatched by Him to "demote" or repudiate His Mother; such an interpretation is obscene. Instead, it teaches how close is the bond uniting the "Head" of the Church to His Mystical "Body":

> For as many of you as have been baptized in Christ, have put on Christ. There is neither Jew nor Greek: there is neither bond nor free: there is neither male nor female. For you are all one in Christ Jesus. (Gal. 3:27-28) That with one mind, and with one mouth, you may glorify God and the Father of Our Lord Jesus Christ. Wherefore receive one another, *as Christ also hath received you* unto the honor of God. (Rom. 15:6–7)

The argument which aims to lessen or deny the exalted place of the Blessed Mother, supposedly based on the words of her Son, is based on a comparison between objects which can *not* be compared – i.e., between the *natural* Mother of Jesus and those who are merely likened to His mother, by way of analogy. If a person is describing his brother, he can list the brother's height, weight, hair color, etc. If he then describes a friend who is "like a brother" to him, he may list the friend's height, weight, etc., but this description in no way describes, applies to, or affects, the *brother*. Jesus, indicating a room full of disciples, may announce that there is His "mother" or "brother", but this does not alter the fact – nor was is meant to – that His divine and human natures were united once and forever in the immaculate womb of the Virgin Mary, a woman blessed among all others.

In Christ, "there is neither male nor female," wrote St. Paul. Yet, he also wrote: "The head of the woman is the man; and the head of Christ is God. . . . But yet neither is the man without the woman, nor the woman without the man, in the Lord." (1 Cor. 11:3,11) The first woman, Eve, was taken from man, but every man is born of a woman. Obviously, then, there is "male" and "female", yet the verses of St. Paul are not contradictory. He does not speak of a natural bond, but a supernatural one, "for you are all one in Christ Jesus," and Jesus "hath received" those who glorify the Father, the faithful "who hear the word of God, and do it." He will receive them, not because they are Jew or Greek, bond or free, male or female, but as *Catholics*, as members of His own Body. He will receive them as "My brother, and My sister, and mother." (Mk. 3:35) As *brethren*, because they are adopted sons of God and coheirs to the kingdom; as *mothers*, because Christ will be *formed* in each one who receives His Spirit.

But there was, and only can be, one "Mother of God": *And she brought forth her first-born Son, and wrapped Him up in swaddling clothes, and laid Him in a manger. . . . Now there stood by the Cross of Jesus His Mother.* Presumptuous souls who wish to place themselves on the same level as the Woman who carried the Savior to Bethlehem in her own womb, carried Him into exile in Egypt, and followed Him to Calvary, would do well to study the quiet dignity and humility of St. Joseph. *He*, alone among men, had the right to seek a special place. He, too, carried the Savior to Bethlehem, to Egypt, and home again – even receiving filial subjection from the Living God – but like his spouse, he wore a self-effacing countenance.

Unlike Our Lady's detractors, filled with specious arguments and circular logic, St. Joseph viewed his wife with nothing but reverence, and he spent his time in nobler, and more profitable, pursuits than questioning her dignity or making comparisons. How can we be so certain of his attitude, when none of his words have been preserved in the Gospels? Scripture is not silent here. St. Matthew relates that St. Joseph was a *just* man: "The desire of the just is all good." (Prov. 11:23) With what high regard would this holy saint have looked upon Mary, after hearing the words of the Angel? – "Fear not to take unto thee Mary thy wife, for that which is conceived in her, is of the *Holy* Ghost."

The spiritual rebirth of sinners is the true "birth" into Life, the birth of those *who are born, not of blood, nor of the will of the flesh, nor the will of man, but of God.* Without it, there is no claiming the spiritual "inheritance" belonging to the coheirs of Christ. Without a rebirth *as children of Mary* – as one of "the rest of her seed" – men cannot become "sons" of God. The inspired texts *never* make reference to the Blessed Virgin in any context which is not characterized by honor and respect.

The members of the Church are called "joint-heirs" of the kingdom, because the Father has placed all things into the hands of His Son. The Son is called "the first-born of every creature", (Col. 1:15) and Jesus said, "All things are delivered to me by My Father." (Mt. 11:27) He is the "first-born" in two ways.

Jesus is the first-born of Mary: *"She brought forth her first-born Son."* This designation does not refer to the number of children in a family, but has both a religious and legal definition: "Thou shalt set apart all that openeth the womb for the Lord . . . And every first-born of men thou shalt redeem with a price." (Ex. 13:12-13) ". . . give him a double-portion of all he hath: for this is the first of his children, and to him are due the first birthrights." (Deut. 21:17)

Of course, even an only child can be a "first-born" son. In honor of Mary's Perpetual Virginity, the phrase "openeth the womb" need only be understood, in her case, to refer to Jesus as the first son to *issue* from her womb. This is the sense in which St. Luke quotes the appropriate text from *The Book of Exodus*, when Mary's "first-born", the Infant Jesus, was taken to the Temple: "They carried Him to Jerusalem, to present Him to the Lord: As it is written in the law of the Lord: *Every male opening the womb shall be called holy to the Lord.*" (Lk. 2:22-23)

By His Resurrection, Our Lord is *first-born* in another sense, ". . . the beginning, the first-born from the dead." (Col. 1:18) This is the foundation for all Hope: "And if Christ be not risen again, your faith is vain, for you are yet in your sins. . . . But now Christ is risen from the dead, *the first-fruits of them that sleep*: for by a man came death, and by a man the resurrection of the dead. . . . Death is swallowed up in victory." (1 Cor. 15:17, 20-21, 54)

The resurrection of the dead, the payment of the debt owed to God since Eden, came by *a man*. God *Incarnate*, God the Son of Mary, rose from the dead, taking human nature with Him – i.e., liberating it from the "empire of death". There is an unbreakable link between Jesus as *first-born* of the Virgin, and as *first-born* from the dead: the immaculate womb of Mary. Mankind is included in this link, for the members of the Church will follow their Head. He rose and, God willing, we hope to rise again, too. He ordained that His Resurrection would occur only because He became human, because He was born of the Virgin. Therefore, all others who would also rise one day to claim their eternal inheritance, will also be "born" of this Virgin: *"Behold thy* Mother" . . . *"This man and that man is born in her."*

Chapter Twenty-Three

Mary's Sacrifice and Her Com-*passion*

Mother and Child forever – Mary's unique place – her suffering on Calvary: Co-Redemptrix – The sacrifice of her maternal rights on Calvary – The New Eve contrasted with the old – The word of the serpent and the word of the angel Gabriel – Distinction between Redeemer and Co-Redemptrix

God rewards His servants according to their merit: "Whatsoever you do, do it from the heart, as to the Lord, and not to men: Knowing that you shall receive of the Lord the reward of inheritance." (Col. 3:23-24) "To every one that hath shall be given, and he shall abound: and from him that hath not, even that which he hath shall be taken from him." (Lk. 19:26) Imagine how these verses apply to Mary and Joseph, who lived and toiled each and every day for one thing only: the security, comfort and happiness of Jesus. Every action they performed was done for the love of Christ, and therefore resounded to the heavens. "Blessed are they that dwell in Thy house, O Lord: they shall praise Thee for ever and ever." (Ps. 83:5) These words were fulfilled perfectly in the holy house at Nazareth.

The Blessed Virgin carried the immeasurable, infinite, omnipotent God in her womb. The bond that exists between a mother and child exists between Jesus and Mary; they are "connected" as *only* a mother and child can be connected. In contemplating Mary, then, we come face to face with someone who has been invited to dwell on the very "frontier" of divinity. Her encounter with God at the Incarnation was not that of the mystic or devout saint, whose piety or contemplation, recognized and rewarded by its Object, can bestow upon them visions, even a brief glimpse of the glory of the Blessed Trinity. Mary became the *Mother* of God, enjoying *every* intimacy and blessing implied by the word.

"When we say that Mary is the Mother of God," observed St. Anselm, "this alone transcends every greatness that can be named or imagined after that of God." Between God and man there stands Jesus Christ, True

God *and* True Man, the High Priest and One Mediator. But, there is a distinct and unique place between Jesus Christ and man, a realm inhabited by one human being only, and logic dictates that, in the created order, our Lady be recognized as more exalted than all creatures except God. Our Lord has many servants, and He can look with pleasure upon martyrs, saints, holy priests and teachers of the Faith, and selfless parents. But, there is only one human being to whom He willingly subjected Himself so as to be wholly dependent upon her for His human existence for nine months and throughout His Infancy and Childhood.

Intercessory prayer is a practice pleasing to God: "I desire therefore, first of all, that supplications, prayers, intercessions, and thanksgivings, be made for all men . . . For this is good and acceptable in the sight of God our Savior." (1 Tim. 2:1,3) The more devout the person who does the interceding, the more pleasing to God is the intercession: "For the continual prayer of a just man availeth much." (Jas. 5:16) "But to me Thy friends, O God, are made exceedingly honorable: their principality is exceedingly strengthened." (Ps. 138:17) Moses spoke to God as a man speaks "to his friend". When the Israelites murmured against him and Aaron, crying out, "Would God that we had died in Egypt," God became angry and threatened to strike them with pestilence. Moses interceded, reminding the Lord of His patience and mercy: "Forgive, I beseech Thee, the sins of this people, according to the greatness of Thy mercy." God replied: "I have forgiven according to *thy* word." (Num. 14:19-20)

The intercessory powers of the Blessed Virgin can not be classified among those of her children, even the most illustrious in sanctity. "How can Power itself refuse you power," asked St. Peter Damian, "when He took His flesh from you." Mary is the Immaculate Conception, a pure creature who loves God with no emotional or sinful impediments. She was proclaimed *Mother of the Church* by her Son from the Cross, and she exercises this Spiritual Maternity as the *Mediatrix of All Graces.* The King of Kings will *never* allow Himself to be outdone in the observation of the Law and Commandments by any earthly monarch. When Our Lady intercedes before Him, the reply of Jesus to her requests can be no less than that of King Solomon to his mother, Bethsabee: "My mother, ask: for I must not turn away thy face." (3 Kg. 2:20)

Our Lady's formidable intercessory powers, her role as *Mediatrix of All Graces*, are GIFTS of God to His Church, gifts arising from such love and charity, they could come only from the Sacred Heart of Jesus, the Heart which shed Its Precious Blood for the restoration of the world. "Mary stands in the presence of her Son, and never ceases to intercede for sinners," wrote St. Bede the Venerable (†735). To demean such a gift is to insult the Giver.

It should come as no surprise that the Blessed Virgin is referred to by the curious title, *Co-Redemptrix*. Already in the *Proto-evangelium*, it was prophesied that the serpent would be crushed by the "Woman" and her "seed", that the Redeemer would come to earth as a man. Jesus did not redeem mankind as an "outsider", as an aloof God acting "in a vacuum": "Husbands, love your wives, as Christ also loved the Church, and delivered Himself up for it." (Eph. 5:25)

The position of Mary in the economy of salvation flows outwards from the Divine Maternity, the basis for all her titles, privileges and prerogatives. Because she is Mother of the *Head*, she is also Mother of the *Body*. On Calvary, her Spiritual Maternity was made manifest, both through her suffering (as Our Lady of Sorrows and Queen of Martyrs), and by the proclamation of her Divine Son (*Behold thy Mother*). Her sharing in the sufferings of Jesus, her "first-born Son", were the "birth pangs" by which a redeemed humanity was generated. Her soul was "pierced" as she contemplated the Crucifixion. Because of her Divine Motherhood, because of her love for Jesus (and the souls to be redeemed by His Blood), she was not merely a *spectator* on Calvary.

The Virgin, therefore, had a maternal "claim" to her Son which permitted her to unite her sufferings to His. She could "offer up" this maternal claim, in *union* with His offering up of Himself, of the human life *she* had given to Him. The sacrifice was Christ's alone; it was He Who redeemed the world by His Passion and death. But Mary could unite her own affections and intentions to His sacrifice, not complementing, augmenting or completing it (as it was superabundant), but *participating* in it to the degree possible for her alone: *I will put enmities between thee and the Woman, and thy seed and her seed. . . . And thy own soul a sword shall pierce, that, out of many hearts, thoughts may be revealed.*

God's love for sinners is the lesson of Calvary: *For God so loved the world, as to give His only begotten Son*. But there is another lesson to be gained, one which resonates with the first. It was summarized by Pope Benedict XV:

> According to the common teaching of the Doctors it was God's design that the Blessed Virgin Mary, apparently absent from the public life of Jesus, should assist Him when He was dying nailed to the Cross. Mary suffered and, as it were, nearly died with her suffering Son; *for the salvation of mankind she renounced her mother's rights* and, as far as it depended on her, offered her Son to placate divine justice; so we may well say that she with Christ redeemed mankind. (*Inter sodalicia*, 1918)

This is carefully worded. Our Lady offered Jesus to the Father "as far as it depended on her." The sacrifice was His to make as Saving Victim and High Priest, but there was something the Woman of Genesis, the Mother of the Redeemer, could do. She "renounced her mother's rights," suffering with her Son in the placating of Divine Justice.

St. Paul described himself as a minister of the Gospel, ". . . who now rejoice in my sufferings for you, and fill up those things that are wanting of the sufferings of Christ, in my flesh, for His Body, which is the Church." (Col. 1:24) Again, the wording is careful, for he says he will fill up what is "wanting" of the sufferings of Christ . . . *for His Body, which is the Church*. There is no question here of any "lack" in the sacrifice of Christ for the atonement of the sins of the world, but of the sufferings befalling the members of the Church.

This suffering is the great enigma confronting rational creatures. Without God, it is nothing more than a useless horror, the ruin of all that seems good to human beings. When human suffering is *joined* to the Passion of Christ, it is used by God for the best of all possible ends. The Suffering of Jesus (the Head) redeemed the world; the sufferings of the members of the Church (His Body) participate in this one saving act of Jesus, filling up not what is "lacking", but what is "wanting" – i.e., an element whose absence is not overtly in evidence, but is desired nonetheless.

Individuals who suffer *with* Christ – in union with Him – receive a multitude of blessings, "always bearing about in our body the mortification of Jesus, that the life also of Jesus may be made manifest in our bodies." (2 Cor. 4:10) Their sacrifices can also benefit others. The blood of the martyrs have irrigated many fields, bringing Christ and His sacraments to those ". . . that sit in darkness, and in the shadow of death." (Lk. 1:79) Countless souls have offered their own trials and illnesses for the suffering souls in purgatory, or the spiritual welfare of family members or friends. Before his conversion, St. Paul ". . . ravaged the Church, entering into the houses, and, dragging away men and women, committed them to prison." (Act. 8:3) He was present at, and received mercy from God on account of, the martyrdom of St. Stephen, who cried out on behalf of his persecutors as he died, "Lord, lay not this sin to their charge."

When St. Paul wrote that it was his joy to *fill up those things that are wanting of the sufferings of Christ, in my flesh, for His Body, which is the Church*, the desired end was the regeneration of sinners, the members of his Lord's Mystical Body. These words apply with even more force to the Blessed Virgin, the *Mother* of this Body, as do the words spoken by her Son at the Last Supper: "A woman, when she is in labor, hath sorrow, because her hour is come; but when she hath brought forth the child, she remembereth no more the anguish, for joy that a man is born into the world." (Jn. 16:21) Jesus said this on the night of His betrayal, and it symbolized both the profound sadness which would afflict the apostles at His death and their joy at His Resurrection. The image also seems to describe the spiritual children brought forth in labor, by His own Passion, *who are born, not of blood, nor of the will of the flesh, nor of the will of man, but of God.* This description of the woman in labor suits Our Lady well: "And thy own soul a sword shall pierce."

Because the redeemed are "sons" of God and "joint-heirs" with Christ, they are also children of Mary, and she loves the Church dearly for that reason, with a truly maternal love. Jesus' description of the woman in labor calls to mind the image of the Sorrowful Mother standing by Him on the first Good Friday:

At the Cross her station keeping,
Stood the mournful mother weeping,
Close to Jesus to the last.
Through her heart, His sorrow sharing,
All His bitter anguish bearing,
Lo, the piercing sword has passed.

(*Stabat Mater*, attributed to Blessed Jacopone da Todi †1306)

According to the common teaching of the Doctors it was God's design that the Blessed Virgin, apparently absent from the public life of Jesus, should assist Him when He was dying nailed to the Cross. Mary suffered and, as it were, nearly died with her suffering Son; for the salvation of mankind she renounced her mother's rights *and, as far as it depended on her, offered her Son to placate divine justice*; so we may well say that she with Christ redeemed mankind. (Pope Benedict XV, *Inter sodalicia*, 1918)

When the supreme hour of the Son came, beside the Cross of Jesus there stood Mary, not merely occupied in contemplating the cruel spectacle, but rejoicing that her only Son was offered for the salvation of mankind; *and so entirely participating in His Passion* that, if it had been possible "she would have gladly borne all the torments that her Son underwent (St. Bonaventure)." (Pope St. Pius X, *Ad diem illum laetissimum*, 1904)

Mary, the best of all mothers, would have taken her Son's sufferings upon herself "if it had been possible;" but it was not. The Lamb of God, and only the Lamb of God, could redeem the world by His Passion and death. However, Our Lady, "as far as it depended on her," (Pope Benedict XV) *could* unite her mother's sorrow to the Son's sufferings and offer it to God for the restoration the world. The Virgin, before St. Paul or *any* disciple of Christ, could *fill up those things that are wanting of the sufferings of Christ, in my flesh, for His Body, which is the Church.* In the bitter anguish of her "first-born Son", Mary's spiritual children, "the rest of her seed", were being generated; there was a supernatural joy supporting her unimaginable sorrow, for she was "not merely occupied in contemplating the cruel spectacle, but rejoicing that her only Son was offered for the salvation of mankind."

The *spirit of the adoption of sons*, which is a hallmark of membership in the True Church founded by Jesus Christ, must include, then, "personal" relationships with both Jesus Christ, the Head of the Church, and with Mary, the Mother of the Church. "For in one Spirit were we all baptized *into one body*," wrote St. Paul, "whether Jews or Gentiles, whether bond or free." (1 Cor. 12:13) If we can speak truly of a "Mystical Body" of Christ, comprised of the individual members of His Church, then we are justified as well in speaking of a "Mystical Womb" of Mary, in which these members, like their Divine Head, come to term:

> It was she who, free from sin either personal or original, always most closely united with her Son, offered Him on Golgotha to the Eternal Father, together with the holocaust of her mother's rights and mother's love, as a new Eve, for all the sons of Adam stained by his pitiful fall, so that she, who in the flesh was the mother of our Head, by the new title also of grief and glory, *in the spirit was made the mother of all His members*. She it was who by very powerful prayers accomplished that the Spirit of the divine Redeemer, already given on the Cross, should be bestowed with wonderful gifts on the day of Pentecost upon the recently risen Church. Finally, she herself by enduring her tremendous griefs with a strong and confident spirit, more than all the faithful of Christ, the true Queen of the martyrs, "filled up those things that are wanting of the sufferings of Christ . . . for His Body, which is the Church" [Col. 1:24]; and she has attended the mystical body of Christ, born of the torn heart of our Savior, with the same mother's care and deep love with which she cherished and nurtured the Infant Jesus nursing in the crib. (Pope Pius XII, *Mystici Corporis*, 1943)

"All we who are united to Christ," wrote Pope St. Pius X, "have issued from the womb of Mary like a body united to His head." By Divine decree, it was necessary that the Mother of the Church be present to *share* in the "labor pains" by which a redeemed humanity was generated, uniting her "*Com*-Passion" to Christ's Passion:

> And a great sign appeared in heaven: A woman clothed with the sun, and the moon under her feet, and on her head a crown of twelve *stars: And being with child, she cried travailing in birth, and was in pain to be delivered.* . . . And she brought forth a man child, who was to rule all nations with an iron rod. . . . And the dragon was angry against the woman: and went to make war with the rest of her seed, who keep the commandments of God, and have the testimony of Jesus Christ.

We are reminded of Genesis here, where the Woman and her seed stand against the serpent. In this magnificent image, the spiritual rebirth of the members of the Church (the Body) is superimposed over the birth of Jesus (the Head), for one and the same Mother gives birth to both. The birth-pangs of the Woman are, of course, not the literal pangs associated with childbirth, for the Mother of God experienced no such tribulations at Bethlehem. They represent both the sorrows of Calvary, and the later persecutions and trials of the Church, and they recall us to the words of Jesus: A *woman, when she is in labor, hath sorrow, because her hour is come*. This is the maternal sorrow experienced by our Lady on Calvary; her natural Son was dying so that her spiritual sons might live. It is an awful thing to see a loved one suffer even for a few moments. For three seemingly endless hours, the Mother of Sorrows "stood by the Cross of Jesus".

The title, *Co-Redemptrix*, belongs to Mary in two ways. Firstly, she gave Jesus the Redeemer to the world. Her cooperation and consent were asked of God, through the Angel Gabriel, before she would be overshadowed by the Holy Ghost, and the celestial courtier did not depart until Mary said, "Be it done to me according to thy word." And so, our Lady was regarded as the *New Eve* by the Fathers of the Church:

> For Eve, a virgin and undefiled, conceived the word of the serpent, and bore disobedience and death. But the Virgin Mary received faith and joy when the Angel Gabriel announced to her the glad tidings that the Spirit of the Lord would come upon her and the power of the Most High would overshadow her, for which reason the Holy One being born of her is the Son of God. And she replied: "Be it done unto me according to thy word." (St. Justin Martyr, †c. 165, *Dialogue with Trypho*)

> Consequently, then, Mary the Virgin is found to be obedient, saying: "Behold, O Lord, your handmaid; be it done to me according to your word." Eve, however, was disobedient; and when yet a virgin, she did not obey. . . . Thus, the knot of Eve's disobedience was loosed by the obedience of Mary. What the virgin Eve had bound in unbelief, the Virgin Mary had loosed through faith. (St. Irenaeus, †c. 202, *Adversus haereses*)

This title of "new" (or second) Eve resonates with St. Paul's description of Jesus as another *Adam*: "Adam, who is a figure of Him that was to come." (Rom. 5:14) "The first man Adam was made into a living soul; the last Adam into a quickening spirit." (1 Cor. 15:45) The first Adam had a helpmate who participated in the fall; in a true reversal of the fall, the "new" Adam would also have a helpmate, a woman who would participate in the Redemption.

The second manner in which the title *Co-Redemptrix* belongs to Our Lady is by virtue of her "*Com*-Passion", by which she united herself to her Son's Passion – the Woman and her seed together again, in the victory against the "empire of death".

"Although God could create the world out of nothing," wrote St. Anselm, "yet when it was lost by sin, He would not repair the evil without the cooperation of Mary." This statement is not extravagant. It is a sober and straightforward look at the economy of salvation. The great misconception concerning the title *Co-Redemptrix* is that, if it is used for Mary, then it must apply also to

Jesus, since at least two people are needed in order to cooperate in any venture; if two people build a house, goes such reasoning, both parties are *equally* "co-builders".

This conclusion is simplistic and leads to muddled thinking. There is no reason to assign any "numerical" value to the *idea* of "cooperation", as though it were a fast rule that, any time two people cooperate in a venture or project, each one's contribution must be valued at exactly "fifty percent" of the achieved result, regardless of their relative positions and roles in the venture. In the matter of personal sacrifice, such attempts to assign "percentage" values to an individual's suffering become even more absurd.

It should be obvious that the role of *Redeemer*, the "One Mediator", *cannot* be parceled out to others. Through the *Hypostatic Union* of divine and human natures in the Person of Jesus, this Redeemer can be both True God and True Man – i.e., a Man capable of paying the debt owed to God since Eden. No one else can "fit the bill" in this matter. However, this fact does not negate the historical certainty that our Lady stood by the Cross of her Son on Calvary, and that she was there by divine decree:

> Do not wonder, brethren, if we say that Mary was martyred in spirit. Remember that St. Paul placed a lack of affection among the great crimes of the Gentiles. This was far from Mary's heart. . . . What sort of reasoning is this that you wonder more at Mary's compassion than at Christ's Passion? He was able to die in body; is she not able to die with Him in her heart? He died because His love is greater than any man's; she died because there is no love like hers among men. (St. Bernard, *First Sermon on the Virgin Mother of God*)

The term *Co-Redemptrix* does NOT apply in any manner to Christ. He is, simply, the Redeemer. In the ransoming of mankind, He did not participate in anyone else's actions or mission. It is the Blessed Virgin Mary who *participated* in the labors of Jesus by uniting her sorrows to His, for the benefit of "the rest of her seed". The fact that Jesus did not "need" His Mother present, or require her "*Com*-Passion" in order to redeem mankind, must bow to another fact: it was because she was present there that our Lord was able to proclaim *formally* her Spiritual Motherhood, which, manifested in her role as *Mediatrix of All Graces*, allows Mary to "mother" the Church in every way. In doing so, she carries out the will and work of her Son: "That they all may be one, as Thou, Father, in me, and I in Thee; that they also may be one in Us." (Jn. 17:21)

Any misconceptions regarding Our Lady's title, *Co-Redemptrix*, are easily righted by taking into account both the definition of the term, and the twofold manner in which it is applied to the Mother of God. We do not call her the "Redemptrix", because the word "Redemption" applies exclusively to the restoration of fallen humanity to friendship with God. *Only the One Who paid the price for this restoration – Jesus Christ – can be called the REDEEMER.* The term "Co-Redemptrix", then, attests to the truth that Mary's share in the Redemption is subordinate to and dependent upon that unique Redemption won by her Son on Calvary. The important word here is "share". A share is something that is *given to* or *bestowed upon* one party by another. Our Lady was given a "place" in the economy of salvation by the Blessed Trinity. This "place" was of such import that she is rightfully called the *Co-redemptrix of mankind* – not because she in any sense "redeemed" the human race, *but because it was divinely ordained that she actively participate in our redemption:*

> As regards the structure of the term "Coredemptrix" we may point out that the prefix "co" is the exact equivalent of the Latin *cum* which means "with", not "equal", as every grammarian knows. For this reason St. Paul could rightly say that we are God's "co-workers" in the process of our sanctification, without in the least equating the efficacy of God's grace with that of our own cooperation. . . . Hence we see no justified fear that the title "Co-redemptrix" will mislead and confuse the less enlightened and the prejudiced. A sensible way to prevent that confusion would seem to be to instruct such people so as to make them more enlightened and less prejudiced. (Fr. Juniper Carol, "Our Lady's Co-redemption" from *Mariology, Vol. II*, 1957)

In God's ineffable wisdom, the consent of the Blessed Virgin to her Divine Maternity – to the Incarnation of the Eternal Word in her womb – was a prerequisite for the restoration of mankind to friendship with its Creator. That same Divine wisdom gave her a place on Calvary, where she was "not just occupied in seeing the dread spectacle [wrote Pope St. Pius X], but actually rejoicing that her Only-Begotten was being offered for the salvation of the human race . . . from this common sharing of sufferings and will, she merited to become most worthily the reparatrix of the lost world."

It is no coincidence that both aspects of the twofold application of the term "Co-redemptrix" to Our Lady refer to her maternal character. Her •*at* to the Angel Gabriel was a consent to her *Divine Maternity*. On Calvary, her "Com-Passion" in response to her Son's Passion, her sorrows as the *Queen of Martyrs*, were the "spiritual birth-pangs" through which a redeemed humanity was generated, *for God counted these maternal sorrows as acceptable to Him*: *"And thy own soul a sword shall pierce, that out of many hearts* thoughts may be revealed." It was on Calvary that Mary's *Spiritual Maternity* was proclaimed by her Son: "Behold thy Mother."

Like all sound Marian doctrine, the Virgin's title of *Co-redemptrix* is grounded in her Divine Maternity. A calm, reasoned look at her place in the created order and in the economy of salvation should make it clear to those of good will that this title is a fitting and proper one, and that anything less would be an injustice to the "Woman of the Protoevangelium" and the *Mother of Sorrows*:

> With her suffering and dying Son she suffered and almost died, so did she surrender her mother's rights over her Son for the salvation of human beings, and to appease the justice of God, so far as pertained to her, she immolated her Son, so that it can be rightly said, that she together with Christ has redeemed the human race. (Pope Benedict XV, *Admodum probatur*, 1917)

Chapter Twenty-Four

Mary's Irresistible Intercessory Power

"WOMAN" IN ARAMAIC, A TITLE OF RESPECT BY WHICH A SON ADDRESSES HIS MOTHER IN PUBLIC – CANA AND THE FIRST MIRACLE – "MY HOUR" – MARY'S POWER WITH GOD

At the Wedding at Cana, when our Lady told her Son that the wine had run out, He replied, "Woman, what is that to me and to thee? My hour is not yet come."

Why did our Lord address His Mother as "Woman"? Some misguided souls choose to see in this term an expression of subdued anger or annoyance on the part of Jesus, but, as always, the truth is much more flattering (and becoming) to the Son of God and Mary:

> The title by which Jesus addressed Mary in His answer is usually translated into English as "Woman", but the words in the original Syro-Chaldaic which Our Lord spoke really meant "Lady", or "Madam", and was the title of respect by which the Hebrew children always addressed their mothers in public. . . . Hence those who would say that Jesus did not show the greatest honor to His holy Mother in the actual terms of His answer are as greatly mistaken as if they would have it that He refused her request. (Rev. Thomas Flynn, "The Queen's Favor," from *Sermons on Our Blessed Lady*, 1919)

Even given the simple, time-hallowed translation, "Woman", there is no reason to attach to it a negative connotation. To do so would be to attribute mere petulance to our Lord. It is obvious that He was not angry or annoyed when He said to the woman of Canaan, "O *woman*, great is thy faith." (Mt. 15:28) Neither do we detect any anger in His words to the Samaritan woman by the well: "*Woman*, believe me, that the hour cometh, when you shall neither on this mountain, nor in Jerusalem, adore the Father." (Jn. 4:21)

In the face of the hypocrisy of the Pharisees, Our Lord will indeed blaze into anger, calling them "whited sepulchers" and "vipers". To imagine Him snapping at His immaculate Mother in public is unthinkable. On the contrary, Jesus will once again address His Mother – the "Woman" of the *Proto-evangelium* and the one "crowned with twelve stars" in the apocalyptic vision – as *Woman*, during the most important event in the history of creation, His sacrifice on Calvary (*Woman*, behold thy son).

The events of this Gospel narrative have been preserved in Sacred Scripture for two reasons. Firstly, because "this beginning of miracles did Jesus in Cana of Galilee, and manifested His glory, and His disciples believed in Him." (Jn. 2:11) Secondly, because it teaches us something important – *crucial* – about our Lady's place in the life of the Church. In this narrative, we are invited to enter yet more deeply into the mystery of Mary:

> And the wine failing, the Mother of Jesus saith to Him: They have no wine. And Jesus saith to her: Woman, what is that to Me and to thee? My hour is not yet come. His Mother saith to the waiters: Whatsoever He shall say to you, do ye. (Jn. 2:3-5)

Our Lord *will* perform a miracle here, and change water into the "good wine" praised by the chief steward. He *will* perform it solely because of His Mother's intercession. Yet, He delays. Why?

And what are we to make of the phrase, "What is that to me and to thee?" This expression has several meanings in the Scriptures. It was used as a protestation against possible hostile measures. When Jephte was asked by the Galaadites to lead the fight against their enemy, the Ammonites, he sent this message to the Ammonite king: "*What hast thou to do with me*, that thou art come against me, to waste my land?" (Jg. 11:12) When our Lord encountered two men possessed by demons in the country of the Gerasens, the demons cried out: "*What have we to do with thee*, Jesus Son of God? Art thou come hither to torment us before the time?" (Mt. 8:29)

This expression is also used in the Scriptures to indicate the denial of a petition. When a man named Semei, a kinsman of Saul, began heaping curses upon King David, one of David's men, Abisai the son of Sarvia, offered to go and cut off the man's head. The king, believing that it was the will of God that he be cursed in such a manner, replied to Abisai: "*What have I to do with you*, ye sons of Sarvia? Let him alone and let him curse." (2 Kg. 16:10) There is no anger or reproach in David's words here, however, for Abisai was one of his most loyal supporters. Our Lord, who fully intended to fulfill His Mother's desire at Cana, spoke to her in a phrase whose implications she would have understood and which would have suggested a turning aside of her petition on behalf of the bride and groom.

The idea of God "delaying" His actions, mercy or justice is encountered often throughout the history of salvation. It permeates the Sacred Scriptures. The Psalms echo with it: "My soul hath fainted after Thy salvation, and in Thy word I have very much hoped. My eyes have failed for Thy word, saying: When wilt Thou comfort me?" (Ps. 118:81-82) The very nature of prophecies is to point to events that will occur in *later* days.

All events unfold in God's good time, and according to His will. Through the mercy of God, the "delays" which are the lot of mortals bound by time and circumstance, become themselves indicators, arrows pointing to a fulfillment even more glorious than expected. Expectation incites the virtues of faith and hope, thereby making the end of the wait even more glorious, even more redolent of divine love and solicitude.

This "waiting in faith" is embodied in the *Paschale Praeconium*, which is chanted on Holy Saturday, and which spans the generations from Adam to Jesus. "O wondrous condescension of thy great kindness in our regard. . . . O happy fault, that was worthy to have such and so great a redeemer." Centuries would pass between the "happy fault" committed in Eden, and the One who atoned for it on behalf of mankind. In the slow passage of the years, God would call a people to Himself, so that St. Peter could one day write: "You were not redeemed with corruptible things . . . but with the precious Blood of Christ." Similarly, when the apostles asked Jesus whether the cause of a certain man's blindness was the result of the man's sins or those of his parents, He replied: "Neither hath this man sinned, nor his parents; but that the works of God should be made manifest in him." (Jn. 9:3)

Delay in the administration of justice or mercy by God is not a sign of rejection. It is meant to *instruct* and to incite the practice of virtue. The man born blind lived his entire life in that state until he met Jesus, at which time "the works of God" were made manifest in him through his healing. When a woman of Canaan cries out to Jesus to cure her possessed daughter, He does not even acknowledge her presence at first. When His disciples ask Him to send her away, Jesus speaks to her: "I was not sent but to the sheep that are lost of the house of Israel." However, the woman persisted in spite of Our Lord's *apparent* refusal:

> But she came and adored Him, saying: Lord help me. Who answering, said: It is not good to take the bread of the children, and to cast it to the dogs. But she said: Yea, Lord; for the whelps also eat of the crumbs that fall from the table of their masters. Then Jesus answering, said to her: O woman, great is thy faith: be it done to thee as thou wilt: and her daughter was cured from that hour. (Mt. 15:25–28)

Our Lord gave this woman the opportunity to make acts of faith, hope and charity, even in the face of a seeming refusal in which He likened her to a cur begging for scraps. Yet, she persisted . . . and Jesus marveled at her faith.

At Cana, our Blessed Mother also practiced the virtues of faith, hope and charity, but to a superlative degree. There was no need for her to dialogue with her Divine Son. In the face of a seeming "refusal", Mary confidently turned to the waiters and said, "Whatsoever He shall say to you, do ye." Unlike the woman of Canaan, our Lady spoke with a true, *maternal* confidence that her Son would not dishonor either her or Himself by violating the Fourth Commandment.

The Cana narrative has been hijacked by our Lady's detractors and twisted into an example of Jesus "putting her in her place", because of His reply – i.e., they perceive in it a supposed Scriptural basis for the rejection of Marian devotion. However, a careful look at this Gospel episode will lead us to a quite different conclusion.

At the Wedding at Cana, Jesus placed His Mother in a situation where she could have taken one of three courses of action: (1) to drop the matter entirely, (2) to continue pleading her case, or (3) to understand that Jesus would respect her intercession, and act accordingly. What are the implications of each of these options?

(1)Had Mary dropped the matter, she – the *Theotokos* who had conversed with an Archangel – would have exhibited less faith than the woman of Canaan. According to St. John, the turning of the water into wine was the "beginning of miracles" which "manifested His glory, and His disciples believed in Him." Had our Lady not interceded *in exactly the manner in which she did*, this miracle would not have taken place.

(2) The incessant pleading which was appropriate from the woman of Canaan on behalf of her daughter was not so for the Mother of God. In the Cana episode, our Lord is an adult. While He had been "subject" to Mary and Joseph during the hidden years at Nazareth, He was now present with His disciples, ready to manifest His glory. Thus, any supposed "rebuke" of Mary by Jesus would express either a grudging (and quite unbecoming) acquiescence by our Lord, as the miracle is performed in the end, anyway, through gritted teeth, or a flightiness on the part of the Virgin, who needlessly insists that her son "do something". There is no way to accept the "rebuke" theory without slandering both the Son of God and the woman to whom the Blessed Trinity had given the name *Kecharitomene*, "Full of Grace".

Our Lord spoke briefly to His Mother. His hour had not yet come. What does this "hour" signify? Elsewhere in St. John's Gospel, the hour refers to the time of Jesus' death and Resurrection: "Before the festival day of the Pasch, Jesus knowing that his hour was come, *that He should pass out of this world to the Father* . . ." (13:1) But, this interpretation raises a question:

> John does not indicate any lack of understanding on Mary's part, [cf. Lk. 2:50 "And they understood not the word that He spoke unto them"]. If she then under-

> stood the word "hour" in reference to His death, how could she have continued the thread of her dialogue with no apparent heed to this meaning? Her words to the waiters are in keeping with her own previous request. It bears no relationship to the death of Christ. . . . There is nothing whatever within the story which suggests a thought of Christ's death. This meaning must rest for its validity on the meaning of the word elsewhere in the gospel after the Cana incident. (From Fr. Michael O'Carroll, *Theotokos: A Theological Encyclopedia of the Blessed Virgin Mary*, 1982)

St. Augustine held that the "hour" was the time in which Jesus would acknowledge His Mother from the Cross:

> Now His hour had come, that hour about which Jesus had mentioned to His Mother when He turned the water into wine. . . . The hour, then so distant, had now arrived, when at the moment of mortal dissolution, He would acknowledge her from whom He had taken mortal flesh. (*Homily on John*)

"This beginning of miracles did Jesus in Cana of Galilee," wrote St. John, "and manifested His glory, and His disciples believed in Him." Taking into account this concise summary of the Cana episode, another interpretation suggests itself, namely, that the "hour" was the time when the Redeemer would finally inaugurate His mission in a *conspicuous* manner:

> The difficulty [in interpreting the *hour* as Jesus' death and Resurrection] consists in the apparent contradiction involved in the fact that Our Lord worked the miracle immediately after having stated that His hour had not yet come – His hour (as the context seems to me on the whole to suggest) *for the working of miracles*. If this be the true meaning of the expression *Mine hour*, it is impossible to accept such an interpretation of the passage as that, for example, of St. Augustine. (Fr. O.R. Vassall-Phillips, *The Mother of Christ*, 1936)

(3) Here is the essence of the event. There are many instances in the Gospels where people literally cried out to Jesus as He passed by, begging for healing and mercy, and He obliged them with great solicitude: "The Son of Man is not come to be ministered unto, but to minister." (Mt. 20:28) The concern of Mary for the young newlyweds was a concern born of charity: "In doing good, let us not fail." (Gal. 6:9) It is ludicrous to suppose that, at Cana, Jesus should take such "offense" merely because it is His *Mother* who brings someone's needs before Him. A grudging acquiescence on the part of Our Lord, at the time He turned the water into wine, would not suit His dignity: "In thy good deeds, make no complaint, and when thou givest any thing, add not grief by an evil word." (Ecclus. 18:15)

When the disciples, caught in a storm at sea, turned to Him in anxiety, our Lord rebuked them before He heeded their cries: "Why are you fearful, O ye of little faith?" (Mt. 8:26) When they were unable to cast a demon from out of a young boy, He cried out, "O incredulous generation . . . how long shall I suffer you?" (Mk. 9:18) How different were things at Cana. There was no rebuke given by our Lord to His Mother, while Mary, who had spoken *and listened* to the Angel Gabriel on the day Christ was made incarnate in her womb by the Holy Ghost, approached Him without any nagging anxiety or doubt.

If the *hour* for miracles, for public manifestations of the Savior's power and glory, had not yet arrived, then Jesus hastened that hour for the simple reason that His Mother had asked it of Him – i.e., to reward her *intercession.* He waited for His Mother to act *with maternal confidence.* His reply to her was calculated to this end, for when God "delays", it is to manifest His glory in a wonderful manner, and these first intimations of the Virgin's powers of intercession and of her solicitude for suffering humanity were, indeed, glorious revelations.

We cannot know the look that passed between Jesus and Mary right after He spoke to her, but the love *and approval* in the Son's eyes caused the Mother to turn immediately to the waiters and say, with no hesitation, "Whatsoever He shall say to you, do ye." At Cana, our Lady saw two things – a need, and the Son she bore in Bethlehem, whose Father is God. Our Lord saw, in addition, the woman He loved as His own Mother, the one who would be hailed by His Church as the *Mediatrix of All Graces.* After Mary spoke her confident words to the waiters, Jesus ordered them to "fill the waterpots with water", demonstrating His *approval* of the Blessed Virgin's intercession by granting her desire. In fact, the entire narrative makes it expressly clear that our Lord rewarded this intercession *for no other reason than that it was His Mother's.*

The events of the Wedding at Cana provide a powerful lesson on the relationship between the Redeemer and the Mother of the Redeemer:

> It was through the portal of Cana in Galilee that Christ issued forth as the promised Messiah, when He wrought His first miracle at His Mother's bidding. It was here that He first designated her as "Woman", saying: "Woman, what is that to Me, and to thee? My hour is not yet come." He was then about to redeem the world and to go out publicly to accomplish the prophecy, *which was fulfilled by "the Woman" and "the seed"*, which are Mary and Jesus Christ. (Fr. A.M. Mayer, *Advanced Mariology*, 1934)

Many saints have interceded for the world; by the grace of God, we are blessed with *many* saints. But, there is only *one* Mother of God. Her honor, her privileges, her mysteries are as unique as the Lady herself. Chief among them is her power of intercession, a power of which St. Peter Damian could boldly say: "Her Son esteems her prayers so greatly, and is so desirous to satisfy her, that when she prays it seems as if she rather commanded than prayed, and was rather a queen than a handmaid."

Knowing that the lesson of Cana would be forever a part of the sacred canon, the Redeemer did speak once to His Mother, allowing her, gently and with no fanfare, to show the world the influence she has over GOD, and to teach one more lesson, as well. Through the intercession of the Blessed Virgin, our Lord manifested His glory. Through her intercession, His disciples believed in Him. "Because God has decided to begin and accomplish His greatest works through the Blessed Virgin ever since He created her," wrote St. Louis de Montfort, "we can safely believe that He will not change His plan in time to come, for He is God and therefore does not change in His thoughts or His way of acting." To this day, our Lady remains the means by which souls approach Jesus and cultivate faith in Him. "Just as no one goes to the Father but by Christ," wrote Richard of St. Laurence (d.1245), "so Christ seems to say of Mary: No one can come to Me unless My Mother draw him by Her prayers."

Chapter Twenty-Five

Mary and the Church

MARY'S MATERNAL LOVE FOR THE CHURCH – THE SACRAMENTS AS CHANNELS OF GRACE – THE PRIESTHOOD AND THE MASS – THE BLESSED VIRGIN'S CONTINUAL PRESENCE IN THE LITURGY OF THE MASS – THE COMMUNION OF SAINTS – THE MASS: CALVARY RE-PRESENTED IN AN UNBLOODY MANNER – THE UNIVERSAL MULTILOCATION OF THE ONE PERFECT SACRIFICE IN EVERY TIME AND PLACE – MARY'S INFLUENCE IN THE SACRAMENT OF PENANCE – HER INSTRUMENTAL CAUSALITY IN THE DISTRIBUTION OF GRACE – "MOTHER OF DIVINE GRACE" – MARY'S "SUPPLIANT OMNIPOTENCE"

The Blessed Virgin labors ceaselessly to cultivate souls, making her own the words of St. Paul: *I am in labor again, until Christ be formed in you*. Her powerful intercession is employed to draw souls nearer to Christ; to dispose the hearts of her children to a more conscientious practice of the True Faith:

> Now Mary, beautiful as the moon, shines brightly as the sun and irradiates life-giving warmth. Whenever we speak of her, or speak to her, let us not forget that she is really our Mother, for through her we received divine life. She gave us Jesus, Himself the Source of grace. Mary is the Mediatrix and Dispenser of graces. . . . Under the sun's light and warmth, plants grow on earth and bear fruit; under the influence and with the help of Mary, that other Sun, good thoughts fructify in souls. . . . Beloved sons and daughters, think over the story of your own lives. Do you not notice therein a pattern of graces received from God? You are then able to add the thought, "Mary took a part in the granting of such graces." Flowers bloomed and fruits ripened in my life thanks to the warming influence of the Woman who is "bright as the Sun." (Pope Pius XII, *A Picture of the Blessed Virgin*, 1953)

For this reason, the Church applies the following Scriptural verses to Mary: "I am the mother of fair love, and of fear, and of knowledge, and of holy hope. In me is all grace of the way and of the truth; in me is all hope of life and of virtue." (Ecclus. 24:24-25) The desire to see men and women oriented towards the good, to want only the best for them, not only materially, but even regarding their characters and dispositions, is very much a *maternal* desire: "Mary is the heart of the Church." (St. Anthony Mary Claret, †1870) This love for the Church is rooted in the love of *Christ* for the Church: "As the Father hath loved Me, I also have loved you." (Jn. 15:9) It would not be amiss, therefore, to picture the Mother's love, using the words of the Father: "As one whom the mother caresseth, so will I comfort you, and you shall be comforted in Jerusalem." (Is. 66:13)

There is no way to enumerate the graces which the Mother of the Church obtains for her children, as they are graces won for us by Jesus Christ, graces bestowed *to* mankind, *from* God, *through* the immaculate hands of Mary:

> Mary's grace was abundant to overflowing and perfect to the last degree, for She gave glory to heaven and God to the earth. She gave joy to the angels and peace to men. She taught the Faith to the nations and put an end to the age-long corruption. "Full of Grace"; that was the Angel's salutation. How then can she who became the Mother of God be anything but the ladder to Paradise, the gate of heaven, the advocate of the world, the terror of demons, the hope of sinners and the true and real Mediatrix of God and men? (St. Lawrence Justinian †1456, *Sermon for the Annunciation*)

The Scriptures teach that the saints, the blessed in heaven, intercede with God for their brethren on earth:

> And another Angel came, and stood before the altar, having a golden censer; and there was given to him much incense, that he should offer of the prayers of all saints upon the golden altar, which is before the throne of God. And the smoke of the incense of the prayers of the saints ascended up before God from the hand of the Angel. (Apoc. 8:3-4)

We are reminded here that this saintly intercession, this "subordinate mediation", is always effected through the merits of Christ, by the fact that the prayers of the saints are offered on a golden *altar* which stands before God's throne. This altar signifies Jesus, Whose merits ascended from the "altar" of the Cross like fragrant incense to the Father: "Christ also hath loved us, and hath delivered Himself for us, an oblation and a sacrifice to God for an odor of sweetness." (Eph. 5:2)

If the saints, our elder brothers and sisters in the Faith, remember us, interceding for us before God, how steadfastly must Mary, endowed with a heart able to nurture the entire world, do so? Our spiritual brothers and sisters will love us with the affection of siblings. Our spiritual Mother will love us with the affection of a *mother.* At Cana, Mary looked into the eyes of her Son – the eyes of *God* – and said, "They have no wine." In heaven, she looks into His eyes still, and knowing that her children are still in need of so much, requests these good things, these graces, consolations, and conversions. Her Son responds with that Divine love for mankind kindled in His Sacred Heart: *My mother ask, for I must not turn away thy face.*

God revealed Himself to Moses as "I am Who am." St. Thomas Aquinas commented on this title: "Now, every name is appointed to signify the nature or essence of a thing. Wherefore it follows that God's very existence itself is His essence or nature." (*Contra Gentiles*) God is the First Cause, the *Principal* Cause which brings things about by its *own* power and efficacy. Creation itself was brought into existence by the Will of God: "For He spoke, and they were made: He commanded, and they were created." (Ps. 148:5)

However, God makes use of *Instrumental* Causes in the accomplishment of His Will and the unfolding of His plans, causes which receive and act upon motion from another. The sacraments are instrumental causes of grace, vehicles for the transmission of grace. Sanctifying grace is administered through instrumental causes: "Amen, amen I say to thee, unless a man be born again of water and the Holy Ghost, he cannot enter into the kingdom of God." (Jn. 3:5) "Receive ye the Holy Ghost. Whose sins you shall forgive, they are forgiven them; and whose sins you shall retain, they are retained." (Jn. 20:22-23)

During the Holy Sacrifice of the Mass, our Lord renews His sacrifice on Calvary in a mystical manner, "extending" it throughout time and space: "For from the rising of the sun even to the going down, My name is great among the Gentiles, and in every place there is sacrifice, and there is offered to My name a clean oblation." (Mal. 1:11) Prescribed sacrifices are synonymous with *priesthood*, the ordained Catholic priesthood which participates in that of the High Priest, Jesus Christ: "The Lord hath sworn and He will not repent: Thou art a priest for ever according to the order of Melchisedech." (Ps. 109:4)

Life-giving, life-restoring sacraments are offered to the world through the Church. Sacramental infusions of sanctifying grace are the province of the Church and her priests, and these infusions also inspire and provide the means to cooperate more fully with the promptings of actual, or "predisposing", grace. However we must not forget the Blessed Virgin when giving thanks for the sacraments and the ministry of priests, the visible causes behind which moves the First Cause. Although Mary is not, nor could she ever be, the source of graces, she is still called "Mediatrix of *All* Graces".

Our Lord's sacrifice on Calvary is the reason why the members of the Church can receive graces during Mass and absolution in the confessional. The members of the Church draw upon the graces won by Jesus like people drawing resources from a treasury. Furthermore, we draw from this treasury not as strangers, but as part of our spiritual inheritance: "You have received the spirit of adoption of sons . . . and if sons, heirs also; heirs indeed of God, and joint-heirs with Christ." (Rom. 8:15,17) Souls redeemed by the Precious Blood enjoy the riches of this treasure-house like Prodigal Sons, feasting in the home of their Father: "They shall be inebriated with the plenty of Thy house; and Thou shalt make them drink of the torrent of Thy pleasure." (Ps. 35.9)

Mary – the *new* Eve, and therefore truly "the mother of all the living" (Gen. 3:20) – provided the Spotless Lamb for the wooden altar of Calvary. With her full consent and an unburdened heart, she bore Him, reared Him, and stood by Him as He died. During each Mass our Lord renews His sacrifice. This renewal is not a repetition, for *Christ was offered once to exhaust the sins of many*, but the one supreme sacrifice offered on Calvary echoes throughout the ages. Like a rock tossed into a lake, it causes ripples which extend outwards in *all* directions – past, present and future. It flowed to the past, allowing the Mother of the Redeemer to be sanctified through her Immaculate Conception "in view of the merits of Jesus Christ" (Pope Pius IX): *She shall crush thy head.* It creates an "eternal present", as each generation to walk the earth is graced with the Real Presence in the Blessed Sacrament, the physical presence of the *Emmanuel* ("God *with* us"): *The bread, which we break, is it not the partaking of the Body of the Lord?* It will flow outward into future years, to souls not yet born in time: "Behold I am with you all the days, even to the consummation of the world." (Mt. 28:20)

At the first Mass, our Lord said to His apostles, His first priests, "Do this for a commemoration of Me." The Redeemer alone was able to satisfy Divine Justice on the Cross, and whenever His sacrifice is renewed mystically (in an unbloody manner) at Mass, it is offered by this same Saving Victim *through the ministry* of men whose priesthood was established at the Last Supper:

> We think that we must call this to mind, namely, that the priest acts in place of the people only for this reason, that he plays the part of Our Lord, Jesus Christ, insofar as He is the Head of all the members, and offers himself for them, and that for this reason he approaches the altar as a minister of Christ, inferior to Christ, but superior to the people. (Pope Pius XII, *Mediator Dei*, 1947)

Ordained priests, successors to the apostles, *offer* the Holy Sacrifice of the Mass. However, as Christ offered Himself a ransom for His *entire* Body, the members of the Church are given a portion and place in this mystical offering, although not in any sacerdotal capacity:

> It is clear that the faithful in Christ offer the sacrifice through the hands of the priest from this, that the minister at the altar plays the part of Christ, as of the Head, making His offering in the name of all His members, whereby indeed it happens that the whole Church is rightly said to offer the oblation of the Victim through Christ. But that the people together with the priest himself offer the sacrifice is *not* established because of this, because the members of the Church, just as the priest

> himself, perform a visible liturgical rite, which belongs only to the minister divinely assigned to this; but for the reason that they *join* their prayer of praise, impetration, expiation, and thanksgiving with the prayers or intentions of the priest, even of the High Priest Himself; so that in the very same oblation of the Victim, also according to an external rite by the priest, *they may be presented to God the Father.* (*Mediator Dei*)

At each Mass offered, graces pour down from heaven, sins are forgiven and hearts are consoled and strengthened. At each Mass offered, the members of the Church can ask pardon and forgiveness, for it is the same Saving Victim Who will present our petitions to the Father. At each Mass offered, we can give *acceptable* praise and thanksgiving to the Father, because this praise will be rendered through His own beloved Son. If there is no priest present, there is no Mass. This unbroken chain which stretches back to the nativity of the God-Man, to the institution of the priesthood, the sacraments and the establishment of the Church, began with Mary's "fiat" to the Archangel, when our High Priest took our nature upon Himself.

The *Co-Redemptrix* who stood beneath the Cross on Calvary has a special place in the "re-presentation" of the sacrifice offered on Catholic altars. When we return in a mystical fashion to Calvary, we behold the Saving Victim, and we also do not neglect the words of that Victim: *Behold thy Mother.* The prayers offered during Mass recognize this place of Mary:

> In the *Confiteor*, the priest and the people plead for the salutary intercession of St. Michael, St. John the Baptist, Sts. Peter and Paul, all the saints and the brethren. This listing of personages begins with the words, "I beseech the Blessed Mary ever virgin . . ." In the *Nicene Creed*, we recall that our hope rests in Jesus Christ, our King, Who was "incarnate by the Holy Ghost of the Virgin Mary."
>
> In the *Suscipe sancta Trinitas*, the priest asks the Blessed Trinity to accept the oblation offered in memory of the

> Passion, Resurrection and Ascension of Jesus, and "in honor of blessed Mary, ever a virgin," and of St. John the Baptist, Sts. Peter and Paul, and of all the saints.
>
> In the *Communicantes*, the members of the Church Militant honor the memory and seek the intercession of the members of the Church Triumphant. It begins, "Having communion with and venerating the memory, first, of the glorious Mary, ever a virgin, mother of Jesus Christ," then includes the apostles and martyrs.
>
> The *Libera nos* implores the protection and aid of God, and expresses trust in the intercession of Sts. Peter, Paul and Andrew, and of all the saints, beginning with "the intercession of the blessed and glorious Mary, ever a virgin, Mother of God."

God is not bound by time or space. The sacrifice of His Son was not meant to suffice only for the people who were alive at the time of the Crucifixion. The First Mass, celebrated by Jesus and the apostles, was not meant to be also the last Mass ever celebrated, a never-to-be-repeated event. On the contrary, Jesus commanded, "Do *this* for a commemoration of Me." Do *this*. The priest offering Mass, "playing the part of Christ", is offering the Mass instituted at the Last Supper, at which our Lord Himself, the High Priest, consecrates the bread and wine, using the lips of men to speak the words; therefore, a priest can rightfully claim that he says "his" Mass. The sacrifice of Jesus on the Cross is not merely "ancient history", an event frozen in the past, but something whose virtue constantly imbues reality like the rays of the sun. Through the mercy of God, each Mass is a return to Calvary:

> The principal excellence of the most Holy Sacrifice of the Mass consists in being essentially, and in the very highest degree, identical with that which was offered on the Cross of Calvary: with this sole difference, that the sacrifice on the Cross was bloody, and made once for all, and did on that one occasion satisfy fully for all the sins of the world; while the sacrifice of the altar is an

> unbloody sacrifice, which can be repeated an infinite number of times, *and was instituted in order to apply in detail that universal ransom which Jesus paid for us on* Calvary. . . . The one threw open the treasury of the merits of Christ Our Lord; the other affords the practical use of that treasury. . . . That same Body, that same Blood, that same Jesus Who then offered Himself upon Calvary, now offers Himself in the Holy Mass. . . . Oh, awful, solemn, and stupendous work! (St. Leonard of Port Maurice, †1751, *The Hidden Treasure: Holy Mass*)

Through the Holy Sacrifice, the members of the Mystical Body of Christ are united to their Head, and to each other, in a spiritual, intimate manner. At Mass, the priest intercedes for each person attending, offering up the praise, prayers and petitions of all who "assist" at Mass by uniting their prayers and intentions to his. In this way, all are united in a particular manner while the mysteries are being celebrated: "Wherefore, we beseech thee, O Lord, to receive this oblation which we Thy servants, *and with us Thy whole family*, offer up to Thee." (the *Hanc igitur*) We are also reminded of our brethren in purgatory: "Be mindful, O Lord, of Thy servants, who have gone before us with the sign of faith. . . . To these, O Lord, and to all who rest in Christ, grant, we beseech Thee, a place of refreshment, light and peace." (the *Commemoration of the Dead*)

The Mass also unites souls on earth with the saints in heaven, who owe their glory and beatitude to the sacrifice made by Jesus on the Cross. The Mass prayers quoted above, in which our Lady is mentioned, make repeated references to the apostles, saints and martyrs.

We are brought close to the angels as well during Mass. "When Mass is being celebrated," wrote St. John Chrysostom, "the Sanctuary is filled with countless angels who adore the Divine Victim immolated on the altar." St. Michael the Archangel is invoked in the *Confiteor*, and in the prayers following the Consecration we find: "We humbly beseech Thee, almighty God, to command that these our offerings be borne by the hands of Thy holy angel to Thine altar on high in the presence of Thy divine Majesty; that as many of us who shall receive the most sacred Body and Blood of Thy Son by partaking thereof from this altar may be filled with every heavenly blessing and grace: Through the same Christ our Lord."

There is a magnificent tapestry of figures engaged during each Mass. There is the priest who, by virtue of his ordination, exercises the awesome power of consecrating the bread and wine, holding the Living God in his hands. There are the vast panoramas of earthbound souls, suffering souls, blessed souls and angels, so different in some ways, yet united in Christ. Some figures in this tapestry "stand out" – i.e., the priest standing before the altar raising the Host and chalice, or the Angel bearing the offerings to the "altar on high". The Blessed Virgin has her own singular place in the unfolding of the Mass, for she is the Mother and Queen of the other figures in the tapestry.

Jesus does not come to our earthly altars as the "Suffering Servant"; He is immolated *mystically* during Mass, "without really dying", wrote St. Leonard of Port Maurice, "at one and the same time really alive and as it were slain – 'I saw a Lamb standing as it were slain'". (Apoc. 5:6) The Sacred Wounds of the Savior, by which mankind were ransomed, will remain forever – "Behold, I have graven thee in My hands" (Is. 49:16) – but the bloodshed, the tears and the anguish of Calvary, the Passion commemorated during Mass, are physically past, transformed at the Resurrection into things of beauty and salvation. As *Co-Redemptrix*, our Lady participated in the immolation of her Son. Just as *His* Wounds remain, eternal symbols of the glorious price paid for the ransom of men, so will the glorious title "Queen of Martyrs" be Mary's forever, even as she stands glorified before Jesus during the celebration of Mass. Her "Com-Passion" has been transformed also, and the radiant Queen stands in the place of the Sorrowful Mother wracked with suffering.

The Mother of God was conceived immaculately in the womb of *her* mother, St. Anne, through the foreseen merits of Christ's sacrifice on Calvary. Each Mass is a "return" to Calvary and, therefore, a joyful reminder to Mary of the privilege of her Immaculate Conception. "Charity never faileth," wrote St. Paul, and the love Mary felt, even through the horrors of Calvary, for the souls being redeemed by her Son was that of a mother for her children. Assumed into heaven and enjoying the Beatific Vision, this "Mother of fair love and of hope" – the *Mediatrix of All Graces* – always remembers these children, understanding better than anyone the plethora of graces with which the Mass is laden.

What are the actions and dispositions of Mary, the Mother of the Church, during the Holy Sacrifice of the Mass?

> If we remember this last will of our dear Savior; if we think of the moment in which the Blessed Virgin was declared the depository of her Son's wishes and the distributor of all His graces; if we remember that this privilege was bestowed upon her whilst her Son was consummating the great sacrifice of atonement upon Mount Calvary, then it will be clear that she executes her Son's wishes most cheerfully, and distributes to us His blessings and graces more abundantly at the very time when the great sacrifice of the Cross is renewed, that is, during the time of the Holy Mass, for then is she at full liberty to distribute to every one as many favors as he is capable of receiving. (Fr. Michael Müller, *The Holy Sacrifice of the Mass*, 1874)

John Gerson addressed these words to Mary: "You are the Mother of the Eucharist. . . . You, more than all others after your Son, were aware of this sacrament hidden from the ages." Truly, as Pope Pius XII taught, the Mother of the Church must take great pleasure to see this Body so intimately bound together during the celebration of Mass:

> Mary has no other desire but to lead men to Christ and to introduce them to the heart of the central mystery of Christianity, that of the Redemption. She continues to give to the Church the Son she brought into the world in Palestine. If she loves to see her children assembled for a stirring manifestation of faith and love, it is to lead them together to the mystical Bread, symbol of unity, of peace and of the eternal joy of heaven. (*Demands of*

> *Consecration to Mary*, Radio Message to the Belgian Marian Congress, 1954)

There is as little cause for Catholics to forget Our Lady during Mass as there is to ignore her presence beneath the Cross on Calvary. We are obliged, by the course of events constituting the "economy of salvation", to feel a sense of gratitude to the Blessed Virgin for her participation in the Redemption. The Cross is, of course, the one unique symbol of this Redemption: "But we preach Christ crucified, unto the Jews indeed a stumbling-block, and unto the Gentiles foolishness." (1 Cor. 1:23) However, from *before the foundation of the world*, it was decreed that another figure would stand in the tableau of Calvary:

> Finally, it was before the eyes of Mary that the divine sacrifice for which she had borne and nurtured the Victim was to be finished. As we contemplate Him in the last and most piteous of these mysteries, we see that "there stood by the Cross of Jesus, Mary, His Mother," who, in a miracle of love, *so that she might receive us as her sons*, offered generously to Divine Justice her own Son, and in her Heart died with Him, stabbed by the sword of sorrow. (Pope Leo XIII, *Jucunda semper*, 1894)

As the Mass extends the sacrifice of the Redeemer throughout time and space, so will the presence of Mary be a part of each Mass celebrated: "As Eve induced man to eat of the forbidden fruit which brought death upon us," wrote St. Peter Damian, "so it is right that Mary should prompt us to eat the Bread which gives us life." Such salutary meditations on our Lady's discreet presence at Mass can never draw the attention of Catholics *away* from Christ, away from the Cross which was the instrument of salvation for the entire world:

> In this, as in so many other things, the Church herself carefully guides the faithful both by word and example. She directs her liturgical prayers sometimes to the triune God, sometimes to Jesus Christ, and then again to the Blessed Virgin Mary, but invariably emphasizes her belief

> in Christ as the sole Mediator by concluding with the words: "through Christ our Lord". (Pohle-Preuss, *Mariology*, 1914)

As the Virgin dispenses graces which draw men to the altar for Mass, so is her beneficial influence present when we avail ourselves of the sacrament of Penance. In this life-restoring sacrament, our Lord forgives sins through the ministry of His priests. Each time sacramental absolution is administered, the Church draws freely from the Treasury of Grace won by Jesus on Calvary: "Those who by sin have fallen away from the received grace of justification, will again be able to be justified when, roused by God through the sacrament of penance, they *by the merit of Christ* shall have attended to the recovery of the grace lost." (The Council of Trent)

When we receive the grace and consolation of the sacrament of Penance, we are justified in expressing gratitude to Mary, after Jesus, for the gift. In his Apocalyptic vision, St. John depicted both the Virgin and the Catholic Church under *one* powerful image, the "Woman clothed with the sun". Rev. Matthias J. Scheeben explained the importance of this Scriptural identification of Mary with the Church in our understanding of the *distribution* of grace:

> By her cooperation in Christ's sacrifice, Mary became the depositary of the merits of the redemption for all mankind and for all times. In the first place she cooperated in imploring the Holy Ghost to hasten His descent upon the infant Church. Likewise, her continuous cooperation must hold as a normal condition for all future fruits of Christ's merits and for the action of the Holy Ghost. By her cooperation in the redemption, Mary became the spiritual mother of all the redeemed. *All the graces of redemption are specifically intended for the communication, the production, the nourishing, and the completion of the life of grace, and for this very reason Mary's continuous and universal cooperation is as natural as that of a physical mother in the rearing of her children.* Finally, the communication of the grace of redemption is linked to the Church in an absolutely universal man-

> ner, so that no one obtains grace without some sort of relation to and cooperation with the Church.
>
> We may conclude from this, first, that Mary is the ideal model of the Church; secondly, that the universal mediation of all graces by the Church cannot exist entirely of itself, if Mary is not regarded as the unfailing Mediatrix of grace. (*Mariology*, Vol. II, 1947)

But if, in the sacrament of Penance, it is the ordained Catholic priest absolving sinners in the name and by the authority of the Blessed Trinity, what place does our Blessed Mother have in this sacramental operation? In other words, in what manner is Mary's *causality* manifested in this sacrament?

Causality is defined as "the act itself of causing, i.e., of actually producing something." There are two ways in which someone can be a *cause*:

> One is called the cause of something even if one has had no direct influence on the achievement of the effect, but has worked on the will of him who did produce the effect: e.g., one did this by giving that person definite advice, or by commanding him, persuading him, begging him, threatening him, or earning it as a reward from him. . . . According to the axiom, the cause of the cause is also cause of the effect, this influence of the will on the doer which makes him do, is rightly called causality; but, because it has not a direct influence on the effect, but only on the *will* of the doer, we call it moral causality.
>
> The other way of using the word cause consists in this, that what we call cause does exercise influence on the effect itself.
>
> The question at issue is whether or not Mary in her universal mediation of grace is or is not a cause with direct action on the effect itself. If she is not, then she is merely moral cause, that is to say, God in that case always and

> everywhere grants every grace for the sake of Mary. . . . If, on the contrary, she is really a cause with direct action on the effect, then God always and everywhere grants every grace *both* for Mary's sake *and* in addition by Mary as an instrument. There is no other alternative possible. (Fr. C. Friethoff, *A Complete Mariology*, 1958)

If the causality of Our Lady with regard to the distribution of graces is a *moral* causality, then it is her *influence* that can be detected whenever graces are administered to mankind, such as that bestowed to the penitent kneeling in the confessional:

> The supernatural life which they [the sacraments] produce in souls flows from that unfailing fountain which began to flow by Her cooperation on Calvary. Furthermore, the sacraments do not reach everybody. Some people receive them, others do not; some approach frequently, others only at long intervals; contrite and fervent souls find in them the means of growing and waxing strong in God's love; others turn them into instruments of death. Whence comes the difference? It is the intercession of Mary that sends us the ministers of Christ and dispenses the mysteries of God; it is She who procures for us the boon of receiving the sacraments; finally, it is She who obtains for us the dispositions needed to approach them holily and to draw from them the fruits of our salvation. We affirm then that there is no limit, no exception, to the universality of the mediation and the intercession of the Holy Virgin. (Rev. Joseph Le Rohellec, *Mary, Mother of Divine Grace*, 1937)

By participating in her Divine Son's Passion (i.e., not complementing or augmenting it in any way), our Lady is said to have merited for us "congruously" (*de congruo*) what Jesus merited for us "condignly" (*de condigno*). "Congruous" elements are those that are marked by a harmonious agreement. A "condign" element is one that is worthy or deserving. Our Lord Jesus Christ is the *only worthy* and *deserving*

Person meriting the title of Redeemer. On Calvary, the Blessed Virgin was in a completely *harmonious agreement* with the Redeemer. Uniting her sorrows to His, she renounced her mother's rights, offering up the Lamb she had reared for the sacrifice on the Cross for the restoration of mankind to friendship with God, for the good of the spiritual progeny bequeathed to her from the Cross. Therefore, when we say that Mary merited graces for us because of her place on Calvary, we do not claim that she merited for us any graces *apart from or in addition* to those merited by Jesus, the very source of grace. What we do claim is that her "Compassion" beneath the Cross must be viewed *in relation to the Passion of Jesus.*

Through His superabundant sacrifice, our Lord made fitting reparation to God. Had there been no other human being present on Calvary during His Crucifixion, the world would still have been redeemed. But, had Mary not been present on Calvary – and present by divine decree – there would have been no "spiritual birth pangs", no Mother of the Church present as a redeemed humanity was generated and the Church born in Blood and water from her Savior's side, no maternal dimension to our spiritual rebirth.

But our Blessed Mother *was* present at the Great sacrifice, and she *did* unite her sorrows to those of her Son. Mankind was being redeemed by the Blood of Christ as Mary stood beneath the Cross. As the Mother of the Redeemer *and* the Mother of the Church, she was called upon to make her own sacrifice on that first Good Friday, and that sacrifice, while never to be confused or identified with that of Jesus, was still tuned to the spiritual benefit of mankind:

> Her cooperation was not necessary to the fact of the redemption, nor to the fullness of it as satisfying and meriting for us eternal life, but as supplemental to the redemption, as God wished it to be, *by a certain added gift and help that was to come to us.* Mary merited not for Herself or for us any graces other than those that Her Son merited on Calvary, but by Her union with Him she merited to become the Mother of His life among men, the Mother of supernatural life, the Mediatrix of

> His graces to mankind. St. Augustine says: "She is the Mother of His members in the spirit. She cooperated by charity towards the birth of faithful children in the Church, who are the members of that Head, Whose Mother She truly is in the flesh." [*De Sanct. Virginitate*] (A.M. Mayer, OSM, *Advanced Mariology*, 1934)

Yet our Lady's place in creation is unique because of her Divine Maternity and all the titles that are grounded in it, such as *Co-Redemptrix* and *Mediatrix of All Graces*. That she acts as a *moral cause* in the distribution of graces, by her influence and prayers, is incontestable. But, can Mary's causality in the distribution of graces be more than a *moral* one? Can it be also a *physical* instrumental causality, a *direct* action on the effects of each and every grace bestowed to men? In the Gospels, we find St. Elizabeth crying out to our Lady at the moment the infant St. John the Baptist was sanctified in her womb: "For behold as soon as the voice of thy salutation sounded in my ears, the infant in my womb leaped for joy." Fr. Reginald Garrigou-Lagrange observed:

> By admitting that Mary not only obtains grace for us by her prayers but transmits it to us by her action, a fuller meaning is given to her titles of treasurer and dispensatrix of all graces. . . . Mary's influence on our souls remains, it is true, shrouded in mystery, but it appears probable that it is more than moral: she seems to enter into the production of grace as a free and knowing instrument, somewhat as a miracle-worker can perform a miracle by his contact and his blessing.
>
> Mary's universal mediation should not be understood as if it meant that no grace is given to us without our having asked it *explicitly* of her; that would be to confuse our prayer to her with her prayer to God. Mary does in fact ask for graces without being invoked explicitly. . . . The *Our Father* can be said without any explicit invocation of Mary; but she is invoked implicitly in it when it is said

> according to the order established by divine providence. . . . All graces without exception come by her mediation. Such is the general law established by divine providence, and there is no known indication of any exceptions. (*The Mother of the Saviour and Our Interior Life*, 1948)

The *Litany of Loreto* addresses Mary as the "Mother of Divine Grace", and her continual cooperation in the distribution of graces, her place as Mother and Mediatrix in the "kingdom of grace", is anchored in the lessons, of Scripture: "Jesus Christ, yesterday, and today; and the same forever". (Heb. 13:8) "Shall not Sion say: This man and that man is born in her? And the Highest Himself hath founded her." (Ps. 86:5)

Our Lord made His Mother *what* she is and placed her *where* she is; therefore, He will not deny her petitions or turn aside from her intercession, for He Himself taught that ". . . every city or house divided against itself shall not stand." (Mt. 12:25) The Church, then, does not hesitate or waver in describing Mary's intercession as *omnipotentia supplex* – "suppliant omnipotence". Accordingly, the children of Mary have reserved some of their most memorable praises for the doctrine of her mediation and distribution of graces:

Blessed is the man, O Virgin Mary,
who loves thy name;
thy grace will comfort his soul.

He will be refreshed as by fountains of water;
thou wilt produce in him the fruits of justice.
Thou alone makest the circuit of the earth;
that thou mayest help those that call upon thee.

Distill upon us the drops of thy sweetness;
for thou art the cupbearer of the sweetness of grace.

He who drinketh from her,
Will spring forth unto life everlasting:
and he will never thirst.

(St. Bonaventure, *Psalter of the BVM*)

> The whole human race prays in the person of Mary. Her whole attitude is expressive and eloquent. There is depth and emotion in her eyes; the gravity of supplication suffuses her beautiful face. Her hands are joined. Her lips quiver. A woman's voice is heard in heaven. Its tone is very soft, well modulated, but also very tenacious and pleading. The eternal Christ recognizes the voice whose pure melody sustained and delighted Him from the Crib to Calvary. . . . Grace is pre-formed in her and receives in her the imprint of a special beauty. All grace and all graces come to us thus canalised and distributed by her, impregnated with that special sweetness which she imparts to all she touches and all she does. (Fr. R. Bernard, *The Mystery of Mary*, 1954)

St. Ambrose (†397) described our Lady as "containing all the delights of Paradise". What else would we expect from the one chosen to be the Mother of God, and, not only of God, but of all mankind? "We shall be filled with the good things of Thy house." (Ps. 64:5) These words seem particularly suited to the spiritual bounty we receive through Mary. Whoever desires to please Christ, to cultivate grace and perseverance, whether priests who speak words of absolution and consecration, or penitents and communicants who live by these holy words, would do well to keep ever in mind our Lady's central place in the daily life of the Church.

Chapter Twenty-Six

Mary's Fullness of Grace

The Holy Ghost inspires praise for Mary in the heart of St. Elizabeth – Jesus redeems, Mary grants – What was the "fullness" of grace in St. Stephen – With Mary "full of grace" is a title – How did Mary "merit" to be the Mother of God? – Her plenitude of grace a gift from God – The ark of the covenant was a prefigure of Our Lady – Parallel comparisons of the reality of Our Lady and the figures of her in Scripture – The Theotokos and the Council of Ephesus

"All Scripture, inspired of God, is profitable to teach, to reprove, to correct, to instruct in justice," wrote St. Paul, "that the man of God may be perfect, furnished to every good work." (2 Tim. 3:16–17) Therefore it is profitable to go to Sacred Scripture as a guide, in order to learn the proper attitude demanded of us by the Blessed Trinity in approaching the one who is at once the beloved Daughter of the Father, Mother of the Son, and Spouse of the Holy Ghost.

St. Elizabeth was a good and holy woman, chosen by God to be the mother of His Son's precursor, St. John the Baptist. What was her attitude before our Lady during the Visitation? St. Luke the Evangelist recorded the scene:

> And it came to pass that when Elizabeth heard the salutation of Mary, the infant leaped in her womb. *And Elizabeth was filled with the Holy Ghost*: And she cried out with a loud voice, and said: "Blessed art thou among women, and blessed is the fruit of thy womb. And whence is this to me, that the Mother of my Lord should come to me?" (Lk. 1:41–43)

St. Elizabeth's attitude towards Mary was one of praise, deep humility and gratitude, spoken *under the direct inspiration of the Holy Ghost*. Here is a precept for the honoring of Mary, taught *directly* by God. Elizabeth spoke from the heart and, as with the prophets of old, God used her voice to proclaim His goodness and bounty – i.e., the gift of our Lady, by whose *mediation* the infant St. John the Baptist was sanctified in his mother's womb, and prepared for his mission. So powerful was Elizabeth's praise of the Mother of God (*the Mother of my Lord*), that it has become part of one of the most cherished prayers the world has ever known: "Blessed art thou among women, and blessed is the fruit of thy womb." Her holy son, too, would never forget that the invaluable gift of his own sanctification was brought to him by the Mother of his Lord.

St. John the Evangelist had a special reason for thanking God for the gift of Mary. He was the one to whom the words, *Behold thy Mother*, were addressed by the dying Jesus on Calvary. Even before the words were spoken, he witnessed the awesome scene where His Lord, indicating him, said to Mary: "Woman, behold thy son." What must have been his feelings at that moment? In the midst of God's own suffering, in the midst of wholesale apostasy and madness, in the midst of death . . . St. John was given the one treasure our Lord had left to give, until His glorious Resurrection. Both mother and disciple knew full well that their new bond, a filial one (meant to contain all the affection indicated by the term), applied to the entire Church, that the Redeemer, speaking from the Cross, was speaking to all men, forever: "*When you shall have lifted up the Son of Man*, then shall you know, that I am He and that I do nothing of myself, *but as the Father hath taught me, these things I speak.*" (Jn. 8:28)

St. John, grateful for this incomparable gift, did not hesitate to express his gratitude to Jesus and his love for Mary: *And from that hour, the disciple took her to his own.* It is not difficult to understand why the young evangelist referred to himself as the disciple "whom Jesus loved." In his acceptance of Mary, there sounds both an echo and a fulfillment of the ancient text: "I purposed therefore to take her to me to live with me: knowing that she will communicate to me of her good things, and will be a comfort in my cares and grief." (Wis. 8:9)

Whenever St. John refers to our Lady in his writings, it is as a *Mother*. At Cana, she is "the Mother of Jesus", a title as profound as it is simple. On Calvary, she is "His Mother". In the *Apocalypse*, she is the "Woman clothed with the sun . . . being with child," the mirror image of the "Woman" prophesied in *The Book of Genesis*. The devout son who took Mary to his own on Calvary looks at the Blessed Virgin and sees the Mother of Jesus . . . sees his own Mother in the order of grace . . . sees the Mother of the Church. Like St. Elizabeth before him, St. John is humbled before the Divine Maternity, and his inspired words are a testament to the glory of Mary's Divine *and* Spiritual maternities; she is "the Mother of Jesus", and she is also the mother of "the rest of her seed", the members of the Church, who "keep the commandments of God, and have the testimony of Jesus Christ." To lack this Spiritual Mother (and the True Church whose own "maternity" is represented by hers) is, quite simply, to lack the testimony of Christ, to disdain His commandments: "Anyone who does not have Mary for his mother, does not have God for his father." (St. Louis de Montfort)

St. John the Evangelist wrote under the inspiration of the Holy Ghost. St. Elizabeth spoke during the Visitation under the influence of the Holy Ghost. Through the words of both of these holy personages, God reveals that we will please Him by loving and honoring Mary and, consequently, displease Him by dishonoring her: "The foolish man despiseth his mother." (Prov. 15:20)

The authentic "Christian" attitude, then, is the one exemplified by St. John in his inspired writings, one which cannot look upon the Virgin Mary without seeing both the Mother of Jesus and *our* own Spiritual Mother, an active mother. This "tandem" of Jesus and Mary is a refrain which haunts the Sacred Scriptures: The Woman and her seed . . . The Beloved and His Spouse . . . The Virgin who will bear a Son . . . The Child and His Mother . . . The Crucified Savior and the Queen of Martyrs together on Calvary . . . The Woman crowned with twelve stars, whose Son will rule all nations.

This refrain, first learned through the cadences of the inspired books, cherished by the apostles and taught to all men of good will, has grown into a symphony of praise over the centuries. It is not in our nature to remain silent in the face of something truly grand, and human sentiment, guided by right reason and Revealed Truth, can do no less than render honor to this "tandem" of Jesus and Mary, a thing as beneficial to souls in a practical sense as it is elevating to contemplate. This was done artfully in a "pilgrim song" of medieval Spain:

Praise Mary, the Virgin Mother,
praise Jesus Christ with all your hearts.

Mary, sanctuary of the world, protect us.
Jesus, our secure refuge, hear us.
Indeed you are our place of refuge,
truly a safe place of shelter.

Jesus, supreme good, source of all truth.
Mary, sweet and tender, most graceful.
In the same way you show your pity to us,
who allow vanity to oppress us.

Mary grants salvation to all.
Jesus redeems the damned.
They fight fiercely for their servants,
enduring hard beatings and blows.

("Mariam Matrem Virginem", from
I Libre Vermell de Montserrat, 14th century)

This is a fine example demonstrating how, at one time, even a popular song could contain a wealth of sound devotional *and doctrinal* material. Jesus *redeems*; Mary *grants*. Here, in the simplest way possible, are expressed the doctrines of the Virgin's participation in our Redemption, and of her role as "distributor" of the graces won by her Son on Calvary. Jesus, the "supreme good, source of all truth", is our *refuge*, the ultimate end of all faith and devotion. Mary, "sweet and tender, most graceful", is our *sanctuary*, the Mother whose mantle protects all wayfarers striving to keep to the road that leads home. In such artistic creations, men and women do no more than emulate the example of those holy personages of the New Testament who were the first to render homage to our Lady, not in the language of prophecy, but as a result of their actual *acquaintance* with her. Each and every Catholic is invited to do likewise . . . and for the same reason.

There are further praises of Mary preserved in the Gospels, praises rendered by God, first, through an angel, and then, by His own mouth. In his account of the Annunciation, St. Luke relates that "the Angel Gabriel was *sent from God* into a city of Galilee, called Nazareth, to a virgin espoused to a man whose name was Joseph." The *fullness of time was come*, when God would send His Son, *made of a woman*. The angel was acting as a messenger; his words were given to him to speak by God, Who had ordained the Incarnation from the Beginning and announced it to the world in Eden. In short, Gabriel's greeting to Mary is *God's greeting to Mary*, delivered by the celestial courtier:

> Hail, full of grace, the Lord is with thee: blessed art thou among women. . . . Thou hast found grace with God.

In *The Acts of the Apostles*, we read that the martyr, St. Stephen, was "full of grace and fortitude". Before this, we are told that the apostles "imposed hands upon" Stephen and six other deacons, men "of good reputation, full of the Holy Ghost." These were men of integrity, wisdom and piety, chosen to serve the material needs of the community; in addition, by the laying on of hands, they were ordained to the sacred ministry.

"And Stephen, full of grace and fortitude, did great wonders and signs among the people." (6:8) Fortitude is one of the Seven Gifts of the Holy Ghost. By relating that St. Stephen was "full of grace", the Scriptures attest to his great sanctity, for, during his martyrdom, "he, being full of the Holy Ghost, looking up steadfastly to heaven, saw the glory of God, and Jesus standing at the right hand of God." (7:55)

While the descriptive phrase, "full of grace", had been applied to others as a means of highlighting their sanctity or piety, it is only with the Blessed Virgin that we find it employed as a *greeting*, in a direct address to someone:

> The Angel salutes Mary with a word, *Kecharitomene*, which I do not remember to have met elsewhere in the Scriptures. Not even to a man has a like word been addressed. "Hail, full of grace." For Mary alone is this reserved. (Origen, *Homily VI*)

The greeting of the Angel Gabriel to Mary was not merely an affirmation that she was justified in the eyes of God, or that God "approved" of her. Destined to be preserved forever in the Gospels, it was a bold statement meant to teach us that the Mother of God was and is *Full of Grace*. In St. Luke's Gospel, the greeting of Gabriel to Mary is rendered by the Greek word, *Kecharitomene*, which was translated as "*gratia plena*" (full of grace) in the Latin Vulgate. Yet even this time-honored translation fails to capture the depths of the word, *Kecharitomene*, which is derived from the root "*charis*" (grace); the one thus addressed is recognized as being, and *always* having been, in the state of grace. Gabriel, then, was the first to speak of the Dogma of the Immaculate Conception, of the glories of Mary's pure soul, and he did so in words given to him by *God*:

> "Full of grace" translates *kecharitomene*, the perfect passive participle of *charitoo*. It denotes one who has been and still is the object of divine benevolence, one who has been favored and continues to be favored by God, one who has been granted supernatural grace and remains in this state. . . . This rendering [full of grace] expresses the conviction of the Church that the divine favor was fully bestowed upon Mary, in the sense that she was ever immune from the least stain of sin and that she abounded in the graces of the supernatural life and in all the gifts and fruits of the Holy Spirit which flow from that life. (Fr. Michael J. Gruenthaner, "Mary in the New Testament," from *Mariology*, Vol. I – Fr. J. Carol, ed., 1955)

> *Kecharitomene* means a woman full of grace endowed not merely with the extrinsic graces proper to her state of life, *but with a full measure of sanctifying grace*, which precedes the grace of vocation, strictly so called, by way of preparation and endowment. Mary was not yet *de facto* the Mother of God when the Angel addressed her as *Kecharitomene*, for she had not yet given her consent. (Pohle-Preuss, *Mariology*, 1953)

St. Luke wrote his Gospel in Greek; our phrases "*Gratia Plena*" and "Full of Grace" are translations of the Greek term, *Kecharitomene*. A very interesting question may be asked concerning the greeting of Gabriel: In what language did the heavenly messenger address our Lady? Did he speak in Aramaic, the common tongue of the time?

Did he speak in Hebrew, the official liturgical language of the children of Israel?

This question is not as important as are its *implications*. St. Luke heard the story of the Annunciation from the lips of Mary herself, for, besides the archangel, she was the only eyewitness to the event. She related to the evangelist the very words spoken to her on that day. When the time came to commit his research on the life of Christ (i.e., his Gospel) to writing, Luke rendered Gabriel's greeting to the Virgin by a word that *in no uncertain terms* expressed her fullness of grace and her Immaculate Conception. *Regardless of the language spoken by Gabriel*, St. Luke's account of the Annunciation is further proof that the Dogma of the Immaculate Conception and the understanding that our Lady is a "Treasury of Graces" are *apostolic* doctrines. St. Luke was inspired by the Holy Ghost when he wrote his Gospel. Furthermore, he would have received from other apostolic sources all the teachings imparted by Jesus Christ to His disciples during the time He remained with them between His Resurrection and Ascension – i.e., the teachings called "Sacred Tradition" today, and which included all the doctrines concerning the Mother of God.

In short, the Angel Gabriel, a messenger from God, visited the Blessed Virgin and addressed her in words which proclaimed the *fact* of her plenitude of grace. Our Lady, in turn, related those words to St. Luke. Luke, then, writing his Gospel in Greek, searched for the word or phrase that would most accurately reproduce the original greeting of the Angel. This phrase, "Full of Grace," is a wonderful testament to the ineffable sanctity of the Blessed Mother. Therefore, anyone who dares to deny either Mary's Immaculate Conception or her plenitude of grace tries to make a liar out of God.

This name, then – *Kecharitomene*, "Full of Grace" – is the secret name of Mary, safeguarded throughout the ages in the bosom of the Blessed Trinity until "the fullness of time was come", and the Angel Gabriel would pronounce it aloud for the first time. Since then, only God alone can know how many times that name, "Full of Grace" has ascended to the vaults of heaven, carrying with it the petitions and gratitude of Mary's spiritual children.

Thou hast found grace with God, announced Gabriel to Mary, again speaking on behalf of his Lord. Of all the millions upon millions of women who would walk the earth, only one would give birth to God Incarnate. What can we say of a woman who could literally "charm" God out of heaven, and into her holy womb? "Thou hast *found* grace with God." Our Lady, the Immaculate Conception, was not a clockwork figure, sanctified and "wound-up" at her conception, so that she might walk the roads of earth blissfully unaware until it was time for the Annunciation. On the contrary, Mary *found* grace with God.

One woman out of millions . . . one particular person, an individual born on a certain day in a certain place; Mary the daughter of Joachim and Anne . . . "found" grace with the Blessed Trinity. This is why it is said, in the writings of Fathers, Doctors and saints that our Lady "merited" the Divine Maternity. "Take as your example blessed Mary," wrote St. Jerome, "whose purity was so great that she merited to be the Mother of the Lord."

In one sense, we cannot say that our Lady merited the Divine Maternity, for then we would be asserting that she *deserved* the Incarnation itself. If this were the case, Mary's merits would need to have been equal to such a reward, and she would have received the Divine Maternity as a reward for her good works. This is not the clear teaching of the Gospels on the "reason" behind the Incarnation: "*For God so loved the world*, as to give His only begotten Son." For this reason, Pope Pius XII referred to Mary and "the Divine Child whom she deserved, albeit through no merit of her own, to bear at Bethlehem." (*Invitation to Cana*, 1956)

The Church makes no claim that the Blessed Virgin deserved the Incarnation itself. However, we do rightfully proclaim that Mary, because of her humility, obedience and purity – i.e., her correspondence with grace – "merited" to be that singular Mother *presupposed* by the Incarnation: "The Blessed Virgin is said to have merited to bear the Lord of all, *not because she merited His becoming man*, but because through grace given her she merited such a degree of purity and sanctity that she *could fittingly be* the Mother of God." (St. Thomas Aquinas)

The Incarnation could not be merited by mankind, but, once it had been decreed, *a Mother would be involved*. The antiphon *Regina Coeli*, sung during Easter season, recognizes our Lady's "claim" to be that Mother: "Queen of Heaven rejoice, alleluia. For He *Whom thou wast made worthy to bear*, alleluia. He has risen, as He said, alleluia."

The Incarnation was the entry into our world of God-made-Man. This could have been effected without the Divine Maternity; Jesus could have appeared on earth as an adult man at any time. However, the love of God for mankind moved Him to become "in all things like as we are, without sin. . . . Because the children are partakers of flesh and blood, He also Himself in like manner partook of the same." (Heb. 4:15,2:14) This is the *reality* of the Incarnation, the bedrock and heart of our Redemption:

> For nowhere doth He take hold of the angels: but of the seed of Abraham He taketh hold. Wherefore it behoved Him in all things to be made like unto His brethren, that He might become a merciful and faithful High Priest with God, that He might be a propitiation for the sins of the people. (Heb. 2:16-17)

God redeemed the world as a Man, as an individual with a name and a face, who was born one day in a certain town, grew up there . . . and died as a ransom for His brethren. This *Man*, like every man, was given a Mother, a young virgin pleasing to God. In the *Nicene Creed*, the Church professes belief in Jesus Christ, "conceived" by the Holy Ghost and "born" of the Virgin Mary. Our Lady, therefore, is called the "Spouse" of the Holy Ghost:

> Among creatures made in God's image, the union brought about by married love is the most intimate of all. In a much more precise, more interior, more essential manner, the Holy Spirit lives in the soul of the Immaculata, in the depths of her very being. . . . The fruit of the love of God and of the Immaculata is Jesus, the Son of God and of man, the Mediator between God and man. (St. Maximilian Kolbe †1943, *Sketches*)

In marriage, the sacramental bond uniting the spouses is not meant to terminate with the birth of offspring. On the contrary, it is meant to be an indissoluble union. The unique bond existing between the

Holy Ghost and Mary also was not meant to terminate at the birth of the Incarnate Word. She remains His Spouse, and she continues to labor with Him for the restoration of souls:

> By the power of the redemption wrought by Christ, the Holy Spirit transforms the souls of men into temples of God; He makes of us the adoptive children of God and heirs of the heavenly kingdom.
>
> Till the end of the world it will be the task of the Holy Spirit to form the new members predestined to glory in the mystical body of Christ. And as St. Louis de Montfort shows, this task is to be carried to completion with Mary, in Mary and through Mary.
>
> Just as the second divine Person appears in His Incarnation as the "seed of the woman", so the Holy Spirit manifests His share in the work of the Redemption through the Immaculate Virgin who, although she is a person entirely distinct from Him, is so intimately associated with Him that our minds cannot understand it. (St. Maximilian Kolbe, *Miles Immaculata I*)

"In the same holy bosom of His most chaste Mother, Christ took to Himself flesh, and united to Himself the spiritual body formed by those who were to believe in Him," wrote Pope St. Pius X. This "marriage" between divine and human nature, consummated in the womb of Mary, was a wedding between Christ and His Church, between the Blessed Trinity and mankind . . . between God and Mary. This is why both the Virgin *and* the Church appear as the Bride, the "Spouse" of the Beloved, in *The Canticle of Canticles*:

> Let my beloved come into His garden, and eat the fruit of His apple trees. I am come into my garden, O my sister, my Spouse, I have gathered my myrrh, with my aromatical spices. . . . I sleep, and my heart watcheth: the voice of my Beloved knocking: Open to me, my sister, my love, my dove, my undefiled. (Cant. 5:1-2)

The language of the Canticles, and many other Old Testament texts, declares that God's love is not an abstract entity, but fully realized *exactly in His relations with His creatures*:

> In the wilderness (as thou hast seen) the Lord thy God hath carried thee, as a man is wont to carry his little son. (Deut. 1:31) O Lord my God, I have cried to Thee, and Thou hast healed me. Thou hast brought forth, O Lord, my soul from hell. (Ps. 29:3-4)

The lament of Jesus over Jerusalem expresses the intensely *personal* nature of the relationship desired by God with his children: "How often would I have gathered thy children as the bird doth her brood under her wings." (Lk. 13:34) The imagery used by Our Lord is very reminiscent of that used in the Old Testament to announce His saving work: "Behold I myself will seek my sheep, and will visit them . . . and will gather them out of the countries, and will bring them to their own land." (Ez. 34:11,13)

The love of Jesus for Mary, then, is not an abstract "appreciation" of the fact that she happens to be His Mother. No one is merely "a face in the crowd" to God: *Before I formed thee in the bowels of thy mother, I knew thee.* A person's entire life and character is set before His eyes: "Ask me of things to come, concerning my children." (Is. 45:11) Mary – Daughter, Mother and Spouse – was cherished by God as a unique *individual* from the Beginning:

> The Lord possessed me in the beginning of His ways, before He made anything from the beginning. I was set up from eternity, and of old before the earth was made. The depths were not as yet, and I was already conceived. (Prov. 8:22-24)

The plenitude of graces bestowed upon the Blessed Virgin from the moment of her conception was a divine gift *for* Mary, but the supernatural benefits conveyed by these graces are treasures which God wishes to bestow upon all His creatures:

> Grace to you and peace be accomplished in the knowledge of God and of Christ Jesus, our Lord: As all things

> of His divine power which appertain to life and godliness are given us, through the knowledge of Him Who hath called us by His own proper glory and virtue. By Whom He hath given us most great and precious promises: that by these you may be made partakers of the divine nature: flying the corruption of that concupiscence which is in the world. (2 Pet. 1:2-4)

However, in accordance with God's will and plans, such powerful graces are not given equally to individual souls: "To every one of us is given grace, according to the measure of the giving of Christ." In her litany, we address Mary as the "Singular Vessel of Devotion", for she gave Jesus to the world, "that you may be made partakers of the divine nature." Out of love, God will send His Son to earth; also out of love, a human woman must say "fiat", *Be it done unto me*, before this will happen.

The true splendor of the Church's devotion to the Blessed Virgin lies *in our recognition of Mary's love for God.* St. Epiphanius underscored this recognition in his refutation of the 4th century *Kollyridian* heresy, whose devotees, mostly women, rendered divine worship to Mary, offering her oblations of small cakes (*kollyra*):

> Yes, Mary's body was holy, but it was not God. Yes, the Virgin was surely a virgin and worthy of honor; however, she was not given for us to adore her. *She herself adored Him Who was born of her flesh*, having descended from heaven and from the bosom of the Father. (*Adversus haereses*)

The Immaculate Conception prepared our Lady for a life devoted to God and her fellow men. But it was *her* heart, *her* will, which turned this devotion into a daily offering of herself, giving such pleasure to the Blessed Trinity. It is no exaggeration, then, to repeat that Mary "charmed" our Lord into seeking out her womb, and no other, when the *fullness of the time was come*:

> He who is not awestruck by this Virgin's spirit and who does not admire her soul is ignorant of how great God is. Heaven trembles, angels quake, creation cannot bear it, nature is helpless – yet a girl carries God in her womb;

> she receives Him into herself and offers Him a dwelling place. (St. Peter Chrysologus †c. 450, *Sermo 140*)

There are great mysteries attending the Mother of God, such as her Immaculate Conception and Assumption, and they, in turn, stem from the most profound of all mysteries: *One* God in Three distinct Persons, and the Incarnation of the Second Divine Person in the womb of a Mother. We are invited by our Lord to ponder His relationship to this Mother, and to do so without getting swamped in esoteric theories. One glance at an icon of the Madonna and Child, with the Holy Infant sitting so serenely and happily on His Mother's arm, or on her lap as upon a perfect throne, is enough to prove the worth of the fine words penned by Caryll Houselander (d. 1954): "It is in Our Lady that God fell in love with Humanity."

These considerations point to one scriptural verse in praise of Mary in which all the others are contained and summarized, for the words came from the mouth of Jesus:

> And it came to pass, as He spoke these things, a certain woman from the crowd, lifting up her voice, said to Him: Blessed is the womb that bore Thee, and the paps that gave Thee suck. But He said: Yea rather, blessed are they who hear the word of God and keep it. (Lk. 11:27-28)

As is sadly to be expected, mean-spirited souls, desirous of projecting their own feelings *onto* Jesus rather than learning *from* Him, imagine that this statement is a veiled warning to steer clear of Marian devotion, to ignore the awesome majesty of the Divine Maternity. Sacred Scripture proves the contrary. The words of St. Elizabeth uttered during the Visitation narrative, uttered after she was "filled with the Holy Ghost", provide eloquent testimony to the fact that the Divine Maternity *must* be honored, if we would please God: *Blessed art thou among women, and blessed is the fruit of thy womb. And whence is this to me, that the Mother of my Lord should come to me?*

The infant Savior rested beneath His Mother's Immaculate Heart for nine months. Wherever Mary went, she carried God with her. Elizabeth praised the mystery of the Incarnation: *Blessed is the fruit of thy womb.* Then, having rendered praise to the Lord, she praises *Mary* directly: "And blessed art thou that hast believed, because those things shall be accomplished that were spoken to thee by the Lord." Here, the depth and power of the Angel Gabriel's greeting to the Virgin is recalled, for Elizabeth says that the words spoken to Mary by *the Lord* will be accomplished; although they were delivered by the Archangel, the words of greeting were God's own words.

St. Elizabeth's praises express the *same* sentiments as those addressed by Jesus to the woman in the crowd. Blessed are they *who hear* the word of God, said Jesus; you have believed those things *that were spoken to thee*, said Elizabeth to Mary. Blessed are they *who keep* the word of God, said our Lord; blessed art thou that *hast believed*, said Elizabeth to Mary.

The mother of St. John the Baptist certainly honored Our Lady through her inspired words. The Angel Gabriel certainly honored Mary at the Annunciation, when he addressed her with the magnificent title, *Kecharitomene*, "Full of Grace". God is Truth and, therefore, can never be accused of displaying self-contradictory behavior. Jesus Christ can *not* have disparaged honor and devotion to His Mother, *after* the Holy Ghost *inspired* the same in St. Elizabeth. The One Who instructed the Angel Gabriel to approach the young Virgin with such lofty regard could not suddenly use a well-meaning woman's outburst of affection as an opportunity to demean His Mother in public, using, in essence, the same words inspired earlier by the Holy Ghost in order *to contradict the sense of those very words*.

However, Jesus *did* use the anonymous woman's outburst to instruct His followers. Having just heard His Mother praised, He rewarded the good intentions of the woman in the crowd both by confirming her praise and elaborating upon it. The woman spoke the truth; the womb of Mary *is* blessed. Even the objects which foreshadowed the Mother of God in the ancient books testify to this blessedness. One such object was the Burning Bush, aflame with the presence of God, yet not consumed by it, just as our Lady bore God in her body without being overcome by the Divine Presence. Moses heard these words spoken from out of this bush: "Put off the shoes from thy feet: for the place whereon thou standest is *holy ground*". (Ex. 3:5) How much holier is the womb of the *Theotokos*?

Another object which foreshadowed the Mother of God was the Ark of the Covenant. The Scriptures relate how a man named Oza, who dared to touch it merely to keep it from falling off a moving cart, was struck dead by God "for his rashness". There is a further lesson here on the importance of honoring holy things *properly*, as God wishes them to be honored. In the procession led by King David, the Ark was carried in a cart, just as the Philistines had done when they returned it to the Levites, after suffering many calamities, such as plague and the destruction of the statue of their "god", Dagon. While the Philistines, the persecutors of Israel, might choose to mount the Ark in a cart, so that they could include propitiatory gifts to the God of Israel, the Levite priests would *carry* the Ark, as they did at the Battle of Jericho. The Ark had rings at its four corners and bars of setim-wood, overlaid with gold, were put ". . . into the rings that were at the sides of the Ark to carry it." (Ex. 37:5) Therefore the use of a cart by David's followers was neglectful and, chastened by the death of Oza, David will later command, "No one ought to carry the Ark of God, but the Levites, whom the Lord hath chosen to carry it." (1 Par. 15:2)

If the Burning Bush stood on "holy ground", and the Ark of the Covenant was deemed worthy of only the highest regard, what of the womb of the Virgin Mary? St. Cyril of Alexandria (†444) addressed our Lady as, "You who gave birth to God and carried under your pure Heart Him Whom space cannot contain." Mary's womb . . . the place where Divinity united Itself to human nature . . . the place where God, the Infinite, rested for nine months . . . *not* blessed? If words, indeed, have any meaning at all, our Lady's womb was the most "blessed" of all places. Her Son knew that, for He had chosen it. The woman in the crowd, observing Jesus, correctly intuited the fact.

In our Lord's reply, then, there is no denigration of the blessedness and holiness of Mary's body or soul. Rather, Jesus wished to praise His Mother's obedience, her intense love of God and willingness to give herself entirely to Him. In doing this, *He is praising the very qualities that moved her to give her "fiat" to the Incarnation.* Before the Son of God would descend to earth, Mary would have to *consent* to become His Mother. She would have to display the greatest faith the world had ever known, and also the most selfless love for both God *and* man that the world had ever known: *The Holy Ghost shall come upon thee, and the power of the most High shall overshadow thee. . . . Be it done to me according to thy word. . . . Blessed are they who hear the word of God, and keep it.* St. Augustine echoed our Lord's own sentiment when he wrote that "the Virgin conceived Him, not by desire, but by faith."

The actual *consent* of the Blessed Virgin to the Incarnation is a thing not to be taken lightly. There is a temptation to consider it a "foregone conclusion", because Mary was so carefully prepared for her role as Mother of God. To believe this is to suggest that noble personages cannot perform noble acts, that the value of a charitable or courageous action is lessened if the one who performs it does so from a generous spirit. This is not only presumption, but it questions the very words of Jesus, "Blessed are they who hear the word of God, and keep it." An individual must *decide* to act upon divine inspiration or instruction, or else there is no merit to his obedience.

"Answer, O sacred Virgin," exclaimed St. Augustine, contemplating the Annunciation, "why delay you the salvation of the world, which depends on your consent?" Gratitude to Christ for His gift of redemption is not expressed by mitigating the circumstances through which He took to Himself that Body which would be given up for the world. The consent of Mary is a key element in the great drama of salvation history, a drama whose focal point is the Annunciation:

> The whole human race, fallen upon its knees, awaits this. Not without reason, for the consolation of the wretched, the redemption of the captive, the deliverance of the condemned, the salvation of all the children of Adam, of all thy race, hangs upon thy lips. Quickly, O Virgin, give thine answer. O Lady, make that reply which the earth, the heavens above and the regions below expect. (St. Bernard, *Homiliae super evangelium "missus est"*)

St. Hesychius of Jerusalem (†c. 451) wrote: "The Ark of Thy sanctification, the Virgin Theotokos surely. If Thou art the pearl then she must be the Ark." The first Ark of the Covenant, made by men from setim-wood, was overlaid with the purest gold "within and without" preparatory to its receiving the divine presence; Mary, created by God, was conceived immaculately, all beautiful interiorly and exteriorly when she received the Son of God into her womb. The first Ark contained the Tables of the Law and the manna of the desert; Mary's womb contained the Divine Judge Himself, Who is the Living Bread that came down from heaven.

The first Ark, the focal point of Israel's spiritual life, gave the people a means by which to apprehend the Presence of the invisible God: "The cloud covered the tabernacle of the testimony, and the glory of the Lord filled it . . . and the majesty of the Lord shining, for the cloud had covered all." (Ex. 40:32-33) Through Mary, the invisible God was given a *body*: "And I saw, and I gave testimony, that this is the Son of God." (Jn. 1:34) "Who is the image of the invisible God." (Col. 1:15)

The identification of the Blessed Virgin with the original Ark of the Covenant is an *apostolic* teaching, preserved in the opening chapter of *The Gospel According to St. Luke*:

St. Luke 1:35
"And the angel answering, said to her: The Holy Ghost shall come upon thee, and the power of the most High shall overshadow thee."

St. Luke 1:41
"And it came to pass that when Elizabeth heard the salutation of Mary, the infant leaped in her womb."

St. Luke 1:43
"And whence is this to me, that the mother of my Lord should come to me?"

St. Luke 1:56
"And Mary abode with her about three months; and she returned to her own house."

Exodus 40:32
"The cloud covered the tabernacle of the testimony, and the glory of the Lord filled it."

2 Kings 6:13-14
"And when they that carried the ark of the Lord had gone six paces, he sacrificed an ox and a ram: And David danced with all his might before the Lord."

2 Kings 6:9
"And David was afraid of the Lord that day, saying: How shall the ark of the Lord come to me?"

2 Kings 6:11-12
"And the ark of the Lord abode in the house of Obededom the Gethite three months: and the Lord blessed Obededom and all his household. And it was told King David, that the Lord had blessed Obededom, and all that he had, because of the ark of God."

The parallels are striking and they do not stem from mere happenstance, for Scripture has its own internal logic: "For what things soever were written, were written for our instruction." (Rom. 15:4) "Now these things were done in a figure of us." (1 Cor. 10:6) The original Ark was covered by the "glory of the Lord"; Mary was *overshadowed* by the Holy Ghost. St. Elizabeth testified that her young cousin was, indeed, the "New Ark", when, inspired by the Holy Ghost, she echoed the words spoken by King David before the first Ark. David danced before the original Ark; St. John the Baptist leaped in the presence of Mary. The first Ark remained in the house of Obededom the Gethite for three months, bringing blessings to his household; Mary remained in Elizabeth's home for "about three months" and brought great blessings to the household, beginning with the sanctification of St. John the Baptist.

St. Epiphanius wrote: "Whoever honors the Lord also honors the holy vessel; who instead dishonors the holy vessel also dishonors his Master. Mary herself is that holy Virgin, that is, the holy vessel." The Scriptures teach clearly that Mary is worthy and deserving of honor and praise, and the lesson is delivered not from one source, but from three. It comes from the lips of a human being (St. Elizabeth), from an angel (Gabriel), and from the Son of God Himself, representing the orders of rational beings in union with their Creator.

To dishonor the sacred "vessel", then, is to dishonor its Maker. In the Old Testament, it is related that King David "danced with all his might before the Lord," that he "and all the house of Israel brought the Ark of the Covenant of the Lord with joyful shouting, and with sound of trumpet." (2 Kg. 6:14-15) This display of fervent devotion angered his wife, Michol:

> And when the Ark of the Lord was come into the city of David, Michol the daughter of Saul, looking out through a window, saw King David leaping and dancing before the Lord: and she despised him in her heart. . . . Therefore Michol the daughter of Saul had no child to the day of her death. (2 Kg. 6:16,23)

In dancing before the *Ark*, David was rendering joyful and fitting praise to *God*. Never mistaking the Ark itself for a divine thing, David understood – since the rules pertaining to the construction and handling of the Ark had been so faithfully recorded and observed – that honoring it was pleasing to God, that God accepts this honor as directed towards Himself, and that God *required* him and his people to render such honor. Thus, Michol's disdain of David's devotion *and its outward manifestations* was directed ultimately to God. Sterility was the price she paid for this contempt.

To this day, a "spiritual sterility" is the price paid by those proud souls who reject or ignore the Blessed Virgin, for it is an *insult* to Christ, and one of the grossest possible, to imagine pleasing Him by despising His Mother. It was impossible to please God by refusing honor to the first Ark; it is impossible to please Him by withholding honor *and veneration* from His "New Ark". Throughout the history of the Catholic Church, there have not been lacking examples of public devotion to Mary – festivals, processions, pilgrimages, etc. There is one that harmonizes well with the story of King David and his effusive display of veneration.

About the year 429, in the cathedral at Constantinople, St. Proclus delivered a stirring homily in which he described our Lady as "the holy *Theotokos* Virgin Mary . . . workshop of the union of natures, marketplace of the saving exchange, bridal chamber in which the Word was wedded to the flesh." Present during this homily was the Patriarch of Constantinople, Nestorius, who rejected the title *Theotokos* ["God-Bearer" or "Mother of God"]. He reasoned erroneously that there was in Christ one moral will formed from a mutual *exchange* of divine and human personalities, with the two natures remaining *distinct*, not united. Therefore, since the properties of a human person cannot be attributed to God, Nestorius concluded that only the title *Christotokos* ["Christ-Bearer" or "Mother of Christ"] could be accorded to Mary, since she generated solely the human nature of Jesus.

This reasoning leads to a separation and segregation of Jesus' divine and human natures, even though it is their *unity* which provided the foundation for the Redemption. This integral union of the divine and hman natures in the one Person of Christ was forged in the womb of Mary. Without that hypostatic union St. Paul could not have inspired to write: "If they had known it, they would never have crucified the Lord of glory." (1 Cor. 2:8) Crucified . . . the Lord of glory. Brought about the death . . . of God.

This dissolution of Christ into a divine and a human person was a denial of Mary's Divine Maternity, and it produced a backlash of protest, led by St. Cyril, Patriarch of Alexandria. In the year 431, an Ecumenical Council was held in Ephesus in order to address the teachings of Nestorius, during which Pope Celestine I instructed his legates to uphold the position of St. Cyril. As a result, Nestorius was excommunicated and removed from his See, and an anathema was pronounced upon anyone who "does not confess that God is truly Emmanuel, and that on this account the Holy Virgin is the Mother of God."

On the evening of June 22, 431, a crowd met the fathers of the Council of Ephesus, after the excommunication of Nestorius. King David and his people had shouted and made joyful music before the first Ark of the Covenant. The people of Ephesus met their bishops, who had just defended the honor of the "new" Ark, with cries of "Praised be the Theotokos." . . . *Praised be the Mother of God!* Pope Pius XI's description of that fateful evening compares favorably with the Scriptural account of David:

> We are told that while the bishops ardently defended the dignity of the Mother of God against Nestorius, the people of Ephesus crowded before the hall where the Council was held. When, toward evening, after a long

> and lively discussion the doors opened and it was solemnly decreed that "Mary was true Mother of God," the devotion of the people was so great that on hearing it they acclaimed the Fathers with an outpouring of joy, and, organizing a procession with blazing torches as signs of faith, they accompanied the bishops to their dwellings. (*Ephesinam Synodum*, 1930)

Another memorable example of this desire – which rests on both natural and supernatural bases – to engage in *public* expressions of devotion to Mary, the "new" Ark, occurred on December 8, 1854, when Blessed Pope Pius IX solemnly defined the Dogma of the Immaculate Conception. Present at the Basilica of St. Peter on that momentous occasion was Cardinal Nicholas Wiseman (d. 1865), Archbishop of Westminster, who set his observations down in a pastoral letter. To compare the attitude of the crowds in Rome with that of the crowds who swarmed through the streets of Ephesus *fourteen hundred years earlier* is to discover a striking continuity. When the time had arrived for the papal definition to be proclaimed, reported Cardinal Wiseman, the Dean of the Sacred College approached the pope, amidst a rapt silence, and formally asked for the pronouncement:

> The Pontiff assented; but called on all to join him in invoking the light and grace of the Holy Spirit at such a solemn moment. He knelt, and in his clear, sonorous, and most musical voice, entoned the hymn, *Veni Creator Spiritus*. The choir sang the verse, and, according to practice, was going to continue, when the entire congregation, not only of assembled Bishops and clergy, but of crowded people, spontaneously and simultaneously, and with admirable harmony, took up the song, and with a voice loud as the song of many waters, but one as the expression of a single heart, filled the whole basilica with such a strain as perhaps never before struck against its golden vaults. It was grand beyond conception; it was sublime; and came nearer the realization of what St. John heard of heavenly music, whose armies

> sing with one accord, than anything which we or others ever before listened to; and it was repeated at each alternate verse, with as perfect regularity as if the whole multitude had been trained to answer the choir. (*Pastoral Letter on the Immaculate Conception*)

The fifth-century Catholics in Ephesus had waited expectantly as the Council Fathers defended the Divine Maternity, then they burst into praise. The nineteenth-century Catholics in Rome had waited in silence as the pope was asked to define the Dogma of the Immaculate Conception, then they raised their voices in a hymn to God. The same sentiment, undiminished by the passage of centuries, animated both crowds, proving that some things do not change – nor are they *meant* to.

Chapter Twenty-Seven

The Magnificat

"MY SOULD DOTH MAGNIFY THE LORD"

The life of the Blessed Virgin Mary, whose praises have been shouted throughout the ages, was a life of service to God, in which the affection of a mother merged seamlessly with the adoration of a creature. As a *mother*, our Lady's one desire was the natural desire to give of herself to her Son. As a *creature*, she understood that all her blessings, graces and privileges were bestowed freely upon her by her God, and she accepted this bounty with gratitude and humility, not as one who *deserves* heavenly favors, but as one who rejoices in God's goodness: "My spirit hath rejoiced in God my Savior. Because He hath regarded the humility of His handmaid."

Mary does not receive praise merely in order to keep it for herself, even though our Lord desires us to honor her with affection: *Honor thy father and thy mother*. She *accepts* our praises, but she *offers* them all to God, on our behalf, for the good of her spiritual children and in thanksgiving for her own superabundant blessings: *My soul doth magnify the Lord.*

Perhaps the greatest testimony to the ultimately "Christocentric" foundations for Marian devotion can be found in this glorious prayer of Mary's, the *Magnificat*, which forms the centerpiece of her Visitation to St. Elizabeth. The Virgin offers this prayer after her cousin says to her, "Blessed art thou among women. . . . Blessed art thou that hast believed." Yes, replies Mary, with gratitude and no semblance of false humility, "all generations *shall* call me blessed." Then, she explains why: "Because He that is mighty hath done great things to me, and holy is His name." Our Lady leads us always *to God*, to the Incarnate God Who was growing in her womb as she uttered her prayer.

The people of ancient Israel were a people raised and nourished by the words of their Patriarchs and prophets; the rhythms and cadences of the Old Testament underscored the daily life of our Lady and her contemporaries the way the "catch phrases" of our mass-media do today. Such phrases and images would have been part of a common vocabulary. In such a society, one need only have referred to an image, say, "Jacob's Ladder" or "the Red Sea", and the person addressed would easily "get the point". Our Lady knew well the sacred texts of her ancestors.

The miraculous nature of our Lord's conception is celebrated in the second line of Mary's prayer, "And my spirit hath rejoiced in God my savior." In *The First Book of Kings*, we find the same thought proclaimed by Anna, a woman who was barren because the Lord "had shut up her womb". Anna prayed that the Lord would not forget His "handmaid" and "she multiplied prayers before the Lord," with the result that she and her husband, Elcana, were able to conceive their son, Samuel. At this she exclaimed, "My heart hath rejoiced in the Lord, and my horn is exalted in my God," (1 Kings 2:1) the *horn* signifying strength or glory.

The phrase spoken by Mary, "My soul doth magnify the Lord, and my spirit hath rejoiced in God, my Savior," echoes a line from the Old Testament book of *Habacuc*. The full impact of her words is lost in translation, however, as the same word in Hebrew means both "Savior" and "Jesus". And, in fact, if we look at the Vulgate Bible, we find that St. Jerome has translated verse 3:18 of *Habacuc* as "I will rejoice in the Lord, and I will joy in God, my Jesus." The Virgin, then, begins her canticle with a *very* personal thanksgiving to God, not merely as a formal nod to the history of her people, but for the inestimable gift of her own Son, the Incarnate Word growing inside her.

Our Lady proclaims, "And holy is His name, and His mercy is from generation unto generations, to them that fear Him." This thought mirrors the words of *Psalm 102*: "But the mercy of the Lord is from eternity and unto eternity upon them that fear Him."

Our Lady proclaims, "He hath scattered the proud in the conceit of their heart. . . . He hath put down the mighty from their seat, and hath exalted the humble." We read in *The Book of Job*: "Who setteth up the humble on high, and comforteth with health those that mourn. . . . Who bringeth to nought the designs of the malignant. . . . He poureth contempt upon princes, and relieveth them that were oppressed." (5:11-12;12:21)

The term "poor" in the Old Testament does not refer solely to financial status; it can allude to a "spiritual" status, to one's humility before God. In *Psalm 68*, our Lord proclaims prophetically in the midst of His Passion, "I am poor and sorrowful; Thy salvation, O God, hath set me up" – His obedience to the Father's will transforms His grim Passion into a thing of supreme glory. In *Psalm 21*, Israel is exhorted to fear and praise God "because He hath not despised the supplication of the poor man. . . . The poor shall eat and be filled" (in Hebrew, *hanavim* – "poor, or quiet and modest men"). These are the ones of whom Jesus said, "Blessed are the poor in spirit, for theirs is the kingdom of heaven." In her canticle, the Blessed Virgin praises God's mercy *and* fidelity to His people (including herself), manifested perfectly in the Son she carried: "Such was the gratitude of the Blessed Virgin . . . far from considering only her own exaltation, she blends her cause with that of the poor and lowly, in order to exalt the universal mercy of God toward all those who recognize their nothingness before Him." (Fr. Emil Neubert, *Mary in Doctrine*, 1954)

Our Lady proclaims, "He hath filled the hungry with good things; and the rich he hath sent empty away." This is a clear echo of *Psalm 106*: "For he hath satisfied the empty soul, and hath filled the hungry soul with good things." When the Virgin speaks of the casting down of the mighty from their seats, of the exaltation of the humble, of the filling of the hungry and the sending away of the rich, she is not preaching politics. She is making a public acknowledgment that " . . . now is the acceptable time . . . now is the day of salvation." (2 Cor. 6:2) The Redeemer is present upon the earth, at last.

Our Lady proclaims, "He hath received Israel His servant, being mindful of His mercy: as He spoke to our fathers, to Abraham and to his seed forever." We read in *The Book of Isaias*: "But thou, Israel, art my servant. . . . I have chosen thee, and have not cast thee away." (41:8,9) Also, in *Psalm 97*: "He hath remembered His mercy and His truth toward the house of Israel." And in *The Book of Genesis*: "He

[Abraham] shall become a great and mighty nation, and in him shall all the nations of the earth be blessed." (18:18)

The *Magnificat* was a spontaneous song of praise, offered by Mary as God rested beneath her heart. It was the first time since the Annunciation that she had broken her prudent silence and proclaimed aloud that God had, indeed, done great things to her:

> She, indeed, must be in perfect peace; for, whilst all those who greet her arrival are but receiving the grace and call of Jesus Christ through her, she actually possesses Him. He lies beneath her heart; and the intense peace and joy that this gives her she pours forth in her glorious hymn. (Bishop Jacques Bossuet, *Sermon on the Feast of the Visitation*)

In Mary's womb, the page separating the Old Dispensation from the New "turned" over, and prophecy and fulfillment became one. It should come as no surprise, therefore, that her canticle is redolent of the Old Testament texts she loved to hear and ponder as she was growing up. The hallowed quotations from the writings of her forefathers, the divine promises enshrined upon the pages of the ancient books, whose flesh-and-blood fulfillment rested in her womb as she sang, provided the ideal phrases with which to praise God. In fact, the *Magnificat* is nothing less than a miniature compendium of salvation history, a harmony of Scriptural echoes spanning the entire history of the Lord's merciful dealings with his people.

Chapter Twenty-Eight

Devotion to Mary Necessary for Salvation

"The Lord is wonderful in His saints" – Devotion to Mary is necessary for salvation – The will of God made manifest at Fatima

"Be humbled in the sight of the Lord," wrote St. James, "and He will exalt you." (4:10) The oft-encountered Protestant fancy that Jesus Christ is somehow "threatened" or offended by devotion rendered to His Mother implies that, while God *will* bestow magnificent spiritual gifts upon His creatures, yet we must pretend this is *not* the case. Such reasoning reduces the panorama of creation down to a two-dimensional schematic, a flat, gray scene in which one man is distinguishable from another only by his physical attributes, since the treasures of grace allotted to each one must be either ignored or denied. In this system, there are no strata, no popes, priests, or saints . . . no sanctification or sacraments . . . no invisible working of the Holy Ghost in and through His creatures . . . ultimately, no merit or majesty.

This is not the teaching of Scripture. "For there is no respect of persons with God", (Rom. 2:11) goes a frequently misunderstood text from the Epistles. Many people, wishing to substitute a vague, democratized "Christianity" in place of the Catholic Faith of the apostles, interpret this to mean that God will not exalt any of His creatures or elevate them to positions of spiritual authority or prominence. The verse, of course, means exactly the *opposite* of this. Just before it appear the words, "But glory, and honor, and peace to every one that worketh good, to the Jew first, and also to the Greek." (Rom. 2:10) God does not "respect" persons in that He will not judge them apart from their works. The Jew, who may be tempted to brandish his descent from Abraham, as well as the Greek, proud of his learning and culture, will be judged by his works: "Who will render to every man according to his works. To them indeed, who according to patience in good work, seek glory and honor and incorruption, eternal life: But to them that are contentious, and who obey not the truth . . . tribulation and anguish upon every soul of man that worketh evil, of the Jew first, and also of the Greek." (Rom. 2:6-9) Why did St. Paul make this distinction? – Precisely because ". . . unto whomsoever much is given, of him much shall be required." (Lk. 12:48)

God may not respect the earthly "status" of a person, but this does not indicate a lack of regard for individuals *as* individuals, for their separate achievements, personalities, merits and works. Those who seek glory, honor and incorruption will not be treated in the same manner as those who reject Truth. St. Paul wrote: "Now there are diversities of graces, but the same Spirit; And there are diversities of ministries, but the same Lord." (1 Cor. 12:4) Jesus said to His apostles, the first Catholic priests, "To you it is given to know the mysteries of the kingdom of heaven: but to them it is not given." (Mt. 13:11) To St. Peter, the first pope, our Lord declared: "I will give to thee the keys of the kingdom of heaven. And whatsoever thou shalt bind upon earth, it shall be bound also in heaven: and whatsoever thou shalt loose upon earth, it shall be loosed also in heaven." (Mt. 16:19) In the *Apocalypse*, St. John teaches that virgins are, among men, ". . . the first-fruits to God and to the Lamb", (14:4) and that special seats of honor are given to the martyrs, who ". . . were beheaded for the testimony of Jesus, and for the word of God." (20:4)

"God is wonderful in His saints," (Ps. 67:36) proclaimed King David, and the Church echoes the sentiment proudly in her *Act of Reparation*, recited after the Benediction of the Blessed Sacrament: "Blessed be God in His angels and in His saints!" The veneration directed towards the power of the angels, or the courage of the martyrs, manifests a recognition of *God's* beauty and might. The angels are radiant because their majesty participates in that of their Creator; the martyrs are victorious because they conquer in, with, and by *Christ*. Still, we recognize these holy personages as individuals, as unique beings with their own names and personalities – St. Michael, St. Raphael, St. Peter, St. Edmund Campion, St. Cecilia, St. Philomena, St. Isaac Jogues, St. Agnes, etc.

"The Lord, Who knows His entire creation well, saw in it nothing like Mary," wrote St. Athanasius, "therefore He chose her to be His Mother." If the Church is admonished to rejoice in the saints, to render thanksgiving and praise to God in the honoring of His faithful servants, how much more do we honor Him by rendering praise and veneration to His Mother? Mary *gave* to the world the Savior Who ennobled the lives of the saints and sanctified their deaths. "Well done, good and faithful servant," (Mt. 25:21) are words which our Lord can say with unfeigned joy to His saints. How much more do these words apply to the Mother of the Redeemer?

The dignity of a creature is proportionate to its proximity to God. This applies both in an *internal* sense – "But without faith it is impossible to please God" (Heb. 11:6) – and in an *external* sense – "Who makest Thy angels spirits: and thy ministers a burning fire." (Ps. 103:4) There can not enter into the presence of God "any thing defiled, or that worketh abomination or maketh a lie." (Apoc. 21:27)

Mary's proximity to God excelled in both senses. As His own Mother, she was closest to Him naturally, but she also possessed a love for Him, a faith in Him, and a desire to adore Him which would remain unequaled. Her dignity, therefore, cannot be compared to that of any other. St. Thomas Aquinas saw in it a reflection of her Son's: "The Blessed Virgin, by becoming the Mother of God, *received* a kind of infinite dignity because God is infinite." This is carefully worded. Our Lady *received* a "kind" of infinite dignity. God receives nothing from anyone; all might and majesty are His by nature. Mary's place as Mother of the Incarnate Word *raises* her to a position in the created order that is unparalleled, where she *receives* her unique dignity. The Marian praises of the Church always recognize the relationship of Mary to the Blessed Trinity: "Blessed be the great *Mother of God*, Mary most holy!"

As Mother of the Church, our Lady is ever solicitous for the welfare of her spiritual children. She intercedes for us, and obtains graces for us. Moreover, knowing that God is pleased by the veneration shown to her, His "New Ark", she also offers up all the Church's Marian praises *to* Him.

The Marian devotion of the True Church is its surety, a defense against heresy and error, against sterility and spiritual pride, against offending God by honoring Him, not as *He* desires it, but as foolish men decide to. The Blessed Virgin herself revealed that God not only *desires* His people to venerate her, but that such veneration has been rendered *necessary* by God. After granting a vision of hell to the young children, Our Lady of Fatima stated quite plainly: "You have seen hell where the souls of poor sinners go. To save them, *God wishes to establish* in the world devotion to my Immaculate Heart."

St. Louis de Montfort wrote of this necessity of Marian devotion:

> We must conclude that, being necessary to God by a necessity which is called "hypothetical", (that is, because God so willed it), the Blessed Virgin is all the more necessary for men to attain their final end. Consequently, we must not place devotion to her on the same level as devotion to the other saints as if it were merely something optional. (*True Devotion to the Blessed Virgin*)

This "hypothetical necessity" is consistent with Mary's titles of *Mediatrix of All Graces, Advocate* and *Mother of the Church*. If she has been made the Dispensatrix of grace by her Son, how can we expect devotion to her to be "optional"? If she is the Mother of the Church – of the Head, Jesus, and of the members, the "rest of her seed" – why presume that someone who disdains this Mother will be granted any share in the "inheritance" of the sons of God?

The Love that was rekindled in Thy womb
sends forth the warmth of the eternal peace
within whose ray this flower has come to bloom.

Here, to us, thou art the noon and scope
of Love revealed; and among mortal men,
the living fountain of eternal hope.

Lady, thou art so near God's reckonings
that who seeks grace and does not first seek thee
would have his wish fly upward without wings.

(Dante Alighieri, *Paradiso*)

In the writings of St. Catherine of Siena (†1380) can be found a powerful testimony to the salvific properties of a heartfelt Marian devotion, rendered in the words of God the Father, Who tells of the reward received by a sinner for veneration shown to the Blessed Virgin:

> For I had not forgotten the reverence and love he had for Mary, My only-begotten Son's most gentle mother. For My goodness, in deference to the Word, has decreed that anyone at all, just or sinner, who holds her in due reverence will never be snatched or devoured by the infernal demon. She is like a bait set out by My goodness to catch My creatures. So it was in mercy that I did this. (*The Dialogue, 139*)

Our souls were created for God, to seek Him out and find Him. Just as the Shepherds and Magi found Him in the arms of His Mother, so will we ever find her at His side. We cannot look upon the Crucified Savior without noticing the Mother who stood by His Cross. Because we are "made" for Christ, then, in a sense, we are also made for Mary. Where it is not stifled by heresy or indifferentism, there is a definite "attraction" for the Blessed Mother planted in the hearts of men and women: *She is like a bait set out by My goodness to catch My creatures*. As a natural mother desires a good life, safety and health for her offspring, so does Mary for her spiritual offspring. Therefore, she draws us to herself to give us *Life*:

> Therefore, my dearest brethren, with every fibre, every feeling of our hearts, with all the affections of our minds, and with all the ardor of our souls, let us honor Mary, *because such is the will of God*, Who would have us to obtain *everything* through the hands of Mary. Such, I say, is the will of God, but intending our advantage. For exercising a provident care for us, her poor children, in all things and through all things, the Virgin Mother calms our trembling fear, enlivens our faith, strengthens our hope, drives away our distrust, raises up our pusillanimity. . . . Assuredly the Son will listen

> to the Mother and the Father will listen to the Son. . . . My brethren, let us seek grace and let us seek it through Mary. (St. Bernard, *Sermon for the Feast of the Nativity of the BVM*)

The Spiritual Motherhood of Mary is a sign of God's boundless love for the world: "God wants everyone, *everyone*, to learn . . . that he who trusts in Mary, will never be abandoned either in this world or in the next." (St. Lawrence of Brindisi, †1619) In fact, to imagine human history without the Blessed Virgin is to picture a barren landscape, for she has warmed the hearts and imaginations of so many, peasants and poets, carpenters and kings, parents, children and artists in untold numbers. The greatest works of human hands and intellects have been created in her honor, and yet, our Lady belongs to *all*, for the same divine mysteries and celestial glory commemorated in the cathedral of Notre Dame can be discerned, in essence, in any simple wood-and-string Rosary.

Knowing our fears, doubts and self-doubts, knowing our thirst for a beauty not devoid of warmth, Jesus Christ, as He hung dying on the Cross, gave His own Mother to us – a *most* awesome gift, from the Giver of awesome gifts. And, as if that were not enough, we get closer to God through this gift. As much as we can appreciate our Lady *for herself*, basking in her purity, her maternal heart and her beauty, in the hope she gives to us in the midst of our difficulties and necessities, there is present always, in addition, the supreme comfort that she will lead us to her Son, that her concern reaches out to embrace the welfare of our very souls.

The Catholic Church, the sole repository of apostolic Truth, has always cherished these salutary teachings. We understand well where our Marian devotions lead, and the benefit we derive from them, and only from them. By the mercy of God, the entire world was again reminded of these truths by the words of the Blessed Virgin herself, spoken at Fatima on June 13, 1917: "My Immaculate Heart will be your refuge *and the way which will lead you to God*."

Chapter Twenty-Nine

The Assumption of the Blessed Mother

THE HANDMAID IS ASSUMED INTO HEAVEN – THE DOGMA AS DEFINED – THE "DORMITION" OF OUR LADY – TESTIMONY OF THE FATHERS AND DOCTORS – "ARISE, O LORD, INTO THY RESTING PLACE, THOU AND THE ARK WHICH THOU HAST SANCTIFIED"

There is no "half-life" or "expiration date" attached to that love for one's parents which is not only pleasing to God, but *commanded* by Him:

> Hearken to thy father, that begot thee: and despise not thy mother when she is old. (Prov. 23:22) Son, support the old age of thy father, and grieve him not in his life, (Ecclus. 3:14)

Thou shalt honor thy mother all the days of her life, was the instruction given to the young Tobias by his father. This lesson was important enough for the elder Tobias to impart it when he believed that his time had come to die. It would be a fickle and unbecoming love on the part of any son to forget his mother after he has grown to adulthood. To attribute such neglect to the Perfect Son, Jesus, is an outrage.

The honor shown to Mary in her Immaculate Conception was an honor with two "edges". It showered grace and blessings on the future Mother of God, which is only right and fitting. It also resounded to the glory of the Son, so that the *Spotless* Lamb, the Saving Victim without blemish, could never be said to have been born of a sinner: "For every tree is known by its fruit. For men do not gather figs from thorns; nor from a bramble bush do they gather the grape." (Lk. 6:44)

At the close of her life, the Holy Virgin, the one who lived for Jesus only, the "handmaid" of the Lord in whom God had accomplished "great things", was further honored by her Divine Son in her glorious Assumption, body and soul, into heaven. This dogma, taught by the Church Fathers, was defined by Pope Pius XII:

> After We have poured forth prayers of supplication again and again to God, and have invoked the light of the Spirit of Truth, for the glory of Almighty God who has lavished His special affection upon the Virgin Mary, for the Honor of her Son, the immortal King of the Ages and the victor over sin and death, for the increase of the glory of that same august Mother, and for the joy and exultation of the entire Church; by the authority of Our Lord Jesus Christ, of the Blessed apostles Peter and Paul, and by Our own authority, We pronounce, declare, and define it to be a divinely revealed dogma: that the Immaculate Mother of God, the ever Virgin Mary, having completed the course of her earthly life, was assumed body and soul into heavenly glory. (*Munificentissimus Deus*, 1950)

For the Honor of her Son, the immortal King of the Ages and the victor over sin and death. Our Lord did not seek among the subjects of the "empire of death" for the Woman who would become His Mother, the Woman of the *Proto-evangelium*. Taking flesh from a true daughter of Eve, the Incarnate Word prepared this daughter, making her a fit dwelling for the Godhead which the entire universe could never contain. Does logic suggest that bodily corruption and the darkness of the grave – "For the wages of sin is death." (Rom. 6:23) ". . . Now the sting of death is sin" (1 Cor. 15:56) – be the lot of this immaculate Mother at the close of her earthly life? Can human reason, informed by the lessons of inspired Scripture, accept that the chains from which she was freed at her conception would become her grim legacy, binding her at the close of her life?

For the glory of Almighty God who has lavished His special affection upon the Virgin Mary. This special affection is a threefold one, rendered to our Lady as Daughter, Mother and Spouse. It is the prototype of the "affection" which God desires to lavish on His *entire* Church: "For no man ever hated his own flesh; but nourisheth and cherisheth it, as also Christ doth the Church." (Eph. 5:29) Before the Church existed in time, however, this divine affection was lavished generously upon an individual who, as *Co-Redemptrix*, would carry in her "mystical womb" the spiritual Body of the Church, as she would carry in her natural womb the human body of the Head of the Church.

It is fitting, therefore, that God's love for His Church be realized principally in His love for Mary. This dual object of God's special "affection" is celebrated in *The Canticle of Canticles*, where Christ prophetically praises the beauty of the *Spouse*, a praise which encompasses both the purity of the Church (*the glorious Church not having spot or wrinkle . . . holy and without blemish*) AND the purity of the Virgin Mother (*the Immaculate Conception*): "How beautiful art thou, my love, how beautiful art thou! Thy eyes are doves' eyes, besides what is hid within. . . . Thou art all fair, O my love, and there is not a spot in thee." (Cant. 4:1,7)

For the increase of the glory of that same august Mother, and for the joy and exultation of the entire Church. The final consideration given by Pope Pius XII for the proclamation of the Dogma of the Assumption is a moving testimony to our Lady's Spiritual Motherhood. The Pontiff identifies the glorious honor rendered to Mary by God with the "joy and exultation" of her spiritual children, the *rest of her seed.* Because of, and by means of, the Incarnation, *supernatural* affection for God, the love of the Israelites of the Old Testament, is bolstered and enhanced by *natural* affection: "And the Word was made flesh, *and dwelt among us.* . . . But I have called you *friends.*" This intimacy with the Savior brings the members of the Church into an intimate relation also with the *Mother* of the Savior:

> As we are debtors to Christ for sharing in some way with us the right, peculiarly His own, of calling God "Father" and possessing Him as such, we are in like manner indebted to Him for His loving generosity in sharing with us the right to call Mary "Mother" and to cherish her as such. . . . No tongue is eloquent enough to put in words what every devout soul feels, namely, how intense is the flame of affectionate and eager charity which glows in Mary, in her who is truly our mother, *not by nature but by the will of Christ.* (Pope Leo XIII, *Magnae Dei Matris*, 1892)

Therefore, the Church rejoices and exults in the recognition and proclamation of Marian dogma, which makes manifest more clearly her privileges and glories. As children of Mary, and brethren ("joint-heirs") of Christ, the members of the Church take pleasure when she is honored, and feel a righteous anger when she is dishonored. This is also the reason why *any* attack on Mary is an attack on Christ's own Church: *And the dragon was angry against the Woman: and went to make war with the rest of her seed.*

The papal definition of the Dogma of the Assumption carefully avoids any speculation on the nature of Mary's death, or as to whether she died at all, and Catholics are thus free to speculate upon the subject with due reverence. However, the consensus of Catholic thought on the matter points to a bodily death (but unattended by any corruption) for our Lady:

> In this way we may hope that she herself, assumed into heavenly glory, will be our advocate before divine goodness and mercy at the hour of our passing, *an hour which she also experienced*, for she made the same journey, not however possessing the grace of God's first creation, but that of Redemption which did not confer bodily immortality in the strict sense of the term. (Pope Pius XI, *Queen of All Saints*, 1933)

This "grace of God's first creation" mentioned by the Holy Father is the state of "original justice", wherein our first parents received, in addition to a *supernatural* bounty of grace in their souls, other endowments of a lower order, but still beyond nature (i.e., *preternatural* gifts):

> Essentially, this state of original justice consisted in the *supernatural* gift of sanctifying grace and the consequent right to the Beatific Vision; to this God had *de facto* attached the *preternatural* gifts, namely: immunity from concupiscence, immunity from ignorance, immunity from suffering and immunity from death. All these preternatural gifts (and therefore the gifts of immortality) were to be enjoyed not only by Adam himself, but also by all his

> descendants on condition that Adam remain faithful to God's command. Unfortunately, Adam did sin and God withdrew these gifts from him and from his posterity.
>
> The fact is that Adam's immortality was granted him in connection with, *but not as effect of*, his original grace. If immortality were the *necessary* effect of grace, then surely Christ Himself would have been immortal, for He possessed grace in a most eminent degree. Yet we know that Christ not only died, but that His death was natural; it was violent, to be sure, as far as extrinsic circumstances were concerned, *but it was natural nevertheless*, as regards intrinsic causes. (Fr. Juniper Carol, "Mary's death," from *Queen of the Universe*, Bro. Stanley G. Mathews, ed., 1957)

"Unless the grain of wheat falling into the ground, die, itself remaineth alone," said Jesus of His own death, "but if it die, it bringeth forth much fruit." (Jn. 12:24-25) These words are not inappropriate when applied to Mary's death. The Resurrection of the Redeemer was made especially glorious because it was preceded by His Passion and death, because "He humbled Himself, becoming obedient unto death, even the death of the Cross."

Mary, the Co-Redemptrix, proclaimed herself the Handmaid of the Lord. If, through her Immaculate Conception, she was indeed the "first-fruits" of the sacrifice on Calvary, and if ". . . the servant is not greater than his Lord," (Jn.13:16) then why can we not view the death of our Lady as the means by which Jesus glorified His Mother *as the first-fruits of the Redemption*, assuming her into heaven after she had undergone bodily death? What sharper blow could the Risen Savior deal to the "empire of death" than to call home to heaven the "Woman" prophesied in Eden as the mortal enemy of that empire . . . and to leave her untainted by any decay or corruption? This is the sentiment behind a prayer from the sixth-century *Gregorian Sacramentary*:

> May today's festivity, O Lord, bring us salutary aid, whereon God's Holy Mother underwent temporal death, *yet could not be held down by the shackles of death*, she who bore Your Son made flesh of her.

Tradition holds that Mary "died of love", that the close of her earthly life was marked by an intense, consuming desire to be reunited with Jesus. Blessed Guerric of Igny († 1157), a contemporary of St. Bernard, picturing the final days of the Blessed Virgin, placed these words on her lips: "I languish with love . . . Jesus is my balm! He is my medicine! Jesus seen as He is in His glory, Jesus held, possessed for ever!" As poetic as the expression "died for love" may sound, it aptly applies to our Lady, for her passing was an event that justly deserves to be called a "prodigy":

> The phoenix dies from the fire, and this holy Lady died of love. The phoenix assembles a funeral pyre of aromatical wood, and placing it on the mountain peak, flaps its wings over this pyre so rapidly that a fire is kindled by the rays of the sun. This Virgin, gathering in her heart the Cross, the crown, the lance of Our Lord, placed them at the summit of her thoughts. Over this pyre she made a great movement of continual meditation, and fire was kindled by the rays of the light of her Son. The phoenix dies in that fire. The Virgin died in this; and it must not be questioned that she had engraven in her heart the instruments of the Passion. . . . Thus died the Mother of Life. (St. Francis de Sales, *Sermon for the Feast of the Assumption*)

The Church Fathers referred to the death of the Blessed Virgin as her *Dormition*, her "falling asleep". Writing of the Assumption, St. Gregory of Tours (†594) described Mary simply as "having completed the course of her earthly life". This is the same language used by Pope Pius XII when he defined the dogma, and he also took care to relate it to the Immaculate Conception:

> Yet according to the general rule, God does not will to grant to the just the full effect of the victory over death until the end of time has come. And so it is that even the bodies of the just are corrupted after death, and only on the last day will they be joined, each to its own glo-

> rious soul. Now God has willed that the Blessed Virgin Mary should be exempted from this general rule. She by an entirely unique privilege, completely overcame sin by her Immaculate Conception, and as a result she was not subject to the law of remaining in the corruption of the grave, and she did not have to wait until the end of time for the redemption of her body. (*Munificentissimus Deus*)

The Fathers recognized that the death of Mary was not an event to be dismissed without respectful consideration. St. Epiphanius was one of the first of the Church Fathers to discuss the close of the Virgin's earthly existence:

> Scripture simply is silent, because of the greatness of the prodigy, in order not to strike the mind of man with excessive wonder. . . . I dare not affirm this with absolute certainty, nor do I say that she remained untouched by death, nor can I confirm whether she died. The Scriptures, which are above human reason, left this question uncertain, out of respect for this honored and admirable vessel. (*Adversus haereses*)

St. Andrew of Crete († c.740) wrote:

> Death, natural to men, also reached her; not, however, to imprison her, as happens to us, or to vanquish her. God forbid! It was only to secure for her the experience of that sleep which comes from on high, leading us up to the object of our hope. . . . It comes in a superior way, and for a reason higher than the reason that obliges us to surrender totally to death. (*Homily 1 on the Dormition*)

The corruption of the grave was not meant for the *Immaculate Conception*, the Mother of God-made-Man. The completion of her earthly life was not a time of sorrow, of pain and anxiety. The Mother of Jesus, who had lived solely for Him, was returning to Him. Sin had never touched her during her life; the wages of sin would not be paid to her at her death. The sweetness of this death was expressed simply, yet movingly, in the *Panegyric for the Dormition of God's Mother*, a homily attributed to St. Modestus, Patriarch of Jerusalem (†634): "She fell asleep, she fell asleep, she fell asleep, she who gave birth to the world's life and resurrection."

An ancient apocryphal text, the *Dormition of the Holy Mother of God*, depicts a scene between our Lady and the Angel Gabriel, in which sound doctrine is conveyed in the angel's moving dialogue:

> Never, you see, in times remote or recent has there appeared in the ranks of men a Virgin Mother of God, never a spiritual child-bearing. In like fashion, your departure too, and the rest that is your falling asleep, has been changed by reason of the fullness of grace that genuinely belongs to you, O Virgin most holy. For this reason sorrow and anguish have vanished from you. And it is hard to know what to say of the place, inexpressible and so delightful, which the Lord has prepared for you and in which glory follows upon glory without interruption.

The Dogma of the Assumption safeguards the dignity of Jesus Christ as True *God*, and as True *Man*. The Holy One born of Mary was not born in pain, a reminder of original sin; He came into the world from a pure womb, a fit dwelling. With all her thoughts and affections directed to God, to the One she gave birth to at Bethlehem, Mary remained free from all sin throughout her life. The Mother of the apostles, of priests, of Christians, would never nourish her spiritual children with tainted nourishment, with "milk" that could ever harm them.

"In Adam, all have sinned," and, therefore, "do need the grace of God." Mary's debt *was* paid by her Son, Who ransomed the entire human race, but hers was paid in a manner befitting her person and place. The Author of *Life* proceeded from her womb, which became a source of "spiritual life" for the entire Church. This immaculate womb remains incorrupt today and forever, for it was the house of God for nine months – even more than a "house", for God took His own human nature *from* Mary. Can anyone imagine a holier place?

> And who, I ask, could believe that the ark of holiness, the dwelling place of the Word of God, the temple of the Holy Ghost, could be reduced to ruin? My soul is filled with horror at the thought that this virginal flesh which had begotten God, had brought Him into the world, had nourished and carried Him, could have been turned into ashes or given over to be food for worms. (St. Robert Bellarmine, *De Assumptione*)

The Assumption of the Mother of God casts a radiant light on the divinity of Jesus, but His humanity is also defended by it. As a human Son, Jesus honors His Mother, desiring that she be with Him in glory. "Who is the child," asks St. Francis de Sales, "who, if he could, would not raise his good mother and place her in Paradise after her decease?" How does the Son, *Who is God risen gloriously from the dead*, "make a return" to His Mother, as is commanded by the Scriptures, for the gift of His human life? Does He reward her with death? Does God repay perfect purity with corruption?

What is the fitting end for Mary, that exquisite human "Tabernacle", of which all others are images? St. John Damascene offered a worthy reply:

> O how could the Font of life be led to life through death? O how could she, who in giving birth surpassed the limits of nature, now yield to nature's laws and have her immaculate body undergo death? . . . It was necessary that the body of the one who preserved her virginity intact in giving birth should also be kept incorrupt after death. It was necessary that she, who carried the Creator in her womb when He was a baby, should dwell among the tabernacles of heaven. (*Homily 1 and 2 on the Dormition*)

Fr. Gerard Manley Hopkins, writing of Mary as the *Rosa Mystica*, described her as a flower that ". . . was made of earth's mould but it went from men's eyes, And its place is a secret and shut in the skies." The English Martyr and poet, St. Robert Southwell (†1595), mused that, at the Assumption of Mary, "Earth rendered up her undeserved prey; heaven claims the right, and bears the prize away." Both poets mention our Lady's earthly origins, while expressing wonder at her Assumption. This combination of natural *and* supernatural recognition and edification is the hallmark of Catholic veneration to the Mother of God.

As taught by Pope Pius XII when he defined the dogma, the Assumption resounds to the glory of God, and also allows the Church to "increase" our Lady's glory, not by adding to it (for mankind can never "improve" upon honor bestowed by God), but by making it better understood and appreciated. Like all Marian dogmas, it draws its substance from Jesus and the one-of-a-kind bond between the Woman *and* her seed: "Arise, O Lord, into Thy resting place: Thou *and* the Ark, which Thou hast sanctified." (Ps. 131:8)

St. Peter, referring to the epistles of St. Paul, wrote that there are contained in them "certain things hard to be understood, which the unlearned and unstable wrest, *as they do also the other Scriptures*, to their own perdition." (2 Pet. 3:16) This is why Christ commands that we *must* go to the Catholic Church, and its teaching Magisterium, if we wish to comprehend both the sacred texts and the truths of the Faith. "To *you* it is given to know the mystery of the kingdom of God," announced Jesus to the apostles, the first members of the ecclesial hierarchy, "but to the rest in parables." (Lk. 8:10) This prudent ordering of affairs by our Lord was arranged in order to protect His flock from error, confusion and spiritual pride.

The Assumption of the Virgin Mary, body and soul, into heaven *is* taught in Scripture, but in an *implicit* manner, as are many doctrinal truths:

> Moreover, the scholastic Doctors have recognized the Assumption of the Virgin Mother of God as something signified, not only in various figures of the Old Testament, but also in that "Woman clothed with the Sun", whom John the Apostle contemplated on the island of Patmos. Similarly they have given special attention to these words of the New Testament: "Hail, full of grace, the Lord is with thee, blessed art thou among women," since they saw, in the mystery of the Assumption, the

> fulfillment of that most perfect grace granted to the Blessed Virgin and the special blessing that countered the curse of Eve. (Pope Pius XII, *Munificentissimus Deus*)

The Blessed Virgin is the *new* "Ark of the Covenant". The first Ark was not destroyed or taken when the Chaldean army tore down the walls of Jerusalem and stormed the city. Sometime before or after the capture of the city, the Ark had been removed by the Prophet Jeremias and brought to Mt. Nebo, the place from which the Lord showed Moses the promised inheritance, ". . . the land, for which I swore to Abraham, Issac, and Jacob, saying: I will give it to thy seed." (Deut. 34:4) *The Second Book of Maccabees* relates the tale:

> And when Jeremias came thither he found a hollow cave: and he carried in thither the tabernacle, and the Ark, and the altar of incense, and so stopped the door. Then some of them that followed him, came up to mark the place: but they could not find it. And when Jeremias perceived it, he blamed them, saying: The place shall be unknown, till God gather together the congregation of the people, and receive them to mercy. (2 Mac. 2:5-7)

The sacred books *do* speak again of the Ark. It is the prelude to the "Great Sign" of the *Apocalypse*:

> And the temple of God was opened in heaven: and the Ark of His testament was seen in His temple, and there were lightnings, and voices, and an earthquake, and great hail. And a great sign appeared in heaven: a Woman clothed with the sun, and the moon under her feet, and on her head a crown of twelve stars. (Apoc. 11:19-12:1)

The Ark is envisioned in heaven, where it is, in effect, "superimposed" over the figure of the Woman. While on earth, it had been kept, hidden by a veil, in the innermost part of the temple, the *Holy of Holies*: "And they shall make me a sanctuary, and I will dwell in the midst of them. . . . And the veil shall be hanged on with rings, and within it thou shalt put the Ark of the testimony, and the sanctuary and the holy of the holies shall be divided with it." (Ex. 25:8; 26:33)

The temple of God "was opened in heaven", says St. John, "and the Ark of His testament was seen." The Ark is with God. It appears with the "Woman clothed with the sun", who symbolizes both the Church and the Blessed Virgin. The Woman, the *Great Sign,* is in heaven. If the original Ark, a structure of wood and metal, was but a "figure", a foreshadowing of Mary, can we ascribe to the holy Mother of God, the living Ark fashioned by God's own hands, any less noble end?

Chapter Thirty

The Most Powerful Queen of Mercy

Mary's universal Queenship – Christ reigns by right and by conquest – Our Lady's conquest at Calvary – Queen of Mercy – Our Advocate – Virgin Most Powerful – The Battle of Lepanto – The message and the stupendous miracle of Fatima – Satan's hatred and fear of Mary – Queen of Angels

Pope Pius XII declared that the definition of the Dogma of the Assumption of Mary resounded to "the Honor of her Son, the immortal *King* of the Ages." Pope Pius XI taught that this Kingship of Christ depends on "that wonderful union" of divine and human natures. He reigns by *right* because He is "to be adored as God by angels and men." However, as Man, our Lord is also said to have "acquired" this kingdom, to have won it by conquest: "But yet what could be more pleasing to us and more pleasant to contemplate than that Christ commands us not only by right of birth but also by an acquired right, that is, of redemption? Would that all forgetful men would recall what price they have cost our Savior." (*Quas primas*, 1925)

The Lord commanded the Prophet Nathan to say to King David: "And when thy days shall be fulfilled, and thou shalt sleep with thy fathers, I will raise up thy seed after thee, which shall proceed out of thy bowels, and I will establish his kingdom." (2 Kg. 7:12) This prophecy relates, in part, to King Solomon, David's son, but it was fulfilled absolutely in Jesus Christ, Who is called the "Son of David" in the Gospels; at the Annunciation, the Angel Gabriel told Mary that her Son would be given "the throne of David His father". One day, after the Pharisees had unsuccessfully attempted to trap Our Lord by putting questions to Him, He turned the tables on them:

> Jesus asked them, saying: What think you of Christ? Whose Son is He? They say to Him: David's. He saith to them: How then doth David in spirit call Him Lord, saying: The Lord said to my Lord, Sit on My right hand,

> until I make Thy enemies Thy footstool? If David then call Him Lord, how is He his son? And no man was able to answer Him a word. (Mt. 22:41-46)

In contemplating the kingdom belonging to the "seed" of David, then, the divinity of Jesus cannot be separated from His humanity:

> Blessed be the God and Father of our Lord Jesus Christ, Who hath blessed us with spiritual blessings in heavenly places, in Christ: *As He chose us in Him, before the foundation of the world*, that we should be holy and unspotted in His sight in charity. (Eph. 1:3-4)

As *Co-Redemptrix*, our Lady was called by her Son to unite her sorrows to His on Calvary, to participate in His redemptive suffering, in the Passion which would ransom her spiritual children. More than any other human being who has ever lived, Mary heeded the admonition which would be written down later by St. Paul: "I beseech you therefore, brethren, by the mercy of God, that you present your bodies a living sacrifice, holy, pleasing unto God." (Rom. 12:1) It is with the image of Mary beneath the Cross on Calvary that St. Peter could have written, "For this is praiseworthy, if, for conscience towards God, a man endure sorrows, suffering wrongfully." (1 Pet. 2:19)

"There is laid up for me a crown of justice," wrote St. Paul, "which the Lord, the just judge, will render to me on that day." (2 Tim. 4:8) God rewards His servants with "the reward of inheritance", (Col. 3:24) a share in His kingdom which is not distributed randomly, but according to merit:

> Every man shall receive his own reward, according to his own labor. . . . One is the glory of the sun, another the glory of the moon, and another the glory of the stars. . . . For star differeth from star in glory. So also is the resurrection of the dead. (1 Cor. 3:8; 15:41-42)

The degree to which our Lady endured sorrows, making of herself a living sacrifice pleasing to God, was never attained by any other creature, for it was never given to anyone else to be the *Mother* of God. "Come, ye blessed of my Father, possess you the kingdom prepared for you *from the foundation of the world*". (Mt. 25:34) These are the words with which Christ will receive His faithful servants into heaven. He will invite them into the kingdom prepared "from the foundation of the world". This is the kingdom that belonged to Him from the Beginning. It belonged to Him by *right*, because of His divinity. It would also belong to Him by *conquest*, because of the Redemption won by Him as Man.

Anyone who enters heaven does so as both a child of the Father *and as a child of Mary*. There is no other way, for our Lord proclaimed His Mother's *Spiritual* Maternity from the Cross. The "adoption of children" is made possible by the fact, firstly, that Jesus and the redeemed have the same Father in heaven (Who has blessed us "in Christ") and, secondly, by the fact that Jesus and the redeemed have the same Mother. As Jesus rules His kingdom both by *right* and *conquest*, we recognize a similar claim to sovereignty on the part of the Mother of Jesus:

> As the first-born daughter of the Father, the perfect Mother of the Word, the beloved Spouse of the Holy Ghost, she is related in virtue of the Hypostatic Union to the whole Most Holy Trinity, to Him who in Himself alone is by essence infinite Majesty, the King of kings, Lord of lords; because she was the Mother of the King divine, of Him to whom from His Mother's womb the Lord God gave the throne of David and eternal kingship in the house of Jacob and who, after asserting in His own right that all power was given to Him in heaven and on earth, He, the Son of God, gave His heavenly Mother a share in His glory, His majesty, His kingship; *because, associated as Mother and Minister to the King of martyrs in the ineffable work of man's Redemption, she is likewise associated with Him forever*, with power so to speak infinite, in the distribution of the graces which flow from the Redemption. . . . And this queenship of hers is essentially motherly, used only for our good. (Pope Pius XII, *Mary's Universal Queenship*, 1946)

The Blessed Virgin is rightfully venerated as *Queen* by the faithful who recognize Jesus as *King*, and for reasons analogous, or similar in some respects, to those by which our Lord's Kingship is recognized. While these reasons could never apply to Mary in the same sense in which they apply to her Son, Who is *Divine*, nevertheless, they express actual, concrete circumstances, for the Queenship of Mary is not merely a "quality" attributed to her because of her intrinsic excellence, by the fact that she is elevated among other women, as one might refer to a lion as "the king of the jungle". She is Queen in a *proper* sense, someone who wields power in the kingdom of Christ.

Jesus Christ is said to reign by *right*, because of His divine nature. Therefore, in one sense, Mary is Queen because she is "the Mother of the King divine, of Him to whom from His Mother's womb the Lord God gave the throne of David and eternal kingship in the house of Jacob," a supreme King who will not allow Himself to be bested in charity or filial devotion by any earthly monarch. In the Scriptures, we read of King Solomon's behavior towards his mother, Bethsabee: "A throne was set for the king's mother, and she sat on his right hand." (3 Kg. 2:19)

Christ is said to reign also by *conquest*, because of the victory won by Him on Calvary. In a very real sense, our Lady can be said to have gained her Queenship also by conquest, insofar as she participated as *Co-Redemptrix* on Calvary. This is what Pope Pius indicated when he referred to Mary as the "Minister to the King of martyrs in the ineffable work of man's Redemption". *Every man shall receive his own reward, according to his own labor.* Would our Lord have allowed His Mother to suffer *with* Him on Calvary, yet refuse, then, to share with her the kingdom won through that suffering? *For star differeth from star in glory. So also is the resurrection of the dead.* Could Jesus, the Judge of the living and the dead, refuse Mary the very honor and place to which she had been invited by the Blessed Trinity when she became the Mother of the Redeemer and *Co-Redemptrix*?

Come ye blessed of my Father, possess the kingdom prepared for you from the foundation of the world. The members of the Church are chosen *in Christ*, "before the foundation of the world"; they will be redeemed by the Precious Blood. But our Lady was chosen to *give* Christ to the world. She was the only one chosen to become a *direct* participant in the Redemption won by her Son – first, through the *Hypostatic Union*, whereby divine and human natures united in her womb and, secondly, by her maternal sorrows on Calvary.

Mary, therefore, will "possess" the kingdom of God, *the kingdom of Jesus her Lord and her Son*, in a manner both fitting to her dignity, and in accord with the promptings of divine justice and the filial love of Christ. "According to the measure of her grace by which she surpassed others on earth," wrote St. Bernardine of Siena, "so great is her singular glory in the kingdom of the blessed."

St. Paul described the various glories of the blessed souls in heaven: "One is the glory of the *sun*, another the glory of the *moon*, and another the glory of the *stars*." It is NO coincidence that these glories seem to be "summed up" in the image of our Lady preserved by St. John, to whom she was entrusted on Calvary: "And a great sign appeared in heaven: A Woman clothed with the *sun*, and the *moon* under her feet, and on her head a crown of twelve *stars*." Is it any wonder the saints have referred to Mary as "God's Masterpiece"?

While Mary's kingdom is co-extensive with her Son's – i.e., they rule it together – there is a particular sphere occupying the Virgin's concern and labors. In the *Salve Regina*, we pray, "Hail, Holy Queen, *Mother of Mercy*, our life, our sweetness and our hope." In 1917, Pope Benedict XV decreed that Mary's title, "Queen of Peace", be added to her Litany. The outstanding, defining character of the Virgin's Queenship is its *maternal* character, as was underscored by Pope Pius XII: "And this queenship of hers is essentially motherly, used only for our good."

Because our Lord gave Mary to us to be our Spiritual Mother, it is right to approach her with a certain "familiarity", taking comfort in that maternal warmth so beautifully evident in the words of Our Lady of Guadalupe to Saint Juan Diego (†1548): "Am I not here who am your Mother? Are you not under my shadow and protection? Am I not your fountain of life? Are you not in the folds of my mantle? In the crossing of my arms? Is there anything else you need?"

There is no person in the court of an earthly monarch who wields as much influence over him as his queen. Ministers, secretaries, courtiers . . . these figures may be valuable assets to a ruler; they may earn his greatest regard and affection. But, in the sphere of *advocacy*, the queen towers above all, for, in the end, all others are still *subjects* of the king, while the queen remains his "consort". The maternal quality of Mary's Queenship, her unique reign as the "Queen of Mercy", comes to the fore in her role as supreme *Advocate* for her children.

As in too many other unfortunate cases, our Lady's detractors attempt to use her role of *Advocate* against her. This particular assault operates on the assumption that one person is being snubbed merely because a certain positive quality is attributed to a different person, with whom the first is somehow connected. Therefore, if we praise a man as being a "good father", yet neglect to say something similar about his wife in the very next breath . . . then, we must be implying that the wife is *not* a good mother. The enemies of Mary, pursuing this train of thought, assume that those who seek her intercession, calling her "Mother of Mercy", must doubt the mercy of Jesus, or lack confidence in Him. As always, such unsound "logic" leads to muddled thinking.

"Advocacy" is merely the pleading of another's cause. It does not imply either that the one *being* petitioned is a tyrant who does not want to grant a request or favor, or that the one *using* an advocate feels this way. A person may deem himself undeserving of favors and may hesitate, out of humility, to present his case. Also, the request may be of such import that the petitioner wishes to use all available means to see that it is presented well.

The practice of advocacy is pleasing to God. When Eliu defended the actions of God to his friend, the sorely afflicted Job, he declared that "God is greater than man"; then, he added: "If there shall be an angel speaking for him, one among thousands, to declare man's uprightness, He shall have mercy on him, and shall say: Deliver him, that he may not go down to corruption: I have found wherein I may be merciful to him." (Job 33:23-24) One who approaches God through an advocate is not making any implied criticism of *God*; on the contrary, he admits his own unworthiness.

The kingdom of God has been established as a *monarchy*. Christ, the Son of God, is King. The Blessed Virgin is the Queen-Mother. The angels and blessed souls constitute the celestial court. The concept of "advocacy" is implicit in the very structuring of this eternal kingdom, and there can be no more efficacious or desirable Advocate than its Queen:

> Mary is the means Our Lord chose to come to us and she is also the means we should choose to go to Him, for she is not like other creatures who tend rather to lead us away from God than towards Him, if we are over-attached to them. Mary's strongest inclination is to unite us to Jesus, her Son, and her Son's strongest wish is that we come to Him through His Blessed Mother. He is pleased and honored just as a king would be pleased and honored if a citizen, wanting to become a better subject and slave of the king, *made himself the slave of the queen*. . . . It is as if a poor peasant, wishing to win the friendship and favor of the king, were to go to the queen and give her an apple – his only possession – for her to offer it to the king. The queen, accepting the peasant's humble gift, puts it on a beautiful golden dish and presents it to the king on behalf of the peasant. The apple in itself would not be a gift worthy of a king, but presented by the queen in person on a dish of gold, it becomes fit for any king. (St. Louis de Montfort, *True Devotion to the Blessed Virgin*)

In addition to an attitude of unfeigned familiarity, it is also meet and fitting to approach our Lady in the attitude of subjects, as those approaching a monarch, the *Great Sign* of St. John's Apocalyptic vision. This "sign", a crowned Woman about to give birth, embodies both the maternal and queenly aspects of the Virgin, and the Church has always intuited and accepted these dual glories with no hesitation or confusion, because, when we approach Mary *as Queen*, we find ourselves drawn, not to power for its own sake, but to a royal might and mien that is always turned towards mankind with an air of great solicitude:

> Happy the day on which the most humble of handmaidens is raised to her position as Queen of heaven and most powerful Mistress of the world. No higher position is possible in Her Son's kingdom. Her throne is right next to Christ's in glory. Happy and venerable is the day on which this

> Queen and Mother is given so powerful and merciful a position that she will ever be our merciful protectress at the throne of the Divine Judge, her Son. (St. Peter Canisius, †1597, *Homily on Mary, the Virgin Mother of God*)

In accord with her spiritual maternity, the all-encompassing, nurturing sovereignty of Mary is manifested in her role as *Mediatrix of All Graces*, by which she is both the "most powerful mistress of the world", as well as our "merciful protectress at the throne of the Divine Judge". As Queen, she is given the right to exercise *authority*, to dispense the graces won by the King "to whomever she desires, when, in what manner, and to what degree she wishes." (St. Bernardine of Siena) As the One Mediator, Jesus is the mediator of graces for all, *including Mary*, and it is *His* privilege to dispose of the Treasury of Grace in any manner He so chooses, and by any means. He has given us the Holy Mass and the sacraments, through which graces flow to earth from heaven; He has given us the ordained priesthood, by whom the Acceptable sacrifice of the Altar is renewed every day and by whose ministry and authority sanctifying grace can be regained through the sacrament of Penance.

Our Lord has also given His Church a Mother and a *merciful* Queen:

> Our great Queen has gone before us, she has gone on, I say, and has been gloriously received, so gloriously that we, her poor servants, walk with confidence after our Lady, crying out to her, "Draw us: we will run after thee to the odor of thy ointments." (Cant. 1:3) . . . She is the Queen of heaven, *she is the Queen of Mercy*, and she is also the Mother of the only-begotten Son of God – a title which more than anything else commends to us the greatness of her power and her loving-kindness: unless perchance there be someone who does not believe that the Son of the Most High honors His Mother, or who hesitates to believe that the very vitals of Mary "have passed into the affection" (Ps. 72:7) of charity, in consequence of having been the home wherein for nine months the "Charity That is from God" (1 Jn. 4:7)

> "dwelt corporeally". (Cf. Col. 2:9) (St. Bernard, *First Sermon for the Feast of the Assumption of the BVM*)

Mary is the Queen of Mercy, but let no one forget "the greatness of her power". She is called the "Virgin Most Powerful" in her Litany, and history testifies to this royal might. On October 7, 1571, the Turkish fleet, threatening "to impose on nearly the whole of Europe the yoke of superstition and barbarity," was defeated by the Catholic forces at the Battle of Lepanto:

> At that time the Supreme Pontiff, St. Pius V, after arousing among all the Christian princes zeal for the common defense, strove, above all, with great ardor to obtain for Christendom the favor of the most powerful Mother of God. So noble an example offered to heaven and earth in those times rallied around him all the minds and hearts of the age. And thus Christ's faithful warriors, prepared to sacrifice their life and blood for the welfare of their faith and their country, proceeded undauntedly to meet their foe near the Gulf of Corinth; while those who were unable to join them formed a band of pious supplicants, who called on Mary and as one saluted her again and again in the words of the Rosary, imploring her to grant victory to their companions engaged in battle. *Our sovereign Lady did grant her aid*; for in the naval battle near the Echinades Islands the Christian fleet gained with no great loss to itself a magnificent victory, in which the enemy was completely routed. (Pope Leo XIII, *Supremi Apostolatus*, 1883)

The inspired books tell of God's command over nature: "Behold the heaven, and the heavens of heavens, the deep, and all the earth, and the things that are in them, shall be moved in His sight." (Ecclus. 16:18) This power was demonstrated by Jesus when He calmed the storm at sea, when "rising up He commanded the winds, and the sea, and there came a great calm." (Mt. 8:26) After this display of divine might, His disciples asked each other "What manner of man is this, for the winds and the sea obey Him?"

The Queen of heaven shares in the King's authority over nature. On a gray, rain-soaked October 13, 1917, tens of thousands of people gathered at the Cova da Iria in Portugal in hopes of seeing a miracle promised by Our Lady of Fatima. Mary appeared to the children, announced herself as the "Lady of the Rosary", and admonished mankind, "Do not offend God anymore, for He is already too greatly offended." As she departed, Lucia cried out to the crowds, "Oh, look at the sun!" It was then that the renowned Miracle of the Sun occurred. Secular newspapers and eyewitnesses, both indifferent and hostile, reported the event, during which the sun revolved like a pinwheel, sent out shafts of multi-colored light and appeared to plunge towards the earth. In her fourth memoir (written in 1941), Sr. Lucia explained her reason for calling out to the crowd: "Opening her hands, [the Lady] made them reflect on the sun, and as she ascended, the reflection of her own light continued to be projected on the sun itself."

"I will fight and overcome my enemies," prayed St. John Damascene to Mary, "with no other buckler than your protection and your all-powerful aid." In recognition of her solicitude, it is natural to turn to the Queen of heaven in times of trial, particularly when courage is put to the test. One of the most ancient prayers to the Virgin, the *Sub Tuum Praesidium* (discovered on papyrus dating from the third century), expresses the desire, universal wherever authentic Christianity flourishes, to take refuge in Mary:

We fly to thy patronage,
O holy Mother of God;
despise not our petitions in our necessities,
but deliver us from all dangers,
O glorious and blessed Virgin.

The men who battled at Lepanto find their literary equivalent in the hero of the medieval epic, *Sir Gawain and the Green Knight*, who carries a shield upon whose inner surface has been painted an image of the Virgin Mary. It is not difficult to imagine this knight whispering a "*Sub Tuum Praesidium*" as he enters the fray, after gazing momentarily upon Mary's countenance for inspiration and fortitude:

And firmly on the Five Wounds all his faith was set
that Christ received on the cross, as the Creed tells us;
and wherever the brave man into battle was come,
on this beyond all things was his earnest thought:
that ever from the Five Joys all his valour he gained
that to heaven's courteous Queen once came from her Child.
For which cause the knight had in comely wise
on the inner side of his shield her image depainted,
that when he cast his eyes thither his courage never failed.

Here is how Christ the King is described in the Scriptures:

> Thou hast made Him a little lower than the angels: Thou hast crowned Him with glory and honor, and hast set Him over the works of Thy hands: Thou hast subjected all things under His feet. For in that He hath subjected all things to Him, He left nothing not subject to Him. (Heb. 2:7-8)

Thou hast made Him a little lower than the angels. This describes God-made-Man, God in His human nature. The Kingship of Christ cannot be separated form this human nature, for it was by His Precious Blood that He despoiled the principalities and powers, "triumphing over them in Himself". (Col. 2:15) *All* creation and creatures are subject to Christ, "That in the name of Jesus every knee should bow, of those that are in heaven, on earth, and under the earth." (Phil. 2:10)

The Kingship of Christ extends over heaven, earth . . . and *under the earth*, hell. Our Lady, therefore, who receives dominion from her Son, is likewise Queen over angels, men . . . and demons. St. Louis de Montfort wrote, "What Lucifer lost by pride, Mary won by humility," a thought which had earlier found expression in a thirteenth-century song by Alfonso the Wise (d. 1284), King of Castile and Leon:

And she was so humble that
He came down from the heavens
where He lived, through her holy
and virtuous body
blessing her with His grace
and with a gift so great

that all who were made sick by
the devil were made well by Her.
(Cantigas de Santa Maria)

Satan's hatred for our Lady is obsessive. She was the one prophesied in Eden: *She shall crush thy head, and thou shalt lie in wait for her heel.* Yet, the only manner in which he can "attack" her – which is *always* an attack on her Divine Son, and therefore of demonic origin – is to assault her children, the members of the Church: *And the dragon was angry against the Woman: and went to make war with the rest of her seed.*

Satan may be the *Prince* of this world – "Now shall the prince of this world be cast out" (Jn. 12:31) – but Mary is the *Queen* of heaven and Earth. The poet François Villon (d. 1463) called her "Lady of heaven, Regent of the Earth, Empress of all the infernal marshes fell." As determined as the serpent and his seed are to "make war" with the seed of the Woman, they remain under her dominion:

> God has given Mary such great power over the evil spirits that, as they have often been forced unwillingly to admit through the lips of possessed persons, they fear one of her pleadings for a soul more than the prayers of all the saints, *and one of her threats more than all their other torments.* (St. Louis de Montfort, *True Devotion to the Blessed Virgin*)

"I do not fear devils," wrote St. Alphonsus Ligouri in a prayer to the Virgin, "for thou art more powerful than the whole of hell." The truth of this has been proven time and time again. St. Bernadette Soubirous († 1879) related how the peaceful silence of Massabielle was broken one day by demonic rantings and noises, and how only one glance from Our Lady of Lourdes was enough to silence the infernal clamoring. Over four centuries before this occurred, St. Bernardine of Siena had referred to Mary as "the ruling mistress of the devils, because she brings them into subjection." Two centuries before that, St. Bonaventure declared that "devils flee before Mary's face as wax melts before the fire." The heavenly hosts, the "good" angels who have been ministers, courtiers and warriors of God since their creation, accept the Queenship of Mary with great satisfaction . . . and *understanding*. Unlike their demonic counterparts, they obey their Creator; His will is their pleasure. Unlike the serpent and his "seed", they rejoiced at the Incarnation: "And the Angel said to them: Fear not; for, behold, I bring you good tidings of great joy." (Lk. 2:10)

Because Mary is the Mother of their Lord and because He loves her as such, then the angels, also, love her gladly and freely as the truly blessed Mother of the Church, and as their Queen. These celestial beings understand well that Jesus and Mary are united forever in a bond established by the Blessed Trinity. When the "Angel of Peace" appeared to Lucia, Jacinta and Francisco in 1916, heralding the appearance of Our Lady of Fatima, he said to them, "The Hearts of Jesus and Mary are attentive to the voice of your supplications," as though to echo the words of the *De Profundis*: "Lord, hear my voice. Let thy ears be attentive to the voice of my supplication." (Ps. 129:2)

Once again, with the appearance of "the Lady of the Rosary" at Fatima, divine solicitude for sinful humanity (whose "voice" cries out in the *De Profundis*) was manifested upon the earth. "The Hearts of Jesus *and Mary* are attentive," announced the angelic courtier clearly. Let this serve as a lesson to all who would dare presume to "separate" the Redeemer and the Mother of the Redeemer.

The "Christocentric" foundation of Marian devotion was highlighted dramatically at Fatima. Before our Lady appeared to the children, the Angel instructed them to make reparation to God for the countless sins by which He is justly offended. Sr. Lucia described the third visit of the celestial messenger:

> He was holding a chalice in his left hand, with the Host suspended above it, from which drops of blood fell into the chalice. Leaving the chalice suspended in the air, the Angel knelt down beside us and made us repeat three times: "Most Holy Trinity, Father, Son, and Holy Ghost, I adore you profoundly, and I offer you the most precious Body, Blood, Soul and Divinity of Jesus Christ, present in all the tabernacles of the world, in reparation for the outrages, sacrileges and indifferences with which He Himself is offended. And through the infinite merits of His most Sacred Heart, *and the Immaculate Heart of Mary*, I beg of You the conversion of poor sinners.

The Virgin will not appear to the three children until they have been carefully instructed to render only the most profound adoration to Jesus Christ in the Blessed Sacrament. We call Fatima a "Marian" apparition because Mary was the principal personage involved, but its end (like that of all authentic apparitions) was *to lead souls to Christ in a spirit of humility and reparation*. The Angel of Peace spoke of our Lord's "infinite merits", the bounty of grace He won for us on Calvary. Yet, he also did not neglect to mention our Co-Redemptrix and Mediatrix: "Through the infinite merits of His most Sacred Heart, *and the Immaculate Heart of* Mary." Such are the lessons taught by angels: "Are they not all ministering spirits, sent to minister for those, who shall receive the inheritance of salvation?" (Heb. 1:14)

St. John Damascene contemplated the joy of all the heavenly Court at Mary's Assumption:

> Today that sacred and living Ark of the living God, in whose womb was conceived the Creator, rests in the temple of the lord, a temple not built by hands. David, her father, leaps for joy, and even the angels join him in exultation. . . . On this feast day the Archangels celebrate, the Virtues glorify God, the Principalities exult and are joined in praise by the Powers. The Dominations rejoice and the Thrones cannot restrain their happiness. Cherubim and Seraphim proclaim her glory. (*Second Sermon on the Dormition of the BVM*)

The blessed souls in heaven take great pleasure in their Queen. They know well that eternal joy is theirs because of the sacrifice of Jesus, and that Our Lady brought the Savior into the world, that she stood by Him on Calvary as the Queen of Martyrs, and that she regards each one of them, not merely as subjects, but as her own children. "The greater glory of the blessed in heaven is, after seeing God, the presence of this most beautiful Queen," wrote St. Peter Damian. While Pope Pius XII reflected on the attitude of these blessed souls at the crowning of Mary: "And Paradise recognized that she was really worthy of receiving honor, glory and rule, because she is full of grace, holier, more beautiful, more exalted, incomparably more so than the greatest saints and angels, taken individually or together." (*Mary's Universal Queenship*, 1946)

The Presence of God, the direct experience of the magnificence of the Blessed Trinity, the reality of an eternity in Heaven – how can the presence of Mary "add" to that? Nothing is "added" to God or His glory by the presence of any creature. The Beatific Vision is the supreme good of heaven: "And I heard a great voice from the throne, saying: Behold the tabernacle of God with men, and He will dwell with them. And they shall be His people; and God Himself with them shall be their God." (Apoc. 21:3)

However, the presence of other holy souls in heaven will constitute a portion of eternal bliss, in the manner of "accessory" goods, non-essential in light of the Presence of God, but a definite component nonetheless: "Behold how good and how pleasant it is for brethren to dwell together in unity." (Ps. 132:1) "I saw a great multitude, which no man could number, of all nations and tribes and peoples and tongues, standing before the throne, and in sight of the Lamb." (Apoc. 7:9)

The abundance and quality of heavenly rewards which comprise the "eternal inheritance" of the Catholic faithful are beyond human description: "Eye hath not seen, nor ear heard, neither hath it entered into the heart of man, what things God hath prepared for them that love Him." (1 Cor. 2:9) When we consider the beauty of Mary, both internal and external . . . when we contemplate her standing beneath her Son's Cross on Calvary . . . when we look back over the ages and see the immeasurable outpouring of love for her which has flowed from human hearts . . . when we think upon the benefits we have received through Mary's Spiritual Motherhood and by her Mediation . . . is it to be wondered at that *her* presence should constitute a unique aspect of eternal happiness?

The physical presence of the "beloved" is always a thing worthy of desire, something to be sought after ardently. *The Canticle of Canticles* depicts the yearning of the Spouse (our Lady and the Church) for Jesus: "I to my Beloved, and His turning is towards me. Come, my Beloved, let us go forth into the field, let us abide in the villages." (7:10-11) In her understanding of the Dogma of the Assumption, the Church apprehends the desire of Jesus, the Son, to have with

Him in heaven the Mother He loves, and this desire is expressed also in the Canticles: "Arise, make haste, my love, my dove, my beautiful one, and come. For winter is now past, the rain is over and gone." (2:10-11) This is the sense behind the very practical words addressed to our Lady by St. Germanus of Constantinople:

> Indeed, as a son looks for and desires his own mother, and the mother delights to live with her son, thus it was right that you also, whose heart was full of motherly love for your Son and God, should return to Him; likewise it was altogether fitting that God, Who for His part had the kind of feelings of love toward you that a son has for a mother, should make you a sharer in His community of life. (*Homily 1 on the Dormition*)

If we desire naturally to spend eternity with those we love, how can we not desire the presence of the "Mother of Fair Love"? How can someone who yearns for Jesus not yearn for Mary as well? *They found the Child with Mary His Mother . . . What therefore God hath joined together, let not man put asunder.* The presence of Mary in heaven reigning as Queen beside her Son, the King of Kings, will certainly enhance the joy of the elect. Knowing, firstly, the love of the Blessed Trinity for Our Lady and, secondly, the love of Mary for all her spiritual sons and daughters, the blessed souls, recalling their own affection for their Spiritual Mother, without which they could not have pleased God, will take delight in this "community of life", in the kingdom ruled by the best of all kings and the finest of all Queens.

St. Andrew of Crete addressed our Blessed Mother in words which are as pragmatic as they are lofty, conveying a fundamental fact about Mary even as they praise her: "Queen of the whole human race, truly faithful to the meaning of your name, you are above all things – except God!" The Blessed Trinity decreed that our world would not have become a redeemed world without Mary. Similarly, our Lord has decreed that heaven would not be "heaven" without her.

Chapter Thirty-One

Our Lady's Wonderful Titles

STAR OF THE SEA – TENDER LOCAL DEVOTIONS TO MARY – TWO THOUSAND YEARS OF DEVOTION – IN THE CHURCH IS FOUND THE "FULL ASSEMBLY OF SAINTS" – MARY IS "THE CAUSE OF OUR JOY" – SHE IS THE "LADDER" OF JACOB'S VISION CONNECTING HEAVEN AND EARTH – TRUE AND FALSE DEVOTION TO MARY – IT IS THE MOTHER OF GOD WHO HAS BECOME OUR MOTHER ALSO – IF MARY BE NOT TRULY GOD'S MOTHER THEN GOD DID NOT TRULY BECOME MAN – OUR LADY IS THE "GREAT SIGN" OF THE APOCALYPSE – TO HONOR GOD'S MASTERPIECE IS TO HONOR GOD

In August of 1613, the composer Claudio Monteverdi underwent auditions for the position of *maestro di capella* of the Basilica of St. Mark's in Venice, the private chapel of the doge and the musical pivot of the renowned seaport city. Understandably, Monteverdi wanted to impress the Procurators of the Basilica and, to this end, one of the compositions he presented was his *Vespro Della Beata Vergine* ("Vespers of the Blessed Virgin"), which had been published three years earlier. It was a monumental work, lasting one and a half hours in duration and containing important stylistic innovations, such as the mixing of psalm settings with extra-liturgical motets, and the inclusion of an appropriate Marian hymn.

Venetian tradition placed the founding of the city on the Feast of the Annunciation, and the Marian hymn set by Monteverdi was "*Ave Maris Stella.*" This title of Mary's, "Star of the Sea", naturally held a special place in the hearts of the people of the great seaport. Under the composer's masterful hand, the familiar plainsong melody is transformed into a moving "sonic painting" for alternating choirs, soloists and instruments. The very first words, sung by a double choir, sound like a respectful summons to our Lady, a reverent, yet confident, calling-out to her: "*Ave Maris Stella, Dei Mater alma, Atque semper Virgo, Felix coeli porta* . . . Hail, star of the sea, mild Mother of God, eternal Virgin, blessed gate of heaven."

The full name of Eton College, founded by King Henry VI in 1440, was "The college Royal of Our Lady of Eton beside Windsor", and the original statutes of this institution prescribed that "every day of the year at a fitting hour of the evening, all the choristers of our royal college, together with the master in chant, shall enter the church at the sound of a bell . . . and these wearing surplices and ranged around a statue of the Blessed Virgin, with candles lighted, shall sing solemnly and to the very best of their skill an antiphon of the Blessed Virgin, with the verse *Ave Maria* and the prayer."

A traditional Breton folk song, *Misteriou Joaius* ("The Joyful Mysteries"), which begins with a greeting to the Virgin, "Full of Grace", tells of the early life of Jesus. It closes with the episode of the finding of the Child in the Temple, and the words, "Your Son remained at the temple, Mary, don't cry anymore."

Here are three instances of the Catholic "Marian" sensibility at work. The story of Monteverdi brings us into the Basilica of St. Mark's, where music that rightfully deserves to be called "celestial" filled the vaulted roofs. It tells of a master composer who, when the time came to give his best, offered a monumental work dedicated to the Blessed Virgin.

In Eton college, located in a land which had once proudly called itself "the Dower of Blessed Mary, the Virgin Mother of God and Queen of heaven," we see how an institution dedicated to the sharpening of the intellect, to the formation of clear, logical thinking, deemed itself best served if it were placed under the patronage of the Mother of God, rendering nightly praises in her honor.

The folk-song from Brittany does not evoke the musical *virtuosi* of early seventeenth-century Venice, or the scholars of Eton. It evokes instead the rural villages of all ages, the sort of landscape in which it would not seem at all out of place to find the Holy Family walking. In place of formal Marian texts which call for only the highest level of artistry in both composition and performance, we encounter in this folk-song the very simple and very human desire to comfort the young mother who would one day be known as the Mother of Sorrows.

It is difficult to imagine such music being written in honor of anyone or anything other than the Blessed Virgin Mary. The voices of her spiritual children can be discerned throughout history, always calling out to her, always hailing her: "*Ave Maria . . . Ave Maris Stella . . . Salve Regina . . . Ave Regina Caelorum.*" Sometimes, she is addressed as Queen: "Hail, Holy Queen . . . Hail, Queen of Heaven." Other times, she is spoken to in more familiar terms: "Remember, O most gracious Virgin Mary. . . . We fly to thy patronage, O holy Mother of God."

"The heart of a fool is as a wheel of a cart: and his thoughts are like a rolling axle-tree." (Ecclus. 33:5) One of the bitter fruits of original sin is a disordering of the passions – inclination to vice, boredom, inconstancy, anxiety. Steadfastness in the struggle for salvation, in the daily battle to follow the commandments and precepts of God, is a gift from God: "I have lifted up my eyes to the mountain from whence help shall come to me. My help is from the Lord, Who made heaven and earth." (Ps. 120: 1-2) "Our God is our refuge and strength: a helper in troubles, which have found us exceedingly." (Ps. 45:1)

In such a "disordered" climate, relieved only by God's mercy, how can we account for two thousand years of veneration offered to the Virgin Mary? Each generation to walk the earth is another generation conceived in original sin, another generation of men and women free to consider the fate of their souls or not, another amalgam of societies oftentimes seeking peace and a fraternal utopia, which, impossible to attain outside of Christ and His Church, is sought there anyway.

By her God-given authority as the sole interpreter of Sacred Scripture and guardian of the Deposit of Faith, the Catholic Church accommodates the following texts to Mary, as words spoken "prophetically" by her, inspired by the Holy Ghost: "And I took root in an honorable people, and in the portion of my God His inheritance, and my abode is in the full assembly of saints." (Ecclus. 24:16) Our Lady is a daughter of King David, a pre-eminent daughter of Israel, the Chosen People of the Old Dispensation. It was in this people that she took "root", and this allowed her Son to be born from the seed of David:

> And there shall come forth a rod out of the root of Jesse, and a flower shall rise up out of his root. (Is. 11:1) Concerning His Son, Who was made to Him of the seed of David, according to the flesh. (Rom. 1:3) He shall be great and shall be called the Son of the most High; and the Lord God shall give unto Him the throne of David, His father; and He shall reign in the house of Jacob forever. (Lk. 1:32)

But there is a fuller meaning to the term "honorable people". Amid the ravages of original sin and concupiscence, there is one way only by which men can become "honorable" – in so far as they are creatures redeemed through the sacrifice of Christ. During Mass, when the priest pours water and wine into the chalice, he prays:

> O God, Who in creating man didst exalt his nature very wonderfully and yet more wonderfully didst establish it anew: by the mystery signified in the mingling of this water and wine grant us to have part in the Godhead of Him Who hath vouchsafed to share our manhood, Jesus Christ, Thy Son, Our Lord, Who liveth and reigneth with Thee in the unity of the Holy Ghost, God, world without end.

There is only one honorable people, or honorable society, in the world, and that is the one expressly founded by Jesus Christ:

> Jesus Christ called upon all mortals, as many as were, and as many as were to be, to follow Him as their leader, and likewise their Savior, not only separately one by one, but also associated and united alike in fact and in mind; one in faith, end, and the means proper to that end, and subject to one and the same power. . . . Therefore, the Church is a society divine in origin, supernatural in its end, and in the means which bring us closest to that end; but inasmuch as it unites with men, it is a human community. (Pope Leo XIII, *Satis cognitum*, 1896)

Therefore, the Church is composed of individual sinners – "But we have this treasure in earthen vessels, that the excellency may be of the power of God, and not of us" (2 Cor. 4:7) – yet, she is called to form a perfect society, the Body and Bride of Christ, "a glorious Church, not having spot or wrinkle, or any such thing . . . holy and without blemish."

The Church, then, is the true embodiment of the "honorable people" foreshadowed by the faithful Israelites of the Old Testament. Faithful Roman Catholics are the fulfillment of God's promise to

Abraham: "Look up to heaven and number the stars, if thou canst. . . . So shall thy seed be." (Gen. 15:5) They are the spiritual descendants of Abraham: "And if you be Christ's, then are you the seed of Abraham, heirs according to the promise." (Gal. 3:29) It was prophesied of this seed that, through it, ". . . all the nations of the earth shall be blessed," (Gen. 18:18) and this has been fulfilled, for it is in the Catholic Church alone that salvation can be found: "One indeed is the universal Church of the faithful, outside of which no one at all is saved." (Pope Innocent III, Lateran Council IV, 1215)

The Blessed Virgin, a descendant of King David, took "root" physically in the honorable people of God, the faithful Israelites who looked for the coming of the Redeemer. She takes "root" spiritually – ineffably and completely – in that honorable society of the Redeemed, the Church foreshadowed continually throughout the Scriptures: "Blessed is the man that feareth the Lord: he shall delight exceedingly in His commandments. His seed shall be mighty upon earth." (Ps. 111:1-2) Jesus Himself would refer to this society, His Church, as a city: "You are the light of the world. A city seated on a mountain cannot be hid." (Mt. 5:14)

"And I took root in an honorable people, and in the portion of my God His inheritance, and my abode is in the full assembly of saints." The Blessed Virgin takes root firmly in the Church, whose sacramental life offers a foretaste of the eternal "inheritance". It is only there, in the "assembly of saints", that true saints, martyrs, teachers and holy personages can be found, for all who toil outside this society founded by Jesus do not remain in Christ: "If anyone abide not in me, he shall be cast forth as a branch, and shall wither." (Jn. 15:6)

Therefore our Lady can truly claim such titles as "Queen of All Saints" and "Queen of Martyrs", for only her children, "who have God for their Father and Mary for their Mother", (St. Louis de Montfort) deserve these glorious designations: "No one, let his almsgiving be as great as it may, no one, even if he pour out his blood for the Name of Christ, can be saved, unless he remain within the bosom and unity of the Catholic Church." (Pope Eugene IV, *Cantate Domino*, 1441) Mary is the Mother of the Church founded by Christ; she is the Mother of the *Catholic* Church.

Marian devotion does not exist in a vacuum. Our Lord took human nature upon Himself in the womb of His Mother, wedding Himself to humanity by means of the awesome Hypostatic Union of divine and human natures. Fr. Leonard Feeney (d. 1978) called this the "great meeting between Time and Eternity, in which Our Blessed Lady was Time's womb, Time's arms, Time's eyes." Christ chose the Blessed Virgin as the means by which He would come to earth to claim His Bride, who would become His own Mystical Body. "And they shall be two in one flesh," (Gen. 2:24) say the Scriptures concerning the sacrament of Matrimony. The Groom (Jesus) and His Bride (the Church) share human nature, the nature of the flesh; more than this, though, they share the same Spirit, making their union complete: "For the law of the spirit of life, in Christ Jesus, hath delivered me from the law of sin and of death. . . . Now if any man have not the Spirit of Christ, he is none of His." (Rom. 8:2,9)

Mankind is intimately related to Jesus, firstly, because He is our Lord and Creator, and again, by nature, a relationship made possible only because of the cooperation of Mary in the Redemption. Jesus is intimately related to the Mother from whom He took His Human nature. Completing this diagram of "intimate relations" is that of mankind to the Blessed Virgin. If our Lady had done nothing else than give Jesus to us, we would still owe all our happiness to her, the "Cause of Our Joy" – and this simply because God had ordained that her cooperation and consent to the Incarnation be a necessary part of the "economy of salvation":

> All nature is created by God, and God is born of Mary. God brought about all things, and Mary brought about God. God created all things, and created Himself through Mary; and thus re-created all that He had created. He who could make all things from nothing would not remake them without Mary. God, therefore, is Father of all created things, and Mary is Mother of all re-created things. . . . Truly, the Lord is with thee, to whom He made all creation along with Himself indebted to such an extent! (St. Anselm, *Oratio 52*)

The history of Creation has witnessed two great *Fiats*, two instances in which the words "let it be done" were spoken, leaving reality altered in their wake through the workings of divine love and mercy. The first time, the words were spoken by God, and the world was created as a result: "The Spirit of God moved over the waters. And God said: Be light made." (Gen. 1:2-3) The second time, the words were spoken by the Blessed Virgin, and the world was re-created as a result: "Behold the handmaid of the Lord; be it done to me according to thy word." (Lk. 1:38)

"The Word did speak, and all things were made," wrote St. Thomas Aquinas; he continued, "Mary did speak, and the Word was made flesh." The Patriarch Jacob had a dream of "a ladder standing upon the earth, and the top thereof touching heaven," on which he observed angels "ascending and descending". (Gen. 28:12) This dream found its fulfillment in the Incarnation. There was to be one "ladder" only which would bridge the infinite space between Divinity and humanity, between heaven and earth: the Blessed Virgin Mary.

Redeemed humanity could justifiably spend eternity honoring Mary solely for her fiat to the Angel Gabriel. Her consent signaled the end of the Time of Expectation and the beginning of the Time of Redemption, for which the earth had been groaning for so many ages; it also signaled the beginning of her labors for and with her Son. This triad of unique relationships existing between Jesus, Mary and the Church ripples outwards, embracing everything in its path:

> The mystery of Christ's immense love for us is revealed with a dazzling brilliance in the fact that the dying Savior bequeathed His Mother to His disciple John in the memorable testament: "Behold thy son." Now, in John, as the Church has constantly taught, Christ designated the whole human race, and in the first rank are they who are joined with Him by faith. (Pope Leo XIII, *Adiutricem populi*, 1895)

God has given us another reason to love Mary. Deriving still from her Divine Maternity, it is a reason presented to each man and woman as an individual bestowal, like the "talents" from the parable.

In this story, a man gave talents to his servants, then left on a journey. Upon his return, he praised the ones who invested the talents, rendering the original bestowal profitable, but he condemned the one who did nothing with the talents, burying them in the ground and forgetting about them.

Our Lady was given to the Church as Spiritual Mother, Advocate, Queen and Mediatrix for our benefit and happiness. Each and every soul is free to make much of this treasure, to watch it yield great spiritual returns, or tuck it away on a shelf, aware of its presence, but doing nothing to glean its riches, like the servant condemned in the parable. What is popularly called Marian "devotion" is actually a combination of things, of practices, attitudes and emotions which are oriented or directed towards one end – the good of the soul. Those who practice it place themselves in a position where they may one day hear the Giver of talents say, "Enter thou into the joy of thy Lord." (Mt. 25:23) Those who reject it, on the contrary, stand to lose all, for God does not reward contempt for his gifts: "Take ye away therefore the talent from him . . . that also which he seemeth to have shall be taken away." (Mt. 25:28-29)

These considerations may sound selfish, as though it were proper to love Mary (and her Son) for the purpose merely of "getting something" in return. This is the unacceptable attitude attributed by St. Louis de Montfort to a self-interested "devotion" to Mary:

> Then there are the *self-interested devotees* who turn to her only to win a court-case, to escape some danger, to be cured of some ailment, or have some similar need satisfied. Except when in need they never think of her. Such people are acceptable neither to God nor to His Mother. (*True Devotion to the Blessed Virgin*)

Included among such false "devotees" are those who would appropriate the Virgin for ends which are inimical to the good of the Catholic Church, for the advancement of modernist or false ecumenical agendas. Such people also "want" something from our Lady – an endorsement of their beliefs and goals. This self-serving attitude is contrasted by St. Louis with authentic devotion to Mary:

> True devotion to Our Lady is interior, that is, it comes from within the mind and the heart and follows from the esteem in which we hold her, the high regard we have for her greatness, and the love we bear her. . . . True devotion to Mary is disinterested. It inspires us to seek God in His Blessed Mother and not ourselves. The true subject of Mary does not serve his illustrious Queen for selfish gain. He does not serve her for temporal or eternal well-being but simply and solely because she has the right to be served and God alone in her. He loves her not so much because she is good to him or because he expects something from her, but simply because she is lovable. (*True Devotion to the Blessed Virgin*)

A disinterested devotion to our Lady will benefit one's soul, for to be a servant of Mary, a son or daughter who recognizes her as mother, is to "seek God in His Blessed Mother", and to serve "God alone in her". There is no discrepancy in loving Mary with affection, and in knowing that such veneration will please God and tend towards the good of one's soul, for each time the members of the Church practice Marian devotion, whether publicly or privately, it is done in accord with the admonition of St. Paul: "All whatsoever you do in word or in work, do all in the name of the Lord Jesus Christ, giving thanks to God and the Father by Him." (Col. 3:17)

That the Virgin is "lovable" in and of herself is only to be expected. Her Immaculate Heart drew God Himself down from heaven to take up His abode beneath it: "Thou hast wounded my heart, my sister, my Spouse, thou hast wounded my heart with one of thy eyes, and with one hair of thy neck." (Cant. 4:9) To hold a filial affection and reverence for Mary is certainly to imitate Christ: "In imitation of Jesus, a Christian should love Mary, and think the best of her. He should have her for mother, and as such love her, serve her, wait upon her, and, like Jesus, be totally subject to her." (St. Anthony Mary Claret, †1870)

Such an imitation can and should become an unconscious act, because, when we ponder the Virgin, we regard not only God's Mother, but our Mother as well. In the normal course of events, whenever children perform a kindly act towards their natural mother, they do not stop beforehand and say, "Now I will do this as a means of obeying the Fourth Commandment." The kindness and concern arise spontaneously, without the need for analysis. Authentic devotion to Mary, then, the only regard for her that is pleasing to God, "comes from within the mind and the heart and follows from the esteem in which we hold her, the high regard we have for her greatness, and the love we bear her."

A spontaneous affection for Mary, coming "from within the mind and the heart", is the standard by which a sound faith is demonstrated. In cases where the Roman Catholic Faith has been compromised through modernism or indifferentism, or rejected formally through heresy or schism, this affection may be either stifled or poorly grounded. In such cases, more analytical studies of Marian doctrine may introduce (or re-introduce) the confused soul to the Mother of God, who will in turn point the way back to her Son. Such a path to the Virgin surely proceeds "from within the mind", but, if the road is traveled with good will, the heart will surely catch up: "She is more precious than all riches: and all the things that are desired, are not to be compared with her." (Prov. 3:15)

After the Crucifix, the defining image of the True Faith is the icon of the Madonna and Child, of the radiant young Mother holding the Infant Savior. The history of civilization teems with many and varied artistic representations of Mary. There are paintings depicting the Madonna and St. Anne, the Coronation of the Madonna, the Enthroned Madonna, the Dormition of Mary, the Immaculate Conception and the Assumption. But it is the image of Mary and the Infant Jesus that sums up all the glories of this Blessed Mother, proclaiming so powerfully, yet so simply, that her place in the created order can only be extraordinary.

These images appeal to the senses, and also to the sentiments. While a certain maudlin or shallow sentimentality, usurping the place of sound, uncompromising doctrine, can be found where the ancient Catholic faith has been diluted, reconfigured, or "reformed", there is no cause to disdain authentic Catholic "sentiment", which is merely a certain well-grounded emotional attitude towards the many manifestations of the Roman Catholic faith: "Thou shalt love the Lord thy God with thy whole heart." (Deut. 6:5) It is not hard to feel this attraction towards our Lord, when we are invited to approach Him intimately in so many ways, the most profound being the reception of Holy Communion during Mass.

Like the Mass, which is rightly called its centerpiece, other facets of Catholic life not only create the "effect", but mirror the reality, that nothing, not time or space, can ever separate us from the love of Christ: *For I am sure that neither death, nor life, nor angels, nor principalities, nor powers, nor things present, nor things to come, nor might, nor height, nor depth, nor any other creature, shall be able to separate us from the love of God, which is in Christ Jesus Our Lord.* During the Holy sacrifice, the millennia which have passed since the Crucifixion drop away, and the graces won on that long-ago day stream forth abundantly. In the sacrament of Penance, we are invited to approach Jesus with the same immediacy as the men who cried out to Him so many centuries ago, "O Lord, Thou Son of David, have mercy on us." (Mt. 20:30) During the recitation of the Rosary, we set before our mind's eye the life of the Savior, deriving fresh inspiration and insight from it with each telling of the beads.

Through His Church, through the Catholic Faith which He left us, Jesus fulfills His promise: *Behold I am with you all days, even to the consummation of the world.* It is fulfilled not through "sentimentality", the belief or supposition that God is near and that we are following Him, but through a sacramental reality, an actual exchange of grace from Head to Body, from Groom to Spouse, which in turn ignites a Catholic sentiment. The time-hallowed phrase, "Holy Mother Church", expresses an objective fact; there is sentiment behind it, but it is not merely "sentimental". It summarizes the difference between belief-systems labeled "Christianity", yet operating outside the sphere of Apostolic authority and discernment, and Roman Catholicism, the faith of the Bride of Christ. Rejection of the Catholic Church, which is a refusal to partake of the sacramental life, is of necessity a rejection of the gifts of grace offered freely by the Head and Groom of the Church to His Body and Spouse. As a consequence of this rejection, grace must be regarded merely as God's "favor", and not a thing capable of transforming the soul; the holder of such a belief can only imagine, if vividly on occasion, God's presence, forgiveness . . . or approval. The Roman Catholic, by contrast, is presented with opportunities to encounter Jesus every day, be it through Mass, the reception of sacramental absolution, the use of sacramentals, etc.

Our Head and Groom, the Lord Who loved His Church enough to suffer and die for her, that she might never taste death, desires that we approach His Mother, and ours, if we would please Him: *Behold thy Mother.* When Jesus gave the Blessed Virgin to us, in the person of St. John the Evangelist (who taught such profound truths concerning her in his *Apocalypse*), He did so in the simplest, clearest words possible, and at the most critical moment in the history of creation. To accept this Mother is to accept the Son: "He that is of God, heareth the words of God." (Jn. 8:47) More than this, it is to accept the Son in the full glory of both His divinity and humanity. It is with deep insight that the poet Coventry Patmore (d. 1896) described Mary as "Our only saviour from an abstract Christ".

From the earliest days of the Church, Mary's Divine Maternity was regarded as the touchstone for truth and orthodoxy, the surety that Jesus was God and Man in one Person. When she is "removed", doctrinal integrity, bereft of its anchor, is cast to the winds. Her sweet presence, and her continuous influence upon the daily lives of those who deem themselves "Christians", is the difference between the true and false manifestations of the Faith founded by her Divine Son:

> I say then, when once we have mastered the idea, that Mary bore, suckled, and handled the Eternal in the form of a child, what limit is conceivable to the rush and flood of thoughts which such a doctrine involves? What awe and surprise must attend upon the knowledge, that a creature has been brought so close to the Divine Essence? It was the creation of a new idea and of a new sympathy, a new faith and worship, when the holy apostles announced that God had become incarnate; and a supreme love and devotion to Him became possible, which seemed hopeless before that revelation. But, besides this, a second range

> of thoughts was opened on mankind, unknown before, and unlike any other, as soon as it was understood that the Incarnate God had a mother. (Cardinal John Henry Newman, *A Letter to the Rev. E. B. Pusey*)

> My Blessed Mother, little Mary of Nazareth, to whom the Angel Gabriel appeared and said, "Hail, full of grace, the Lord is with thee; blessed art thou among women," is the Mother of God. She is the Mother of the only God I adore. She is the Mother of my Emmanuel, and if her Child is not God, then I have no God to adore. This washout of a world had in it one sublime success. Quantitatively, the world did not give much to God. But in quality, it gave Him a girl so transcendently beautiful, so responsive to the slightest wish of His heart on any and every term, that she was worthy to be called His masterpiece of creation. Without Mary, none of us would love God. We would reverence Him, and fear Him; but we would never speak to Him as Our Father; never ask Him for His Divine Child as our daily Bread; and we would never say, "Holy Mary, Mother of God, pray for us sinners now and at the hour of our death. Amen." (Fr. Leonard Feeney, *Bread of Life*, 1952)

What can be said of those professed followers of Jesus who, holding still to the doctrines of leaders who had rejected His Church, revel either in their contempt, or complete indifference, towards the Blessed Virgin, the Mother of Jesus? No reply other than God's own words is necessary. "If I say the truth to you," asked our Lord of the Pharisees, "why do you not believe Me?" (Jn. 8:46) *Behold thy Mother!*

The Woman of the Apocalyptic vision was called the Great Sign by St. John. She is the standard beneath which the faithful rally: *She brought forth a Man Child, Who was to rule all nations with an iron rod.* There are two sides to this finely-embroidered banner. On one side is represented the "Woman" as the Blessed Virgin, who "brought forth her first-born Son". She gave birth to "the Way, the Truth and the Life", the King of Kings. On the other side is represented the

"Woman" as the Roman Catholic Church, generating and nourishing spiritual children through Baptism and the sacraments, forming a "perfect society" that is the ideal of all other earthly societies.

These two representations of the "Woman" are inseparable, as are the divine and human natures of Jesus, and the divine and human components of the Church which mirror them. Mary is the Mother of Jesus forever, and the Mother of Christians forever:

> How is it that you do not belong to the Virgin's birth, if you are members of Christ? Mary gave birth to our head; the Church gave birth to you. Indeed, the Church also is virgin and mother; mother because of her womb of charity, virgin because of the integrity of her faith and piety. (St. Augustine, *Sermo 192*)

Considering this, the words of St. John take on a heightened sense of the ominous: "And when the dragon saw that he was cast unto the earth, he persecuted the woman, who brought forth the man child." (Apoc. 12:13) Satan, "cast unto the earth", defeated by St. Michael the Archangel, harbors an unquenchable hatred for the "Woman" in both of her representations. Despising the Incarnation, he hates the one who brought it about by her "fiat", and he attacks her and her Son through the members of the Church, offspring of Mary and brethren of Jesus.

Because the "Marian" and "Ecclesial" interpretations of the Woman Clothed with the Sun are inseparable, our Lady is referred to as the "Image" or "Model" of the Church. To despise Mary is to despise the Church founded by Christ; similarly, to despise the Church is tantamount to despising Mary and her Son. We read that "the dragon persecuted the woman," and we recall the Proto-evangelium and the enmities set between the serpent and the Woman. The persecutions of the early Church by the Emperor Diocletian, the ongoing battle waged by the enemies of Catholicism . . . all trials are included here.

The Great Sign has been given to us as both a standard of orthodoxy beneath which to rally, and a protection against error and heresy. Whenever the Dragon – Satan – attacks or persecutes the "Woman", he rages against Christ Himself. Therefore, Scripture, inspired by the

Holy Ghost, records these words, which the Church applies to Mary: "He that shall find me, shall find life, and shall have salvation from the Lord: But he that shall sin against me, shall hurt his own soul. All that hate me love death." (Prov. 8:35-36) Death is the devil's domain, Life that of the Sovereign Virgin. It is impossible to live with one foot in both, to despise or ignore the Mother, yet "love" the Son: "He that is not with me, is against me." (Mt. 12:30)

Because of this divinely-ordered state of affairs, we must go to Mary if we desire a "personal relationship" with Jesus. Behind all the magnificent theology of the past two millennia, behind the summas, treatises and compendiums, rests the truth embodied in the icon of Madonna and Child. All the Truth the world will ever need can be found there. Hope enough to last until the end of time can be found there. Both the source of Beauty, and its grandest manifestations, can be found there:

> There it pleased Him who shaped all life, the Holy Ghost, to dwell in her treasure-house – bright on her breast shone the radiant Child who was the beginning of all light. (*A Brave-Hearted Maid*, Old English poem)

To gaze, as did the shepherds and the Magi, upon this living icon of Madonna and Child, is like gazing at the most beautiful ring ever crafted, because it was designed by God. Our eyes go immediately to the precious "gem" which forms the centerpiece of this ring: *You shall find the Infant wrapped in swaddling clothes.* To look into this Infant's eyes is to look into the eyes of God; to receive His caress is to feel God's own touch. Many generations trod the earth, hoping for a glimpse of that face, for a sound from that Child's lips. His coming added a new depth to the very idea of joy: *I bring you tidings of great joy, that shall be to all the people: For, this day, is born to you a Savior, Who is Christ the Lord.*

If this ring, made by God, was to be perfect in every respect, what of the setting chosen to hold this invaluable gem? After our eyes have feasted upon the Infant Lord, hearts pounding at the proximity of such majestic humility, we dare to raise them to the radiant visage of the Woman holding Him . . . and discover therein a new cause for wonder. On her face is an expression which no artist can ever capture fully. There is a certain solemnity there, but not a distant regard; after all, she holds God in her lap. There is warm, unfeigned pleasure there, as well; after all, she is looking down at her Son.

The master painter or sculptor would pause, if asked to capture the expression of the Madonna in marble or on canvas. The master musician would also pause, wondering what possible combination of voices and instruments could express a charm too human to be purely celestial, yet "heavenly" nonetheless. The poet would pause, as well, running through a lifetime of stored phrases and imagery, to find there a string of words that could depict something so new – "For the Lord hath created a new thing upon the earth: A WOMAN SHALL COMPASS A MAN" – yet figured in the most universally cherished of images, a mother and her newborn: "And entering into the house, they found the Child with Mary His Mother."

It would perhaps strike us, then, that there is only one description of the Virgin-Mother that could ever do her justice, because its author was God and its words were so perfectly crafted and joined, they deserved to be spoken by an angel: "Full of Grace, the Lord is with thee: blessed art thou among women."

In the natural order, we tend to admire the creator of a fine statue or painting in our admiration of the work itself. If his work moves us to any degree, we pay the artist an unconscious tribute each time we gaze upon it. To consider the beauty, interior and exterior, of Mary is to contemplate a work of art fashioned by God Himself: "For by the greatness of the beauty, and of the creature, the creator of them may be seen, so as to be known thereby." (Wis. 13:5)

Our Lady always directs us to her maker. In the history of art, she is often depicted doing this very thing. In the Catacombs of Priscilla, one of the most ancient cemeteries of the Roman Church, can be found a picture of our Lady seated with the Christ Child, while a prophet (probably either Balaam or Isaias) points to a star above her head. In a large class of icons known by the Greek designation, *Hodegetria* (i.e., "Guide of the Way)," of which the renowned "Our Lady of Czestochowa" is an example, Mary holds the Infant in her left arm, as though inviting us to contemplate Him.

In the *Mater Misericordiae* representations, votive Madonnas commissioned and displayed in return for favors granted, the Infant, seated in His Mother's lap, leans forward in an attitude of solicitude, while in those labeled *Sancta Dei Genetrix*, the Virgin and Child are enthroned, and the lap of Mary, the "Seat of Wisdom", becomes a most fitting throne for the King of Glory. The humanity of the Savior is brought out with real heart in the paintings classified under the designation *Mater Admirabilis*, where our Lady does not look down from a celestial seat, but stands or sits peacefully, holding the Infant Redeemer, as though the two had sat for a portrait. In the *Madre Pia* depictions, Mary adores Jesus, regarding the Divinity of her Son with great devotion.

Even when the Divine Child is not depicted, His presence permeates artistic renderings of His Mother. In paintings of the *Immaculate Conception*, Mary is often depicted as the "Woman" of the Apocalypse, standing on the moon, the head of the serpent under her heel, and crowned with stars. There is a celestial quality to these representations, with angels surrounding the perfect Woman who will become the Mother of God. We see her exterior beauty, but we are drawn to consider the beauty of her soul, the privilege of the Immaculate Conception, and the One of Whom she said, "He that is mighty hath done great things to me." In the paintings labeled *Misericordiae*, the absence of the Divine Child highlights the Spiritual Motherhood, which causes Mary to love and protect all her children. Here, the Virgin is depicted as patroness or protectress, with her mantle extended over the people seeking refuge beneath it. While her Son is not figured here, these images recall the words of Jesus, *Behold thy Mother,* instilling in the viewer the same sense of comfort expressed in the verses addressed to our Lady by Giovanni Boccaccio (d. 1375):

I trust in thee with that same trust of old,
Fixed in the ancient love and reverence
Which now I tell as I have always told.
Guide thou my journey, strengthen my pretense
To reach with thee at last the blessed fold
Thy Son prepares His flock in recompense.

(The Queen of the Angels)

Little wonder, then, that the Blessed Virgin's physical beauty is so often lauded in tandem with the beauty of her soul. In the Person of Jesus Christ, we adore humanity and divinity united. In the Catholic Church, we recognize both a divine and human constitution. In Mary, we admire the human woman who became the Mother of God. We wonder at her immaculate soul, and render fitting praise to the pure body in which God rested, with great complacency, for nine months, and which He would not allow the corruption of the grave to touch. If we are honest with ourselves, we will be moved to ask the same question that was asked once by St. Ambrose: "Now, who could be nobler than the Mother of God? Who more splendid than she, whom Splendor chose?"

High praises of Mary's physical beauty allow mankind to express affection and regard for the unique Mother given to us by Christ. We can add nothing to our Lady's heavenly glory, but her maternal heart will always appreciate the praises and esteem of her spiritual children. We can, then, please her and, in so doing, please her Son, Who has honored her as only God can. The benefit is always ours: *He that honoreth his mother is as one that layeth up a treasure.*

Moreover, praise of Mary's beauty (both interior and exterior) is taught by the precepts of Scripture, in the words addressed prophetically by Jesus to His Mother: "How beautiful art thou, my love, how beautiful art thou. . . . Thou art all fair, O my love, and there is not a spot in thee. . . . Who is she that cometh forth as the morning rising, fair as the moon, bright as the sun, terrible as an army set in array?" (Cant. 4:1,7; 6:9)

Terrible as an army set in array. Our Lord does not neglect to mention the royal might accorded to His Queen, the one whose heel rests on the serpent's head, who stood by her Son's Cross on Calvary, and who continues to prove our surest defense against all error, as she did in the very first centuries of the Catholic Faith, when her Divine Maternity safeguarded both the humanity and the divinity of Jesus from the early doctrinal innovators.

Dante Alighieri described Mary's beauty as one of the delights of Paradise, lighting up heaven as the east stands out from the west at dawn:

> *And as the sky is brightest in that region*
> *where we on earth expect to see the shaft*
> *of the chariot so badly steered by Phaeton,*

While to one side and the other it grows dim –
just so that peaceful oriflamme lit the center
and faded equally along either rim.

And in the center, great wings spread apart,
more than a thousand festive angels shone,
each one distinct in radiance and in art.

I saw there, smiling at this song and sport,
her whose beauty entered like a bliss
into the eyes of all that sainted court.

(*Paradiso*)

The words of St. Peter Damian already quoted, written two centuries before Dante's epic, sound like a commentary on it: "The greatest glory of the blessed in heaven is, after seeing God, the presence of this most beautiful Queen." G. K. Chesterton (d. 1936) described Mary's countenance as one "that none had ever looked on without loving," and he envisages the angelic hosts greeting her as she is crowned after her Assumption:

Our Lady went into a strange country
And they crowned her for a queen,
For she needed never to be stayed or questioned
But only seen;
And they were broken down under unbearable beauty
As we have been."

(*Regina Angelorum*)

When we consider the interior beauty of Mary, we give thanks to the God Who created her: "For in her is the spirit of understanding: holy, one, manifold, subtle, eloquent, active, undefiled, sure, sweet, loving that which is good, quick, which nothing hindereth, beneficient, gentle, kind, steadfast." (Wis. 7:22-23) Our recognition of her exterior beauty rests on a similar consideration:

> Surely in His own Mother's countenance God has gathered together all the splendors of His Divine artistry. Mary's glance! Mary's smile! Mary's sweetness!

> The majesty of Mary, Queen of heaven and earth! As the moon shines resplendent in the dark heavens, so is Mary's beauty set apart from all other beauties, which are but shadows beside her. Mary is the most beautiful of God's creatures. (Pope Pius XII, *A Picture of the Blessed Virgin*, 1953)

If we are attracted to this Mother, the attraction is a gift from God. If we honor her, we render only a shadow of that rendered by Him Who made her the Immaculate Conception and the Queen of heaven and earth. If we praise her, we render only a shadow of that rendered by Him, Who became her Son. If we love her, it is in imitation of that love for her felt "from before the foundation of the world" by the Blessed Trinity as Father, Son and Spouse:

> The Mother of God is a creature. It follows that all she is, she has from God. But she is God's most perfect creature. For this reason, the homage paid to her is, by the very nature of the case, paid to God himself . . . The more we pay homage to the divine perfections found in Mary, the more perfect is our homage to God; this is perfectly in order, since God created her in the highest state of perfection. (St. Maximilian Kolbe, *Conference*, April 9, 1938)

This recognition of God's regard for Mary, which forms the undercurrent of that found in ordinary men and women wherever a sound faith flourishes, was captured in verse by Coventry Patmore:

Desire of Him whom all things else desire!
Bush aye with Him as He with thee on fire!
Neither in His great Deed nor on His throne –
O, folly of Love, the intense
Last culmination of Intelligence, –
Him seem'd it good that God should be alone!
Basking in unborn laughter of thy lips,
Ere the world was, with absolute delight
His Infinite reposed in thy Finite;

Well-match'd: He, universal being's Spring,
And thou, in whom art gather'd up the ends of everything!

(*The Child's Purchase: A Prologue*)

It would be highly unusual, if not distinctly unnatural, for mankind to have such strong and lasting feelings for this Woman, so favored by God, and not be intrigued by her:

> And did not the All-wise know the human heart when He took to Himself a Mother? Did He not anticipate our emotion at the sight of such an exaltation in one so simple and so lowly? If He had not meant her to exert that wonderful influence in His Church, which she has in the event exerted, I will use a bold word, He it is who has perverted us. If she is not to attract our homage, why did He make her solitary in her greatness amid His vast creation? If it be idolatry in us to let our affections respond to our faith, He would not have made her what she is, or He would not have told us that He had so made her. (Cardinal John Henry Newman, *The Blessed Virgin Mary*)

The very existence of the apocryphal books are proof of this very human interest. The writers of those ancient texts portrayed the birth of Mary, her childhood, her espousal, her death and Assumption. In the midst of many fanciful, even vulgar and doctrinally treacherous, episodes can be found passages worthy of their subject, such as this description from *The Gospel of Pseudo-Matthew*:

> Now Mary was in admiration with all the people of Israel. When she was three years old, she walked with so firm a step, spoke so perfectly, and was so assiduous in the praises of God, that all were astonished at her, and marveled. . . . And her face was beautiful and splendid, to such a degree that scarcely any one could look upon her countenance.

Descriptions of the Mother of God, apart from those preserved in the apocrypha, are not lacking; in fact, they can be found throughout the Church's history. Sometimes, they focus on her physical characteristics; other times, on her demeanor and behavior. In his ecclesiastical history, Nicephorus Callistus (d.c. 1335) included a description of our Lady attributed to a fourth-century account by St. Epiphanius, and derived from a more ancient source:

> She was of middle stature; her face oval; her eyes brilliant, and of an olive tint; her eyebrows arched and black; her hair was of a pale brown; her complexion fair as wheat. She spoke little, but she spoke freely and affably; she was not troubled in her speech, but grave, courteous, tranquil. Her dress was without ornament, and in her deportment was nothing lax or feeble.

Venerable Maria of Agreda (d. 1665), a nun and mystic, wrote this description of the Virgin as she appeared at the time of the Annunciation:

> The bodily shape of the heavenly Queen was well proportioned and taller than is usual with other maidens of her age; yet extremely elegant and perfect in all its parts. Her face was rather more oblong than round, gracious and beautiful, without leanness or grossness; its complexion clear, yet of a slightly brownish hue; her forehead spacious yet symmetrical; her eyebrows perfectly arched; her eyes large and serious, of incredible and ineffable beauty and dovelike sweetness, dark in color with a mixture tending toward green; her nose straight and well shaped; her mouth small, with red-colored lips, neither too thin nor too thick. All the gifts of nature in Her were so symmetrical and beautiful, that no other human being had the like. (*The Mystical City of God*)

In 1842, Alphonse Ratisbonne, a young Jewish man with a law degree, a partnership in his uncle's bank, and a betrothed spouse, traveled to Rome for pleasure, where he met up with Theodore de Bussières, a friend of his brother (a sibling who had earned the enmity of Alphonse and his family by converting to Catholicism and becoming a priest). Despite Alphonse's hostility towards Roman Catholicism, he accepted a friendly challenge from de Bussières to wear a medal of the Blessed Virgin and pray the Memorare. One day, while accompanying de Bussières to a small Church to make arrangements for a funeral, Ratisbonne experienced there the vision that would change his life, and find him ending his own days as a Catholic priest:

> The Church of San Andrea delle Fratte is small and poor; at that hour it was almost deserted. I think I was almost the only person in it, and there was no work of art to attract my attention. I was looking around mechanically, without any definite thought or purpose; I remember only a black dog, which bounded and jumped before me as I moved about. Suddenly the dog disappeared. The whole church disappeared; I saw nothing further. Or rather, O my God, I saw only one object!
>
> And how should I speak of it? No words of man can even attempt to utter the unutterable. All description, however sublime, must be only a degradation of the ineffable reality. I lay prostrate, my heart completely absorbed and lost, when de Bussières recalled me to life. I could not answer his questions, but I grasped my medal and kissed the image of the Virgin, radiant with grace. It was indeed her very self. (*The Narrative of Marie-Alphonse Ratisbonne*)

As far as depictions of Mary's physical characteristics go, of particular interest are those related by the visionaries who have been privileged to see and converse with her in the apparitions approved by the Church. Mélanie Calvat described Our Lady of La Salette (1846):

> Her face was majestic, imposing, but not imposing in the manner of the Lord's here below ... Her gaze was soft and penetrating. Her eyes seemed to speak to mine ... The Holy Virgin was all beauty and love; the sight of her overwhelmed me ... everything radiated the majesty, the splendor, the magnificence of a Queen beyond compare.

When asked by a child whether Our Lady of Lourdes (1858) was "lovely", St. Bernadette Soubirous replied, "Oh, yes, so lovely that, when you have seen her once, you would willingly die to see her again!" Blessed Jacinta Marto (†1920), one of the young Fatima visionaries, described the Virgin as "a beautiful lady", and Sr. Lucia described her first vision of Our Lady of Fatima (1917), in which the radiance of the celestial Queen shone forth: "We beheld a Lady all dressed in white. She was more brilliant than the sun, and radiated a light more clear and intense than a crystal glass filled with sparkling water, when the rays of the burning sun shine through it."

More brilliant than the sun. We have encountered this description before and, at Fatima, God once again set His seal on the Church's authoritative interpretation of Scripture. Sr. Lucia's eyewitness account of the Virgin's appearance resonates and harmonizes completely with both St. John's description of the "Woman clothed with the Sun", and the following Marian image from the Psalms: "The Queen stood on Thy right hand, in gilded clothing." (Ps. 44:10)

Mary's character has been praised since the time of the Fathers and offered as an object for inspiration and imitation. St. Athanasius wrote:

> Mary was a pure virgin . . . she loved to do good works . . . she gave generously to the needy what surplus she had earned by the work of her hands . . . she prayed to God as one person speaks to another . . . her speech was reflective and her voice subdued. (*Letter to Virgins*)

St. Ambrose wrote:

> Imagine! In this one Virgin every species of virtue shines forth. The peace of modesty, the triumph of faith, and the service of obedience are there. A Virgin in the home, a companion in work, a mother in the Temple! Need I say anything of her almost supernatural fasts and vigils, practically forgetting nature's demands in her love of God? She slept when necessary; she ate, more to avoid illness than out of desire for tempting foods. How many she has inspired to good works! (*On Virginity*)

The triumph of faith. This is a magnificent way in which to describe the faith of the young Virgin who gave her consent to the Angel Gabriel for the restoration of the world. But, there was also found in her every species of virtue: intellectual acumen devoid of pride, courage devoid of haughtiness, modesty devoid of timidity. These gifts are evident in one passage from the Gospels which, ironically, is used against the Mother of Jesus by her detractors. It relates how the Child had remained behind in the Temple after the Passover:

> And when He was twelve years old, they going up into Jerusalem according to the custom of the feast, and having fulfilled the days, when they returned the Child Jesus remained in Jerusalem; and His parents knew it not.
>
> And thinking that He was in the company, they came a day's journey, and sought Him among their kinsfolks and acquaintance. And not finding Him, they returned into Jerusalem, seeking Him. (Lk. 2:42-45)

In his biographical study of the Blessed Virgin, Rev. B. Rohner provided background information for this Gospel episode:

> Three times a year, on the feasts of Easter [i.e., the Pasch], Pentecost, and the Tabernacles, were the men of Israel obliged to make a pilgrimage to the city containing the Ark of the Covenant, which since King David's time had rested within the walls of Jerusalem.* (Ex. 34:23) Women were not required to make this visit to the Temple, yet the most pious among them, and of course Mary, made it voluntarily out of devotion. . . . Every boy in Israel, on reaching his twelfth year, was by law declared to be "of age". He emerged from childhood and, to some extent, from his parent's guardianship, and was admitted as a sufficiently grown and matured member of the Israelite community. He was also now obliged to perform all religious exercises.

* Publisher's Note: the Ark of the Covenant was taken out of the Temple by the priest/prophet Jeremias before the Persians wasted Jerusalem, burning the old Temple to the ground, in 587 B.C.

> In these pilgrimages of the Israelites the men and women usually traveled in separate bands, each sex by themselves. The children were at liberty to travel in either band. Thus it happened that when returning from Jerusalem, Mary supposed her Child was with St. Joseph, while he on the other hand, believed Him to be with Mary. Each journeyed through the whole length of the day happy with the thought of meeting Him at night, when preparing to make their encampment in the tents. How astonished, then, and alarmed they must have been at not finding Him at the expected time and place! (*Life of the Blessed Virgin*, 1897)

On reflection, this is one of the more curious episodes recorded in the Gospels. Here, the Perfect Son causes His parents real anguish. How can this behavior be explained in light of the Fourth Commandment and the admonition of St. Paul: "Children, obey your parents in all things." (Col. 3:20)

The miracle of the Divine Maternity was made possible because of Mary's fiat. Before the Son of God descended into her womb by the working of the Holy Ghost, there was the young Virgin, hearing and accepting the words of the Archangel, freely devoting her entire life and being to the service of God. This is the active, penetrating faith of Mary, which would be publicly acknowledged by her Son: "Yea rather, blessed are they who hear the word of God, and keep it."

When our Lady consented to the Divine Maternity, she was consenting, not only to bear the Redeemer, but to a share in His work: "And thy own soul a sword shall pierce." This work, which was nothing less than the restoration of fallen humanity, was accomplished through the Passion and death of the Savior. To share in the labors of the Redeemer is to be ready to "fill up those things that are wanting of the sufferings of Christ." This is the essence of the question posed by our Lord to Sts. James and John: "Can you drink the chalice that I shall drink?" (Mt. 20:22)

The Blessed Virgin was pre-eminent among the disciples of her Son. She was by His side when Herod's hired killers sought to murder

Him along with the Holy Innocents; she was by His side when Simeon uttered his foreboding prophecies; she was by His side when He hung in agony on the Cross. She was a "disciple" of Jesus, to be sure – "Behold the handmaid of the Lord" – but the term flared into an unheard of brilliance when applied to her. If the following words of St. Paul describe the apostles and Disciples of Jesus, then they must surely apply in full measure to the Theotokos:

> We suffer tribulation, but are not distressed; we are straitened, but are not destitute. We suffer persecution, but are not forsaken; we are cast down, but we perish not: always bearing about in our body the mortification of Jesus, that the life also of Jesus may be made manifest in our bodies. (2 Cor. 4:8-10)

St. Paul speaks of bearing the "mortification" of Jesus in his body; Mary carried in her body the "emptying" of the Eternal Word, whereby He "took the form of a servant, being made in likeness of men." St. Paul speaks of the "life" of Jesus being made manifest in his body; the humanity of the God-Man, the means by which the Blessed Trinity would restore life to a dead world, was generated and made manifest in the body of Mary. St. Paul writes of tribulation, straitened circumstances and persecution. Our Lady was well acquainted with these things as she gazed upon the poor manger in which lay the newborn King, as she and St. Joseph carried the Infant Savior across the desert miles into Egypt and worked to sustain themselves there, as she "stood by the Cross of Jesus", without even the comfort of Joseph in the face of such an ordeal.

When we ponder the details of the life of the Blessed Virgin Mary, we cannot isolate them from the work of the Redeemer, or the "economy of salvation". She is bound up with it, her life eternally intertwined with His.

The Gospel narrative continues:

> And thinking that He was in the company, they came a day's journey, and sought Him among their kinsfolks and acquaintance. And not finding Him, they returned into Jerusalem, seeking Him.

> And it came to pass that, after three days, they found Him in the temple, sitting in the midst of the doctors, hearing them, and asking them questions. And all that heard Him were astonished at His wisdom and His answers.
>
> And seeing Him, they wondered. And His Mother said to Him: Son, why hast Thou done so to us? Behold Thy father and I have sought Thee sorrowing.
>
> And He said to them: How is it that you sought Me? Did you not know, that I must be about My Father's business? And they understood not the word that He spoke unto them.
>
> And He went down with them, and came to Nazareth, and was subject to them. And His Mother kept all these words in her heart. And Jesus advanced in wisdom, and age, and grace with God and men. (Lk. 2:44-52)

The Son of God and Mary offers no other reply to his worried Mother than the simple "I must be about my Father's business." One day in the future, He will speak of this "business":

> This is the will of the Father Who sent Me: that of all that He hath given Me I should lose nothing, but should raise it up again in the last day. And this is the will of my Father that sent me: that every one who seeth the Son, and believeth in Him, may have life everlasting, and I will raise Him up in the last day. (Jn. 6:39-40)

It was Mary's consent to the Incarnation that enabled mankind to see the Son, when "the Word was made flesh, and dwelt among us," and her intimate connection to Christ and His mission would not end as He grew "in age and grace with God and men". Certainly, the outward expression of their relationship would change, for it was Jesus Himself who quoted these words from Genesis: "For this cause shall a man leave father and mother, and shall cleave to his wife, and they two shall be in one flesh." (Mt. 19:5) Our Lord, too, had a "Bride", on whose account He would leave the home that He had shared with Mary for so many years:

> Let us be glad and rejoice, and give glory to Him; for the marriage of the Lamb is come, and His wife hath prepared herself. (Apoc. 19:7)

This "Bride" is the Church: "Husbands, love your wives, as Christ also loved the Church, and delivered Himself up for it . . . that He might present it to Himself a glorious Church, not having spot or wrinkle, or any such thing." Our Lord referred to Himself as a "bridegroom" – "But the days will come, when the bridegroom shall be taken away from them, then shall they fast in those days." (Lk. 5:35) He would "cleave" to this Bride, who, through the awesome union whereby humanity and divinity joined at the moment of the Incarnation, had become "one flesh" with the Bridegroom: "Therefore, in the same holy bosom of His most chaste Mother, Christ took to Himself flesh, and united to Himself the spiritual body formed by those who were to believe in Him." (Pope St. Pius X)

Pope St. Pius X described the relationship of the Redeemer and His Mother on Calvary as a "community of will and suffering", but our Lady's trials did not begin there. As with any natural mother, the circumstances surrounding Mary's motherhood changed as the seasons brought her Son to maturity, and closer to His hour: "And as He increases in age, she changes her working, but not her love." (Dame Juliana of Norwich, d. 1415) As Jesus matured, the occasions for her participation with Him in the "community of will and suffering" would progress in their intensity.

For all the dangers of the Flight into Egypt, Mary could take comfort in the fact that her Son never left the arms of her or St. Joseph. When the youthful Jesus remained behind in the Temple, the pangs would increase; Mary and Joseph would be physically separated from Him for three days. Finally, on Calvary, our Lady would stand beneath the ultimate horror, but a horror transformed into the living icon of salvation – the Redeemer of the world dying upon the Cross and, standing beneath the Cross, the Co-Redemptrix, the Mother both of "Sorrows" and of "Divine Grace".

"Did you not know that I must be about my Father's business?" As our Lord made this reply to His Mother in the Temple, we can imagine another, unspoken question passing between them: "Can you drink the chalice that I shall drink?"

> The depth and extent of the Mystery of the Redemption will be revealed to her only gradually. She is glad to have found Jesus again. But in her joy sounds many an overtone of sadness yet to come. (Fr. Reginald Garrigou-Lagrange, *The Mother of the Saviour and Our Interior Life*)

On Calvary, Mary would taste of this chalice to the utmost degree that a human being could. The episode of the Finding of her Son in the Temple was partly a preparation for that day. It was also partly a foreshadowing of the Resurrection. St. Luke tells us that Mary "kept all these words in her heart". She would have meditated on this incident and related it to the apostles, who would also "lose" their Lord on the eve of Good Friday, and "find" Him again three days later.

And they understood not the word that He spoke unto them. If the Blessed Virgin were really an active participant in the economy of salvation, if she were such a pivotal figure in the life of Jesus, how could St. Luke tell us that she was in the dark concerning our Lord's reply? If she really knew who and what her Son was, wouldn't His statement about doing His heavenly Father's business be crystal clear? Such doubts enter far too easily into the minds of our Lady's detractors, but they are dispatched with little effort.

Firstly, the Blessed Virgin *was* absolutely knowledgeable concerning the nature of her Son. The Angel Gabriel had announced it in the plainest of terms: "And therefore also the Holy which shall be born of thee shall be called the Son of God." Our Lady knew who the Father of Jesus was; therefore, Jesus' reference to this "Father" cannot be the aspect of this scene which could have caused any lack of understanding.

Secondly, our Lady knew that her Son had been given to her so that she might give Him to the world – i.e., He had a mission. Even before Simeon's prophecy of Jesus being set "for the resurrection of many in Israel", Mary heard the words of Gabriel: "The Lord God shall give unto Him the throne of David His father . . . and of His kingdom there shall be no end." This is clear "Messianic" imagery, whose implications Mary would have grasped with no difficulty. Therefore, Jesus' reference to His Father's "business" also could not have been the cause of any lack of understanding.

We know that Mary lived a life of faith; St. Elizabeth said to her, "Blessed art thou that hast believed." St. Irenaeus taught that "the evil done by Eve's incredulity was remedied by Mary's faith," and the thought was echoed by other Church Fathers. Because of her freely chosen role of Theotokos, this faith of Mary's was unparalleled, yet it did not rob her of the merit to be gained by exercising it as a virtue:

> Mary understood explicitly more revealed truths and understood them more profoundly than any other creature, both because she was inspired by God in a singular way and because she was closely associated with the work of redemption. . . . Although she had extraordinary faith in the Blessed Trinity, the Incarnation, the divinity of Christ, and His mission as Redeemer, she did not understand all of the circumstances of these mysteries from the beginning. (Fr. Gregory Alastruey, *The Blessed Virgin Mary*, Vol.1, 1963)

Our Lady had consented to become the Mother of God's own Son. She consented, therefore, to raise Him and make a home for Him. When our Lord remained behind in the Temple, He was still a boy, humanly speaking. The normal reaction for a mother, any mother, at the sudden and unexplained disappearance of her child is deep concern. Mary knew that Jesus would one day leave her home to begin His Father's "business". Before her, though, was the practical situation of her Son, still too young (in His humanity) to be alone in the world, mysteriously absent; the responsibility for the care and safety of this Son belonged to her. That she and St. Joseph should find Him speaking of holy matters in the Temple was not a source of confusion. The unusual circumstances in which He did so was the reason "they understood not the word that He spoke unto them."

The end of this Gospel narrative bears out this conclusion. What happens after Mary and Joseph retrieve the young Jesus from the Temple? "And He went down with them, and came to Nazareth, and was subject to them. And His Mother kept all these words in her heart." (Lk. 2:51) At that time, our Lord, according to the human nature He had freely chosen, was still young, still "subject" to His parents. So, He returned home with them. The concern and, even, confusion, of His parents was absolutely justified and in keeping with the normal order of things.

In no way can this episode be given any honest interpretation which mars the integrity of the Blessed Virgin. Mary's detractors, though, would place her in an impossible situation. If she worries about her Son, then she is "ill-informed", or is somehow unaware she gave birth to God! If she does not worry about Him, believing that He is God, then she behaves with presumption. The truth, as recorded by St. Luke, shows that the Mother of Jesus displayed neither ignorance nor presumption in the Temple. She was not confused at the words of the young Redeemer, who came to earth to do His Father's will: "This day is born to you a Savior, Who is Christ, the Lord." (Lk. 2:11) Nor did she feel that she was "above" worrying about her Child, as though her exalted position as Mother of God, as one blessed and full of grace, exempted her from trials and suffering: *And thy own soul a sword shall pierce.*

Our Lady replies to her detractors with simple, unadorned truth, the Truth of her Divine Maternity, embodied in her words to Jesus: "Thy father and I have sought Thee sorrowing." Her sincere concern for her young Son, and her subsequent relief upon finding Him, are eloquent testimonies to the depth of her maternal feelings. Would the Blessed Trinity have settled for anything less in the Mother of the Incarnate Word?

Moreover, this event, and the reply of our Lord to Mary's thoroughly justifiable concern, would serve as a continual source of meditation for her. In the years to come, people would marvel at Jesus' words:

> And when the sabbath was come, He began to teach in the synagogue: and many hearing Him were in admiration at His doctrine, saying: How came this man by all these things. (Mk. 6:2)

Mary would hear such things and think back to the time when Jesus remained behind in the Temple, speaking and listening to the doctors, ". . . and all that heard Him were astonished at His wisdom and His answers." (Lk. 2:47)

Chapter Thirty-Two

A Portrait of Mary

The seven gifts of the Holy Ghost manifest in Mary – The description of St. Catherine Laboure – The Hail Mary – The Rosary – Mary's request for fifteen minutes in her company on first Saturday – The Litany of Loreto – Mary in prophecy – How can Mary suffer while in the Beatific Vision of God? – Mary in the Bible – Mary is always there interceding – Jesus and Mary in Capharnaum: the disciples observe the Son's devotion to His mother – Mary is a "living gospel" – the Holy Name of Mary

The virtues of the Blessed Virgin, lauded by Catholic writers since the time of the apostles, and meditated upon even more than her physical beauty, are displayed to full effect in the Gospels. The idea, fostered mainly by Protestant apologists, that the Scriptures do not tell us much about the Mother of God, is an erroneous one. Everything we need to know has been provided, starting with the most important piece of information, her Divine Maternity: *And she brought forth her first-born Son, and wrapped Him up in swaddling clothes, and laid Him in a manger.*

When the inspired books of the Old Testament are read correctly – i.e., under the guidance of the Church which preserved and holds the sole right of interpreting them – a wealth of "Marian" references, beginning with *The Book Of Genesis* (and culminating in the New Testament with St. John's *Apocalypse*), can be discerned clearly. In the Gospels, we are "introduced" to the Woman for whom the prophets dreamed, the rod from which would bloom the Savior. The accounts of the Evangelists provide a rich portrait of Mary, in which can be noted a flowering of the Seven Gifts of the Holy Ghost in her pure soul:

> 1. *Charity* – "Mary, rising up in those days, went into the hill country with haste into a city of Juda. And she entered into the house of Zachary, and saluted Elizabeth. . . . And the wine failing, the Mother of Jesus saith to Him: They have no wine."
>
> 2. *Understanding* – "Mary kept all these words, pondering them in her heart."

3. *Counsel* – "How shall this be done, because I know not man?"

4. *Fortitude* – "And she brought forth her first-born Son, and wrapped Him up in swaddling clothes, and laid Him in a manger, because there was no room for them in the inn. . . . Arise, and take the Child and His Mother, and fly into Egypt, and be there until I shall tell thee. . . . There stood by the Cross of Jesus, His Mother."

5. *Knowledge* – "For behold, from henceforth all generations shall call me blessed. Because He that is mighty hath done great things to me. . . . His Mother saith to the waiters: Whatsoever He shall say to you, do ye."

6. *Piety* – "After the days of her purification according to the law of Moses were accomplished, they carried Him to Jerusalem, to present Him to the Lord. . . . His parents went every year to Jerusalem, at the solemn day of the Pasch. . . . The apostles were persevering with one mind in prayer with the women, and with Mary the Mother of Jesus, and with His brethren."

7. *Fear of the Lord* – "Who, having heard, was troubled at his saying, and thought within herself what manner of salutation this should be."

Mary's Spiritual Maternity makes her eminently approachable; it underscores St. Louis de Montfort's words that true devotion to our Lady "comes from within the mind and the heart and follows from the esteem in which we hold her, the high regard we have for her greatness, and the love we bear her." This love is a gift from God, but one not meant to be treated like an old print, kept behind a glass frame and glanced at occasionally. Mary is our Queen, and the Mediatrix of All Graces. Her maternal heart is tuned to give; our filial hearts should be tuned to receive. Like millions of Catholics who came before us, we go to Mary with our needs, with our sorrows and desires, with the confidence expressed by St. John Vianney (†1859):

> The heart of this good Mother is all love and mercy; she desires only to see us happy. We have only to turn to her to be heard. . . . All that the Son asks of the Father is granted Him. All that the Mother asks of the Son is in like manner granted to her. When we have handled something fragrant, our hands perfume whatever they touch: let our prayers pass through the hands of the Holy Virgin; she will perfume them. (*The Little Catechism on the Blessed Virgin*)

To be able to approach Jesus through Mary, to have her present our prayers to Him "perfumed" by their contact with the immaculate hands of the Mystical Rose, is a great mercy afforded to mankind by our Redeemer. Too often, when the realization of our sins and failings steals upon us like a thief in the night, we are tempted to repeat to Our Lord the words of St. Peter, "Depart from me, for I am a sinful man, O Lord." (Lk. 5:8) The devil is called "the Accuser of our brethren" by St. John, and the realization of sinfulness can cut deep. It is a great comfort, then, to approach Jesus at the side of the one in whom He took such delight, beneath whose Heart and in whose arms He reposed as an Infant, whose face He looked upon as a beacon amid the murk of Calvary, and with whom He so gladly shares His entire kingdom. This is the hope – hope in the Woman loved by the Blessed Trinity as Daughter, Mother and Spouse – summarized in verse by Petrarch (d. 1374):

Virgin most holy, Full of grace, that wast
Exalted by thy deep, true humbleness
To heaven, whence thou my orison dost hear;
Thou broughtest forth the Fount of tenderness
And Sun of justice, who the world, when lost
In errors dense and dark, made bright and clear.
Three names thou linkest, that are sweet and dear –
Mother and Child and Bride.
O Virgin, glorified
Queen of that Lord who to this earthly sphere,
Loosing our bonds, brought liberty with bliss;
True Comforter, impart

Peace to my heart,
By those blest wounds of his.

(*Twenty-Ninth Ode*)

The Church refers to the Blessed Virgin as the "Gate of heaven". In the *Ave Regina Cœlorum*, she is called "the gate through which the Light rose over the earth". In the *Alma Redemptoris Mater*, she is called the "open door of heaven". The Redeemer came down to earth through this gate; the redeemed must pass through it to reach heaven. God passed through this gate and entered Time; human beings pass through it to enter Eternity:

The Gate that opens, yet secures
God's inmost sanctuary;
Gate of the one true Dawn art thou,
Gate of the one sweet Eden,
Gate of the angels into earth,
The Gate of souls to heaven."

(Fr. Frederick Faber, d. 1863, *The Happy Gate of heaven*)

Daily concourse with the Mother of God is one of the most beautiful facets of Catholic life, and our Lord invites us to approach this "Gate" each and every day: *My Immaculate Heart will be your refuge and the way which will lead you to God.* She is Mother, Mediatrix and an Advocate of such power, her Son takes His pleasure in rewarding her intercession on our behalf. The scope of these powers of intercession was portrayed dramatically during her apparition to St. Catherine Laboure (†1876), who described her second vision of Our Lady of the Miraculous Medal:

> Her height was medium, and Her countenance, indescribably beautiful. She was dressed in a robe the color of the dawn, high-necked, with plain sleeves. Her head was covered with a white veil, which floated over Her shoulders down to her feet. She wore a narrow lace band round her hair. Her face was not concealed. Her feet

> rested upon a globe, or rather one half of a globe, for that was all that could be seen. Her hands which were on a level with Her waist, held in an easy manner another globe, a figure of the world. Her eyes were raised to heaven, and Her countenance beamed with light as She offered the globe to Our Lord.
>
> Suddenly Her fingers were covered with rings and most beautiful precious stones. Rays of dazzling light gleamed forth from them, and the whole of Her figure was enveloped in such radiance that Her feet and robe were no longer visible. . . . As I was busy contemplating Her, the Blessed Virgin fixed Her eyes upon me, and a voice said in the depths of my heart: "This globe which you see represents the whole world, especially France, and each person in particular . . ."
>
> The Blessed Virgin added: "Behold the symbol of the graces I shed upon those who ask me for them." And She made me understand how pleasant it was to pray to the Blessed Virgin, how generous She is to all who implore Her intercession . . . how many favors She grants to those who ask Her for them with confidence and the joy that She experienced in granting graces!

In this apparition, the globe represents the world and each person in the world; it symbolizes Mary's universal mediation. Graces – rays of dazzling light – stream forth from her hands, where her Son has placed them. Like a good mother, she experiences joy when assisting her children.

To approach Mary daily, with attitudes of veneration (towards her Divine Maternity and Queenship) and filial familiarity (towards her Spiritual Motherhood), is to go to the surest means by which to realize the "goal" of the Catholic life: "My little children, of whom I am in labor again, until Christ be formed in you." St. Augustine declared that our Lady is "worthy to be called the mold of God". Mary, who "formed" Jesus in her womb, desires also to "form" her other children as brethren of Christ sharing the same Spirit. Therefore, she is regarded as the "mold" wherein Christians are formed:

> Please note that I say that saints are molded in Mary. There is a vast difference between carving a statue by blows of hammer and chisel and making a statue by using a mold. . . . Those who accept this little-known secret of grace which I offer them can rightly be compared to smelters and molders who have discovered the beautiful mold of Mary where Jesus was so divinely and so naturally formed. They do not rely on their own skill but on the perfection of the mold. They cast and lose themselves in Mary where they become true models of her Son. . . . But remember that only molten and liquified substances may be poured into a mold. That means that you must crush and melt down the old Adam in you if you wish to acquire the likeness of the new Adam in Mary. (St. Louis de Montfort, *True Devotion to the Blessed Virgin*)

Concupiscence, anxiety, preoccupation – with such burdens on the soul, the thought of becoming "conformed" to Christ seems more like a pious convention than a possible reality. Yet, we are told repeatedly in the Scriptures that it can be done, and that it will be done. Even in the face of nagging doubt, then, people of good will are left with one alternative only: to believe it can be, and to seek it by all available means. The best way, of course, to seek conformity to Jesus is through Mary, His Mother and ours: "All we who are united to Christ . . . have issued from the womb of Mary like a body united to His Head." (Pope St. Pius X) Not only will she dispense necessary graces, but she will watch over us daily, encourage, assist and intercede for us. Mary bore one Son according to nature, and lavished all her love on Him. Her affection for the Mystical Body of that Son reflects this focused and intense affection, imparting to it an "exclusive" quality, in which each soul is treated as though it were the only one she watched over: *As long as you did it to one of these my least brethren, you did it to me.* In this way, Mary, her heart full of charity, reflects the love of Jesus for the Church: *As the Father hath loved Me, I also have loved you.*

Liquid poured into a mold takes time to set, and a soul, bruised by sin, takes time to achieve the likeness of Christ. This is why Perseverance is so often admonished: "Therefore, my beloved brethren, be ye steadfast and unmovable; always abounding in the work of the Lord, knowing that your labor is not in vain in the Lord." (1 Cor. 15:58)

The great struggle for people of good will is to keep always in mind that their labors are "not in vain in the Lord". Small victories against sin and temptation do not seem like much, as they are too often seemingly negated by larger failures. But, in truth, they are not "negated". They have been noted by the One Who fell beneath the burden of the Cross, the burden of our sins, on the Via Dolorosa, the One Who said ". . . the very hairs of your head are all numbered." (Mt. 10:30) One glance at a Crucifix reveals the face of a Lord Who does not desire the destruction of His children, the annihilation of those who share His own human nature: "It is not the will of your Father, Who is in heaven, that one of these little ones should perish." (Mt. 18:14) " . . . Father, I will that where I am, they also whom Thou hast given Me may be with Me." (Jn. 17:24)

There is nothing in creation that is more symbolic of Hope, more redolent with the possibility of good things for even the most wretched soul, than the face of the Crucified Savior:

> They that hope in the Lord shall renew their strength, they shall take wings as eagles, they shall run and not be weary, they shall walk and not faint. (Is. 40:31) Let not your heart be troubled, nor let it be afraid. (Jn. 14:27)

The Holy Face of the Crucified One was formed in the womb of Mary, and His features resemble hers to the highest degree, because Christ, with no human father participating in His human generation, took all His humanity from His Mother. This holy, precious "mold", whereby the sons and daughters of the Church are formed – this sacred womb in which, like their Head before them, the members of the Church are born into their eternal inheritance – this Mother from whose hands flow a dazzling stream of graces – this is a "hope" given to us by the very Source of Hope.

We are invited to approach the Blessed Virgin every day of our lives and we are offered many means by which to do so: the Rosary, the Little Office of the Blessed Virgin, the Angelus, the Brown Scapular, the Five First Saturdays of Reparation, the Litany of Loreto, the Miraculous Medal, the writings of the saints on Mary, Consecration to Jesus through Mary (as taught by St. Louis de Montfort), etc. In addition to these, we can speak heartfelt words to her anytime of the day, anywhere, for any reason, confident that she is glad to listen with full attention and solicitude.

The Hail Mary, the "Angelic Salutation", is a prayer especially pleasing to God, as is evident by the fact that the first part of the prayer was "composed" by God Himself: *Hail, Full of Grace, the Lord is with thee: blessed art thou among women.* The familiar words were spoken by the Angel Gabriel at the Annunciation, praises offered by the Blessed Trinity through the heavenly messenger. *Blessed art thou among women, and blessed is the fruit of thy womb.* These praises, which repeat again Mary's exalted place among all others, were spoken by St. Elizabeth under divine inspiration, after she "was filled with the Holy Ghost". The first part of the Hail Mary is, then, a gift from God, the same One Who gave us the Our Father. Each time it is recited, it honors and celebrates the most important event in creation: the Incarnation. Thus, it also celebrates the great mercy of God towards mankind, something which deserves to be remembered and honored every day.

The second part of the Hail Mary reflects the Church's joy in Mary's title, Theotokos, "Mother of God". It was a title first proclaimed publicly by the inspired St. Elizabeth, during the Visitation: "And whence is this to me, that the *Mother of my Lord* should come to me?" It was defended and proclaimed at the Council of Ephesus (431): "If anyone does not confess that God is truly Emmanuel, and that on this account the Holy Virgin is the Mother of God (for according to the flesh she gave birth to the Word of God become flesh by birth), let him be anathema." It has been honored since the Middle Ages in the Litany of the Saints, where Mary is the first to be invoked after God:

> Holy Trinity, one God, Have mercy on us.
> Holy Mary, Pray for us.
> Holy Mother of God, Pray for us.

Holy Mary, Mother of God, pray for us sinners now and the hour of our death. The second part of the Hail Mary summarizes our hope in Mary, the Mother of God – the Mother of the Redeemer. We can approach her with confidence "now", for the graces we require daily and the comfort that sustains us in this vale of tears, and "at the hour of our death", for assistance and strength in final perseverance.

It should come as no surprise that the Hail Mary contains two parts, one "composed" by God, and the other, a response to the first, added by the Church, for Mary is the Mother of God *and* the Mother of the Church. Because God prays to no one, the first part of the Hail Mary does not contain supplications or petitions. It is a greeting to the Virgin, and describes her plenitude of grace, her singular place among all rational creatures – i.e., the riches bestowed upon Mary by her Son. In the second part, the Church replies with supplications; recognizing the place and position of God's Mother and ours, we fly to her for protection and assistance. St. Louis de Montfort referred to the Hail Mary as "a most concise summary of all that Catholic theology teaches about the Blessed Virgin."

The recitation of even a single Hail Mary can be of great spiritual benefit. The world owes all its happiness to the Incarnation, when Jesus came to restore mankind to friendship with its Creator. Our Lady, who was prepared for the Incarnation by her Immaculate Conception, renders even greater praise to God for that miraculous event; on the day of the Annunciation she was raised to the dignity of Mother of God. Each Hail Mary offered to her is, therefore, always referred to God:

> When we praise and bless Our Lady by saying the Angelic Salutation she always passes on these praises to Almighty God in the same way she did when she was praised by Saint Elizabeth. The latter blessed her in her most elevated dignity as Mother of God and Our Lady immediately returned these praises to God by her beautiful Magnificat. (St. Louis de Montfort, *The Secret of the Rosary*)

"Since the work of salvation began with the Angelic Salutation," wrote St. Dominic (†1221), the great champion of the Rosary, "the salvation of each one of us in particular is attached to this prayer."

Who can gauge the value of even one Hail Mary, of the effect upon Jesus of this reminder of His Incarnation, offered to Him by His own Mother on our behalf? As she offers these prayers to Him, He gazes with love at the one beneath whose Heart, of all hearts that were ever created, He chose to rest as an Infant, dependent upon her for nourishment, for safety, for His human life.

Of what import, then, is the Hail Mary? St. Louis de Montfort did not mince words when he put it into perspective:

> The heretics, all of whom are children of the devil and clearly bear the sign of God's reprobation, have a horror of the Hail Mary. They still say the Our Father but never the Hail Mary; they would rather wear a poisonous snake around their necks than wear a scapular or carry a rosary. . . . My Hail Mary, my Rosary of fifteen or five decades, is the prayer and the infallible touchstone by which I can tell those who are led by the Spirit of God from those who are deceived by the devil. . . . The Hail Mary is a blessed dew that falls from heaven upon the souls of the predestinate. It gives them a marvelous spiritual fertility so that they can grow in all virtues. The more the garden of the soul is watered by this prayer the more enlightened one's intellect becomes, the more zealous his heart, and the stronger his armor against his spiritual enemies. (*The Secret of the Rosary*)

A blessed dew . . . a marvelous spiritual fertility . . . the Garden of the soul is watered by this prayer. It is impossible to read these descriptions and not recall that our Lady is known as the "Aqueduct" of grace.

If prayer is the means by which grace is petitioned, an occasion when our Mother and Advocate "reminds God of His covenant and causes Him to be mindful of His mercy," then the Rosary is surely the most valuable weapon in the arsenal of prayer. "Among the public prayers which we profitably address to the Virgin Mother of God," wrote Pope Pius XI, "the holy rosary occupies a special and exceptional place." He continued:

> This logically follows from the very flowers from which this mystic garland is woven. What more appropriate and more holy prayers can be found? The prime prayer is the one which our Redeemer Himself uttered when His disciples asked Him: "Lord, teach us to pray." It is assuredly a very holy prayer which, while giving glory to God to the best of our ability, also provides for all the needs of our body and soul. How can the Eternal Father refuse to come to our aid when we pray to Him with the very words of His Son?
>
> The other prayer is the Angelic Salutation, which begins with the eulogy of the Archangel Gabriel and of St. Elizabeth, and concludes with that very pious supplication by which we implore the help of the Blessed Virgin now and at the hour of our death. To these invocations, said aloud, there is added the contemplation of the sacred mysteries which bring the joys, sorrows and triumphs of Jesus Christ and of His Mother before our very eyes, as it were, so that we derive relief from them and comfort in our sorrows. Following those most holy examples, we are encouraged to ascend to the happiness of the heavenly fatherland by ever higher degrees of virtue. (*Ingravescentibus malis*, 1937)

During the recitation of the Rosary, verbal prayer (of praise and petition) is joined to meditations on the story of mankind's Redemption, the life of Christ and the mysteries of the Virgin Mother of God: "I remembered the works of the Lord: for I will be mindful of Thy wonders from the beginning. And I will meditate on all Thy works: and will be employed in Thy inventions." (Ps. 76:12-13) Encompassed within this ancient devotion is the entire story of "the Way, the Truth and the Life," the foundation of all possible joy and hope. As the Mysteries are contemplated, the life of the Savior unfolds in a tapestry of memory, contemplation, prayer and supplication. It is a perfect devotion, rendered by mind and body. It takes the intellect, heart, voice and hands – the things by which men create, in imitation of God – and occupies them in the service of contemplating the glorious works of the Blessed Trinity. Pope Julius III (1550-1555) called the Rosary "the glory of the Roman Church".

With its multi-layered prayers, meditations, supplications, and expressions of divine praise, the Rosary is a finely-honed sword which has been wielded against both the spiritual and temporal enemies of the Church:

> This devotion, so great and so confident, to the august Queen of heaven has never shone forth with such brilliance as when the militant Church of God has seemed to be endangered by the violence of widespread heresy, by intolerable moral corruption, or by the attacks of powerful enemies. Ancient and modern history and the more sacred annals of the Church bear witness to public and private supplications addressed to the Mother of God, to the help she has granted in return, and to the peace and tranquillity which she has obtained from God. Hence her illustrious titles of "Help of Christians", "Consolation of the Afflicted", "Our Power in War", "Queen of Victory", "Queen of Peace". And among these is specially worthy of note that familiar title of the Rosary by which the signal benefits she has gained for the whole of Christendom have been solemnly commemorated. (Pope Leo XIII, *Supremi Apostolatus*, 1883)

The violence of widespread heresy, moral corruption and diabolical assaults are not lacking in any era. On May 13, 1917, Our Lady of Fatima said, "Pray the Rosary every day to obtain peace for the world, and the end of the war." She repeated this desire during her apparitions of June, July, August, September and October, and she also taught the young visionaries to add this prayer after each mystery: "O my Jesus, forgive us our sins, save us from the fires of hell. Lead all souls to heaven, especially those who are most in need of Thy mercy." On October 13, 1917, she announced, "I am the Lady of the Rosary. Continue always to pray the Rosary every day."

On December 10, 1925, the Child Jesus and Our Lady appeared to Sr. Lucia at her convent in Pontevedra. The Child said to the nun: "Have pity on the heart of your most Holy Mother. It is covered with thorns which ungrateful men place therein at every moment and there is no one to remove them by an act of reparation." It is the Child Who appeared, as though to underscore the Motherhood of Mary, who is described as "your most Holy Mother" to Sr. Lucia. The Virgin, holding a thorn-wreathed Heart, spoke similarly, in truly Catholic words which testify to the virtue and power of the Mass, Holy Communion, Confession and the Rosary:

> See, my daughter, my Heart, surrounded by thorns with which ungrateful men wound it at every moment by their blasphemies and ingratitude. Do you, at least, console me and announce that I promise to assist at the hour of death with all the graces necessary for salvation, all those who, on the first Saturday of five consecutive months, confess, receive Holy Communion, recite five decades of the rosary and keep me company for fifteen minutes while meditating on the mysteries of the rosary, with the intention of making reparation to me.

Keep me company for fifteen minutes. Can any treatise on the Spiritual Maternity convey the affections of Mary's heart better than this simple request? A mother enjoys the company of her children and it is the smallest gestures on their part that bring the most satisfaction. Our Lady does not ask for monumental displays of endurance, only for a special monthly visit of fifteen minutes. The "Five First Saturdays of Reparation", by which the requests related to Sr. Lucia by our Blessed Mother are fulfilled, allow the members of the Church to gain great spiritual benefits, while also consoling Mary for the blasphemies committed against her Immaculate Conception, her Divine Maternity and her Perpetual Virginity, as well as those committed by people who dishonor her images and, sadly, teach children nothing but contempt or indifference towards her.

The Little Office of the Blessed Virgin was a popular devotion among the laity until the end of the Middle Ages. The volume commonly referred to as the "Book of Hours", found in the libraries of monarchs and in the hands of men and women staring out over the centuries from their portraits, was this "Little Office" of the Virgin Mary. Like the Divine Office prayed by priests and religious, it divided each day into canonical "hours" of prayer, including hymns, psalms, lessons and, according to season, the proper Marian antiphons (the anthems *Alma Redemptoris Mater*, *Ave Regina Cœlorum*, *Regina Cœli*, and *Salve Regina*).

Throughout the various hours of the Little Office, the Psalms which praise God and rejoice in His mercy are introduced by short antiphons which are minute repositories of Marian doctrine:

> Behold, Mary hath borne us the Savior, whom John beholding, exclaimed: "Behold the Lamb of God, behold Him who taketh away the sins of the world."
>
> In the bush which Moses saw unconsumed, we acknowledge thy admirable virginity preserved: intercede for us, O Mother of God.
>
> Mary was taken up into heaven, the angels rejoice and with praises bless the Lord.
>
> Rejoice, O Virgin Mary, thou alone hast destroyed all heresies in the whole world.

Such were the lofty sentiments and doctrinal truths imbibed daily by so many people in the Middle Ages, ordinary souls readily viewed askance by the children of a technological age, who too often confuse the mere accumulation of data with wisdom. However, Scripture teaches that ". . . the fear of the Lord is the beginning of wisdom." (Ecclus. 1:16) What are the fruits of this true wisdom which can only be found in a holy fear of God? – "Wisdom shall distribute knowledge, and understanding of prudence: and exalteth the glory of them that hold her. . . . Ye that fear the Lord, hope in Him: and mercy shall come to you for your delight." (Ecclus. 1:24;2:9)

The Litany of Loreto (or the "Litany of the Blessed Virgin") was approved by Pope Sixtus V in 1587, but originated centuries earlier.

This collection of Marian titles is interesting in a number of ways. It enshrines both Old and New Testament imagery to form an expansive verbal tapestry, offering a panoramic view of the Blessed Mother's place in salvation history. She is invoked not only as *Holy Mother of God* and *Mother of the Church*, but also as *Ark of the Covenant* and *Tower of David*. The divisions between the "Testaments" melt away in this Litany, and the plan of our Redemption seems to flow across the centuries uninterruptedly, with logic and thoroughness. The holy womb of the Mother of God, the first of all Tabernacles, is superimposed over the original Ark of the Covenant, which foreshadowed it, and all the proper connections come to light.

The structure of the litany makes these connections evident. The invocations are layered in a deliberate manner. It begins with Mary's maternal titles: *Mother of Christ*, *Mother Most Admirable*, *Mother of Good Counsel*, etc. From the maternal titles, the Litany moves on to the titles praising her virginity: *Virgin Most Prudent*, *Virgin Most Renowned*, *Virgin Most Powerful*, etc. This is the logical progression.

Since our Lady's Divine Motherhood forms the basis of ALL her glories and privileges, it is right to invoke this Maternity at the start of the Litany. By doing so, the Incarnation is planted as the bedrock, the very reason for our veneration of the Lady who presented the God-Man to us, clothed in visible flesh. This Divine Motherhood points inescapably to a Virginal Motherhood, to the purity which must accompany the conception and birth of Him Whom the Angel Gabriel would describe as "the Son of the Most High". Moreover, this virginal purity must be abiding, "perpetual", otherwise there is no consistency to God's actions. If our Lady's purity were not an abiding one, then we would find God carefully planning the Virginal Conception and Birth of His Son from the beginning of time, only to have this honored, divinely-bestowed purity discarded at the first opportunity.

Mary's virginity is not merely an incidental attribute, necessary at one time only to ensure a virgin birth for the Savior, and summarily discarded. On the contrary, it is an essential characteristic of hers, for "she was a virgin not in body only, but in mind also." (St. Ambrose) It defines her, and the litany recognizes this fact and defends it, when it addresses her as *Holy Virgin of Virgins*.

After these praises of Mary's motherhood and virginity, the Litany of Loreto praises the roles bestowed on Mary as a result of this Virginal Maternity, invoking her under such titles as *Seat of Wisdom*, *Gate of heaven*, *Refuge of Sinners*, while not ignoring some allusions to her mystery and beauty: *Cause of our Joy*, *Mystical Rose*, *Morning Star*, etc. The Litany closes, fittingly enough (both doctrinally and chronologically), with invocations of Mary's Queenship: *Queen of Angels*, *Queen of All Saints*, *Queen Assumed into heaven*, etc. The devotion which begins by calling out to the Holy Mother of God, closes with an appeal to the Queen of Peace, just as the Rosary opens with the Annunciation (the First Joyful Mystery) and closes with the heavenly Coronation of Mary (the Fifth Glorious Mystery). The image of a modest young girl giving her "yes" to the Archangel on behalf of the world, and thereby becoming the Mother of God, is transformed into that of a powerful Queen reigning over this redeemed world at the side of her Son and Lord: again, a logical progression.

Through daily commerce with the Blessed Virgin, the faithful will obtain necessary and useful knowledge, tending towards the good of the soul, even while fostering a greater love for God and a desire for amendment: "They that fear the Lord, will seek after the things that are pleasing to Him: and they that love Him, shall be filled with His law. They that fear the Lord, will prepare their hearts, and in His sight will sanctify their souls." (Ecclus. 2:19-20)

To learn what is pleasing to God and to prepare hearts which He may sanctify, and in which He may dwell, are pursuits which prepare souls to claim their eternal inheritance: "If anyone love Me, He will keep My word, and My Father will love him, and We will come to him, and will make Our abode with him." (Jn. 14:23) At Fatima, Our Lady revealed that her Immaculate Heart, so beloved by the Blessed Trinity, is the means by which she will lead souls to God. After allowing the visionaries a glimpse of hell, she said, "You have seen hell where the souls of poor sinners go. To save them, God wishes to establish in the world devotion to my Immaculate Heart." (July 13, 1917)

God wishes to establish in the world devotion to my Immaculate Heart. Devotion to the Virgin, the "Gate of heaven", are prerequisites for pleasing God:

> She glorifieth her nobility by being conversant with God: yea and the Lord of all things hath loved her. For it is she that teacheth the knowledge of God, and is the chooser of His works. . . . I purposed therefore to take her to me to live with me: knowing that she will communicate to me of her good things, and will be a comfort in my cares and grief. (Wis. 8:3-4,9)

I purposed therefore to take her to me to live with me. These words describe the actions of St. John the Evangelist, after Mary was given to him (and the entire Church) as Mother on Calvary: "And from that hour the disciple took her to his own." Each member of the Church is meant to imitate the Apostle, taking Mary "to his own". This Blessed Mother is conversant with God and can teach the knowledge of God as no one else can, for she was and remains more intimately bound to the Three Divine Persons than anyone else; she is the chooser of His works, to whom Jesus gives the authority of dispensing the graces He won for us. Of Mary, it can be said with no exaggeration that the Lord of all things hath loved her as He loves no one else – as His Mother. The vigilant and generous Mediatrix of All Graces will always communicate to us of her good things, which are nothing less than the graces merited by the Redeemer and, furthermore, she will carry out her task with a loving heart that will be a comfort in our cares and grief. The inspired Scriptures describe her well.

Again and again, the Church, by her Apostolic authority and discernment, discovers in the phrases of the Old Testament the prophetic "voice" of Mary, encouraging, instructing and admonishing the Church, her spiritual sons and daughters:

> Now, therefore, ye children, hear me: Blessed are they that keep my ways. Hear instruction and be wise, and refuse it not. Blessed is that man that heareth me, and that watcheth daily at my gates, and waiteth at the posts of my doors. He that shall find me, shall find life, and shall have salvation from the Lord . . . Whosoever is a little one, let him come to me. (Prov. 8:32-35;9:4)

Whosoever is a little one, let him come to me. We are told the same thing by Jesus: "Suffer the little children to come to me, and forbid them not; for of such is the kingdom of God. Amen I say to you, whosoever shall not receive the kingdom of God as a little child, shall not enter into it." (Mk. 10:14-15)

All the heresies promulgated throughout the ages were instigated by men who rebelled at the thought of childlike submission to God, to His Church, His Vicar, and the doctrines safeguarded by them. *Non Serviam* ("I will not serve"), the "credo" of Lucifer, is also that of the apostate, the heretic, the schismatic, the modernist, even of the one completely indifferent to religion in any form. The reformer or innovator who has proudly shrugged off the "chains" of Catholicism has little in common with the Lord who washed the feet of His disciples, instructing them that ". . . the servant is not greater than his lord; neither is the apostle greater than He that sent him." (Jn. 13:16) This Lord is God, but a God of Whom it could be said: "And whereas indeed He was the Son of God, He learned obedience by the things which He suffered." (Heb. 5:8)

It is an awesome lesson in humility when God allows Himself to be described in the Scriptures as one who "learned obedience". A filial submission to Jesus through Mary, of the 'joint-heirs" of Christ to their own spiritual Mother, is the embodiment of receiving the kingdom of God "as a little child". Through this worthy, beneficial and necessary devotion, the members of the Church "learn obedience" in imitation of their Head, by conforming their wills and hearts to the desire of the Father, Who wishes us to honor and obey the Mother given to us by the Son as His "last will and testament" from the Cross: "The mystery of Christ's immense love for us is revealed with dazzling brilliance in the fact that the dying Savior bequeathed His Mother to His disciple John in the memorable testament: 'Behold thy son'." (Pope Leo XIII)

When the Church recognizes and acknowledges the Blessed Virgin as the "Destroyer of All Heresies", she is not seeking fanfare for its own sake. In the earliest days of the Church, the target of choice among heretics was the Person of Jesus Christ, and they spent their time and energy in denying His Divinity, His humanity, or in deliberately confusing the manner in which the two natures were united.

The Virginal Maternity of Mary silenced them all, and taught that Jesus is both True God and True Man.

In the early days of Protestantism, praises of the Blessed Virgin still sounded from the lips of some of its proponents. Martin Luther called Mary "the fairest gem in all of Christendom . . . the supreme empress and queen, far exalted above all nobility, wisdom and holiness." Yet, this is the man who would one day call the Roman Catholic Church, of which our Lady is the Mother and Image, "an arch-whore of the devil". Pretty words spoken about Mary are meaningless if they are not accompanied by a trust in her intercession and a desire to submit to her guidance, knowing that she can only lead us to, and never away from, Jesus. Can there be any doubt that, had Luther embraced and sought the assistance and guidance of the "supreme empress and queen" he seemed at one time to regard so highly, he would never have fallen into, or continued in, the consuming heresy he unleashed upon an all-too willing world?

Can someone love our Lady and say, as Luther did all too often, such vile things about the Church? No, because the Church is the Mystical Body of Christ, the Son of God and Mary. When our Lady regards the Church, she regards Jesus and, as it is one of her joys to lead people to Him, she will teach and inspire nothing but love for the Church: *Ye children, hear me. . . . Hear instruction, and be wise, and refuse it not.* So profound is the love of Mary for the Catholic Church that, on September 19, 1846, she appeared at LaSalette sitting "with her head in her hands", and she spoke sadly the words, "I have suffered all the time for the rest of you!"

How can the Queen of heaven and earth "suffer" while enjoying heavenly bliss, the Beatific Vision? Our Blessed Mother clearly stated that she suffered "for the rest of you". She spoke then of grievous afflictions which would beset the Church, of the loss of faith, the defection of priests, the rise of false religions and the trials of the pope. It is not on her own account that our Lady grieves, for she has no reason to. Far from it, for she has been blessed and glorified as no other human being ever will be. However, let no one imagine for a moment that the Sacred Heart of Jesus or the Immaculate Heart of His Mother are mere representations, "religious" icons devoid of substance or feeling. They beat, and they beat in tandem.

St. Augustine described our Lord and His Mother as two mystical harps. "What sounded on the one," he wrote, "also sounded on the other, even though no one touched it." St. John Eudes compared the hearts of Jesus and Mary to harps whose strings vibrate in unison, creating one melody, instruments foreshadowed by the harp of their illustrious ancestor, King David:

> These two Hearts and these two Harps are nevertheless so closely attuned that in a certain sense they constitute one single harp, vibrating in unison, giving forth but one sound and one song, singing the same canticle of love. If the first sounds a canticle of praise, the second echoes it with its own chords. If the Heart of Jesus loves God the Father, Mary's Heart unites in that love; if the Heart of Jesus pours itself out in thanksgiving before the Most Holy Trinity, Mary's Heart sings an identical hymn of gratitude. The Heart of Mary loves and hates all that the Heart of Jesus loves and hates. What rejoices the Son's Heart rejoices the Heart of the Mother as well; what crucifies the Heart of the Son likewise nails the Mother's Heart to the Cross. (*The Admirable Heart of Mary*)

Our Lord, reigning in heaven, said to St. Paul, before the conversion of the future Apostle: *Saul, Saul, why dost thou persecute Me?* He said to St. Margaret Mary Alacoque (†1690): "I wish thy heart to serve Me as a refuge wherein I may withdraw and take My delight when sinners persecute and drive Me from theirs." The Crucifix does not reveal a distant, aloof God, remaining concealed and indifferent behind an impenetrable shield of Divinity. "He came unto His own," says St. John. Our Lord delights to be with His people, with the sons of men, and will delight always to be with them: *I am with you all days, even to the consummation of the world.* This God is neither the indistinct, contradictory phantom of "non-Catholic Christianity", nor the ethereal, neo-pagan nature-spirits of modernist folklore. Our Lord can be offended by the ingratitude of men, and He can take pleasure in hearts which turn to Him.

Our Lady was proclaimed "universal" Mother by her Son on Calvary. Therefore, like Jesus, she is intimately involved in our lives.

Without compromising any of her present glory, she feels the vicissitudes of her children, enjoying their affection, sorrowing at their errors and miseries, and grieving at their ingratitude to God . . . and to her. During the Presentation in the Temple, Simeon said to Mary, "And thy own soul a sword shall pierce, that, out of many hearts, thoughts may be revealed." (Lk. 2:35) This indicates, firstly, that the man of good will seeks Christ, even though He is the "sign which shall be contradicted", and, secondly, that opposition to Jesus, culminating on Calvary, would bring great grief to His Mother.

There is another meaning to Simeon's statement. Our Lord was physically pierced on Calvary: "One of the soldiers with a spear opened His side, and immediately there came out blood and water." (Jn. 19:34) It was His suffering, His Passion, His Crucifixion . . . His sacrifice . . . that redeemed mankind, making complete and perfect atonement to the Father for our sins. Our Blessed Mother was "pierced" also, but not physically (for a soul cannot be stabbed with a weapon). She is the Co-Redemptrix of mankind; she was pierced "spiritually" when she united her sorrows to the redemptive sufferings of Jesus on the Cross. Only one person, the Redeemer, can be physically pierced; only one person, the Co-Redemptrix, can be spiritually pierced. The Redeemer dies for the world; the Co-Redemptrix joins in this offering, suffering also for love of her children, "the rest of her seed".

Therefore, the thoughts or dispositions of hearts are revealed at the piercing of Mary's soul. Those who regard the inspired Gospels knowledgeably cannot ignore the Sorrowful Mother standing beneath her Son's Cross. Simeon's words, prophetic at the time they were spoken, now bid us to recall Mary's place on Calvary. Anyone refusing to acknowledge that she stood there as a "participant", by Divine decree, exposes a heart that is opposed to Christ, that is in "contradiction" to His desires and ways. By contrast, the loyal son or daughter of the Virgin, recognizing her titles and prerogatives in their plenitude, reveals a heart willing to receive and welcome the Blessed Trinity, a heart which seeks, not to add further pain and "contradiction" to the Mother of God and men, but to console her.

One of the most appealing facets, to both the intellect and sentiments, of the True Faith is the manner in which it bridges heaven and earth. During the Mass, the celestial and terrestrial realms merge as the Lamb of God descends anew to earth, to the altar, under the appearance of Bread and Wine. The womb of our Lady, the very Image of the Church, was the first bridge between heaven and earth, the ladder by which the Second Divine Person descended to earth, to humanity.

The Incarnation made God one of us by nature, and it made Mary the Mother of us in the order of grace. Practically speaking, then, we are truly related to God, not only as creatures, but as "brethren", as adopted sons of God and "joint-heirs" with Christ. Speaking just as practically, we are truly related to Mary by a filial bond which, though spiritual, encompasses every aspect of our lives, body and soul, because the foundation of this bond is the Divine Maternity – i.e., its foundation is Christ, ". . . for Whom are all things, and by Whom are all things." (Heb. 2:10)

The Lord Who said "without Me you can do nothing" is the Lord Who gave us the Blessed Virgin to be our Mother and Queen, our Mediatrix and Advocate. How logical, then, is the Catholic belief that we must go to Jesus through Mary, that this unique "tandem" is a mighty work of God, established since "before the foundation of the world". This is the essence of the Total Consecration taught by St. Louis de Montfort:

> God the Son wishes to form Himself, and, in a manner of speaking, become incarnate every day in His members through His dear Mother. To her He said, "Take Israel for your inheritance." (Ecclus. 24:13) It is as if He said, 'God the Father has given me as heritage all the nations of the earth, all men good and evil, predestinate and reprobate. To the good I shall be father and advocate, to the bad a just avenger, but to all I shall be a judge. But you, my dear Mother, will have for your heritage and possession only the predestinate represented by Israel. As their loving Mother, you will give them birth, feed them and rear them. As their Queen, you will lead, govern and defend them.'

Saint Louis goes on to explain, as is only to be expected, the rejection of God's desires and ways brings with it certain inevitable consequences:

> An infallible and unmistakable sign by which we can distinguish a heretic, a man of false doctrine, an enemy of God, from one of God's true friends is that the heretic and the hardened sinner show nothing but contempt and indifference for Our Lady, and endeavor, by word or example, openly and insidiously – sometimes under specious pretexts – to belittle the love and veneration shown to her. God the Father has not told Mary to dwell in them because they are, alas, other Esaus (i.e., those who have rejected their precious spiritual birthright).

The acceptance of God's desires and ways will, of course, bring other consequences:

> When Mary has taken root in a soul she produces in it wonders of grace which only she can produce; for she alone is the fruitful Virgin who never had and never will have her equal in purity and fruitfulness. Together with the Holy Ghost, Mary produced the greatest thing that ever was or ever will be: a God-Man. She will consequently produce the marvels which will be seen in the latter times. The formation and the education of the great saints who will come at the end of the world are reserved for her, for only this singular and wondrous Virgin can produce in union with the Holy Ghost singular and wondrous things. When the Holy Ghost, her Spouse, finds Mary in a soul, He hastens there and enters fully into it. He gives Himself generously to that soul according to the place it has given to His Spouse. (*True Devotion to the Blessed Virgin*)

The Scriptures teach clearly that, throughout the most critical events in the earthly life of the Savior, our Lady was present, and not as a mere spectator. The story of our Redemption, the story of Christ, is also a "Marian" tale:

I will put enmities between thee and the Woman, and thy seed and her seed: she shall crush thy head, and thou shalt lie in wait for her heel. . . . Behold a Virgin shall conceive, and bear a Son, and His name shall be called Emmanuel.

The Angel Gabriel was sent from God into a city of Galilee, called Nazareth, to a virgin espoused to a man whose name was Joseph, of the house of David; and the virgin's name was Mary.

And it came to pass, that when Elizabeth heard the salutation of Mary, the infant leaped in her womb.

And entering into the house, they found the Child with Mary His Mother, and falling down they adored Him.

Arise, and take the Child and His Mother, and fly into Egypt: and be there until I shall tell thee.

And He went down with them, and came to Nazareth, and was subject to them. And His Mother kept all these words in her heart.

And the third day, there was a marriage in Cana of Galilee: and the Mother of Jesus was there. . . . This beginning of miracles did Jesus in Cana of Galilee.

Now there stood by the Cross of Jesus, His Mother . . . And thy own soul a sword shall pierce that out of many hearts, thoughts may be revealed.

When Jesus therefore had seen His Mother and the disciple standing whom He loved, He saith to His Mother: Woman, behold thy son. After that, He saith to the disciple: Behold thy Mother. And from that hour, the disciple took her to his own.

This place of Mary beside her Son places her also at the side of the Church, from its infancy to the present:

> They went up into an upper room, where abode Peter and John, James and Andrew, Philip and Thomas, Bartholomew and Matthew, James of Alpheus, and Simon Zelotes, and Jude the brother of James. All these were persevering with one mind in prayer with the women, and Mary the Mother of Jesus, and with His Brethren. . . . And there appeared to them parted tongues as it were of fire, and it sat upon every one of them: And they were all filled with the Holy Ghost.

> And the dragon was angry against the Woman: and went to make war with the rest of her seed, who keep the commandments of God, and have the testimony of Jesus Christ.

St. John ended his Gospel by informing his readers that "there are also many other things which Jesus did" which are not detailed in the Scriptures, enough to fill countless volumes. The fundamentals of Catholic doctrine are preserved in the Gospels – original sin, the Divinity and Resurrection of Jesus, the establishment of the Mass and the sacraments, the Trinitarian nature of God, Marian doctrines, etc.

In addition, we are told that ". . . all Scripture, inspired of God, is profitable to teach, to reprove, to correct, to instruct in justice, that the man of God may be perfect, furnished to every good work." (2 Tim. 3:16-17) Christ is the Source from Whom flows all the riches, all the authority and all the truth contained in the Gospels. To ignore His living presence, even for a moment, while reading the holy books is to render them useless, or turn them into historical curiosities. The disciples walking along the road to Emmaus after their Lord's Crucifixion knew the Scriptures, had heard them all their lives ; but the sacred texts availed them nothing until the risen Christ appeared to them and, ". . . beginning at Moses and all the prophets, He expounded to them in all the Scriptures the things that were concerning Him." (Lk. 24:27)

"Brethren, stand fast," wrote St. Paul, "and hold the traditions which you have learned, whether by word, or by our epistle." (2 Thes. 2:14) The situation has not changed since that day Jesus walked with His disciples and taught them the meaning of the holy books. During the Last Supper, He told the apostles: "I have yet many things to say to you:

but you cannot bear them now. But when He, the Spirit of truth, is come, He will teach you all truth." (Jn. 16:12-13) The apostles would go through their great trial, the betrayal of the Master by one of their own, and their subsequent abandonment of Jesus. They had learned much before the Passion, but, after their misery had turned to joy and their Lord was with them again, they would learn even more. Our Lord spent forty days with His disciples before His Ascension into heaven. Would He not have spoken of the Mass, the sacraments, the priesthood, the papacy . . . and of the Mother of the Church?

The intercessory powers of the Blessed Virgin were proclaimed to the world at Cana, and God only knows how often her intercession alone has made the difference in the lives of men even while she still walked the earth:

> We see the Virgin Mother standing on Calvary at the foot of her Son's Cross. On each side of Jesus a condemned criminal is suspended to a gibbet. Both are about to pay with their lives the penalty of a long career of robbery and crime. Alas! The failing faculties of which they still have the free use are employed by them to fill up the measure of their iniquity; they utter blasphemies against the innocent Victim who is agonizing in their midst. But suddenly a complete change takes place in the heart of one of them; penitently he addresses Jesus thus: Lord, remember me when Thou shalt come into Thy kingdom. And Jesus does not delay in pronouncing the solemn decree of pardon: This day thou shalt be with Me in Paradise. Whence comes so sudden a change in this hardened sinner? Through Mary! The sacred writers proclaim it; it is because Mary has prayed for him that he is converted. The intercession of the Mother of God opens for him the gates of a blissful eternity. (Cardinal Alexis Henry M. Lepicier, *Behold Thy Mother!,* 1935)

Our Lady prayed with and for the infant Church after the Ascension of Jesus into heaven; in fact, St. Luke mentions her by name in *The Acts of the Apostles*: "All these [the apostles] were persevering with one mind in prayer with the women, and Mary, the Mother of Jesus, and His brethren." (1:14) She was present on Pentecost, when parted tongues of flame descended upon the apostles, and "... they were all filled with the Holy Ghost, and they began to speak with divers tongues." (Act. 2:4) Recognizing the efficacy and scope of Mary's intercession with our Lord, and how pleasing it is to Him to honor her by granting her requests, the Church also recognizes the fruits of her Mother's intercession on that day when the Church first manifested herself visibly, when Apostolic preaching commenced, when St. Peter, who had denied his Lord three times, stood before the crowds in Jerusalem and boldly proclaimed the death and Resurrection of the Savior:

> You know well the intimate and wonderful relations existing between her [the Blessed Virgin] and the Holy Ghost, so that she is justly called His Spouse. Her intercession was of great avail both in the mystery of the Incarnation and in the coming of the Holy Ghost upon the apostles. (Pope Leo XIII, *Divinum illud*, 1897)

In addition to her role as intercessor, we find another reason for the Virgin's presence during Pentecost. Through her Immaculate Conception, she had been sanctified at the very moment she was conceived in the womb of her mother, St. Anne. This was done to prepare her for her Divine Maternity. At the Annunciation, this Maternity, awaited since the time of Adam and Eve, became an historical fact.

St. John recorded that, after Jesus had performed His first public miracle at Cana, "He went down to Capharnaum, He and His Mother, and His brethren, and His disciples, and they remained there not many days." (2:12) Here, at the very beginning of the Redeemer's public ministry, we find our Lady, not at a discreet distance from her Son, as we will encounter her later on in the Gospel narratives (until Calvary), but among this group of disciples who had come to "believe" in Jesus – i.e., who were witnesses of His divine nature and power.

Those precious days spent at Capharnaum in the presence of Jesus and Mary surely had a profound affect on the disciples; they certainly made an impression on the young Evangelist. The disciples would have observed first-hand the respect and honor accorded to Mary by Jesus; they would have listened to the words which passed between Mother and Son; and, they would have taken note of our Lady's demeanor, the manner of one to whom Christ was everything, but who expressed this complete devotion in the most natural of ways.

No doubt, it was during those few precious days at Capharnaum that the disciples of Jesus began to intuit that the Mother of their Lord was someone . . . unique. It was then that a genuine affection and regard for her would have begun stirring in their hearts. And, most likely, it was then also that they first began to intuit, to however small a degree, that she would somehow be a "mother" to them as well.

On Calvary, Jesus proclaimed this "Spiritual Motherhood" when He proclaimed Mary the "Mother of the Church" and, therefore, there is something eminently fitting about her presence at Pentecost. The Virgin was present at the "beginning of miracles" at Cana, when that small group of disciples, the seed which would blossom into the Catholic Church, banded together and made their way to Capharnaum. At Pentecost, this Church, was, as it were, made "manifest" for all the world to see, and our Lady is there again, but here there is no need to "intuit" her Spiritual Motherhood. "The Paraclete, the Holy Ghost, Whom the Father will send in my name, He will teach you all truth," said our Lord at the Last Supper, "and bring all things to your mind, whatsoever I shall have said to you." (Jn. 14:26) On Pentecost, the Holy Ghost, descending once more upon our Lady, offered to the world a visible "manifestation" of Jesus' words on Calvary: *Behold thy Mother.* The infant Church has taken her first steps . . . and the Mother of the Church is right beside her:

> Peter presided over the assembly in the cenacle. Under his direction Matthias was elected in the place of the traitor Judas. Mary's influence was of a different kind: discreet, amiable, irresistible – surely things would not have gone on so well without her – an influence without parallel, namely, that of the Mother of the Church. The Holy Ghost descended anew upon the Blessed Virgin. He had come upon her and overshadowed her since

> the first moment of her Immaculate Conception. He had come upon her with more power at the moment of the Annunciation. Now He came again to complete as it were her maternity, to make her Mother of the Church, the prolongation of Christ, which was founded on that day. (Rev. Peter A. Resch, *Our Blessed Mother: Outlines of Mariology*, 1939)

Through the Evangelists, a record of the Savior's life, death and Resurrection – the Gospels – would be preserved, written down for all the world to see. The charism of infallibility was given to them while they wrote their books: "The Paraclete, the Holy Ghost, Whom the Father will send in My name, He will teach you all things, and bring all things to your mind, whatsoever I shall have said to you."

It is the living Christ Who makes the Scriptures live. It is His Spirit which guides His Church towards the correct interpretations of the sacred texts; it is His life and mission that has been preserved by the Evangelists. St. Matthew began his Gospel with the words, "The book of the generation of Jesus Christ, the Son of David, the son of Abraham." St. Mark wrote, "The beginning of the Gospel of Jesus Christ, the Son of God." St. John wrote, "In the beginning was the Word, and the Word was with God, and the Word was God." St. Luke spent more time introducing his account:

> Forasmuch as many have taken in hand to set forth in order a narrative of the things that have been accomplished among us; according as they have delivered them unto us, who from the beginning were eyewitnesses and ministers of the word: It seemed good to me also, having diligently attained to all things from the beginning, to write to thee.

There is also a "fifth" Gospel, a living Gospel, on the pages of whose heart is written the complete story of Jesus Christ. She was an eyewitness, the only eyewitness "from the beginning", and the apostles spoke to her, listened to her and learned from her. She is "the only worthy repository of His secrets", wrote St. Padre Pio (†1968). One of the Evangelists, the one who remarked that he had studied his subject "diligently", wrote of her: "Mary kept all these words, pondering them in her heart." (Lk. 2:19) And, again: "His Mother kept all these words in her heart." (Lk. 2:51) The Blessed Virgin Mary is this Living Gospel:

> Who more than His Mother could have a far-reaching knowledge of the admirable mysteries of the birth and childhood of Christ, and above all the mystery of the Incarnation, which is the beginning and the foundation of faith? She not only "kept in her heart" the events of Bethlehem and what took place in Jerusalem in the Temple of the Lord, but sharing as she did the thoughts and the secret wishes of Christ, she may be said to have lived the very life of her Son. Hence nobody ever knew Christ so profoundly as she did, and nobody can ever be more competent as a guide and teacher of the knowledge of Christ. (Pope St. Pius X, *Ad diem illum laetissimum*, 1904)

The Evangelists relate how the Divine Infant traveled to Egypt and lived there with His Mother and St. Joseph, and how He returned to the land of His birth and grew up "subject to them". For three decades, a time referred to as the "Hidden Life" of the Redeemer, the Holy Family spent their days in work, in meals, in conversation, in prayer, in the celebration of the Passover, in the enjoyment of the weddings, births and good fortune of relatives and neighbors, and in the sharing of the sorrows of death, including that of the most noble husband, father and guardian of them all, St. Joseph. There were times of relaxation, and times when the vicissitudes of living under Roman subjugation brought rumor and ill-feeling to many of their neighbors. The earthly domicile of the Incarnate Word, a beacon of grace, was, nevertheless, a blissfully normal home:

> Mary knew the joys and sorrows of the family; she knew also the happy and the sad events, the fatigue of daily

> work, the discomforts and sadness of poverty, separation's rending of heart. But she also tasted the ineffable joys of family life, rejoicing in the purest love of a most chaste spouse, and the smiles and tenderness of a Son who was at the same time the Son of God. (Pope Pius XII, *Patroness of the Family*, 1939)

"Learn of me, because I am meek, and humble of heart: and you shall find rest to your souls," (Mt. 11:29) said our Lord. The Son of God, the Promised One, could have spent His days living in the desert as an ascetic, like St. John the Baptist, receiving those who sought Him out to question Him. He could have come to earth as a prince or an earthly ruler, a man of influence and prestige. He could have lived as a renowned religious scholar, the author of treatises and commentaries. But, He chose another way: "Is not this the carpenter, the Son of Mary?" (Mk. 6:3) ". . . Is not this Jesus, the son of Joseph, whose father and mother we know?" (Jn. 6:42)

"Heaven is my throne, and the earth my foot-stool," (Is. 66:1) says the Lord. The world, and everything in it, belonged to Jesus even before the foundation of the world. He orders creation as He wills, and accomplishes His designs to perfection. He chose to spend all but three years of His earthly life with the Blessed Virgin, leaving her side only as His "hour" approached. The prime lesson of the "Hidden Life at Nazareth" is a simple one: It is good to spend every day with Mary. This truth is not wrested from the sacred texts or concocted from irrelevant data. The Son of God imparted it to us by His own life:

> God-made-Man found freedom in imprisoning Himself in her womb. He displayed power in allowing Himself to be borne by this young maiden. He found His glory and that of His Father in hiding His splendors from all creatures here below and revealing them only to Mary. He glorified His independence and His majesty in depending upon this lovable virgin in His conception, His birth, His presentation in the temple, and in the thirty years of His hidden life. Even at His death she had to be present so that He might be united with

> her in one sacrifice and be immolated with her consent to the eternal Father, just as formerly Isaac was offered in sacrifice by Abraham when he accepted the will of God. It was Mary who nursed Him, fed Him, cared for Him, reared Him, and sacrificed Him for us.
>
> Our good Master stooped to enclose Himself in the womb of the Blessed Virgin, a captive and loving slave, and to make Himself subject to her for thirty years. As I said earlier, the human mind is bewildered when it reflects seriously upon this conduct of Incarnate Wisdom. . . . Consumed with the desire to give glory to God, His Father, and save the human race, He saw no better or shorter way to do so than by submitting completely to Mary. He did this not just for the first eight, ten, or fifteen years of His life like other children, but for thirty years. He gave more glory to God, His Father, during all those years of submission and dependence than He would have given by spending them working miracles, preaching far and wide, and converting all mankind. Otherwise He would have done all these things. (St. Louis de Montfort, *True Devotion to the Blessed Virgin*)

The method by which a Catholic can make the Total Consecration is taught in St. Louis de Montfort's spiritual classic, *True Devotion to the Blessed Virgin*. While it is common to use the phrase "Total Consecration to Mary", the end of this powerful devotion is, of course, Jesus Christ:

> Since we live in an age of pride when a great number of haughty scholars, with proud and critical minds, find fault even with long-established and sound devotions, it is better to speak of "slavery of Jesus in Mary" and to call oneself "slave of Jesus" rather than "slave of Mary". We then avoid giving any pretext for criticism. In this way, we name this devotion after its ultimate end which is Jesus, rather than after the way and the means to arrive there,

> which is Mary. However, we can very well use either term without any scruple, as I myself do. . . . It would be easier to separate light from the sun than Mary from Jesus. So united are they, that Our Lord may be called "Jesus of Mary", and His Mother "Mary of Jesus". (*ibid.*)

Through this Consecration to Jesus through Mary, everything is placed confidently in the hands of our Mother and Queen. All goods, material and spiritual, the merits of all good actions . . . everything one has is given to Jesus through Mary. All things are done through Mary, with Mary, in Mary and for Mary, the better to do them through, with, in and for Jesus. St. Louis de Montfort explains the reason for placing all things in the Virgin's safekeeping:

> Pour into the bosom and heart of Mary all your precious possessions, all your graces and virtues. She is a spiritual vessel, a vessel of honor, a singular vessel of devotion. Ever since God personally hid Himself with all His perfections in this vessel, it has become completely spiritual, and the spiritual abode of all spiritual souls. It has become honorable and has been the throne of honor for the greatest saints in heaven. It has become outstanding in devotion and the home of those renowned for gentleness, grace and virtue. Moreover, it has become as rich as a house of gold, as strong as a tower of David and as pure as a tower of ivory. (*ibid.*)

The practical, salutary results of placing oneself daily, and completely, into Mary's keeping are set down in the plainest of language by St. Louis:

> You never think of Mary without Mary thinking of God for you. You never praise or honor Mary without Mary joining you in praising and honoring God. Mary is entirely relative to God. . . . She is an echo of God, speaking and repeating only God. If you say "Mary," she says "God". When St. Elizabeth praised Mary, calling her

> blessed because she had believed, Mary, the faithful echo of God, responded with her Canticle, "My soul doth magnify the Lord." (*ibid.*)

You never think of Mary without Mary thinking of God for you. The very name of Mary evokes that of her Son. "O name of Mary!" exclaimed St. Anthony of Padua (†1231), "joy in the heart, honey in the mouth, melody to the ear of her devout clients." In the melody of this holy name can be discerned both simplicity and grandeur, the familiarity of the hearth and the mysteries of heaven, and scholars throughout the ages have pondered its meaning.

The name Mary is Miryam in Hebrew; it was the name of the sister of Moses. It means "bitterness" (Hebrew, *merur*) and the ancient rabbinical scholars, perceiving in it a symbol of Israel's slavery in Egypt, held that Miryam was given the name because she was born during the oppression of the Israelites. The sister of Moses was a "type", or a foreshadowing, of the Blessed Virgin, as Moses was a "type" of Christ. Miryam, a prophetess, supported her brother, the liberator of their people, and sang a canticle of thanksgiving after the safe crossing of the Red Sea and the destruction of Pharaoh's army. Through her cooperation with Jesus, the supreme "Liberator" of His people (from slavery to the "empire of death"), our Lady, who prophesied that all generations would call her blessed and sang a canticle of joy during her Visitation to St. Elizabeth, became the true "antitype" (fulfillment) of Miryam, the fullest expression and realization of the courageous woman standing at the side of, and laboring with, the one who comes to bring liberty to captives.

Other meanings for the name Mary which have been put forth and cherished over the centuries are *Star of the Sea*, *Lady* (in the regal sense, as in Lord and Lady), *Myrrh of the Sea*, *Enlightener*, *Bitter Sea* (a reflection of her Seven Sorrows), the *Exalted One* and, on the supposition that the name has Egyptian roots, the *Beloved of God* (*meryt* = much loved). Also proposed are the meanings "fleshy" or "robust" (Hebrew, *mara*), on the supposition that, in the East, descriptions implying corpulence were used to indicate beauty and fecundity. The Psalms describe the Church in this manner, indicating both fruitfulness and the spiritual gifts of the Holy Ghost: "The mountain of God is a fat mountain. A curdled mountain, a fat mountain. . . . A mountain in which God is well pleased to dwell." (Ps. 67:16-17) This resonates with the prophecy of Isaias concerning the New Dispensation (and the Church), and with the words of our Lord: "And in the last days the mountain of the house of the Lord shall be prepared on the top of the mountains, and it shall be exalted above the hills, and all nations shall flow unto it." (2:2) "You are the light of the world. A city that is set on a mountain cannot be hid." (Mt. 5:14)

These varied interpretations for the name "Mary" recall our Lady's sorrows, her blessedness, her beauty, her powers of mediation and her sovereignty, and as such they are found in the writings of the saints. However, even in the absence of such speculations, the name of Mary holds a special place in the history of the world, and in the hearts of men. It was secreted in the bosom of the Blessed Trinity since before the foundation of the world beside the sacred name of Jesus. "Whoever names Mary," wrote St. John Eudes, "names the most brilliant ornament of the house of God."

Before the Incarnation, the name of the Living God was deemed unpronounceable by the children of Israel, out of reverence. When it appeared in the Scriptures, they would read the word "Adonai" (Lord):

> And the Lord spoke to Moses, saying: I am the Lord That appeared to Abraham, to Isaac, and to Jacob, by the name of God Almighty: and my name ADONAI I did not shew them. (Ex. 6:2-3)

At the Incarnation, the Second Person of the Blessed Trinity took to Himself a name: "And after eight days were accomplished, that the Child should be circumcised: *His name was called Jesus.*" (Lk. 2:21) It is the name of the "seed" prophesied in Eden, Who would come to save His people. It is the name by which we address the Redeemer, God-made-Man, and it remains, and always will remain, the one word which summarizes all that is perfect and glorious in the created order, "that in the name of Jesus, every knee should bow of those that are in heaven, on earth, and under the earth." (Phil. 2:10)

The name of Mary, the "Woman" also prophesied in Eden, summarizes all that is perfect and glorious among the redeemed. Our Lady has been assumed into heaven, where she reigns as Queen by the side of her Son, but, here on earth, her name rests in Catholic hearts like a dazzling gem in a silk-lined vault:

Hail, holy Queen of humble hearts!
We in thy praise will have our parts.
Thy precious Name shall be Thy self to us; and we
With holy care will keep it by us. We to the last
Will hold it fast
And no Assumption shall deny us.
All the sweetest show'res
Of our fairest flow'res
Will we strow upon it.
Though our sweets cannot make
It sweeter, they can take
Themselves new sweetness from it.
Maria, men and angels sing
Maria, mother of our King.

(Richard Crashaw, d. 1649,
On the Glorious Assumption of Our Blessed Lady)

Each time someone recalls, in prayer, the Incarnation of the Word and the Redemption of mankind, the name of the Mother of the Church soars aloft to the vault of heaven: *Hail Mary, Full of grace, the Lord is with thee.* It is spoken countless times each day by countless souls, yet it always sounds sweet, bright as a newly-minted coin. "Your name, O Mother of God, is filled with divine graces and blessings," wrote St. Methodius (†847).

"May the last movement of my tongue," prayed St. Germanus of Constantinople, "be to pronounce the name of the Mother of God." This name is, truly, honey in the mouth and music to the ear, and God alone knows how many saints – and sinners – have whispered it with their final breath: *Holy Mary, Mother of God, pray for us sinners, now and at the hour of our death.*

Chapter Thirty-Three

"Of Mary Never Enough"

JESUS IS THE "WAY"; IN MARY IS "ALL GRACE OF THE WAY" – JESUS IS THE "LIFE"; IN MARY IS ALL HOPE OF LIFE" – MORE BEAUTIFUL POEMS IN PRAISE OF MARY – MARY IS THE "BAIT" SELECTED BY GOD TO CATCH SOULS – THE UNNATURAL PERVERSITY OF DISDAIN FOR THE MOTHER OF JESUS – THE GOOD HEART REJOICES WHEN REFLECTING ON THE MADONNA AND CHILD – MARY IS A LIVING, LOVING, PERSON, NOT A TOPIC – THE HOLY STANDARD: "OF MARY NEVER ENOUGH" – FATHER FABER ON THE MUTUAL LOVE OF MOTHER AND SON

Approaching Jesus through the Blessed Virgin, which is the basis of the Total Consecration, is also the essence of all Catholic Marian devotions, great and small. Our hearts are drawn to Mary for her own sake, because of her nobility, her goodness, and because she is our spiritual Mother. Whenever we speak to her, we do so with the understanding that she will never treat our words, or wants, as unworthy to be presented to Christ. We often ask our Lady explicitly to intercede for us: "O clement, O loving, O sweet Virgin Mary. Pray for us, O Holy Mother of God, that we may be made worthy of the promises of Christ."

However, even when we are not explicit, when we render private prayers of praise or gratitude to Mary, we understand that our thoughts and our words will be directed to Christ, and with the intercession of our Lady added. Therefore, to go to Mary with needs is to beseech the mercy of Christ; to go to Mary with praises is to honor God; to go to Mary in gratitude is to thank God for His works, a thing that is "truly meet and just, right and profitable, for us, at all times, and in all places" to do, according to the Preface of the Mass.

Our Lord desires that no one be excluded from the comfort and assistance of His Mother: "I am the Mother of fair love, and of fear, and of knowledge, and of holy hope. In me is all grace of the way and of the truth; in me is all hope of life and of virtue." (Ecclus 24:24-25) In these words, we do not hear Mary's prophetic voice saying the words which only her Divine Son could say: "I am the Way, and the Truth, and the Life. No man cometh to the Father, but by Me." (Jn. 14:6) Instead, we hear her say, "In me is all grace of the way, in me is all hope of life and virtue."

I am the Way, and the Truth, and the Life, are the words spoken by Jesus, the Fountain of life. *In me is all hope of life*, are sentiments rightly belonging to Mary, the "Aqueduct" by which the Fountain nourishes the world. Because God wills that we receive all graces through her, our salvation is in her hands, literally: "As no man goes to the Father but by the Son, so no one goes to Christ except through His Mother." (Pope Leo XIII) Such is the plan set in place by the Blessed Trinity, and one that will not change, for it is the Woman (representing Mary and the Church), expecting a Child, who is called the "Great Sign" by St. John the Evangelist.

The Church has great reason to rejoice in Mary, Mother and Queen. The great paintings, statues, cathedrals, musical compositions, poems and hymns created in her honor are more than matched by the private devotions rendered to her every day. This attraction to her, instilled in the hearts of men and women of all times and circumstances, finds its first object in our shared nature. Mary is one of us:

We've built so many towers in our skies,
So often flung the great stones up for her
To ease the heart's full need, and be a praise
To stand above the years' long pondering;
So often have we turned the litanies,
Strung out so many garlands, while her bells
Have called to us, and kneeling we have sighed
In such dear confidence . . .
We scarce remember
Now that once this name was spoken softly
In a time before the Aves rang.
Perhaps across some threshold it was said,
So casually, by one who called to her, "Mary".
Then, she might have turned and come,
Obedient from where the children played
Together in the dusk: and no one knew
That more was said than just a young girl's name.

(Fr. John W. Lynch, *A Woman Wrapped in Silence*)

She is also a holy personage, the Mother of Christ, sharing in the sovereignty of His kingdom, and we sense that we are safe near her. And more. Jesus said, "Come to Me, all you that labor, and are burdened, and I will refresh you. . . . You shall find rest to your souls." (Mt. 11:28-29) Through Mary, this "rest", this security, bathes mankind:

You are the dawn that appears
before God and lights up
the skies, and You deserve
his company.
And I would like
to see You at his side, as
I would be safe,
and at rest, where You are
with God, where You are the dawn.

(King Alfonso the Wise, *Dawn of All Dawns*)

Think, O sick toiler, when the night
Comes on thee, sad and infinite,
Think, sometimes, 'tis our own Lady
Spreads her blue mantle over thee,
And folds the earth, a wearied thing,
Beneath its gentle shadowing;
Then rest a little; and in sleep
Forget to weep, forget to weep!

(Francis Thompson, d. 1907,
Lines for a Drawing of Our Lady of the Night)

Mary is a Mother, warm and solicitous; she is a Queen, regal and powerful. The Church honors her in both of these magnificent titles, for they are two sides of a coin, and one seems only to enhance the other. Mankind receives from Our Lady the maternal affections of a Mother, and the constant favors of a Queen. Her influence upon history is not merely a thing of the past, a happy offshoot of a time when the True Faith flourished unhindered by social or political impediments. On the contrary, as the world witnessed at Fatima, the necessity for devotion to the Mother of God only increases as the ages roll by:

> I declare that, considering things as they are, because God has decided to begin and accomplish His greatest works through the Blessed Virgin ever since He created her, we can safely believe that He will not change His plan in the time to come, for He is God and therefore does not change in His thoughts or His way of acting.
>
> God the Father gave His only Son to the world only through Mary. . . . The Son of God became man for our salvation, but only in Mary and through Mary. . . . God the Holy Ghost, Who does not produce any divine person, became fruitful through Mary whom He espoused. It was with her, in her and of her that He produced His masterpiece, God-made-Man, and that He produces every day until the end of the world the members of the Body of this adorable Head.
>
> God therefore wishes to reveal Mary, His masterpiece, and make her more known in these latter times. . . . In these latter times Mary must shine forth more than ever in mercy, power and grace: in mercy, to bring back and welcome lovingly the poor sinners and wanderers who are to be converted and return to the Catholic Church; in power, to combat the enemies of God who will rise up menacingly to seduce and crush by promises and threats all those who oppose them; finally, she must shine forth in grace to inspire and support the valiant soldiers and loyal servants of Jesus Christ who are fighting for His cause. (St. Louis de Montfort, *True Devotion to the Blessed Virgin*)

This "bait" selected by God to catch souls, as we find Mary likened to in the writings of St. Catherine of Siena, was created to love and to be loved, to love her God as a Son, and mankind as her "other" children – and to be loved both by God and men as a Mother. She has been called our Lady down through the ages, and there is a world of affection hidden in that simple title. It reflects the attraction of sinful hearts to the Immaculate Heart, for the perfume of the "Mystical Rose" is of such virtue and power, that it can attract hardened sinners as well as those who place few obstacles in the way of grace. This affection is reciprocated by the Lady herself, who will remember the words of Jesus, *Behold thy son*, each time she regards one of her spiritual children.

The enemies of Jesus and Mary have made of the Blessed Mother a phantasm, an object to be feared and avoided. Some treat her with outward disdain, preaching and writing against her and her privileges and prerogatives. Misguided "theological" studies, agenda-laden Biblical exegesies, even passionate, though ultimately unconvincing, professions of allegiance to the honor of Jesus Christ – all these tools are employed by such people for the unnatural, indeed perverse, object of creating a surreal scenario in which our Lord either disdains or ignores His Mother, the very "Woman" whose presence permeates the sacred texts from beginning to end!

> For she is a vapor of the power of God, and a certain pure emanation of the glory of the Almighty. . . . For she is the brightness of eternal light, and the unspotted mirror of God's majesty, and the image of His goodness. . . . For she is more beautiful than the sun, and above all the order of the stars. (Wisdom 7:25,26,29)

Others affect a quiet disdain, and would appear shocked if informed that their attitude towards the Mother of God was lacking in respect. But there are two ways to show contempt. One can hurl insults at another person . . . or one can deliberately refuse to acknowledge the other's claims or titles. One disgruntled subject can describe a king as a bad ruler. Another subject can say to the king, "You are no king at all . . . you're no better than the rest of us." The one who, while claiming to honor Christ, refuses to acknowledge the Mother of Christ as Queen and Mother, can lay claim to no more authentic "Christian" sentiment than the one who preaches or writes against her. To deny Marian doctrine is to deny Truth: Scriptural truth, truth promulgated by the Church's authoritative teaching Magisterium

. . . even defined truths that have been revealed by God through the infallible pronouncements which only the Vicar of Christ can make.

A question may rightfully be asked here of Protestants, who have made dismissal or denigration of the Holy Virgin a tenet of their belief systems, and of those Catholics who are willing to sacrifice or set aside their doctrinal legacy for the sake of some collusion with those outside the Church in the name of false "ecumenism". What manner of "spirit" will prompt men and women to view the radiant Madonna with anything other than feelings of intense joy, and a desire to belong to her, to offer devotion to her? It is a question worth pondering, and carefully at that.

Because of her unique place in the created order, the Mother of God – the Gate of Heaven – is the best and surest of means by which to approach Jesus Christ. This is true also when we reflect upon the Redemption, and the One Who effected it on our behalf. To gaze into the finely crafted portals of this "gate", designed by God Himself, is to view the sacred mysteries of God-made-Man from a vantage point other than which none can be closer or offer a clearer panorama:

> Whence is this to me that the Mother of my Lord should be loved by me? But how could I fail to love this marvel of life? The Birth of the Word is eternal, unchanging; it was, it is, it always will be. The birth which is thine, O blessed Mother of God, I gaze upon it as I should gaze upon an immense lake on an island which the boundless sea holds encompassed from all sides: it is the birth of God surrounded by a more immense birth of God; Thou art, O blessed Lady, the island containing the one and contained by the other. From thee, as from a point of vantage, I hope to contemplate forever the two Lives in Which the happiness of all created intellects lies, the Life that is born in eternity and the Life that was born in time. (Abbot Anscar Vonier, *The Divine Motherhood*, 1921)

The movement of the heart towards Marian devotion is not precipitated by one's level of education or imagination; it is not the result of a conscious adherence to a theological principal, and it can flourish even where cultural incentives have been lacking. When someone enjoys a moving piece of music, he does not have to stop listening in order to lecture himself on how much the music should be affecting him. Similarly, a mind receptive to Truth can "experience" our Lady in an uninterrupted flow of regard and affection. Both she and her Son will see to this:

> When you approach the time for reading about Mary Immaculate, always remember that you are entering into contact with a living, loving person. . . . It is a fine thing to study Mariology; but let us never forget that we will get to understand Mary much better through humble prayer, through the loving experience of our daily lives, than through learned definitions, distinctions and arguments, even though we must not neglect these latter. (St. Maximilian Kolbe)

We encounter a moving example of this natural "movement" of the affections towards our Lady in the autobiography of St. Teresa of Avila (†1582):

> I remember that, when my mother died, I was twelve years of age or a little less. When I began to realize what I had lost, I went in my distress to an image of Our Lady and with many tears besought her to be a mother to me. Though I did this in simplicity, I believe it was of some avail to me; for whenever I have commended myself to this Sovereign Virgin, I have been conscious of her aid.

"*De Maria Numquam Satis*," proclaimed the saints. *Of Mary, there is never enough.* To say that we have praised her enough is to say that we have praised the works of God enough. To say that we have honored her enough is to say that we have honored enough the One Who Redeemed us as her Son. To say that we have plumbed her depths is to say that we have plumbed the depths of the ocean, after merely scooping up a handful of water. To suggest that we have written enough about her, or contemplated too much her doctrines, would be like suggesting that we have discovered all the mysteries of all celestial phenomena, merely because we have glimpsed the moon through a telescope:

> If we think of her deep love of Jesus, it is only to delight in its interminable magnificence. It is beyond our definitions, out of the sphere of our comprehension. We make wild comparisons of all angels and of all saints, indulge in fanciful arithmetic, repeat our superlatives, but we only do so to convince ourselves more satisfactorily that it is all beyond us, just as a man uses violence with himself to be sure he is awake. Yet the dimensions of that love do not reach to the dimensions of her Compassion, because there is another love yet, to which it marvelously outstretches. It is the deep love of Jesus for her.
>
> Who can tell it? Who can speak of it even figuratively, for where is our figure to come from? Yet the breadth, and the depth, and the height of that love of Jesus for His Mother are the only true dimensions of her Compassion. Here are five abysses, five measures, five standards: His sufferings, His beauty, men's cruelty, her deep love of Him, His deep love of her. We must do our poor best with them all, and we shall reach a view of our Blessed Mother's Compassion which will be good for us and acceptable to her, but it will be below the truth.
>
> A work which Jesus and Mary made together, out of God's wrath, and man's sin, and the Hypostatic Union, and the sinlessness of a pure creature, must be a marvel about which at best we can but stammer, and lovingly go wrong; and such a work is Mary's Compassion. (Fr. Frederick William Faber, *The Foot of the Cross,* 1857)

A work which Jesus and Mary made together. If we turn our eyes to Bethlehem, we find there the Mother and her Son. If we look towards Calvary, we find there also the Mother and her Son. When we remember the earthly life of Jesus Christ, we cannot help but remember the Virgin Mary as well:

> Here we are treading on very holy ground indeed – nothing can be more mysterious than the relations of the Incarnate God with his Blessed Mother, as he led her soul step by step to heights of sanctity far above our mortal ken, through sorrows unimaginable – from earth to heaven that she might, when life was past, be crowned by his Hand Queen of Angels and of men. (Rev. O.R. Vassall-Phillips, *Mary, The Mother of God*, 1928)

To our great consolation and benefit, we will, if taught correctly in the ways of God, find once again the Mother and her Son when we dare to lift our eyes to that place called "the holy city, the new Jerusalem", and hope against hope for a place within its walls:

Mother full of gentle virtues,
maiden patient and well-taught,
I am in the bonds of thy love
and I am all drawn to thee.
Shield me, yea, from the devil,
as thou art free and will and may,
and help me to my life's end
and the joining I have sought with thy Son.

(*Edi be thu, heven-queene,* medieval English hymn)

When mankind can render to the Blessed Virgin Mary even one iota of the honor bestowed upon her by God when He made her the Mother of His only-begotten Son, then we may say that we have just begun to regard her realistically, let alone excessively: "And yet in truth we must still say with the saints, *De Maria numquam satis*: We have still not praised, exalted, honored, loved and served Mary adequately. She is worthy of even more praise, respect, love and service." (St. Louis de Montfort)

The son or daughter of Mary comes from a long, long line of sons and daughters of Mary, all flesh and blood creatures, not paragons. Jesus

Christ is the King of heaven and earth, yet we approach Him as sinners, unworthy. Whereas an earthly ruler may give a cool reception to a supplicant, the King of Kings, instead, holds out a hand upon which is engraved a Wound made by the nail when He was crucified on Calvary. No ruler can love us as Christ does.

The Blessed Virgin is Queen of heaven and earth. In mankind, she beholds souls so cherished by her Son that He bore the weight of the Cross for them. No ruler can love us as Mary does.

The pages of Sacred Scripture are alight with the Presence of Jesus Christ, the awaited Redeemer: "For I am God, and there is no God beside, neither is there the like to Me. . . . I have brought My justice near, it shall not be far off: and My salvation shall not tarry." (Is. 46:9,12) There is another presence whose silhouette is cast upon the ancient inspired texts, and it cannot be separated from that of the Desired of the Nations: "Therefore will He give them up till the time wherein she that travaileth shall bring forth." (Mi. 5:3)

Our hearts were made for God. They strain against the shackles of mortality, fighting, falling, rising. Underneath every sin, underneath every victory, is a soul making its way home. An unfettered affection for the Mother of God and men belongs also in our hearts, and it should run deep, because we belong to Jesus *and* Mary. If the sheep will recognize their Master's voice, how can they fail to be moved by that other voice, the one which the Master Himself listened to on earth with such pleasure, and which He regards today with no less complacency . . . the voice of Mary, His Mother and ours?

Our Lady wears a crown in a strange country,
The crown he gave,
But she has not forgotten to call to her old companions,
To call and crave;
And to hear her calling, a man might arise and thunder
On the doors of the grave.

(G.K. Chesterton, *Regina Angelorum*)

Mark Alessio
Born 1955, New York City

Since 1996, Mr. Alessio has been a frequent contributor to *Catholic Family News* and *The Remnant.* He has also published articles for *The Angelus*, *From The Housetops* and *The New Triumph.*

1992 His short-story, "From the Depths," was adapted into a radio drama and broadcast on WCVE-FM (Public Radio 88.9FM in Richmond, Virginia). It was rebroadcast yearly until 1994.

2002 His short-story, "One for the Road," appeared in a hardcover collection entitled *The Muse in the Bottle* (Citadel Press).

2002 Alessio wrote the Introduction for the 2nd Edition of the book, *Of Mary There Is Never Enough* by William L. Biersach (published by Catholic Treasures).

Mr. Alessio has also contributed to an upcoming book on film noir, which is as yet untitled.